MORTAL ERROR

MORTAL ERROR

THE SHOT THAT KILLED JFK

BONAR MENNINGER

SIDGWICK & JACKSON

LONDON

First published in Great Britain in 1992
by Sidgwick & Jackson Limited

Published in association with St. Martin's Press Inc,
175 Fifth Avenue, New York, NY 10010

ISBN 0-283-06136-7

Printed by Billing and Sons Ltd,
Worcester
for Sidgwick & Jackson Limited
18–21 Cavaye Place
London SW10 9PG

Dedicated to Ann Cain and Katie Donahue

CONTENTS

ACKNOWLEDGMENTS

Special thanks to Nick Beltrante for a great news tip, the late Ralph Reppert for showing the way, Howard and Katie Donahue for casting their lot with me, Alfred Glossbrenner for sound book-writing advice, Mark Heschmeyer for an early thumbs-up, Jean Gibbons for her knowledge of the publishing world, Lola Butcher and Andy Cline for their real-time editing and faithful support, Bruce Kilkenny for his weapons expertise, the workers of the Arlington County Public Library, main branch, and the Fairfax County Public Library, Sherwood branch, for their cordial assistance, Chuck Ortleb for linking me up with St. Martin's, Marty Lobel, for helping us get a contract, Michael Denneny for taking a chance on this project and seeing it through to the end and for his outstanding editing, Keith Kahla for his steadfast service on the New York front, Paul Sleven for his relentless attention to detail, David Kaye for his intellectual acuity, Tom McCormack for getting involved in this project and for publishing this book, Dan Margolies for his vote of confidence, Ari Bavel for his mathematical prowess, Mark Pawlosky for getting me to D.C. and for years of good advice, Marvin Arth for encouraging words and a job way back when, Col. and Mrs. Ashton Crosby, for years of friendship and encouragement, my mom, Catherine Menninger, for her wise counsel, my dad, Roy Menninger, for his insight and crunch-time technical aid, my brother, Eric, and my sisters, Ariel and Heather, for believing in me, my friends in Kansas, Missouri and northern New Hampshire and everyone else who wished me well, and most of all, through it all, thanks to my wife and best friend, Ann Cain, who kept hope alive, a roof overhead, and food on the table for twenty long months.

—BONAR MENNINGER
Kansas City
January 21, 1992

LIST OF DRAWINGS

LIST OF ILLUSTRATIONS
IN THE PHOTO SECTION

MORTAL ERROR

1

A CHANCE
TELEPHONE CALL

FATE SOMETIMES HOLDS A MAN IN CHECK until his moment arrives. Hidden skills and talents lie dormant for years, only to surface after a chance encounter or extraordinary event. It is a common phenomenon but no less dramatic each time it occurs.

So it was for Howard Donahue. Donahue was a salesman most of his career. For years, he supplied pharmaceutical products to drugstores around Baltimore; later he sold missile components to defense firms across the South. After that, Donahue realized a lifelong dream and opened a gun shop.

But Donahue's real calling was detective work. His abilities in this area did not emerge until he was middle-aged, and had it not been for a chance encounter in the spring of 1967, they probably wouldn't have surfaced at all.

What Howard Donahue did—part-time, on weekends, over the course of twenty-five years—was investigate the assassination of President John F. Kennedy. In this he was no different from thousands of other amateur sleuths. Except that, unlike others, Donahue possessed considerable knowledge of firearms and ballistics and a remarkable ability to imagine and understand. In time, these traits allowed him to spot inconsistencies in the evidence that virtually everyone else had missed. So Donahue pulled the string. And kept pulling until, in the end, the vast tapestry of fact, fiction, and paranoid fantasy surrounding Kennedy's death unraveled in his hands.

Donahue's startling opinion about what happened on November 22, 1963, remains unconventional in the extreme. It is controversial. It is also profoundly compelling, because more than any theory ever put forth about Kennedy's death, Donahue's understanding is grounded in facts and evidence alone.

What Donahue discovered was this: The bullet that slammed into Kennedy's skull could not have been fired by Lee Harvey Oswald.

Donahue understood who actually pulled the trigger. And he saw why this savage irony had remained buried for so long.

Donahue's conclusions grew from a lifetime's experience with firearms. From his earliest boyhood days, Howard was fascinated by hunting and guns. That passion took hold in the woods and hills around Malone, New York, where Howard was born in 1922, the middle son of Michael and Mildred Donahue. Howard's father was a successful advertising executive who'd opened his own agency in the small upstate town; his mother was a friendly, easygoing woman who had grown up on a farm.

Michael Donahue's firm thrived through the twenties, but with the onset of the Depression revenues dried up and closed the business down. In 1932, Michael Donahue accepted a job with a manufacturing firm in Baltimore, Maryland. Although he had been forced to terminate his business in upstate New York, the elder Donahue had insulated himself well against the Depression. As a result, the family was able to settle in a fashionable district near the sleepy town of Towson, just north of Baltimore.

Howard didn't always get along with his father, a cold, austere man, and his emerging personality favored his mother's. He was a charming, happy-go-lucky kid; a neighbor sustained the boy's interest in hunting and fishing, and before long the outdoors were the ruling obsession in young Howard's life. Spring afternoons would find him fishing for bass and trout in the ponds and creeks beyond Towson or hunting rabbits past the edge of town. In summer, Howard returned to upstate New York to hunt squirrels and fish with his uncle on the family farm.

Even as a boy, Howard combined his interest in firearms with a natural mechanical ability. At age eleven, he traded his Flexible Flyer sled for a defective .22 caliber rifle. The gun's barrel had been drilled off center, making it woefully inaccurate. Howard trued the gun by simply pounding the sight slightly to the left. He was soon the best shot in the neighborhood. By his early teens, Howard was consistently winning top honors in National Rifle Association junior marksman competitions in Baltimore and eastern Maryland. When he wasn't competing, he could most often be found tinkering in his bedroom with shotguns and rifles or taking target practice in the fields beyond Towson.

Donahue's graduation from high school came in the spring of 1940 as German tanks slashed across Europe. That fall, Howard entered the University of Maryland to study engineering. When the Japanese attacked Pearl Harbor, Howard enlisted in the Army Air Corps Reserves and waited to be called up. Word came down in the spring of '43.

Donahue spent the better part of the next year training as a bomber pilot at airfields across the South. In May of 1944, the twenty-one-year-old lieutenant shipped out. He arrived in England just after D day and was assigned to the Eighth Air Force as a B-17 Flying Fortress copilot, based at Bassingborn, England, thirty miles north of London.

All told, Donahue would fly thirty-five combat missions over Europe before the war ended. He was never wounded, but he saw men maimed and killed all around him. In September 1944, on a mission to bomb an I.G. Farben chemical plant in Ludwigshafen, Germany, the captain of Donahue's aircraft was struck in the skull by a piece of antiaircraft shell. The pilot slumped over the bomber's controls and the plane pitched down toward a B-17 flying nearby in tight formation.

When Howard tried to pull the pilot off the control yoke, the semiconscious, pain-crazed man went berserk. Donahue finally kicked the right rudder to steer the plane off the collision course, even as he continued to grapple with the wounded man. The top turret gunner soon helped restrain the pilot, and although two of the B-17's four engines were shot out, Donahue managed to limp the plane back to England.

The young airman's quick reactions and coolness getting home saved the lives of at least eighteen men, including nine in the unsuspecting bomber Donahue's aircraft almost collided with as well as the pilot, who mercifully recovered from his wound. For his efforts, Howard was awarded the Distinguished Flying Cross, one of the highest commendations in the Army Air Corps. The official citation noted his display of "courage, coolness and tenacity of purpose" over Ludwigshafen. By the time he returned to Maryland, Donahue had earned seven air medals, the Distinguished Flying Cross ETO (European Theater of Operations) with five battle stars, the Victory in Europe medal, and the Presidential Unit citation, making him one of the state's most decorated flyers of the war. He was discharged with the rank of first lieutenant.

In 1948, Howard reenrolled in the University of Maryland. He opted to study medicine this time around and joined the Delta Sigma Phi fraternity. However, after facing death daily for months, Howard found it difficult to take school or anything else very seriously; he enjoyed himself too much and his grades suffered.

As he struggled with life and school, Howard renewed his friendship with a childhood companion named Catherine Wood. The Wood and Donahue families had lived within a mile of each other through the 1930s and the two children had often played together growing up. But the attractive, articulate brunette of 1948 bore scant resemblance to the freckle-faced girl Howard used to bedevil at the neighborhood swimming pool through the long summers of childhood. Katie was strong, independent, and opinionated, and she'd had the time of her life during the war—working at the local USO club and dancing many a night away at military balls around Baltimore.

Howard and Katie were married in June of 1949. As part of their verbal prenuptial agreement, Katie made a solemn promise never to interfere with Howard's hunting and fishing trips.

The newlyweds settled in College Park near the University of Maryland campus. Katie held down two jobs while Howard completed his studies. In 1951, he graduated with a bachelor's degree in psychology. Howard then applied to the University of Maryland School of Medicine, but the competition was tough due to all the returned veterans and Howard's grades kept him out. Though he stood a fighting chance elsewhere, Howard wouldn't apply to a medical school out of state. All that he loved—his family, his friends, his hunting and fishing—were in Maryland.

And so, after trying a couple of jobs, Donahue settled down and went to work for one of the large pharmaceutical firms that dotted the Baltimore area. The couple moved back to Towson and before long bought a modest brick row house on the GI Bill a mile from the center of town. In the winter of 1951, Katie gave birth to a daughter, Colleen. Like millions of young veteran's families, the Donahues worked hard to put the war behind them and pursue their version of the American dream. During this period, Howard spent an increasing amount of time tinkering with guns—repairing or modifying them for friends and neighbors—and his mechanical talent soon evolved into a remarkable inventiveness as a gunsmith.

Typical were the modifications he designed for the popular Winchester Model 50 and Model 59 12-gauge shotguns. While well made, the guns had a tendency to "blowback" noxious powder gas when fired. Katie had complained of this after a couple of particularly nasty days of skeet shooting. Howard made some calculations and had a machine shop cut him several precisely measured stainless steel rings. Installed in the firing chamber of the Winchester, the rings eliminated the blowback problems and also made the guns less likely to foul.

Realizing there were thousands of Winchester shotguns across America, Howard formed Maryland Research Co. and began advertising his invention in hunting magazines. Over the next twenty years, he would modify more than three hundred of the guns at thirty-five dollars a crack.

With extra income from his weapons business and a steady paycheck from the pharmaceutical company, life was good enough for the Donahues as the 1950s passed.

Politically, however, Howard and Katie were often at odds. No more rock-ribbed Republican had ever lived than Howard's father, and at least in that respect, Howard took after him—voting twice for Eisenhower. Katie, however, was ill at ease. She sensed a dangerous slide in the country through the long, complacent years of the Eisenhower presidency. As a result, John F. Kennedy's candidacy for President in 1960 appealed to her a great deal. Like many

Americans, Katie was charmed by this handsome and self-confident man and inspired by his rhetoric. Here, she believed, was a leader for the future.

Kennedy's margin of victory was one of the narrowest in American history. Katie was overjoyed; Howard, though irritated, quickly put the election behind him for the more immediate concerns of supporting a family. His sales job for the pharmaceutical company kept him on the road a good deal of the time. It was not an easy life, but his genuine personality made him an effective salesman and the commissions paid the bills.

Katie, meanwhile, decided to put to work a realtor's license she had earned several years earlier, since her daughter Colleen was in sixth grade now and able to look after herself when school finished each day. Katie was a natural; she had a presence that inspired trust, she was sharp, and before long she was pulling down nice commissions selling homes around Towson.

On Friday afternoon, November 22, 1963, Katie was getting dressed to run out to the grocery store. She'd invited a fellow realtor over for dinner. As it happened, Howard was home that day following a spell on the road. He was working in the basement when the doorbell rang.

"I'll get it," he called to Katie upstairs.

At the door was Earl Young, a neighbor and friend. He was ashen-faced.

"Kennedy's been shot in Dallas," Young stammered. "I just heard it on the radio."

To those not yet born in the autumn of 1963 or too young to remember, it is difficult to convey the effect President Kennedy's assassination had on the nation and the world. It was a cataclysmic event; a tidal wave that roared out of Dallas across the wires and by word of mouth to every corner of the world, spreading gloom in its wake.

The Donahues went through with dinner that Friday night, but Katie couldn't stop her tears. All through the long weekend the family sat hypnotized as the images hurtled into the nation's memory: *Air Force One* bringing the dead President home, rolling through the cold night at Andrews Air Force Base; the lines waiting in the bitter cold for a glimpse of the President's casket at the Capitol; Lee Harvey Oswald's gut-shot death in the crowded basement of Dallas police headquarters; and finally, the austere beauty of the funeral march as it wound its way through Washington toward the Potomac and the Virginia hills beyond.

For the Donahues and the country, the days mercifully turned to months and the months became years. Although the horror and pain of the assassination receded into the less-threatening domain of history, the circumstances surrounding Kennedy's death soon became a maelstrom that showed no sign of abating with the passage of time.

Donahue didn't pay much attention to the increasingly lurid speculation about who or what may have been behind the killing. Kennedy was dead. That was it. Nothing he or anyone else could do would change it.

And then one day in the spring of 1967, Howard received a telephone call that would, from the vantage point of the distant future, emerge as a major turning point in his life—the first faint pull that would draw him inexorably back to those grim days of November 1963.

Howard was middle-aged by now. His thick black hair had turned silvery gray and he had added a few pounds since the war. He wasn't wealthy, but he made a decent living and he was well known across eastern Maryland as a dead-eye marksman, ballistics expert, and gunsmith.

He was out running errands on a raw Saturday morning in late May when he remembered he had some bills to mail. He'd just picked them up and was headed out the door again when the telephone rang. On the other end of the line was an old hunting pal, Bill Fitchett. Fitchett asked if Howard wanted to come shooting that afternoon. The details were sketchy. It seemed someone was conducting a rifle study. They needed the participation of a wide variety of marksmen.

Howard didn't need to be asked twice. He assumed the test involved a murder investigation or a court case, and he was always looking for an excuse to go shooting. Before long, Fitchett and his brother, Somerset, pulled up out front. Howard piled in and the group headed for Bel Air, where they met the Fitchetts' brother-in-law, John Dinning. All expert shots, the men had a quick bite to eat and then made for sprawling H. P. White Ballistics Laboratory, a half-hour drive to the north.

H. P. White at the time was the largest independent weapons testing laboratory in the country, a complex located on nearly one hundred acres, with numerous outdoor and indoor firing ranges. The lab's primary function was to conduct controlled, scientific weapons studies for clients ranging from firearms manufacturers to insurance companies and law enforcement agencies.

Once inside the H. P. White compound, the four men were led to a firing range in the basement of one of the lab buildings. Technicians there instructed each man to fire three shots from a high-powered rifle lying on a table nearby. The group was still in the dark about the specifics of the test.

But if Donahue didn't yet know what the test was about, one glance at the rifle gave him a clue. He immediately recognized the gun as a Model 31/98 6.5 millimeter Mannlicher-Carcano, the weapon Lee Harvey Oswald had used to kill Kennedy three and a half years before. The shoddily made World War II surplus Italian rifle was no state-of-the-art firearm, but, as events in Dallas had shown, it was lethal.

Gradually, through conversation with the lab's chief technician, it emerged that the marksmen had been brought to H. P. White to test-fire the gun in an attempt to duplicate Oswald's performance in Dallas. In the fall of 1964, the Warren Commission, which had been appointed by President Johnson to investigate the assassination, had concluded Oswald had acted alone in killing the President. One of Oswald's shots had missed, the Warren Commission had said, one had hit the President in the neck, and the third had shattered the right side of Kennedy's head.

Central to these findings was the assertion that Oswald was indeed capable of firing the Carcano three times in the space of 5.6 seconds, the approximate elapsed time of the shooting based on an analysis of Abraham Zapruder's home movie of the murder.

Commission critics—and there were many by 1967—thought this a dubious proposition. They found it hard to believe that Oswald or anyone else could have fired three rounds from the unwieldy Carcano within the allotted time frame. Oswald was no expert marksman, and the gun's bolt action was notoriously stiff and hard to operate.

These doubts, in fact, had been fanned by the Warren Commission's own tests. Of the three professional marksmen used by the Commission to try to duplicate Oswald's performance, only one was able to fire three shots within the required amount of time. And none of the group had fired at a moving target, let alone scored two direct hits as Oswald had.[1] CBS News had commissioned the study in which Donahue was now a participant in an attempt to lay this fundamental question to rest. If it was indeed physically impossible for trained marksmen to fire the gun as fast as Oswald allegedly had, then the results would go a long way toward proving that Oswald hadn't acted alone.

The gun provided for the marksmen that day was, like Oswald's, equipped with a makeshift sling and a cheap Japanese four-power scope mounted slightly off center to the left. As was the case with all Carcanos, the gun's action required that the marksman slam the bolt hard with the heel of the hand in order to drive a shell into the chamber.

Donahue and the others were initially instructed to fire three sets of three shots at a target about 150 feet away in the basement firing range. Donahue was skeptical about just what this could prove. He noticed some of the lights on the firing range weren't working, making accurate shooting more difficult. And the targets themselves were already riddled with holes. There would be no way to tell where the shots hit. He pointed out these problems to one of the technicians. Not to worry, the technician said. This part of the test was designed only to acquaint the marksmen with the gun. The real work came next.

A total of eleven marksmen were participating in the test. Half the group had already shot the day before. Of the eleven, three were employees of the H. P. White Laboratory, three were Maryland state police officers, one was a weapons engineer (Donahue), one a ballistics technician, two were sportsmen, and one was an ex-paratrooper just back from Vietnam.[2] None had been informed ahead of time about the nature of the test. CBS News directors apparently believed that if any of the riflemen had a chance to practice, the results of the demonstration would be worthless. And none would be paid for their time no matter how well they shot.

After each man had test-fired the Carcano, Donahue's group headed for a remote area on the H. P. White compound. Here, much to their amazement, they found a functional mock-up of the Dealey Plaza site in Dallas where Kennedy had been killed. CBS had erected a sixty-foot wooden tower to simulate Oswald's perch on the sixth floor of the Texas School Book Depository. Beneath it ran a narrow-gauge railroad track that stretched for several hundred feet down a slight grade. A small vehicle powered by an electric motor was mounted on the makeshift track; inside it was a silhouette target of a man's head and shoulders.

It was obvious that considerable thought and expense had gone into construction of the mock-up. To CBS and the country, it just might be worth it. For the first time, a Carcano test firing would be conducted in realistic fashion—at a moving target from the same height from which Oswald had fired.

Donahue climbed the rickety ladder to a small wooden platform at the top of the tower. Already there were three policemen, several television crew members, a camera, and considerable TV equipment. Several heavy crates were also scattered around, as had been the case in Dallas. A plank nailed across one edge of the roost simulated the fourteen-and-a-half-inch windowsill Oswald had fired from. Donahue noticed two of the police officers wore pistol expert medals and a third sported a sharpshooter medal. They would shoot first.

They fired from various positions, Donahue recalled. "Some moved the boxes around to use as rifle rests. Everybody had a lot of trouble stabilizing the rifle. The bolt action was so clumsy that after a man squeezed off a shot, ejected the empty cartridge and rammed in a new one with the stiff bolt mechanism, his rifle remained nowhere near on-target and he had to find the target in his scope sight all over again."*

The designers of the firing range had placed two stakes alongside the railroad track. The first represented the initial instant Oswald would have had a clear shot at Kennedy; the second marked the position of the limousine at the time the final shot hit home. The

---

*All Donahue quotes in this chapter about the CBS reenactment are from an interview with Donahue that appeared in the *Baltimore Sun Sunday Magazine*, May 1, 1977.

marksmen were told they could not fire until the vehicle passed the first stake at eleven miles an hour, the speed the limousine had been traveling in Dallas that day. Any shot fired after the second stake would not count.

By the time Donahue's chance to shoot came, the weather had turned for the worse. A light rain began to fall and the tower swayed slightly in the wind. At five feet nine inches tall and 159 pounds, Donahue was almost exactly the same size as Oswald. He decided for that reason to fire from a position the assassin might have used: a deep kneel, with his right leg tucked under him and his left hand steadying the rifle on the windowsill. He wrapped the gun's sling tightly over and under his left arm to further stabilize the gun.

Donahue drew a bead and fired as the electric cart passed the first stake, but the weapon jammed and he was unable to free the bolt before the vehicle motored beyond the second stake. In his second attempt, Donahue fumbled with the sticky bolt mechanism and managed to get off only two shots. Both were hits. He would get one more chance.

"In my third series of three, I fired the split second the target passed the first stake," Donahue recalled. "With my right hand, I hit the bolt handle to eject. It was stuck again. Realizing how little time I had, I hit the bolt with all the force possible, ejecting the empty.

"I felt more than half my time had passed when I slammed the bolt forward to insert the second round, picked up the target in the cross hairs and fired."

Even as the rifle recoiled, Donahue brought up his right hand, hit the bolt to eject the spent shell, slammed it forward, drew a bead and fired his final shot.

"We've got a good one!" one of the target spotters below shouted as Howard stood up from his sniper's crouch. Remarkably, Donahue's shots had all hit within a three-inch circle on the target's head. More importantly, the elapsed time from first shot to last was only 4.8 seconds, well under the 5.6-second maximum. A second timer measured the elapsed time of the shooting at 5.2 seconds, but still within the range.

The rain began to come down harder and the test was concluded. It was not until several weeks later that Donahue learned that out of the eleven men who had participated in the test, he was the only one able to better Oswald's performance, though several others had equaled it.

He received a congratulatory letter from Leslie Midgley, a CBS executive producer. "While your performance with the Mannlicher-Carcano was outstanding and impressive, I'm afraid it will take much more to 'dispel once and for all' the many theories of multiple assassins," Midgley wrote.

A CBS News special centered around the test and anchored by veteran newsman Walter Cronkite ran over four successive nights beginning Sunday, June 25, 1967. A central conclusion of the CBS investigation was that the Zapruder film was probably running slower than the Warren Commission believed and thus Oswald actually had more than 5.6 seconds to fire off three shots. In any case, the carefully controlled shooting experiment had shown the Carcano could, in fact, be fired more rapidly and accurately than previously thought.

"These points strengthen the Warren Report's basic finding," Cronkite said at the broadcast's conclusion. "They significantly weaken a central contention of the critics—their contention that Oswald could not have done it because he did not have enough time to fire. . . . Did Lee Harvey Oswald shoot the President? CBS News concludes that he did."[3]

No mention was made during the broadcast of Howard's singular performance with the Carcano, but there was a small write-up in the *Baltimore News-American*'s June 26, 1967, edition. Beneath a picture of an unidentified marksman sighting the Carcano and an insert photo of a 6.5 millimeter bullet, the *News-American* reported:

> CBS-TV commissioned the H. P. White ballistic laboratory in Bel Air to determine by actual firing if Lee Oswald could have fired his rifle as fast and as rapidly as the Warren Report credited him—and a Baltimore man, Howard Donahue, proved that he could—three shots in 5.2 seconds, bolt action.

Donahue's shooting prowess with the Carcano was soon known in the gun shops and shooting clubs around Baltimore. As a result, Donahue was approached later that summer by an editor from *True* magazine with a proposition: Since he was knowledgeable about firearms and ballistics and the only marksman to ever better Oswald's performance, would Howard be interested in writing an article for the magazine supporting the Warren Commission's conclusions?

Donahue agreed to take on the assignment, but he told the editor he needed to do a little research first.

"I just want to be sure they're right," he said.

2
THE WARREN REPORT

ACTUALLY, DONAHUE DIDN'T NEED MUCH CONVINCING ABOUT the veracity of the Warren Report. True, there had been more than a few books raising questions about the Commission's motives, methods, and findings. Some had gone so far as to argue, with varying degrees of clarity, that the assassination was the work of conspirators. But Donahue dismissed these attacks. He assumed they were the work of cynical writers who cared less about finding the facts of Kennedy's death than they did about making money. Besides, Donahue had fought for his country in the war. The idea that his own government would deceive him, as these books suggested, was so farfetched as to be absurd. In Communist Russia or Red China, undoubtedly. But not in the United States.

Still, Donahue decided to examine several of the contrary theories, if for no other reason than to shoot them down in the *True* article. But first he would learn all he could about the Warren Commission and its explanation of Kennedy's death.

The Commission had been formed only seven days after the assassination. President Lyndon Johnson was desperate to allay fears even then—particularly in Europe—that the shooting was the work of conspirators.[1] He knew he had to act fast. He also knew that it was essential that a man of unimpeachable integrity head the blue-ribbon panel. Johnson figured Supreme Court Chief Justice Earl Warren was that man. A onetime vice presidential candidate with Thomas Dewey and a former governor of California, Chief Justice Warren had led the Supreme Court in its pioneering *Brown versus the Topeka Board of Education* decision in 1954. The ruling undermined the multitude of separate-but-equal race laws in the country and proved a primary catalyst for the civil rights movement that would sweep across America during the next twenty years.

Warren had admired the young President Kennedy, but even

though outraged and saddened by Kennedy's death, he initially turned down Johnson's request, which was delivered by Deputy Attorney General Nicholas Katzenbach and Solicitor General Archibald Cox. Warren told the Justice Department officials he didn't think it appropriate for one branch of government to be employed by another branch.[2]

Johnson was not about to buy this, however, and few politicians could be more persuasive. The President spoke of the grave risks the country faced if the facts surrounding the assassination were never brought to light. He cagily appealed to Warren's sense of duty, honor, and patriotism.[3]

"Mr. Chief Justice, you were a soldier in World War One," Johnson said. "There's nothing you then did that compares with what you can do now for your country. As your Commander-in-Chief, I am ordering you back into service."[4]

And so Warren agreed. He and six other distinguished current or former government officials were sworn in to investigate the assassination on November 28, 1963. Joining Warren were Senator John Sherman Cooper of Kentucky, Allen Dulles, a former Central Intelligence Agency director, Congressman Gerald Ford of Michigan, John McCloy, assistant secretary of war during World War II, Senator Richard Russell of Georgia, and Congressman Hale Boggs of Louisiana.

The President's mandate to the Commission read:

> . . . Examine the evidence developed by the Federal Bureau of Investigation and any additional evidence that may hereafter come to light or be uncovered by federal or state authorities; to make further investigation as the Commission finds desirable; to evaluate all the facts and circumstances surrounding such assassination, including the subsequent violent death of the man charged with the assassination, and to report to me its findings and conclusions.[5]

To execute this task, the Commission had at its disposal fourteen attorneys as well as a number of government staffers. The group would also have access to the vast resources of the FBI and the federal government as a whole.[6] In the early months of the probe, the Commission directed requests for any information on the assassination, Oswald, or Jack Ruby, Oswald's killer, to no less than ten major departments of the federal government, fourteen of its independent agencies or commissions, and four congressional committees.[7]

The Commission itself would interview 522 witnesses over the ten-month life of the investigation. Of that number, 94 testified in person before members of the Commission, 395 were questioned by members of the Commission's staff, 61 submitted sworn affidavits, and 2 gave statements.[8]

For the most part, though, the Commission relied on information generated by the FBI. A massive FBI probe was launched immediately after the killing, and eighty special agents were temporarily detailed to the Dallas field office to assist in the work. Five volumes worth of the Bureau's initial findings were submitted to the Commission on December 9, 1963.[9] In the months that followed, Bureau gumshoes continued to sleuth on behalf of the Commission. FBI agents would conduct a phenomenal 25,000 interviews or reinterviews of persons having information of possible relevance to the case by the time the Warren Commission's work was finished in the autumn of 1964.[10]

As the documents poured in, Commission attorneys divided into groups to tackle particular aspects of the case—analyzing and summarizing the data, organizing the facts and sorting out unresolved questions. The commissioners themselves periodically reviewed these efforts and continued to direct the overall thrust of the probe, although staff attorneys did virtually all the real work.

The Commission had initially planned to submit its final report to the President by June 1, 1964. But as winter passed into spring, it was apparent this deadline would go unmet. Investigators worked furiously through the summer months. With autumn closing in, pressure intensified from Johnson's aides to complete the report before the impending November presidential election.[11]

The Warren Commission Report was finally submitted to President Johnson and a waiting world on September 24, 1964. It was 888 pages long. Transcripts from the Commission's interviews filled an additional fifteen volumes, while exhibits were presented in ten more. To the immediate relief of most—and the enduring skepticism of some—the Commission's account of the killing differed only in degree from the conclusions reached by the Dallas police within hours of the assassination. Lee Harvey Oswald acted alone in killing the President, the Commission said. Oswald fired three shots from the sixth floor of his place of employment, the Texas School Book Depository: One shot missed, one hit Kennedy in the neck, and one struck the President in the head.

The Commission further asserted that the assassin's death two days later at the hands of Jack Ruby, a small-time strip joint operator—for all its ominous appearances—was purely an impulsive act of a man driven temporarily insane with grief.

If the Commission had been unable to uncover any new facts that proved Oswald's guilt beyond all reasonable doubt, most observers conceded the evidence it did have against the twenty-four-year-old ex-Marine was powerful. Furthermore, the information seemed to be presented with such authority, lucidity, and attention to detail as to convince all but the most cynical of Oswald's solitary role in the killing. Commission authors seemingly used every available fact to painstakingly reconstruct the principal characters and events in the drama. Then, in an understated, almost literary style, they demonstrated how the abiding forces of fate and chance intervened at crucial intervals to push the tale toward its sorrowful end.

The tragedy, the Commission reported in straight, emotionless prose, was set in motion on the evening of November 21, when Lee Harvey Oswald hitched a ride with coworker Buell Wesley Frazier to the home of Oswald's estranged wife in Irving, a suburb fifteen miles from Dallas. Oswald told Frazier he needed to get some curtain rods for his rented room in Dallas.[12] He would stay overnight and ride back to Dallas with Frazier in the morning.

Frazier picked up Oswald the next day and noticed he carried a long, bulky object wrapped in brown paper. When Frazier asked what was in the package, Oswald told him it was the curtain rods.[13] Hidden in the brown paper, of course, was the Mannlicher-Carcano rifle Oswald had purchased under the name "A. Hidell" for $21.45 in March of 1963 from a mail-order house in Chicago, according to the Commission.[14]

At 11:40 A.M., Kennedy's plane touched down at Dallas's Love Field. Dallas was the fourth stop on what was turning out to be a grueling three-day political swing across Texas. The President had come to Texas to settle a factional dispute within the Texas Democratic party. Kennedy also hoped to boost his popularity in an extremely conservative state he had barely won in 1960; the President was particularly anxious to endear himself to the city of Dallas, a right-wing enclave he'd in fact lost in the election three years before.[15]

After greeting a crowd of more than one thousand supporters on the tarmac, Kennedy and a motorcade of nearly twenty vehicles left the airport and headed for the Dallas Trade Mart. Kennedy would address a group of business and civic leaders at a luncheon there. Among those riding in the presidential procession that day were Vice President Johnson, Texas Governor John Connally, Senator Ralph Yarborough, the men's wives, and a Secret Service contingent, as well as a host of local dignitaries, press, and other political hangers-on.

Kennedy's aides were overjoyed as the motorcade made its way through the canyons of downtown. The crowds were six deep and ardent in their apparent affection for Kennedy and his wife. Even the most optimistic member of Kennedy's party had not envisioned such a turnout.[16]

The day had started cool and drizzly but by late morning the sky cleared and a strong prairie breeze was pushing out of the west. The sixty-eight-degree temperature was hot for November. At the end of Main Street, the primary east-west corridor through downtown, Kennedy's motorcade swung right onto Houston and then, a block later, made an acute left-hand turn onto Elm Street, directly beneath the Texas School Book Depository and five minutes from the Trade Mart.

Governor Connally's wife was riding with her husband in the presidential car, and she too was elated by the size and warmth of the crowds. There had been concern that an incident might mar the President's visit to the city. Now, with the motorcade almost over, Mrs. Connally turned to Kennedy and gushed with pride and relief. "Mr. President, you can't say Dallas doesn't love you."

In his characteristic Harvard accent, Kennedy replied, "That is very obvious."[17]

The clock on the huge Hertz Rent-a-Car sign atop the book depository read twelve-thirty when Oswald squeezed the trigger from his sniper's nest of boxes on the building's sixth floor. The President's car was dropping slowly down and away from the building toward a railroad overpass just west of downtown.

The Commission concluded this first shot in all probability struck Kennedy at the base of his neck and exited the President's throat just below his larynx. The same bullet then slammed into Governor Connally's right side, shattered a rib, exited his chest, went through his right wrist and, almost spent, lodged in his left thigh. A few seconds later, another shot entered the back of Kennedy's head and blasted out the right front portion of his skull.

The Commission did equivocate somewhat on the sequence of events: The consensus among witnesses was that three shots were fired. But since the Commission had concluded a single bullet wounded both Kennedy and Connally and a second hit Kennedy in the head, the evidence seemed to dictate that one shot missed.[18]

This view was seemingly strengthened by the fact that a witness who'd been standing down by the underpass was slightly wounded by an apparent bullet fragment, and there was also a bullet nick in the pavement nearby.

Whether the miss that slammed into the concrete and wounded James Tague was the first, second, or third shot fired, the Commission in the end could not say with absolute certainty. It did, however, feel confident enough to state that the preponderance of evidence suggested the first shot was the one that hit Kennedy in the neck, the second was the miss and the third smashed the President's skull.[19]

Reading this, Donahue was convinced. Among the facts that seemed to point unswervingly to Oswald's guilt:

- A 6.5 millimeter rifle owned by Oswald was found on the sixth floor of the Texas School Book Depository.[20]
- Three empty 6.5 millimeter shells were discovered nearby.[21]
- Oswald's palm print was lifted from the gun.[22]
- Oswald worked at the book depository.[23]
- At least one witness saw a man of Oswald's description aiming a rifle to fire from the sixth-floor window.[24]
- Oswald disappeared from the book depository immediately after the assassination.[25]
- Witnesses identified him as the killer of a Dallas police

officer slain an hour and forty-five minutes after the assassination in another part of the city.[26]

- Four ejected .38 caliber shells were found under a bush near where the officer died.[27]
- Witnesses saw Oswald open a pistol and shake the shells out after the shooting.[28]
- The shells were ballistically matched to Oswald's Smith & Wesson .38 Special.
- The gun was in Oswald's possession at the time of his arrest.[29]
- Oswald resisted arrest in a movie theater after the police officer was shot, even as he exclaimed, "Well, it's all over now."[30]
- Oswald's jacket was found in a parking lot between the site where the police officer was murdered and the movie theater where the arrest was made.[31]
- Oswald's wife confirmed her husband had attempted to kill retired Army general and right-wing activist Edwin Walker in April 1963, thereby "demonstrating Oswald's disposition to take human life."[32]
- A 6.5 millimeter bullet fired from Oswald's gun was found at Parkland Hospital after it apparently dropped from Governor Connally's thigh.[33]

Yet if the evidence was impressive, investigators still lacked a clear motive for Oswald's act. Donahue, however, found the picture the Commission painted of Oswald's life in the months and years before the shooting compelling in its pathos, and he was inclined to agree with investigators: Such circumstances could have easily poisoned Oswald's character and spawned a bitter man with little to lose by killing the President.

On this central question of motive, the Commission wrote:

Indications of Oswald's motivation may be obtained from a study of the events, relationships and influences which appear to have been significant in shaping his character and in guiding him.

Perhaps the most outstanding conclusion of such a study is that Oswald was profoundly alienated from the world in which he lived. His life was characterized by isolation, frustration and failure. He had very few, if any, close relationships with other people and he appeared to have great difficulty in finding a meaningful place in the world.[34]

That world began for Oswald in New Orleans on October 18, 1939. His father, an insurance premium collector, died of a heart attack two months before Lee was born. His mother subsequently put Lee, his brother, and a half-brother in an orphanage for a time. She later reclaimed them and the family moved to Dallas.[35] They were poor.

When Oswald was thirteen, the family uprooted again and moved to New York City. Classmates made fun of Oswald's southern accent and western dress. He began to stay away from school. Truancy charges were brought. He spent three weeks in a youth detention center. Doctors reported Oswald had a vivid fantasy life, "turning around the topics of omnipotence and power, through which he tries to compensate for his present shortcomings and frustrations."[36]

The Commission wrote: "The reports of the New York authorities indicate that Lee's mother gave him very little affection and did not serve as any sort of substitute for a father. Furthermore she did not appear to understand her own relationship to Lee's psychological problems."[37]

After a year and a half in New York, the family moved back to New Orleans. In school, Oswald was teased again, now because of the northern accent he had acquired while living in New York.[38]

"Several witnesses testified that Lee Oswald was not aggressive," the Commission reported. "He was, however, involved in some fights. Once a group of white boys beat him up for sitting in the Negro section of a bus, which he apparently did simply out of ignorance."[39]

Lee's IQ was 118. He had a learning disability. He was a wretched speller.[40] He finished the ninth grade and joined the Marines soon after his seventeenth birthday in October 1956. He did not adjust well to military life. His career was hindered by "his attitude that he was a man of great ability and intelligence and that many of his superiors in the Marine Corps were not sufficiently competent to give him orders," the Commission wrote.[41]

He was sloppy in his personal habits and appearance. Acquaintances believed he labored under a persecution complex. He attempted to garner sympathy. Fellow soldiers nicknamed him "Ozzie Rabbit" after a children's cartoon character. He accidentally shot himself with a pistol.[42]

He began to study Marxism in the service. He read Russian newspapers, studied the language, and showed an interest in what was happening in the Soviet Union.[43]

In September 1959, Oswald quit the Marine Corps, ostensibly to care for his ailing mother. He then booked passage on a ship to Europe, traveled to Finland via Le Havre, France, and London, and promptly defected to the Soviet Union.[44] He cabled his brother to say that the Soviet Union was a country that "I have always considered to be my own" and that he would "never return to the United States which is a country I hate."[45]

His brother responded by assuring Lee he would not renounce him for defecting. Oswald in turn sent another cable, explaining on what terms he would accept his brother's support:

> 1. In the event of war I would kill *any* american who put a uniform on in the defence of the american government—any american.

2. That in my own mind I have no attachment's of any kind in the U.S.

3. That I want to, and I shall, live a normal happy and peaceful life in the Soviet Union *for the rest of my life*.

4. that my mother and you are (in spite of what the newspaper said) *not* objects of affection, but only examples of workers in the U.S.[46]

Once in Russia, however, Oswald was stunned to find he was not welcomed as a hero by Soviet authorities. They told him to get out of the country. He slit his wrists. Oswald wrote in his "Historic Diary":

I am shocked!! My dreams! . . . I have waited for two year to be accepted. My fondes dreams are shattered because of a petty offial . . . I decide to end it. Soak rist in cold water to numb the pain, Than slash my leftwrist. Than plaug wrist into bathtum of hot water . . . Somewhere, a violin plays, as I wacth my life whirl away. I think to myself "How easy to Die" and "A Sweet Death, (to violins)"[47]

Oswald was discovered by his government-provided translator before he bled to death. He spent a week in a hospital. Soviet officials eventually relented and allowed him to stay. He tried to renounce his American citizenship, but U.S. embassy officials told him to come back in a few days to fill out the proper papers.[48] He never did. Had Oswald succeeded in giving up his citizenship, he would probably have never been able to reenter the United States.

Oswald was sent to work at a television factory in Minsk. He met a girl and married her. Marina Oswald confided to a friend later that in Russia, "everyone hated him."[49] In time Oswald became increasingly disillusioned with the grim life under communism, and in June of 1962 he was finally allowed to return to the Dallas–Fort Worth area after fifteen months of haggling with U.S. embassy officials in Moscow.[50]

Back in the States, Oswald bounced from job to job. In April of 1963, he moved to New Orleans. In May, he went to work as a greaser and oiler of coffee machines. In July, he was fired. Despite his newfound aversion to communism, Oswald became involved in Fair Play for Cuba, a pro-Castro organization.[51]

In the early fall of '63, Oswald traveled briefly to Mexico, apparently in an unsuccessful attempt to get a visa to visit Cuba.[52] He then returned to Dallas in October and found a job at the Texas School Book Depository.

A little over a month later, he was dead.

According to the Commission, then, the long and short of it was that there was no evidence pointing to the involvement of anyone else in Oswald's decision to kill the President. He was simply a

twisted loser or "lone nut," as he quickly became known to the press
and the world.

Oswald's death by gunfire in the crowded police headquarters
basement two days after the assassination, of course, raised a host of
questions the Commission had no choice but to address. Did his
killer, Jack Ruby, know Oswald? Had a conspiracy gone awry? Were
the Dallas police involved? Was Oswald silenced? Were foreign
powers mixed up in it? Was Oswald just a "patsy," as he claimed to
newsmen?

Investigators reconstructed Ruby's movements and actions from
November 21 to November 24 on the premise that "if Jack Ruby
were involved in a conspiracy, his activities and associations during
this period would, in some way, have reflected the conspiratorial
relationship."[53]

This reconstruction revealed a tawdry picture of a struggling night-
club owner going about the daily business of his life. The day before
the shooting, Ruby met with an attorney to discuss problems he was
having with federal tax authorities. He owed the Internal Revenue
Service in excess of $44,000.[54] Ruby also visited a Dallas County
assistant district attorney to complain about a bounced check a friend
had passed at one of his clubs. Earlier, he met with authorities about
a peace bond he'd been obliged to put up after he'd fought with one
of his strippers.[55]

On the twenty-second, Ruby was putting together advertisements
for his two clubs, the Vegas and the Carousel, at the *Dallas Morning
News* when word came in that Kennedy had been shot. John
Newnam, an advertising department employee, described Ruby's
reaction to the news as one of "stunned disbelief." Another employee said Ruby appeared "obviously shaken, and an ashen color—
just very pale" as he sat silently with a dazed expression on his
face.[56]

Friends, club employees, and acquaintances who had contact with
Ruby over the next forty-eight hours told the Commission that Ruby
seemed extremely distraught over the President's killing. To a Chicago acquaintance, Ruby said, "I've got to do something about this."
The friend was unsure whether Ruby was referring to the assassination or to the failure of other Dallas strip joint operators to close
down in mourning on Saturday night, November 23.[57]

After the murder, Ruby became highly agitated about a black-
bordered advertisement that ran in the Dallas morning paper the day
of the assassination attacking Kennedy's purported liberal positions.
A billboard in Dallas calling for the impeachment of Supreme Court
Justice Earl Warren likewise angered him considerably.[58]

By his own admission to the Warren Commission, Ruby was driven
to shoot Oswald after reading in the newspaper on Sunday morning,
November 24, that Jackie Kennedy would probably have to come
back to Dallas to testify against Oswald: ". . . [S]uddenly the feeling,

the emotional feeling came within me that someone owed this debt to our beloved President to save her the ordeal of coming back," Ruby said. "I don't know why that came through my mind."[59]

As for the possibility that Ruby and Oswald knew each other, the Commission categorically ruled it out.

> . . . [T]here have been numerous specific allegations that Oswald was seen in the company of Ruby prior to November 22, often at Ruby's Carousel Club. All such allegations have been investigated, but the Commission has found none which merits credence.
>
> In all but a few instances where the Commission was able to trace the claim to its source, the person responsible for the report either denied making it or admitted that he had no basis for the original allegation. Frequently those responsible for the allegations have proved to be persons of erratic memory or dubious mental stability.[60]

The Commission also gave little credence to suggestions that Ruby might have had ties to organized crime. A short section in the Warren Report was dedicated to the subject. In it, the Commission stated that any links Ruby may have had with the mob were undoubtedly limited to the professional gamblers who frequented his clubs. Law enforcement agencies, the Commission wrote, had thoroughly investigated the matter and were satisfied that Ruby was in no way affiliated with La Cosa Nostra families then operating in the United States.

As he finished reading the Warren Report, Howard Donahue was no more inclined to believe the Commission's critics than before. The Commission's exhaustive account of the events and people in Dallas seemed more than sufficient in his mind to resolve any doubts that may have existed.

Still, fairness required that he examine both sides of the story. He knew that for his *True* article to be credible, he would have to deal with the arguments made by those who did not believe the government's explanation of the killing.

And so, buying a little more time from his editor, Donahue found every book he could on the assassination and started to read.

3
THE CRITICS

FOR ALL OF DONAHUE'S CONFIDENCE IN THE Warren Report, he and others like him were fast becoming a minority by the mid-1960s. A survey conducted by *The Washington Post* in October 1966 found that 60 percent of the American people rejected the "main arguments" of the Warren Commission's findings and had "deep and abiding doubts about the official explanation" of the assassination.[1] This skepticism was driven by, and in turn, driving, a tremendous amount of written material about Kennedy's death. By the time Donahue began his research, dozens of articles and close to twenty books had been written on the murder.[2] Most were sharply critical of the Warren Report.

In tone and content, the books ranged from the sensationalistic to the scholarly, while their titles often reflected competing conspiracy theories that seemed to mushroom monthly in the dark, uncertain aftermath of the shooting: *Oswald: Assassin or Fall Guy?, The Second Oswald, Inquest, Whitewash I—The Report on the Warren Report, Whitewash II—The FBI–Secret Service Cover-Up, Rush to Judgment, The Bastard Bullet.*

Alleged conspirators ranged from disgruntled Cubans to the Russians to the Central Intelligence Agency, organized crime, right-wing fanatics, or any combination of the above. Writers sustained these theories with what they claimed were a host of unanswered questions, bizarre coincidences and outright contradictions in the Warren Commission's findings. The red flags emerged after reporters and writers began scrutinizing the Commission's twenty-six volumes of transcripts and evidence and after they started talking to witnesses the Commission chose not to hear.

One of the areas of greatest doubt centered on what quickly and derisively became known as the Commission's "magic bullet" theory: the claim that both Connally and Kennedy were wounded by the same bullet, probably the first Oswald fired. According to the critics, the bullet trajectory through both men didn't even line up, and in any case, Connally himself testified he was hit by the second shot fired, not the first. Connally said he heard the first shot and was beginning to turn, trying to determine where the sound came from, when a second bullet hit him.[3]

The Zapruder film, as well as the testimony of others, seemed to back up the governor on this crucial point. As the President's limousine emerged in the film from behind a highway sign on Elm Street, Kennedy appeared to be grabbing his throat and was obviously hit. Connally, however, still looked normal and did not crumple from his wound until nearly two seconds later. The Commission asserted the governor probably had a delayed reaction to his wounds, but given the severity of the injuries, many critics didn't buy it.

Another overarching difficulty with the magic bullet theory was how the slug found at Parkland Hospital could have crashed through both Kennedy and Connally and emerged virtually undamaged.[4] And while the Warren Report implied there was no doubt the bullet had fallen from Connally's thigh wound, Darrell Tomlinson, the hospital employee who found it, was by no means certain the slug came from Connally's stretcher. Several carts were parked in the area where the bullet was discovered, and it wasn't even clear Connally's stretcher was out of the emergency room at the time the bullet was found. Commission lawyers pressed Tomlinson on this point, but Tomlinson held his ground and would say only that the bullet *could* have come from Connally's stretcher.

"I am going to tell you all I can, and I'm not going to tell you something I can't lay down and sleep at night with either," Tomlinson said.[5]

There was also a multitude of questions surrounding the grassy knoll just west of the book depository. Many witnesses ran to the area just after the shots were fired and at least thirty-three subsequently reported they believed the shots came from the knoll.[6]

More to the point, one man even said he saw a puff of smoke on the knoll at the time of the shooting.[7] Another, Lee Bowers, told the Commission he noticed two men standing behind the fence along the top of the knoll just before the assassination. Bowers was a railroad employee who worked in a switching yard tower several hundred feet north of the knoll.[8] His view of the area was unsurpassed.

Bowers later told Mark Lane, author of *Rush to Judgment,* that as the shots rang out, "a flash or light or smoke or . . . something out of the ordinary" caught his eye in the vicinity of where the two men had stood.[9]

Before that, in the twenty minutes prior to the shooting, Bowers noticed three cars drive down a dead-end street running in front of the book depository and into the area behind the knoll.[10] "The [first] car proceeded in front of the school depository, down across two or three tracks and circled the area in front of the tower and to the west of the tower as if he was searching for a way out, or was checking the area, and then proceeded back through the only way he could, the same outlet he came into," Bowers said.

He described the vehicle as a muddy 1959 blue and white Oldsmobile station wagon with out-of-state license tags and a Goldwater for President sticker on the bumper. Soon after, a black 1957 Ford drove through the same area. According to Bowers, the driver "seemed to have a mike or telephone or something that gave the appearance of that at least." Finally, just a few minutes before the assassination, a white 1961 or 1962 Chevrolet motored slowly through the parking lot beyond the knoll. Like the station wagon, Bowers said, the Chevy was muddy and had out-of-state tags.

The presence of the men and the automobiles behind the knoll certainly seemed suspicious. Yet little weight was given to Bowers's testimony and no serious attempt was made by the Commission to locate or identify either the vehicles, their owners, or the two men.

Other questions were raised by the witnesses the Commission never called. Carolyn Walther, who stood with a friend fifty to sixty feet south of the corner of Elm and Houston, noticed two men on the fourth or fifth floor of the book depository just before the shooting started. One of the men wore a white shirt, had blond hair, and was holding what appeared to be a short-barrelled sub-machine gun.[11]

Steelworker Richard Randolph Carr reported that immediately after the assassination, he saw two men sprint from the rear of the book depository and drive away in a Rambler station wagon.[12]

And Bill and Gayle Newman, who were standing just a few feet from Kennedy when the final shot hit, both repeatedly asserted the shots came from directly behind them, from the grassy knoll.[13]

Then there were the questions raised in the testimony of witnesses the Commission did call. H. L. Brennan, hailed as the Commission's most important witness by Congressman Gerald Ford, reported seeing a man matching Oswald's description aim his rifle from a sixth-floor book depository window. Apparently, it was Brennan's description that led to Oswald's arrest. Strangely, though, Brennan heard only two shots, not the three the Commission said were fired.[14]

Likewise, several ear-witnesses deep inside the book depository reported hearing only one or two shots.[15] Bonnie Ray Williams, a depository employee who watched the motorcade with several co-workers from the fifth-floor window directly below Oswald's perch, told the FBI on the afternoon of the twenty-second that he heard only two shots fired above him.[16]

Months later, however, Williams testified that actually he heard three shots; that in the excitement of the twenty-second he'd mistakenly told the FBI he heard only two.[17]

In any event, what was one to make of the reports of a so-called "second Oswald" that filtered into Dallas law enforcement offices in the weeks following the assassination? A gun dealer in Irving told investigators a man named Oswald left a rifle to have it mounted with a telescopic sight in the first two weeks of November.[18] Yet the gun Lee Harvey Oswald used to kill the President was purchased with the sight attached.[19]

At least six people reported seeing a man resembling Oswald practicing at rifle ranges in the Dallas area through the fall of 1963 with a gun "perhaps identical to Oswald's Mannlicher-Carcano." According to the Commission, however, there was no evidence proving Oswald ever went to the ranges in question that autumn.[20]

Albert Bogard, a salesman with a Lincoln-Mercury dealer in Dallas, said that on November 9 a man who gave his name as Lee Oswald took a test drive in a new car at seventy miles an hour on a nearby freeway. The problem was the "real" Oswald did not know how to drive. Bogard nonetheless said he recognized the man to be Oswald from photographs that appeared in the newspapers after the assassination.[21]

The Commission eventually decided Oswald could not have been involved in these sightings or encounters.[22] But that, critics said, was precisely the point. In any case, the Commission made no effort to find out who this person or persons might have been or why they would want to establish sightings of "Oswald" in the weeks prior to the assassination.

Finally, there was the prolonged and bitter controversy surrounding the President's wounds and his examination by doctors in Dallas and in Bethesda, Maryland, where the Kennedy autopsy was conducted. Doctors in Dallas initially told the press that the frontal wound in Kennedy's neck may have been one of entry.[23] This obviously destroyed the one-gunman scenario, and Commission investigators subsequently suggested the doctors might have been mistaken. Most of them eventually concluded they had been.[24]

The Bethesda autopsy itself was conducted by a doctor who had virtually no experience with gunshot victims.[25] Not surprisingly, the procedure was rife with errors. And what possible reason, critics asked, would the doctor have had for burning his autopsy notes two days after the operation was complete?[26]

A host of other troubling questions raised by the critics included:

- Why was the gun found at the depository initially described as a 7.65 millimeter German Mauser, when Oswald's gun was clearly stamped "Cal. 6.5—Made Italy"? Were two guns found in the book depository?[27]
- Why did the Commission discount the testimony of veteran reporter Seth Kantor, who swore he saw and talked to Jack Ruby at Parkland Hospital just after the shooting?[28] Did Ruby plant the "magic bullet"?
- Why did the Commission never mention that the slaying of the Dallas police officer, J. D. Tippit, occurred just two

blocks from Ruby's apartment? Was Oswald on his way to see Ruby when the policeman stopped him?[29]

- How was Ruby able to penetrate the basement of the Dallas police station to kill Oswald? It was a fact that Ruby knew a number of police officers. Did they let him in? Were police involved in a plot to kill Kennedy and silence Oswald?[30]
- Along the same lines, how did Ruby manage to arrive at the police station at the precise moment Oswald was passing through? Oswald's transfer had originally been scheduled for 10:00 A.M. that Sunday morning. Did someone tell Ruby the transfer wouldn't take place until 11:20?[31] Or was his timely appearance just luck?

One of the broad complaints about the Warren Report centered on the Commission's methodology and apparent preconceived notions about the assassination. Harold Weisberg spoke for many when he wrote the following passage in his 1965 book *Whitewash I—The Report on the Warren Report*:

Did the Commission ever consider that anyone other than Lee Harvey Oswald could have been the assassin? Neither in the Report or anywhere else is there even any indication that the Commission ever seriously considered such a possibility. Oswald himself denied having shot anybody. The Report concludes his denial was not credible because the Commission considered him a liar.

Whether or not Oswald actually was a liar, the fact remains that the Commission ruled out the possibility of anyone else being the assassin of President Kennedy. This was the widely but not officially reported conclusion of the massive FBI report turned over to the Commission. It was the conclusion of the Dallas police. Perhaps it was even the fact. **But in determining before it held its hearings that it would not diligently seek out all other possibilities, the Commission conducted an inquiry with a built-in verdict.** It converted its function from one which would "uncover all the facts" to one that could have but a single purpose: To validate the conclusion that Oswald was the lone and unassisted assassin. This can scarcely be called the premise for an impartial and unbiased investigation.[32]

Of the books critical of the Commission written in the first five years after the shooting, Donahue found *Six Seconds in Dallas* by Josiah Thompson among the most compelling. The book had just been published in the fall of 1967. Thompson's effort was obviously thoroughly researched and included a wide variety of graphs, photographs, and other visual aids. Much of *Six Seconds* focused on the author's analysis of Abraham Zapruder's home movie of the assassination.

This analysis, Thompson concluded, revealed two essential points that proved the shooting was the work of more than one gunman: First, a frame-by-frame study of the film showed that Connally was indeed not hit until between ½ and 1½ seconds after Kennedy was. Given that the minimum firing time between Carcano shots was 2.3 seconds, the governor's wound—according to Thompson—came too late to be from the same bullet and too soon to have been a second bullet from the same rifle.[33]

Second, the film showed Kennedy's head move slightly forward and then violently backward as the final shot struck. According to Thompson, this motion proved that the President was hit in the head simultaneously with two shots: one from the front and one from the rear.[34] "If, as the Commission had said, the [last] shot came from the rear, then the force of the blow could be expected to jolt Kennedy forward, not **backward** as clearly appeared on the film," Thompson wrote.[35]

Thompson's final thesis was that

> three assassins fired four shots from three different locations. The first and third shots were from the depository—most likely from the sixth-floor, southeast-corner window later identified by the Warren Commission as the sniper's nest. The second shot, wounding the governor, was fired from the east side of Dealey Plaza—most likely from a building rooftop. The fourth and final shot was fired from a point near the corner of the stockade fence [on the grassy knoll] north of Elm Street.[36]

As he read Thompson's book and others and studied the skeptics' arguments and assertions, Donahue's loyalty to the Warren Commission diminished somewhat. The critics were right: There were too many omissions and seemingly arbitrary conclusions in the Warren Report, and too many questions left begging.

But at the same time, Donahue was struck by the fact that although these authors were writing with ostensible authority about a gunshot murder, few, if any, apparently had any experience with firearms or ballistics. Mark Lane, author of *Rush to Judgment,* was an attorney and former New York State assemblyman.[37] Harold Weisburg, the dean of the critics and author of the *Whitewash* series, was a government intelligence analyst–turned–goose farmer.[38] Sylvan Fox, who wrote *The Unanswered Questions About President Kennedy's Assassination,* was a Pulitzer Prize–winning reporter.[39] And for all his analytical skills, Thompson, author of *Six Seconds in Dallas,* was a philosophy professor.[40]

To Donahue, this lack of firearms training was all too apparent. In none of the books could he find a thoughtful, rigorous analysis of the ballistic evidence. Most of the authors, he believed, instead relied on ballistic generalizations and often outright fallacies to support their arguments. Others played down or ignored evidence that didn't support their particular bent on the killing.

This tendency to misunderstand the evidence or see it as a kind of rolling Rorschach test open to any number of interpretations, in Donahue's view, fostered many widespread misconceptions that seemed only to strengthen with the passage of time.

One example were the terms "master rifleman,"[41] and "superb marksman"[42] mentioned by incredulous writers in connection with Lee Harvey Oswald's performance in Dallas. Donahue knew Oswald's shooting was mediocre at best: The distance Oswald fired from was not that great and out of the three shots he supposedly got off, one missed the presidential limousine entirely.

Another fallacy, widely accepted as fact once it was reported, was that the Mannlicher-Carcano rifle required a minimum of 2.3 seconds for bolt action between shots. Thomas Buchanan wrote the following in his 1965 book *Who Killed Kennedy?* "It is doubtful if a single man exists who could have fired this weapon with the skill required [in the time required.] But if the feat is possible, it is, in the opinion of the experts, a superlative performance which requires one of the world's best marksmen . . ."[43]

Donahue wouldn't have minded being known as "one of the world's best marksmen," but he realized Buchanan's phrase and others like it were products of sheer ignorance. In the 1967 CBS reenactment, Donahue had been able to fire his last two shots in about two and a half seconds each. And the time it took him to fire all three was well under 5.6 seconds—the time between the first and third shot as calculated by the Warren Commission.

Yet another misconception that later on enjoyed wide currency was the belief that the 6.5 millimeter cartridge was a low-to-medium-powered military bullet incapable of penetrating both Kennedy and Connally.[44] In fact, Donahue knew the cartridge was extremely powerful. The Carcano had been produced as Italy's primary infantry weapon in the first half of the twentieth century, and its heavy bullet had been designed for deep penetration in house-to-house fighting or firing from a long distance. The round's muzzle velocity was 2,234 feet per second; more than twice the speed of a common .22 caliber bullet.

In the 1950s, African big-game hunter Koromojo Bell had demonstrated the weapon's lethal punch by using a Carcano-type rifle and cartridge to kill scores of elephants with single head shots. Donahue's confidence in the penetrating power of the Carcano was confirmed in later years by photographs of a 6.5 millimeter round passing through forty-seven inches of pine board.[45]

Even Thompson, whom Donahue considered to be the most conscientious and scholarly of the critics, made highly suspect forensic and ballistic conclusions central to his thesis that Kennedy was hit by multiple gunmen. According to Thompson, the slight forward, and, a fraction of a second later, violent backward movement of Kennedy's head revealed in the Zapruder film proved virtually simultaneous shots from front and rear.

Donahue knew there were no hard and fast rules about the way the human body reacted when hit by gunfire. He was inclined to believe the head movement could have just as easily been caused by a neuromuscular reaction. In any case, the movement of Kennedy's head alone, whatever it meant, hardly seemed like evidence conclusive enough to support the proposition that a second or third gunman was involved.

Donahue reorganized the data he'd gathered and looked it over once again. While less inclined to believe the Warren Report, he nonetheless found most of the critics' work to be worthless from a ballistics standpoint. Consequently, he decided that henceforth he would focus solely on the ballistic and forensic aspects of the assassination. Let others concern themselves with the tangle of conspiracy theories spun from the killing. How could Donahue ever know the true relationship between Oswald and Ruby, or whether there was a conspiracy? To make such a judgment would require a vast investigative apparatus, thousands of man-hours and a lot of luck.

Instead, by limiting his study to the ballistic and forensic evidence, Donahue would stay with what he knew best. He'd accumulated a vast amount of experience with guns and bullets over the years. And from longtime friendships with police detectives and his pre-med courses in college, he'd developed a fair understanding of forensic science.

Witnesses might offer conflicting testimony, but the irreducible facts remained unchanged: The Kennedy assassination was fundamentally a story of gunshots that killed one human being and wounded another. If Donahue could satisfy himself as to sequence and origin of the shots and the nature of the wounds they caused, it might go a long way toward proving how John Kennedy really died.

Judging by the ignorance revealed in everything he'd read so far, Donahue figured there just might be key pieces of evidence out there that had been overlooked or misunderstood. If such evidence was available, he was determined to find it.

4

THE SINGLE BULLET THEORY

DONAHUE BEGAN HIS STUDY BY FIRST ADDRESSING in detail the question of whether Oswald's first shot could have performed the way the Warren Commission said it did.

According to the Commission, the bullet struck Kennedy at the base of the neck just to the right of the spine. It then exited his throat below the Adam's apple, struck Connally beneath and behind the right armpit, shattered four inches of Connally's fifth rib, exited below his right nipple, crashed through the governor's right wrist and finally lodged two inches deep in his left thigh.[1]

Donahue had already shown the Carcano rifle was capable of being fired accurately three times in well under six seconds. And he knew the gun had more than enough penetrating power to push a bullet through both Kennedy and Connally. Therefore, he decided four other primary questions needed to be answered in the affirmative before the single bullet theory could be proven correct:

- First, was the bullet's apparent trajectory consistent with the way Kennedy and Connally were positioned?
- Second, were the wounds themselves compatible with the trajectory?
- Third, could the bullet recovered at Parkland, if it did come from Connally, really have done so much damage and remained essentially intact?
- And fourth, did the Warren Commission's single bullet theory agree with eyewitness reports and photographic evidence?

As to the first question, critics often argued that the men's relative positions in the limousine categorically ruled out the single bullet theory. This belief was based in large part on a Warren Commission photograph, known as Commission exhibit, or CE, number 697.[2] (See illustration 1.)

CE 697 showed a side view of the presidential limousine taken seconds before the shots rang out. In the picture, Kennedy and Connally appear to be perfectly aligned along the right side of the car's interior. Skeptics seized on this and asked how, given the men's respective attitudes, a bullet slanting down from the right rear could have pierced the President's throat, then inexplicably made a sharp right turn and entered Connally's back on the extreme right side. (See illustration 2.)

Donahue knew such a dogleg, or "bumblebee turn," was impossible. On this point he was inclined to agree with the skeptics. He then decided to go down to the National Archives in Washington to study the assassination photographs there. Among the dozens of pictures, one caught his attention.

The photo was a top-view interior shot of the limousine; the car was empty. Donahue was immediately struck by the positioning of the jump seats the Connallys had ridden in. Far from being in direct line with the President's and Jackie's respective places in the back seat, as CE 697 seemed to show, the small folding seats were actually situated very close to the center of the car, hard against the drive shaft tunnel. (See illustration 3.) As a result, at least six inches separated the outer edge of each folding seat from the car doors. Furthermore, it was clear the jump seats were installed on sliding runners mounted directly to the floorboard. Hence, they were also considerably lower than the bench seat on which the Kennedys rode.

Obviously Connally was actually sitting lower and much farther inboard than where he'd appeared to be in CE 697. Apparently, the picture had created the optical illusion that Kennedy and Connally were aligned. This was confirmed when Donahue studied several other photographs taken of the limousine from different angles prior to the shooting; pictures that did not make their way into the Warren Report. (See illustration 4.)

In each one, Connally is clearly closer to the car's center line than Kennedy. And though a physically large man, Connally is also shown without question to be seated below the President; his six-foot-two-inch frame packed tightly in the seat and his knees drawn up. As well, stills from the Zapruder film taken seconds before the first bullet hit showed Kennedy seated on the extreme right side of the rear seat, waving to the crowd. This position further distanced him, laterally, from Connally.

Using the photographs as a guide, Donahue made his own sketch of the men's actual positions at the time the bullet hit. Sure enough, by placing Connally farther inboard and lower and turned slightly to the right, Donahue found the bullet's trajectory from the book depository sixth-floor window lined up perfectly. The slug's impossible dogleg was eliminated. (See illustration 5.)

That the critics made no mention of the other limousine photos and, most importantly, the critical top view of the empty car showing the actual positions of the seats was, to Donahue, an example of flawed, incomplete analysis being passed off as the truth. Using basic skills of observation and deduction, he'd resolved one of the major arguments leveled against the Commission's magic bullet.

The irony of this was not lost on him. Though Donahue was increasingly inclined to believe the Commission may have been hiding something, for the second time (the CBS reenactment being the first) he had single-handedly backed up the Warren Report on a key point.

Of course, Donahue realized resolution of the positioning issue was meaningless unless the wounds themselves lined up with the trajectory. Resolving this question would be much more difficult, since virtually all of the crucial evidence was locked away from the public and since statements by the medical team in Dallas and the autopsy doctors in Maryland seemed hopelessly at odds.

The much publicized saga surrounding the medical record of the assassination began shortly after the presidential limousine screeched to a halt in front of Parkland Memorial Hospital less than five minutes after the shooting. Dr. Charles Carrico was the first doctor to examine Kennedy as the President was being wheeled into the hospital. Carrico observed two wounds: a small bullet wound in the front lower neck and a large, gaping wound in the President's head.[3] He also noted that Kennedy "was blue-white or ashen in color, had slow, agonal spasmodic respiration without any coordination; made no voluntary movements; had his eyes open with the pupils dilated without any reaction to light; evidenced no palpable pulse; and had a few chest sounds which were thought to be heart beats."[4]

No less than twelve doctors were soon at work on the President and Governor Connally. This group included four general surgeons, four anesthesiologists, the hospital's chief neurologist, a urological surgeon, an oral surgeon, and a heart specialist.[5]

Surgeon Malcolm Perry saw the President was having great difficulty breathing and immediately performed a tracheotomy, opening the throat slightly on either side of the neck wound. He then reinserted a respirator tube Carrico had previously placed in the wound to assist the President's breathing.[6] Unfortunately, Perry's incision irrevocably altered the appearance of the neck wound. This fact would produce major confusion in Bethesda hours later and chronic controversy in the years ahead.

The confusion would be compounded by the fact that the Dallas doctors never examined Kennedy's back and hence were unaware of the wound below the nape of his neck.[7] Having seen only the wounds to the President's throat and head, doctors speculated at a wild news conference on the afternoon of the twenty-second that the neck injury could have been caused by a bullet entering from the front.[8] This scenario, of course, ruled out the possibility that only one gunman was involved in the slaying. Naturally, the press jumped on the doctors' statements.

The plot thickened after the President's body arrived for the autopsy at the Bethesda Naval Hospital shortly after 7:30 P.M. on the night of the twenty-second. Commander James Humes, director of laboratories at the Naval Medical Center, was in charge of the procedure. Assisting him were Commander J. Thornton Boswell, chief of pathology at the Naval Medical School, and later, Colonel Pierre Finck, chief of the Wounds Ballistics Branch of the nearby Armed Forces Institute of Pathology. Humes and Boswell were eminently qualified to perform autopsies on individuals who had died from disease. But neither had any experience in gunshot wound cases. Finck, on the other hand, did have experience with gunshot wounds.[9] But he was not in charge.

Witnessing the autopsy on behalf of their respective agencies were two FBI agents from the Baltimore field office, James Sibert and Francis O'Neill, and four Secret Service agents from the late President's protection detail.[10]

The first of the many questions that would come back to haunt the autopsy results surfaced when Humes examined the back wound. According to a report prepared later that evening by agents Sibert and O'Neill and circulated the next day to FBI offices, Humes probed the back wound with his finger and found "that the trajectory of the missile entering at this point had entered at a downward position of 45 to 60 degrees." The agents also reported that Humes had determined "the distance traveled by this missile was a short distance inasmuch as the end of the opening could be felt with the finger."[11]

This was startling information. If the bullet entered at a downward, 45-to-60-degree slant and the end of the wound path could be felt with a finger, how was it possible that the same bullet could continue on to exit the President's throat? Months later, the Commission testimony of Secret Service agent Roy Kellerman confirmed the FBI agents' account of the examination.

"[Finck] was probing inside the shoulder with his instrument and I said, 'Colonel, where did it go?' He said, 'There are no lanes for an outlet of this entry in this man's shoulder.' "[12]

Later on during the autopsy, word was passed to the doctors that a bullet had been recovered at Parkland Hospital.[13] Equipped with this information, Humes promptly concluded that there was a ready explanation for the apparent lack of a path through the President's back: The slug had gone only a short distance and then worked its way out of the President's body during cardiopulmonary resuscitation attempts.[14]

Humes consequently did no dissection to determine exactly where the bullet had gone. In fact, Dr. Finck later said that the autopsy doctors were ordered not to perform a bullet tracking procedure, "but I don't remember by whom."[15]

As for the wound in the throat, as far as Humes was concerned, there wasn't one. He assumed the cut in the President's neck was simply a tracheotomy.[16] It wasn't until the following morning, long after the autopsy was finished, that Humes talked to Dr. Perry in Dallas and learned of the gunshot wound beneath the President's Adam's apple.[17]

According to Perry, Humes sounded momentarily taken aback and then exclaimed, "So that's it!"[18] Clearly, this information would force Humes to radically rethink his conclusions about how the President had been struck. But by then it was too late to perform a tracking procedure to reveal the actual path of the bullet. Kennedy's body had been sent to the funeral home.

Facing this dilemma, Humes spent most of that weekend writing his autopsy report so as to conform to the evidence; namely, that a bullet traversed the President's neck from back to front. On Sunday morning, he burned his original autopsy notes in the fireplace at his home.[19] Humes years later would assert that he did this because the notes were bloodstained and he was concerned they might end up on public display.[20]

For its part, the Warren Commission eventually stated that the autopsy doctors had been unable to find a bullet path through Kennedy's back because the slug had passed neatly between the gap separating the large strap muscles in the President's upper torso.[21]

If these machinations weren't already enough to throw the results of the entire autopsy procedure into doubt, there were also serious questions about where the bullet wound in Kennedy's back was actually located. Humes described it as being five and a half inches from the tip of the right shoulder and approximately the same distance below the right mastoid process, the bony point immediately behind the ear.[22] This put the wound about two inches below the nape of the neck and just to the right of the spine. Yet this reported location was contradicted by two seemingly unimpeachable pieces of evidence.

The first was a chart made by Dr. Boswell during the autopsy that purported to show the locations of the President's various wounds. The chart included front and rear drawings of a human body. On the rear view, Boswell marked the back wound several inches below where the autopsy report described it to be. This was odd, since the marking placed the entrance wound *far below* the exit wound in the neck.[23] In so doing, it put the bullet on an upward trajectory and thereby destroyed the assertion that Kennedy and Connally were hit by the same shot coming down from the book depository. (See illustration 6.)

Boswell would later say the drawing was only meant to mark the approximate location of the back wound and that obviously he had mistakenly marked the wound too low.[24]

Still, a second piece of evidence—the President's clothes—seemed to confirm Boswell's location of the back wound. Measurements made by FBI special agent Robert Frazier showed the bullet hole in the President's coat to be 5⅜ inches below the top of the collar and 1¾ inches to the right of the midline. The holes in Kennedy's shirt, meanwhile, were 5¾ inches below the collar and 1⅛ inches to the right of the midline.[25] These holes as described by Frazier (and confirmed by photographs of the coat and shirt) were almost exactly where Boswell had placed the wound on the autopsy sheet.[26] To most, the measurements, the photos and Boswell's autopsy sheet notation offered clear evidence that the back shot did in fact come in below the neck wound.

Faced with the incongruity, the Commission decided that since Kennedy was waving when the bullet struck, his coat and shirt were riding up higher on his back than would normally have been the case.[27] Ergo, the holes in the President's clothes were consistent with Humes's higher, "correct" location of the back wound.

This question could have been quickly resolved had the Warren Commission seen fit to release photographs of the wound. But because of fears the pictures might be commercially exploited,[28] the Commission did not, and it wasn't until 1978 that the matter was finally laid to rest.

The House subcommittee investigating the assassination that year had realistic paintings made of the President's wounds directly from the autopsy photographs and also went to great lengths to make sure the photographs were not fakes and had not been altered. The picture of the President's back, as it turned out, placed the wound exactly where Humes had said it was.[29] (See illustration 7.) Kennedy's raised right hand had indeed apparently pulled his coat high on his shoulder at the time the bullet hit. This was subsequently confirmed by a motorcade photograph discovered by assassination researcher Dr. John Lattimer, which clearly showed Kennedy's coat riding up on his back prior to the shooting.[30] An alternative possibility was that Kennedy was leaning farther forward than most realized when the bullet struck in the back. In any event, the photo of the wound's location did not lie; the seeming incompatibility of the holes in the jacket and shirt were accounted for and the apparent shot from below eliminated.

Of course, Donahue didn't know any of this in late 1967. But he did have access to the doctors' descriptions of the neck and back wounds' appearance and other ballistic evidence from the President's clothing, and he continued to sift the data.

Humes and his team described the wound in the President's back as an oval, approximately seven millimeters by four millimeters, with sharply delineated, clean edges. No problem there; this description was typical of a wound of entry. The appearance of the wound in Kennedy's throat, however (before it was altered by the tracheotomy), was described by Carrico of the Parkland staff in similar terms, i.e., "rather round" and free of the "jagged edges or stellate lacerations" normally associated with exit wounds.[31] Dr. Perry estimated the bullet hole's diameter as between three and five millimeters.[32]

Another Parkland doctor, Ronald Jones, told the Commission that:

> The hole was very small and relatively clean cut, as you would see in a bullet that is entering rather than exiting from a patient. If this were an exit wound, you would think that it exited at a very low velocity to produce no more damage than this had done, and if this were a missile of high velocity, you would expect more of an explosive type of exit wound, with more tissue destruction than this appeared to have on superficial examination.[33]

Jones's troubling conclusion that the throat wound seemed to be one of entry was bolstered by the results of a test conducted in early 1964 at the Army's Edgewood Arsenal in Maryland by Dr. Alfred Olivier, a researcher in wound ballistics. In the test, Olivier fired three 6.5mm Carcano rounds through a simulated human neck, consisting of fourteen centimeters of goat meat held between goat skin and clothing. Olivier's goal was to determine the size of exit holes a 6.5 Carcano bullet made.[34]

While Olivier's entrance holes were the same size as the one in Kennedy's back, he found the smallest exit hole to be 10 millimeters in diameter, more than twice as large as the wound at the front of the President's throat.[35]

Here then, critics loudly claimed, was irrefutable evidence that the neck shot came from the front. And one of the Warren Commission's own experts had proved it.

Once again, however, it didn't take Donahue long to spot a fundamental error in the way critics had interpreted the data. Unlike the goat meat, the flesh on Kennedy's neck was surrounded and restrained by his buttoned shirt collar. As a result, Kennedy's skin stretched as the bullet pushed through from the inside—but only until it was tight against the collar. At that point the bullet punctured the skin, leaving a neat, clean hole, much like a sharp stick would when passing through a taut sheet of rubber.

Had the collar been unbuttoned, the bullet would have pushed the skin out much farther, to the point of extreme elasticity, and then broken through in a tearing fashion that would have left a more typical exit hole: larger, with torn, ragged edges. This conclusion was confirmed by Lattimer, a New York urologist, in his 1980 book *Kennedy and Lincoln: Medical & Ballistic Comparisons of Their Assassinations*.[36]

To Donahue, the fact that the restraining effect of the shirt collar had not occurred to Jones, Olivier, the critics—or for that matter, the Warren Commission itself—was another example of the flawed analysis that seemed to characterize so much of assassination research.

In any event, the FBI's examination of the bullet hole on the front of the President's shirt offered final, irrefutable proof that the bullet had passed from back to front, in Donahue's view. According to the FBI, the cloth fibers surrounding the hole were pressed out, not in. This showed the cloth was carried forward as the bullet made its way through the shirt from the rear.[37] Conversely, the fibers around the hole on the back of the shirt were pressed in, confirming the back wound was one of entrance.[38]

As he concluded his analysis of the medical evidence, Donahue lastly considered the appearance and characteristics of Connally's back wound. Critics had pointed to two apparent inconsistencies here. First, the wound was elliptical in shape,[39] unlike the entrance wound in Kennedy's back. Second, although Donahue had already satisfied himself that Kennedy's neck wound and Connally's back wound lined up, the channel through the governor's chest nonetheless dropped off at a 27-degree angle,[40] a declination 10 degrees sharper than the calculated slope through Kennedy's throat.[41]

This latter fact led skeptics to argue that the governor may have actually been wounded by a second gunman firing from a different location.[42]

Again, however, Donahue realized that the critics' analysis was based on an imperfect understanding of ballistics. It is a fact that bullets almost always yaw, or wobble on the vertical axis, after passing through a solid or semisolid object. The wobble effect is the result of friction and disruption created by, in this case, the bullet's course through the President's neck. Therefore, this yawing in all likelihood caused the bullet to strike Connally out of square, or at an angle somewhat less than perpendicular. In so doing, the bullet left an oval-shaped wound and proceeded downward on a slightly altered course. This was the explanation of the governor's wound offered by the Warren Commission, and Donahue's experience with weapons led him to believe they were absolutely correct—at least on this point.[43] As far as Donahue was concerned, the appearance and angle of the governor's wound offered more proof, not less, that the bullet that struck Connally had first passed through the President's neck.

What did the mass of medical evidence prove? Donahue looked at the data again. If Humes's location of the back wound was correct, the shots lined up: The wound in Kennedy's back was consistent with an entrance wound; the wound in his neck consistent with an exit wound; the wound in Connally's back consistent with an entrance wound of a wobbling, yawing bullet.

Left unexplained were the apparent discrepancies in the character of the President's back wound: According to the examination by Humes and Finck, the wound channel headed downward at a 45-to-60-degree angle, while the end of it could be felt just several inches into the back. This was strange. Still, Donahue figured the bullet's true channel may have been obscured by the fact that, in death,

Kennedy's back muscles were completely relaxed. As well, Kennedy's supine position facedown on the autopsy table bore little resemblance to his position when the bullet struck: At the time of the shot, his arm was apparently raised, thereby stretching the muscles and tissue of the upper back. In death, these muscles eased back into their normal position and may well have distorted or obscured the trajectory. And then, too, there was the Warren Commission's conclusion that the bullet passed between the back muscles and left no discernible track at all.

All three explanations were within the realm of possibility. The bottom line was that no tracking procedure was done to determine the actual course of the bullet. The question, therefore, could never be answered unequivocally one way or the other. Nonetheless, Donahue was convinced that the rest of the medical evidence, plus the direction of the fibers around the holes in the President's shirt, reasonably supported the contention that Kennedy and Connally were hit by the same bullet.

But could that slug really have been the "pristine" or "magic" bullet recovered at Parkland, seemingly undamaged even though it passed through two men and caused seven wounds? To critics, this was preposterous, particularly in view of the fact that when the Army's Dr. Olivier fired a 6.5 Carcano round through the wrist of a cadaver in an attempt to simulate Connally's wrist wound, the bullet emerged smashed and badly deformed.[44]

Donahue went back to the archives. Under the supervision of archivist Marion Johnson, he personally examined the pristine bullet, known as CE 399. Much to his astonishment, the bullet was by no means undamaged, as Commission critics claimed. To the trained eye, the jacketed slug was obviously somewhat bent and severely flattened, so much so that a small amount of lead had been extruded from the bullet's base. Clearly, it had hit something. (See illustrations 8, 9, and 10.)

Donahue next reviewed what he knew about military bullets in general and the 6.5mm Carcano round in particular. By the time of the American Civil War, the flintlock musket carried by most soldiers in the American Revolution had been made obsolete by the rifle. Unlike the flintlock, which fired a low-velocity round lead ball, Civil War weapons used a larger gunpowder charge that propelled a newly invented, cone-shaped bullet at much greater velocity. Because of its hollow base and cone shape, the bullet expanded snugly against the spiraled grooves cut inside the barrel—the rifling—as it left the weapon. This spun the bullet and gave it a gyroscopic effect that held the round on its intended course, making the rifle extremely accurate, and also carried the lead a far greater distance than the old flintlock balls.

Predictably, the consequences of this breakthrough were carnage. Civil War surgeons quickly discovered that wounds caused by the new high-velocity projectiles were characterized by the exceptional damage they did. The bullet's soft lead flattened out as the slug struck flesh, then the deformed, now-larger mass plowed through tissue, bone, or anything else in its way. The effect was a gaping and, if it hit the torso, usually fatal wound.

The Geneva Convention of 1922 therefore determined that henceforth all military bullets would be required to be encased with a strong metal jacket. The so-called full-metal jacket would prevent the bullet's lead core from flattening and wreaking such havoc, and, in so doing, reduce fatalities caused by wounds sustained in combat.

The Mannlicher-Carcano bullet of the type Oswald fired was manufactured according to the specifications of the Geneva Convention. While its jacket was made primarily of copper and zinc, it was every bit as strong as later jackets made of mild steel. The 6.5mm's thick, tough exterior, therefore, was specifically designed to be highly resistant to breaking up or expanding. This did not mean that the bullet was impervious to fragmentation, however, and Donahue knew it would be damaged if it hit a large bone, such as the femur or, obviously, an even harder material such as concrete or brick.

All well and good, but how could such an understanding of the bullet's inherent strength be reconciled with the results of Olivier's test, which showed the bullet was badly smashed after being fired through the wrist of the cadaver in a wound presumably similar to the one Connally suffered?

The answer was simple. For the second time, Donahue spotted a fundamental flaw in the way Olivier had conducted his shooting experiments. The problem was this: The Warren Commission's expert fired the bullet into the cadaver wrist at nearly maximum velocity, or 2,200 feet per second.

Oswald's bullet, on the other hand, had first transversed Kennedy's neck and Connally's back. Both of these wounds created friction that slowed the bullet considerably before it struck the governor's wrist. Donahue estimated the bullet's velocity had fallen off from 2,200 feet per second to around 1,400 to 1,700 feet per second after passing through the President's neck. The subsequent penetration of Connally's back, the impact with his fifth rib, and the force required to push the bullet out the governor's body dramatically reduced the velocity again, probably to no more than 700 to 900 feet per second.

Ergo, physics suggested that the bullet was traveling at less than a third of its original speed when it finally pierced Connally's wrist. This speed was consistent with the superficial wound Connally suffered in his thigh when the bullet finally came to a halt.

Had Olivier fired his test bullet through the neck of one cadaver, through the torso of a second and finally into the wrist of a third, chances are the slug would have appeared much as CE 399 did.

To his credit, Olivier realized this and subsequently did additional simulations for the Warren Commission that showed the bullet would have indeed slowed and therefore remained intact after penetrating the President's neck and Connally's body.[45]

Having resolved that the bullet (CE 399) could have passed through both men and stayed in one piece, Donahue next looked at the question of the fragments found in the governor's wrist and thigh. Critics believed they could never have come from the bullet in question.[46]

An unfired 6.5mm slug weighs between 160 and 161 grains. The bullet found at Parkland weighed 158.6 grains.[47] The overriding question, then, was whether there were more than 1.4 to 2.4 grains of metal found in the governor's body.

An empirical answer did not exist. Not all of the fragments had been removed from Connally's body and some of those that were apparently were lost.[48] Asked to speculate on whether CE 399 could have caused Connally's wrist and thigh wounds after viewing the governor's X rays, doctors Humes and Finck said they thought not, since there appeared to be more than three grains of metal left behind by the bullet.[49]

The doctor who actually attended to Connally's wrist wound, however, said the amount of metal left there "would have to be weighed in micrograms," or the equivalent of a postage stamp; the implication being that the amount was so minuscule that it could have easily been three grains or less.[50]

Like the question of the wound channel through the President's back, the fragment debate could never be completely resolved. But again, Donahue concluded, at least on this point, the Commission's explanation was within the realm of possibility.

Another question that would go unanswered was whether this bullet, Commission exhibit 399, had even come from Connally's stretcher. To Donahue, the most likely explanation on this point was Josiah Thompson's suggestion in *Six Seconds in Dallas*: A hospital employee may have surreptitiously picked up the bullet as a souvenir and then, having second thoughts about the wisdom of such a move, placed the slug where it would later be found by authorities.[51]

Who could say for sure?

The most telling evidence of all concerning CE 399 was the FBI test that showed marks on the bullet exactly matched the rifling grooves in the barrel of Oswald's Carcano.[52] This was the ballistic equivalent of matching fingerprints, and to Donahue, seemed as close to conclusive proof as one could get as to the origin of the magic bullet. The results of the rifling comparison, however, were seldom mentioned by the critics.

But if Donahue was now convinced the Commission's single bullet theory was correct, he still needed to reconcile that belief with the available photographic and eyewitness evidence. Frame 225 in the Zapruder film is the first to show the President emerging from behind a highway sign that had momentarily blocked Zapruder's view. As

Kennedy appears, he seems to be grabbing his throat and is clearly reacting to a wound. Based on estimates of the President's reaction time, along with the fact that each frame of the film was one-eighteenth of a second, the Warren Commission calculated that the first shot struck very soon after Zapruder frame 210.[53]

This impact time, however, does not jibe with Connally's reaction. When the governor comes into view from behind the sign, he turns slightly to his right and then again calmly faces forward, hat in hand, seemingly unhurt. It is not until frame 238, a second and a half later, that Connally reacts to his wound. His shoulder collapses, his cheeks puff out, his hair flies. Critics therefore asked, If a single shot had penetrated Kennedy and Connally, how could this mysterious time lag between the two men's reactions be explained?

The Commission's response: "There was conceivably a delayed reaction between the time the bullet struck [Connally] and the time he realized that he was hit, despite the fact that the bullet struck a glancing blow to a rib and penetrated his wrist bone."[54]

Maybe so. But Thompson's work in *Six Seconds in Dallas* seriously undermined this proposition. Thompson asked Dr. Charles Gregory, the surgeon who had operated on Connally's wrist, about the physiology of Connally's massive exhalation of air as shown by the governor's puffed cheeks in Zapruder frame 238. According to Gregory, "a necessary consequence of the shot through [Connally's] chest would be a compression of the chest wall and an involuntary opening of the epiglottis followed by escaping air forcing open his mouth."[55]

Gregory went on to estimate the interval between impact of the shot and this involuntary physical reaction would have been no more than one-quarter to one-half a second.[56] The facts therefore required that the bullet struck Connally only a fraction of a second before his cheeks puffed out. Yet the Warren Commission maintained the shot actually came a full second and a half earlier. On top of this troubling contradiction was Connally's own testimony. The governor was absolutely certain he was not hit by the first shot.

> We had just made the turn, well, when I heard what I thought was a shot. I heard this noise which I immediately took to be a rifle shot. I instinctively turned to my right because the sound appeared to come from over my right shoulder, and I saw nothing unusual except just people in the crowd, but I did not catch the President in the corner of my eye, and I was interested because once I heard the shot in my own mind I identified it as a rifle shot, and I immediately—the only thought that crossed my mind was that this is an assassination attempt.
>
> So I looked, failing to see him, I was turning to look back over my left shoulder into the back seat, but I never got that far in my turn. I got about in the position I am in now facing you, looking a little bit to the left of center, and then I felt like someone hit me in the back.[57]

Commission assistant counsel Arlen Specter asked Connally specifically which shot hit him.

CONNALLY: The second one.
SPECTER: And what is your reason for that conclusion, sir?
CONNALLY: Well, in my judgment, it just couldn't conceivably have been the first one because I heard the sound of the shot. In the first place, I don't know anything about the velocity of this particular bullet, but any rifle has a velocity that exceeds the speed of sound, and when I heard the sound of that first shot, that bullet had already reached where I was, or had reached that far, and after I heard that shot, I had the time to turn to my right, and start to turn to my left before I felt anything.

It is not conceivable to me that I could have been hit by the first bullet, and then I felt the blow from something which was obviously a bullet, which I assumed was a bullet, and I never heard the second shot, didn't hear it.[58]

Another eyewitness account cast a long shadow over the single bullet theory. Secret Service agent Roy Kellerman was riding in the right front seat of the presidential limousine as the motorcade made its way through Dallas.

Kennedy, according to Kellerman, cried out, "My God! I'm hit!" just after the first shot.[59]

This made no sense at all. If the first shot cut through Kennedy's throat and windpipe as the Commission asserted, the President wouldn't have been able to say anything. Could Kellerman have been mistaken? No one else in the presidential limousine apparently heard the President's exclamation. Commission attorney Specter pushed Kellerman:

SPECTER: With relationship to that first noise that you have described, when did you hear his voice?
KELLERMAN: His voice?
SPECTER: We will start with his voice.
KELLERMAN: OK. From the noise of which I was in the process of turning to determine where it was or what it was, it carried on right then. Why I am so positive, gentlemen, that it was his voice—there is only one man in that back seat that was from Boston, and the accents carried very clearly.
SPECTER: Well, had you become familiar with the president's voice prior to that day?
KELLERMAN: Yes; very much so.

SPECTER: And what was the basis for your becoming familiar
                with his voice prior to that day?
KELLERMAN: I had been with him for three years.
SPECTER: And had you talked with him on a very frequent basis
                during the course of that association?
KELLERMAN: He was a very free man to talk to; yes. He knew most
                all the men, most everybody who worked in the
                White House as well as everywhere, and he would
                call you.
SPECTER: And from your experience would you say that you
                could recognize his voice?
KELLERMAN: Very much, sir; I would.[60]

Donahue didn't know what to make of it. He was convinced the
ballistic and medical evidence surrounding the single bullet theory
was coherent, logical, and consistent, at least when interpreted
correctly. But he could not explain the governor's implausible delayed reaction to the shot, Connally's own testimony, and finally,
Kellerman's memory about what may have been the President's last
words.

Surely Dr. Gregory didn't make up his explanation about the timing
involved in Connally's involuntary exhalation of air. And it seemed
equally unlikely that Connally or Kellerman were mistaken in their
recollections. Both men seemed adamant about what they had heard.

Something was missing. Something didn't fit.

5
THE HEAD SHOT

FACED WITH CONNALLY'S AND KELLERMAN'S MYSTERIOUS testimony and the strange time lag between when the bullet supposedly struck the governor and when Connally reacted to his wounds, Donahue decided to put the single bullet question aside. Perhaps an answer would emerge. In the meantime, he would focus his attention on the shot that hit Kennedy in the head.

At first glance, the evidence surrounding the head shot seemed straightforward enough, at least compared to the controversy that engulfed the President's neck wound.

According to the Commission's analysis of the Zapruder film and two other, lesser-quality, home movies made that day, the fatal bullet struck Kennedy at a point 231 feet west of the intersection of Houston and Elm Street.[1] This put the distance between the President and Oswald's roost in the book depository at just over 265 feet.[2] Accordingly, the Commission calculated that the shot came down at a declination of just under 16 degrees.[3]

Oddly, Donahue could not find in the Report any explicit statement about the angle from right to left, from Oswald to the midline of the car. The Texas Book Depository window was behind the car, but not directly behind; it was slightly to the right, so Oswald's bullet had to come from right to left. Lacking any other data, he decided to use Josiah Thompson's assertion that the angle was 6 degrees, which seemed reasonable (although Donahue was puzzled to notice Thompson said the angle of declination was only 12 degrees, not 16 as in the Report[4]).

Donahue then considered the Warren Report's artist renderings of the head wound—drawings only, because no X rays or autopsy photographs were available to the public in early 1968. But stills from the Zapruder film were available, and Donahue compared them to the drawings.

According to the Warren Report, the bullet entered the back of

Kennedy's head and disintegrated, blowing out the upper right portion of the skull from about an inch and a half above his ear upward to within two inches of the top of his head. The wound appeared to extend four to five inches front-to-back, from just above his hairline in the front to a little behind his ear. There were many tiny, irregular bullet fragments through the brain and embedded in the interior of the skull.[5] The Report asserted that larger pieces of the same bullet were found on the floor of the presidential limousine.[6]

This account sounded plausible enough, but as Donahue studied the details, he slowly tumbled to a strange inconsistency in the government's explanation.

The bullet's trajectory made no sense.

A slug coming in at a 6-degree angle from right to left and down at 16 degrees should have exited through the President's face—somewhere in the area of the right eye, forehead, or nose. Yet the actual exit wound was in the upper right portion of the skull.

It was true that Kennedy's head was tilted down and slightly to the left at the time of impact, according to Zapruder 312, the frame exposed an instant before the bullet struck. (By Z-313, one-eighteenth of a second after Z-312, Kennedy's skull is already destroyed.) Using Zapruder 312 as a guide, Donahue estimated the President's head was nodding forward perhaps 10 or 11 degrees and turned, at most, 15 degrees to the left. This position would have necessarily raised the exit wound and shifted it to the right.

But not nearly far enough, Donahue thought, to cause the wound Kennedy suffered. Unless Kennedy's head was turned much farther to the left—and clearly from Zapruder 312 (see illustration 19) it was not—Oswald's bullet would have had to exit through the face on the right side. To argue otherwise would be to suggest that the bullet made a sharp right turn as it passed through the brain. Donahue did not believe such a movement was ballistically possible.

He next examined Dr. Humes's location of the entrance wound on the back of Kennedy's head. Perhaps this would help explain the inconsistency. The Report drawings and Dr. Humes's autopsy put the entrance hole one inch to the right and "somewhat above the occipital protuberance."[7] Donahue dug out an old anatomy textbook from his college days and noted that the occipital protuberance is the bony bump at the base of the skull in the back, just above the neck.

This didn't make any sense, thought Donahue; if the wound was this low on the back of the head, and the bullet was coming *down* at an angle of 16 degrees. . . .

Realizing he needed to make a three-dimensional model to understand the bullet's trajectory through the skull, Donahue went to a local medical supply store and bought a plaster skull.

The first thing to do was to drill a hole of entrance. Going back to the autopsy report, he found Humes's description of the wound's location maddeningly imprecise. Presumably "somewhat above" the occipital protuberance meant less than an inch above, since Humes used one inch to measure the lateral distance. If the vertical distance had been at least one inch, surely the pathologist would have said so. Donahue decided he would put the entrance wound where the various Report sketches seemed, however roughly, to place it.

Admittedly, the drawings did not instill confidence. The Report's principal rendering of the shot's path through the skull did indeed maintain a 16-degree downward angle, but it did so only by tilting Kennedy's head forward about 60 degrees. (See drawing 1.) The Zapruder picture of Kennedy in frame 312 showed this was preposterous; Donahue judged the tilt in Zapruder 312 to be 10 or 11 degrees. (Ten years later the Select Committee on Assassinations of the House of Representatives would come to the same judgment.)

Then came the question of where to place the outshoot hole. The Commission text and the autopsy report were of no help. The only drawing that addressed the question was the one with the vastly tilted head, and it put the outshoot on the right side of the skull about halfway between the top of the ear and the top of the head. There was no documentation for this choice of exit point.

The omission, though frustrating, was more understandable than the vagueness about the entrance hole, since the bullet broke into many pieces and shattered a large portion of bone. Donahue inferred that there were, in effect, many exit points.

He therefore chose an exit spot near the center of the huge opening, roughly where the Report drawing had it. Donahue reasoned that a bullet breaking up along this plane would easily account for the area of damage done to Kennedy's skull. Because the large head wound was created by a shower of fragments, there was, in 1968, no other way of deciding where the bullet would have emerged (if it had remained intact) than picking the center of that area of destruction. His plan was to drill this exit hole and push a long wooden dowel through both openings. Then, using Zapruder 312, he would position the skull as it appeared to be at the moment of impact. All this done, he could discern a line of trajectory—the course of the incoming bullet—and trace it back to its source.

But even as he was drilling the hole he knew it would not support the Warren Commission Report. He could foresee that with the head tilted at 10 or 11 degrees and the bullet coming down at 16 degrees and hitting the alleged entrance point, it would exit on the face, around the level of Kennedy's nose. If it exited in a shower of fragments, everything from the eyes to the mouth would be gone. And this clearly had not happened. (When the autopsy photos finally surfaced in the eighties, they showed no damage to Kennedy's face.)

Donahue then drilled a second exit hole, pushed a long wooden dowel through both holes to represent the bullet's path, and, using Zapruder frame 312, positioned the skull as Kennedy's head would have been at the moment of impact.

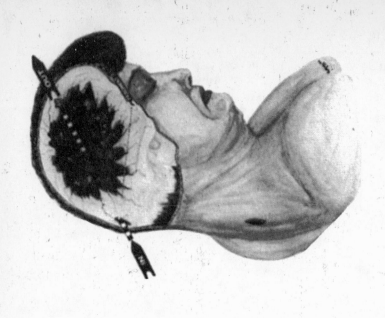

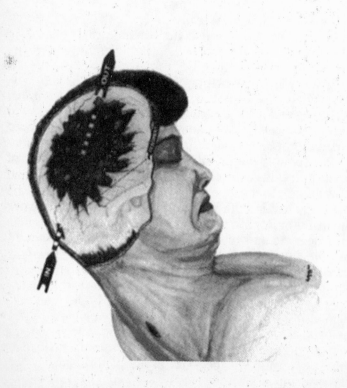

1. Warren Commission drawing of the line of fire through Kennedy's skull (left). The head in the drawing is tilted nearly 60° forward. Rearranged to correspond to the House Select Committee's 11° forward tilt (right), the drawing matches Donahue's original skull models.

Donahue was surprised at what this simple but effective simulation revealed. According to the path dictated by the attitude of the dowel, the shot that hit Kennedy in the head came from the trunk of the presidential limousine! (See drawing 2.)

Donahue again checked Humes's entrance wound location against his own. The results were unchanged. The bullet came up from the trunk. This, of course, was absurd. Impossible. Yet the alternative seemed equally so.

If one accepted that the hole Humes located on the back of Kennedy's skull was caused by a bullet fired by Oswald, then the bullet struck Kennedy on a downward, 16-degree angle, banked up like a pool ball and made a quick right turn to exit the skull near the right front—at a higher level than where it went in.

Donahue was stunned. In one afternoon's work, his confidence in the Warren Report was effectively destroyed. There was no possible way the Commission stance on the source of the head shot could be correct. But his own conclusion—that the shot came from the trunk— was even more absurd.

Humes must have misplaced the location of the entrance wound. Nothing else made sense. Given Humes's questionable performance in other aspects of the autopsy—his failure to dissect the neck wound, his failure to measure the wounds against fixed body "landmarks," and his failure to identify the throat wound—one more significant error didn't seem so improbable.

What did seem improbable was the apparent fact that no one else had picked up so massive a fault in the Warren Report. With all the uncountable man-hours spent by the Commission's team in compiling twenty-six volumes of evidence and analysis, followed by dozens more volumes of skeptical scrutiny by critics of the Report, no one seemed to have brought to bear a trained ballistics look at the head shot. All of their trajectory-analysis energies seemed to have been expended on the neck shot.

Donahue was reasonably proud of his expertise in the field of firearms, but he didn't judge himself some kind of genius. If he had figured out something all these experts had missed, it was, he thought, because they had simply not done the nuts and bolts work of analyzing the head shot's trajectory.

Yet even if Humes had mistakenly located the entrance wound, and it looked as if that was the case, still unresolved was the larger question of how a bullet coming down from the right rear could have blown out the *right* upper top of the skull.

As Donahue pondered this problem, he was struck by another subtle, but equally stark, inconsistency in the government's explanation of the head wound. The problem was this: If one was to believe the Commission, the first bullet to hit Kennedy pierced his neck and went on to inflict extensive damage to the bone and flesh of Governor Connally. For all that, the bullet (CE 399) remained essentially intact.

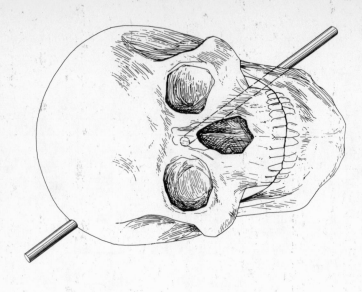

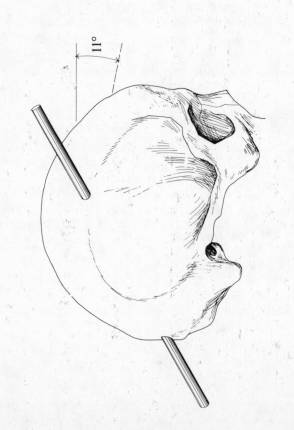

11°

2. Side view (tilted forward at 11°) and front view of Donahue's skull models based on Humes's incorrect inshoot contained in the Warren Commission Report. They indicate a line of fire coming from the trunk of Kennedy's limousine.

Donahue already accepted this explanation, given that the Carcano round was a full metal–jacketed bullet specifically designed not to fragment or expand.

But precisely for this reason he could not understand how exactly the same kind of bullet, fired from exactly the same weapon six seconds later, could have exploded in a hail of lead that shattered the President's skull and left an exit portal the size of a small plate.

How differently could two supposedly identical pieces of ammunition perform?

To Donahue, the second round appeared to have acted not as a bullet encased in a thick metal jacket would have, but more like a frangible, soft or hollow-nosed missile with a thin metal jacket traveling at extremely high velocity. Unlike full metal–jacketed bullets, soft or hollow-nose missiles are specifically designed to flatten and disintegrate in order to inflict the kind of shattering wounds the Geneva Convention sought to outlaw in the 1920s.

Donahue was willing to concede that the Carcano bullet, the full-metal jacket notwithstanding, probably would have broken up to some extent after piercing the skull and hitting the brain. Although the Carcano's thick casing was specifically designed to hold the lead core together, the bullet's impact against the thick, dense bone of the skull might have split the jacket and the split would have widened as the bullet spun through the brain.

Still, the resulting fragments would have been much larger and far less numerous than the ones found in Kennedy's skull: two or three large pieces at the most. The Carcano round simply did not have the velocity—either rotational, from the rifling in the gun barrel, or linear, from the gunpowder charge in the shell—to completely shred the thick metal jacket and disintegrate the lead inside upon impact.

Yet Humes had reported "multiple minute metal fragments" embedded in the skull and brain along the apparent flight path of the bullet.[8] Numerous, tiny fragments? It didn't make sense.

The startling fact was that the bullet that hit Kennedy's head had not behaved like a full metal–jacketed round at all. A great number of tiny lead fragments was characteristic of a completely different kind of bullet, one spinning with far greater speed and hence exhibiting much more centrifugal force upon impact.

Little light could be shed on this mystery by studying the external appearance of Kennedy's wound. Regardless of whether the bullet was a full-metal jacket or a soft or hollow-point round specifically designed to fragment, a large area of damage would probably have resulted. Any bullet traveling at least 2,000 feet per second will push a broad shock wave ahead of it as the slug moves through the semiliquid material of the brain, and this shock wave would be capable of rupturing the skull wall across a wide area.

For weeks, Donahue studied the Warren Report volumes in vain for a detailed explanation of how Oswald's two bullets could have

behaved so differently. The discrepancy, of course, could be explained if Oswald's second round had been a hollow-point bullet. But
this seemed unlikely. The Commission determined that all three spent
shells found at the depository came from the same lot of full metal–
jacketed 6.5 millimeter ammunition manufactured by East Alton,
Illinois–based Western Cartridge Co.[9]

Donahue next weighed the possibility that the head shot might
have come from the front. A number of critics argued that the sharp
backward movement of the President's head at the time of impact as
seen in the Zapruder film indicated this. Could a frontal shot account
for the wound's size, location, and characteristics?

Only if the gun fired had been a shotgun, Donahue thought. Unlike
a rifle, which fires a single bullet, a shotgun sprays dozens of small
lead or steel pellets that fan out as they move away from the gun's
muzzle. This makes a shotgun tremendously lethal at close range,
but because the pellets are extremely light, they rapidly lose velocity
after about thirty yards.

Consequently, if a shotgun caused a wound the size of the one on
the top and side of Kennedy's head, it would have had to have been
fired from no more than a few yards away. The grassy knoll where
many witnesses believed the shots originated was nearly forty yards
from where the President was hit. And nobody reported anyone with
a 12-gauge lurking at the curb along Elm Street. More to the point,
no round, uniform shotgun pellets were found in Kennedy's brain or
skull. Only tiny, irregular shards of metal.

Could any other type of weapon fired from the front have caused
the President's wound? No way, as far as Donahue was concerned.
Nothing except a bullet pushing through from the rear could have
burst the President's skull open the way it did.

But what about the grassy knoll? According to Thompson's research in *Six Seconds in Dallas*, 33 out of 66 witnesses reporting on
the direction of the shots thought the bullets came from the knoll.[10]
This suggestion raised two questions in Donahue's mind. First, if
someone did fire from the knoll, where did the bullet go? It did not
go into Kennedy's body. The characteristics of both the President's
neck wound and the head wound ruled that out. Therefore, the shot
must have missed. Yet none of the spectators in the line of fire along
Elm Street was hit by errant bullets. Nor was the side of the car
struck. And no one but Kennedy and Connally was hit in the car, and
Connally was clearly hit from behind.

If a stray shot coming in from the right front did somehow manage
to miss the President, his wife, the car, and nearby spectators, it
might well have slammed into the pavement beyond the limousine.
Surely such a bullet chip in the concrete would have attracted the
attention of the police and spectators who swarmed over the area in
the minutes and hours after the shooting.

Furthermore, what kind of hit man would miss a relatively easy shot from a little over one hundred feet away? The second question Donahue contemplated was, assuming a gunman was on the knoll, how did he escape? A large number of spectators and several police officers swarmed up the rise within seconds of the shooting. Behind the knoll was a parking lot, and beyond that, a railroad yard. Within a minute or two, the entire area was covered with police officers and witnesses.

It seemed improbable a gunman could have dodged so many pursuers, particularly the railroad workers running over from the triple overpass. They had the area behind the fence in view within a few seconds of the final shot and arrived there soon after. It was true that Jean Hill—standing directly across the street from the grassy knoll—said she saw a man moving rapidly away from the knoll toward the railroad tracks immediately after the shots rang out.[11]

". . . he was the only thing moving up there," Hill said.[12]

Still, none who converged on the knoll from the railroad overpass or from Elm Street apparently saw this man. And Lee Bowers, the railroader working in the switching tower behind the knoll, didn't see him. Donahue knew he couldn't rule out the possibility of a gunman on the knoll. For one thing, there was the strange testimony of several witnesses who claimed they encountered a man who identified himself as a Secret Service agent in the area immediately after the shooting.[13] In fact, the Secret Service had no agents detailed to the knoll before or just after the shooting.[14] Perhaps this "agent" was really a gunman. Such a scenario could explain the lightning getaway.

But to Donahue, the fact remained that with the exception of these curious reports and the ear-witnesses' testimony, nothing in the evidence pointed to a gunman on the knoll. Regarding the apparent direction of the sound of the shots, Donahue's long experience with weapons led him to agree with the contents of a memo written by Warren Commission assistant counsel Melvin Eisenberg to staff investigators on March 7, 1964.

Donahue found it in *The Scavengers and the Critics of the Warren Report,* an obscure 1967 book by Richard Warren Lewis and Lawrence Schiller that defended the Commission's findings.

In the memo, Eisenberg wrote:

> . . . a mass of evidence has been collected concerning the aural observation of bystanders. The purpose of this memorandum is to point out that very little weight can be assigned to this category of evidence.
>
> A leading firearms textbook states flatly that "Little credence . . . should be put in what anyone says about a shot or even a number of shots." This results from two interrelated factors: the difficulty of accurate perception of the sound of gunshots, and the acoustics of gunshots.
>
> **Perception.** The sound of a shot comes upon a witness suddenly and

often unexpectedly. The witness is not "ready" to record his perception. The same is usually true of subsequent shots following hard on the heels of the first. For these reasons such sounds "are generally extremely inaccurately recorded in [one's] memory."

The perception of distance is as unreliable as the perception of number: "The observation of a sound is often unclear and subjective. A loud noise may appear to have been produced nearby, while a weak sound may seem to have been transmitted from some distance. This difficulty of estimating the distance from the site at which the sound is produced to the place where it is heard is increased considerably if the sound is of a nature unknown to the listener."

Similarly, as to the characteristics of the sound: "Another subject frequently discussed in criminal cases is the report made by various types of weapons. People will go into court and swear on occasion that a weapon fired was a certain type and even make and model. Unless a great many other factors are known, such evidence may be sincere but it is utterly ridiculous."

Acoustics. Apart from the difficulty of accurately recording aural perceptions of gunshots, the acoustics of gunshots are such that the witness' perceptions may lead him to draw inaccurate conclusions.

> **(a) Number of Shots.** The firing of a bullet causes **three** noises: (1) the muzzle blast, caused by the smashing of the hot gases which propel the bullet into the relatively stable air at the gun's muzzle; (2) the noise of the bullet, caused by the shock wave built up ahead of the bullet's nose as it travels through air; (3) the noise caused by the impact of the bullet into its target. Each of these noises can be quite sharp and may be perceived as separate "shots" by an inexperienced or confused witness.
>
> **(b) Direction.** If a bullet travels faster than the speed of sound, the acoustics are such that the observer at right angles to the path of the bullet may perceive the shot to have been fired from a site somewhere **opposite to him.**

It must be emphasized that the above discussion is not merely theoretical, but is based upon the analysis and observations of professional criminal investigators. Furthermore this testimony is borne out by the very fact that the testimony of the bystanders to the assassination varies enormously.[15]

Reluctant to give too much credence to the ear-witness accounts, Donahue went back to the medical reports prepared by the doctors in Dallas and Bethesda to see if they might offer some additional clue about the origin of the head wound. Once again, however, the information provided by the two camps was contradictory and incomplete.

Strangely, a number of Dallas doctors located the massive head wound at the rear of the President's head. According to Dr. Robert N. McClelland, "the right posterior portion of the skull had been extremely blasted."[16]

Dr. Ronald Coy Jones described "what appeared to be an exit wound in the posterior portion of the skull."[17]

Dr. Gene Akin said that the "back of the right occipital-parietal portion of his head was shattered, with brain substance extruding."[18]

These descriptions were at odds with where Doctors Humes and Boswell located the wound during the autopsy, and also contradicted the Zapruder film, which clearly showed the right *front* portion of Kennedy's head exploding.

Once again, contradictions in the medical reports offered rich fodder for those who suspected the President was shot from the front. Author David Lifton eventually postulated the bizarre thesis that the differences in the doctors' descriptions proved Kennedy's wounds had been surgically altered by the time the President's body arrived in Bethesda on the evening of the twenty-second.

As was the case with the mislocation of the President's back wound, many years would pass before the head wound controversy could seemingly be resolved. In November 1988, the public television program *NOVA* brought together four of the doctors who attended Kennedy in Dallas as part of a television special marking the twenty-fifth anniversary of the assassination. Each of these physicians had originally reported the wound to be at the back of the President's head.

One by one, the doctors were given the opportunity to study color photographs of the President's wound taken during the autopsy to see if the pictures conformed to their recollections. After hours of scrutiny at the National Archives, each doctor reported the pictures did indeed reflect what they saw that day in Dallas.

Said Dr. Paul Peters, "[My inaccurate observations about the head wound in 1963] shows how even a trained observer can make an error in a moment of urgency."

But even with this admission there continued to be those who believed a large exit wound did exist in the back of Kennedy's head, and that evidence of it had been systematically covered up.

In the 1989 best-seller *High Treason,* authors Robert J. Groden and Harrison E. Livingstone asserted that photographs of the back of Kennedy's head were altered to obliterate evidence of a large exit wound. They also claimed that because a frontal autopsy X ray of Kennedy's skull showed damage in the area of his right eye, and because autopsy photographs showed no externally visible wound in that area, the X ray could not have been of President Kennedy.

Finally, according to the writers, a large number of Parkland Hospital personnel and several Bethesda autopsy staffers interviewed in the 1980s all asserted that there most definitely was a large exit hole or defect, nearly four inches square, in the right-rear portion of Kennedy's head.

Around this information, Groden and Livingstone built a case that Kennedy was shot from the front as well as the rear and, therefore, a massive conspiracy was behind the assassination. The two writers, however, were extremely selective in the information they did present. Their interpretation of both the X rays and photographs ignored a number of critically important facts.

First, the damaged right eye area on the X ray, though perhaps appearing to a layman to be completely blown out, was in fact consistent with the wound Kennedy suffered, according to a group of independent physicians who examined the X rays and photographs in 1968, as well as those physicians who looked at the evidence ten years later for the 1978 congressional investigation of the assassination. The orbit, or bone ring surrounding the eye, is often severely fractured in gunshot wounds to the head without any externally visible damage.

More importantly, forensic anthropologists who provided outside expertise to the 1978 committee conducted extensive comparisons between the X rays in question and X rays taken of President Kennedy before the assassination. These examinations revealed that the two sets of pictures unequivocally were of the same man, since every bone develops in a slightly different way and, therefore, each human skull is unique. For example, the sinus cavities vary so markedly in size and shape from one person to another that forensic pathologists refer to their configuration as "sinus prints." Courts throughout the world have long accepted the matching of predeath and postdeath sinus X rays as evidence for the positive identification of unknown bodies.

The committee's forensic anthropologists reported that not only did the sinuses on both sets of Kennedy X rays match, but so did the cranial sutures (the joints uniting the bones of the skull), the location and arrangement of vascular grooves, and the honeycomblike air cells of the mastoid bone.

Finally, forensic dentists compared dental X rays taken before the shooting with the teeth visible in the postmortem X ray and likewise found exact matches.

As for the autopsy photographs that Livingstone and Groden claimed to be fakes, outside experts working for the '78 committee again went to considerable lengths to determine the authenticity of the pictures and concluded beyond a doubt that the pictures were genuine.

Perhaps the sole legitimate area of doubt raised by *High Treason* involved the interviews done with Parkland medical personnel, many of whom allegedly claimed a large exit wound was visible in the rear. On this score, the only conclusion one can draw, given the authenticity of the X rays showing otherwise, is that the staffers at the hospital were wrong.

The fact is, the physicians in Dallas never turned the President's body over and hence were unaware of the bullet hole in his upper back. Ergo, in the heat of the moment, as they struggled to save the President's life, it is doubtful that anything more than a cursory examination was made of the back of Kennedy's head. Moreover, the brain, blood, and fluid from the exit wound on the side of the skull undoubtedly oozed out and down, and may well have contributed to the impression that the wound was in the rear.

Donahue, of course, knew none of this in early 1968. But he did have access to a photograph taken by Mary Moorman, a witness who stood on the south side of Elm Street only fifteen feet or so from Kennedy's location at the time of the fatal shot. Moorman's picture (see illustration 23), generally accepted as taken just after the bullet struck the President in the head, shows no large exit wound behind the right ear.

Similarly, although the Zapruder film graphically showed the massive explosion of exiting brain, blood, and bone at the right front of the President's head, no similar exit explosion is seen at the rear. And in frames of the film taken after the bullet struck, Kennedy turns to reveal nearly all of the rear portion of his head. Once again, no exit wound can be seen.

And if there truly was an exit wound on the right rear of Kennedy's head, where was the coinciding entrance wound? Taking into account the position of the head and assuming a straight-line trajectory, the entrance wound would have to be somewhere in the face. Nobody reported that the President was shot here. And where was the gunman who would have had to fire this shot? Standing on the triple overpass alongside a couple of police officers and a dozen spectators?

Not likely.

What Donahue did see all too clearly on the Zapruder film was the horror that unfolded in the limousine that day: The presidential limo emerges from behind a highway sign that momentarily blocks Zapruder's view and Kennedy's elbows are high and his hands clenched from the wound through the neck; his body held erect by the back brace he wore, Jackie turns and reaches out her hand and the seconds drift, then Kennedy's hands and elbows fall and his head slowly droops, as if a perception of doom flickers momentarily through his brain and then . . .

An exploding pink cloud envelops Kennedy's head like a scarlet halo against the green grass of Dealey Plaza and the President crashes backward in the seat like a boxer against the ropes, lingers upright for a moment, then topples slowly into Jackie's lap. (See illustrations 16–22.)

And where his hair used to be, from above his right ear all the way to his temple, there is no hair at all. Instead the whole right front of Kennedy's head is an appalling mass of white and red tissue glistening in the hot Texas sun. A huge flap of scalp and bone hangs grotesquely

down from the wound and another piece of the President's skull
several inches square flies up and lands on the trunk of the big
Lincoln. Jackie scrambles out of the seat to retrieve it. Secret Service
agent Clint Hill, who jumped from the running board of the follow-up
car at the sound of gunfire, scrambles onto the trunk deck, pushes
Mrs. Kennedy back into the seat and covers the First Lady and
President with his body. But Hill is too late—the damage is done and
the limousine slips into the darkness of the triple underpass under
the railroad tracks.

As Donahue reached a stopping point in his study of this sorrowful
and grisly scene, he reviewed his conclusions.

So far, his inquiry had uncovered two crippling problems in the
government's claim that Lee Harvey Oswald fired the shot that struck
Kennedy in the head: 1) the apparent trajectory of the bullet did not
seem to match the location of Oswald's sniper's nest, and 2) the type
of bullet fired was totally at odds with the rounds Oswald was known
to have used.

These were serious defects that defied explanation. Like the time
delay between Kennedy's and Connally's reaction to the single bullet,
the evidence surrounding the head shot was as ominous as it was
enigmatic.

For the first time, the legitimate possibility that another gunman
fired the fatal head shot entered Donahue's mind.

6
A FORTUITOUS ENCOUNTER

DONAHUE TELEPHONED THE EDITOR HE'D BEEN WORKING with at *True* magazine and told him he wouldn't be able to finish the article endorsing the Warren Commission's conclusions after all.

"I found a few inconsistencies in the Warren Report and I don't know if I'll be able to resolve them," Donahue said. He added with a laugh, "If I stay with this and figure it out, I'll be back in touch."

Actually, Donahue had no plans for abandoning his work. In just eight months, working on weekends and evenings in his cluttered basement den, he had been able to construct a rebuttal to the critics of the Commission's single bullet theory that effectively destroyed their principal arguments. More important, he was sure he'd identified two serious flaws in the government's explanation of the head wound, flaws those same critics has missed entirely.

Still, lacking further data—or a correction to Humes's placement of the entry wound—Donahue was stymied in his analysis of the vertical aspect of the head-shot trajectory. He was sure the Report's account was wrong. There was no realistic ballistic explanation for a rifle bullet coming down from the rear and then, after entering the skull, making so sharp an upward turn as to exit near the top of the head, considerably higher than where it went in. It is true a bullet can be deflected slightly by an encounter with bone, but to nothing like the degree required by the Warren Commission's trajectory. And it is true bone and tissue can even cause a bullet to yaw. But to understand yaw, Donahue thought, picture a car skidding on ice: Sure, its *attitude* can be more or less out of line, but its *direction* perseveres forward.

Since the downward trajectory remained problematic for Donahue, he turned his mind once again to the matter of the trajectory on the horizontal plane—that is, the question of the angle of fire as it would be seen from above.

Once again, he was faced with difficulties. The problem was, the angle in from Oswald at the rear was right to left. But the route of the bullet through Kennedy's head was markedly left to right. According to Josiah Thompson, the Oswald-to-Kennedy angle was 6 degrees right to left, relative to the straight-ahead direction of the car. Looking at the Report's sketch of the exit portal of the head wound and recalling Humes's location of the entry hole (one inch to the right of the occipital bone), Donahue estimated the angle of the bullet's trajectory through the head could be as much as 20 degrees left to right. This inshoot-to-outshoot angle, however, was not relative to the forward line of the car, the direction in which Kennedy was *traveling*, but to the midline of his head, the direction in which Kennedy was *looking*. Donahue knew that he had to account for the fact that the President appeared to be turned somewhat to the left.

Looking at images of Kennedy at or just before the head shot, particularly Zapruder 312, Donahue thought a consensus would put the angle his head was turned at the moment of impact at 15 degrees or so to the left.

Given these numbers, the arithmetic/geometry of the horizontal trajectory became possible to calculate. If the head had been facing straight forward, a bullet from Oswald would have followed a path through the skull that came out 6 degrees to the left of where it came in (relative to the center line of the head). But the head was *not* facing straight forward, it was turned 15 degrees to the left. Consequently the path through the skull should have terminated 9 degrees to the right of where it came in (in relation to the midline of Kennedy's skull). But, again, the Report's own drawing suggested the bullet came out as much as 20 degrees to the right of where it entered (relative to the midline of Kennedy's skull), not 9 degrees. Simple geometry seemed to show the Warren Report's trajectory was impossible.

Therefore, and Donahue was loath to admit it, the only explanation for the position of Kennedy's exit wound was that the shot had not come from the right rear but from the left rear, from a second gunman located somewhere over the President's left shoulder.

Pulling out an aerial photograph of Dealey Plaza, Donahue studied possible sniper positions behind and to the left of where the fatal bullet struck. There were two adjacent buildings that fit the bill: the Criminal Courts Building and the Dallas County Records Building.

Both were government office buildings. To Donahue, it seemed unlikely that a gunman could have fired from either one of these and escaped detection. The exception, perhaps, would have been had the gunman been on the roof. But attributing the shot to the roof of either building resurrected part of the same problem that surfaced when one attempted to pin the fatal shot on Oswald. The Records Building was the same height as the book depository, seven stories, and the Courts Building was taller yet, nine stories. Consequently, a shot fired from the roof of either building would have had to come down at an angle at least as steep as Oswald's purported shot.

Of course, this again required that a bullet descending at 16 degrees or better would suddenly ascend once it hit the President so as to exit at the top right of his skull, and Donahue knew no ballistics expert would accept this once he focused on it. As was the case with the trajectory from the book depository, ballistics would seem to require that a shot fired from either rooftop would exit through Kennedy's face.

Donahue was frustrated. He could speculate as much as he wanted to, but the fact was that unless he could establish beyond a doubt where the entrance wound was located on the back of Kennedy's head, it would be impossible to determine the actual trajectory of the bullet and hence the location of the weapon that fired the shot.

He shifted his mind back to the question of the disintegrating, fragmenting bullet. Who would use such lethal ammunition? At least one possibility crossed Donahue's mind.

Bodyguards.

Donahue knew that the type of penetrating military bullet fired by Oswald, though a good choice for a sniper, would never be used by bodyguards or anyone else who might have to fire into a crowd. A full metal–jacketed Carcano bullet could pass through three or four people and possibly kill a fifth.

A frangible, self-destructive bullet fired from, say, an automatic rifle, on the other hand, would be the ideal round for a bodyguard, since it would achieve the protector's two most important goals: The shot would instantly immobilize the enemy by creating a massive wound, and in so doing the bullet would disintegrate and go no farther to injure anyone else.

Bodyguards.

Intrigued by the thought, Donahue recalled what he knew about big-city police department shooting probes. In cases where more than one weapon may have been involved, investigators known as shooting teams routinely collect all the guns present, including those of police officers, check to see if the guns have been fired and, if so, how many times, examine any bullets or shell casings found, attempt to locate any nearby bullet holes in walls, cars, doors, furniture, et cetera, and examine all wounds to determine which weapon might have caused them.

These investigations reveal all too often that in many cases police officers mistakenly fire on and occasionally kill each other in the wild confusion of a shootout. Hence, officers involved are sequestered, forbidden to contact each other and thoroughly interrogated under oath.

With this in mind, Donahue wrote a letter to the Secret Service. He asked for the names of the agents who rode in the car behind the President that day, if they were still agents and if so in what capacity, what weapons they had carried, their caliber, and what if any changes had been made in the agency's weapons requirements since the assassination.

A letter came back some weeks later from James Rowley, the director of the Secret Service. According to Rowley, the President's follow-up car was driven by Samuel Kinney. Riding with Kinney were Emory Roberts, Clinton Hill, William McIntyre, John Ready, Paul Landis, Glen Bennett, and George Hickey. All were Secret Service special agents. Dave Powers and Kenneth O'Donnell, close advisors to the President and members of Kennedy's "Irish Mafia," were also in the car.

Oddly, Rowley's letter did not address Donahue's questions about the weapons agents carried. Donahue wrote back. In time, he received a second reply stating that as a matter of policy, the Secret Service did not disclose the types of weapons it used, other than the .38 caliber revolvers issued to all agents. The letter went on to emphasize that no shots had been fired by the Secret Service at the time of the assassination.

So Donahue ruminated, studying and reexamining the evidence. Weeks passed but he got no closer to establishing the origin of the fatal shot. In the meantime, he had a living to make—selling the latest drugs and health care products to doctors' offices and pharmacies around the mid-Atlantic region. To that end, Donahue stopped in to make his usual sales call at B. T. Smith's Pharmacy in downtown Baltimore one March morning in 1968.

Bernie Smith was a rotund man with an easy smile. Between filling out orders and chatting about Bernie's latest diet or health food kick, Donahue casually mentioned he'd been poking into the Kennedy assassination.

Smith looked up.*

"You ought to talk to my neighbor," he said. "Russell Fisher. He's the state medical examiner. A couple of months ago he went to Washington on some kind of investigation about the assassination. I'm not sure what it was. I think it had to do with that deal going on down in New Orleans. He might be worth talking to, though."

Donahue asked Smith to see if he could set up an appointment with Fisher. Smith called several days later and told Donahue the pathologist would be happy to talk with him. He suggested the three men gather at Smith's home in north Baltimore.

"Go ahead and give him a call to set up a time," Smith said.

Donahue rang up the medical examiner and the men agreed to rendezvous the following Saturday afternoon. Briefly, Fisher explained his connection to the Kennedy case. A month or so earlier, Attorney General Ramsey Clark had pulled together a panel of three pathologists and one radiologist to examine the X rays and photographs made during Kennedy's autopsy. Fisher had been among this group. According to Fisher, Clark's goal had been to reaffirm the

---

*The following conversations have been reconstructed from the recollections of Howard Donahue.

findings of the Warren Commission and throw cold water on increasingly lurid speculation about the assassination then coming out of "that affair in New Orleans."

"I'll look forward to talking with you," Fisher said as he signed off. "You might be interested in what we found."

Donahue could hardly contain his excitement as the week began. Surely Fisher could provide some kind of answer about the strange and contradictory evidence surrounding the President's head wound.

The "affair in New Orleans" to which Fisher had alluded was the notorious probe into the Kennedy assassination then being conducted by Orleans Parish District Attorney Jim Garrison (the basis for Oliver Stone's 1991 film, *JFK*). In February 1967, the *New Orleans States-Item* stunned the world with the revelation that Garrison had launched a criminal probe into an alleged conspiracy behind the Kennedy killing based out of Louisiana and Texas.[1] At the center of this investigation was David Ferrie, a shadowy former Eastern Airlines pilot and private investigator. New Orleans police apparently received two tips shortly after Kennedy was killed alleging that Ferrie may have somehow been involved in the shooting: He'd been Oswald's Civil Air Patrol commander in New Orleans, and he'd also made a mysterious trip to Texas just after the assassination.[2]

The authorities, including the FBI and Warren Commission investigators, had pursued this information and conducted interviews with Ferrie and others in New Orleans in December 1963.[3] However, they soon determined the tips had been without merit. While it was true Ferrie had briefly been Oswald's commanding officer in the Civil Air Patrol, the two men had not known each other.[4]

But by late 1966, District Attorney Garrison was apparently convinced there was more to the alleged Ferrie connection than the Commission's cursory check had revealed. He launched his own investigation in October of that year.[5] After the story broke, Garrison fumed that the publicity would put off arrests in the case for weeks, maybe months. Nevertheless, he seemed to relish his newfound notoriety. As reporters from around the world descended on New Orleans, Garrison spoke freely and confidently about the investigation's prospects for success.[6] "There is no question there will be arrests, charges and convictions," Garrison said.[7]

But a scant four days after the Garrison story broke, prime suspect Ferrie turned up dead. The coroner ruled he died of natural causes—a brain hemorrhage. A note found in his apartment near the body seemed to cast doubt on this conclusion, however.[8] It read, in part, "to leave this life for me, is a sweet prospect. I find nothing in it that is desirable, and on the other hand, everything that is loathsome."[9]

If Garrison's conspiracy case was dealt a major blow by Ferrie's death, the tall, barrel-chested D.A. didn't show it. Instead, he brazenly claimed the assassination had been "solved." Yet once again he cautioned that it might take "months or years" to work out details in order to make arrests.[10]

In fact, the first arrest came less than two weeks later. On March 1, Garrison picked up a prominent New Orleans businessman, Clay Shaw, on charges of conspiracy to kill the President.[11] According to Garrison, an informant who'd been administered sodium pentothal claimed that Shaw, Ferrie, and Oswald plotted the assassination at a meeting in New Orleans in September 1963.

The case grew even more sensational with oblique disclosures that Shaw was a homosexual and that investigators found chains, whips, a black hood, cape, and other sadomasochistic paraphernalia in his home.[12]

But when it became apparent the headline-grabbing district attorney couldn't back up his allegations against Shaw with more relevant evidence, the weight of public and media opinion quickly began swinging away from Garrison. Before long, the American Civil Liberties Union was decrying the "Roman circus" atmosphere surrounding the New Orleans probe.[13] On March 5, *The New York Times* ran a cartoon depicting Garrison as a chagrined-looking male stripper covering his private parts with feathers.[14] Across the stage behind this pathetic figure were banners that proclaimed, "Startling revelations that can not be revealed!" and "Sensational disclosures too sensational to disclose!"

As the spring of 1967 drifted into summer, allegations that Garrison offered to pay a witness for evidence against Shaw further deepened suspicions about the methods of the probe.[15] Soon after, one of Garrison's top investigators quit the case, angrily asserting that there was no truth to any of Garrison's conspiracy allegations.[16]

Newsweek magazine reported the only conspiracy was the one that existed in Garrison's mind.[17] *The New York Times,* in a decision reflecting the stock editors now put in Garrison, on May 24 buried the D.A.'s latest pronouncement in the case at the bottom of page 50—beneath New York area wedding announcements. In this brief item, Garrison claimed "guerrilla fighters shooting in a crossfire" from three locations killed Kennedy.[18] Farfetched, perhaps, but on at least one point, Garrison seemed to be stumbling toward the truth.

"It appears [the assassins] used frangible bullets," Garrison said. ". . . Frangible bullets explode into little pieces."

The flamboyant D.A. was convinced by autumn that the Kennedy conspiracy involved pro-Castro Cubans, the Central Intelligence Agency, the Mafia, certain members of the Dallas police department and for good measure, "a handful of oil-rich psychotic individuals."[19] In December, Garrison further refined his understanding of shooting. Now he claimed Kennedy was shot with a .45 caliber pistol by a gunman hiding in a sewer manhole.[20]

This increasingly frenzied and bizarre speculation—along with the publication of Josiah Thompson's book *Six Seconds in Dallas* in November—apparently prompted the following letter to Attorney General Clark from J. Thornton Boswell, one of the three doctors who had presided over the Kennedy autopsy on November 22.[21] For years, critics had savaged the work the doctors did that night. It seems that by early 1968, Boswell had had enough:

January 26, 1968

Dear Mr. Attorney General:

As you are aware, the autopsy findings in the case of the late President John F. Kennedy, including X-rays and photographs, have been the subject of continuing controversy and speculation. Dr. Humes and I, as the Pathologists concerned, have felt for some time that an impartial board of experts including pathologists and radiologists should examine the available material.

If such a board were to be nominated in an attempt to resolve many of the allegations concerning the autopsy report, it might wish to question the autopsy participants before more time elapses and memory fades; therefore, it would be my hope that such a board would be convened at an early date. Dr. Humes and I would make ourselves available at the request of such a board.

I hope that this letter will not be considered presumptuous, but this matter is of great concern to us, and I believe to the country as well. Your attention to this matter will be greatly appreciated.

Respectfully, J. Thornton Boswell, M.D.

Clark had expressed skepticism bordering on contempt for Garrison's investigation throughout 1967,[22] and in Boswell's plea for vindication he no doubt saw an opportunity to discredit the Warren Report critics and Garrison in particular once and for all.

The attorney general moved quickly. Within a month, a panel was appointed that would presumably accomplish the task at hand. In recruiting Dr. Russell Fisher to head the effort, the attorney general found an excellent man for the job. Fisher was a leader in the field of forensic pathology. He'd been the Maryland chief medical examiner since 1949 and was well known nationwide for applying new methods of chemical analysis to the autopsy process.[23] These procedures improved the accuracy of autopsy results and eventually became standard practice around the world.

Joining Fisher on the four-member panel was another Maryland medical pioneer, Dr. Russell Morgan, head of the radiology department at John Hopkins University School of Medicine. Like Fisher, Morgan was a respected leader in his field. He had been responsible for developing a number of improvements in the quality and safety of radiology, including the instantaneous X-ray machine, a timing device that shut down the machine the instant the film was exposed and thus limited the patient's exposure to harmful radiation.[24]

The other panel members were Dr. William H. Carnes, a professor

of pathology at the University of Utah and a member of the state's
Medical Examiner Commission, and Dr. Alan Mortiz, a professor of
pathology at Case Western Reserve University in Cleveland.[25]

The panel, then, was well qualified in its role as the first group
outside the government to gain access to the controversial autopsy
materials. That Donahue would now be privy to what this panel had
found, just weeks after their work had finished, was a great stroke of
good luck.

Saturday finally arrived. Donahue collected some of his notes on
the assassination, particularly the information he'd put together on
the discrepancies surrounding the head shot, and went to see Fisher.

Fisher was a large, soft-spoken man. He wore glasses and smoked
a pipe. After coffee and small talk, Fisher explained that the panel
had viewed the assassination material at the National Archives on
February 26 and 27 under the supervision of the chief archivist.

This material, Fisher said, included forty-five photos taken during
autopsy, fourteen X rays, the President's clothes, the Zapruder film,
two other lesser-quality home movies of the assassination as well as
CE 399, the bullet recovered at Parkland hospital.*

"And . . ." Donahue asked casually, "what did you find?"

"Well, for one thing, the bullet that hit him in the head disintegrated completely. We saw nearly forty fragments throughout the
right cerebral hemisphere and embedded in the interior of the skull.
A lot of them were no bigger than the point of a pen, and the largest
was about the size of the nail on your little finger.

"Another thing," Fisher continued, "was that the entrance wound
on the back of the skull wasn't where it was supposed to be. Humes
placed it an inch to the right and somewhat above the external
occipital protuberance, but we measured it from the X rays and found
it was actually four inches above the occipital protuberance and an
inch to the right of the midline."

Donahue was flabbergasted. Here was the confirmation he'd been
looking for. The bullet had indeed explosively disintegrated into
dozens of tiny fragments. And Humes had in fact mislocated the
entrance wound. According to Fisher's information, the bullet actually entered way up at the top of Kennedy's head, just to the right of
the cowlick area. An inch or two higher and the shot would have
missed the President completely.

That wasn't all. Humes had also failed to report precisely the shape
and extent of the exit wound. Moreover, according to Fisher, the
panel had agreed that at least one major fragment of bullet had exited
much farther forward than the Warren Report's sketches had suggested.

Fisher went on to say the panel had observed a curious metal

*The following conversation has been reconstructed from the recollections of Howard Dona-
hue.

fragment embedded on the outer table of the skull just beneath the entrance wound. He described it as round and about 6.5 millimeters in diameter, and noted there had been no mention of this fragment in the original autopsy report.

"Where could it have come from?" Donahue asked.

"Well, we thought it looked like a ricochet fragment," Fisher replied. He drew a picture of the fragment's approximate size and location.

Donahue tried to digest what he was hearing. A ricochet, another shot . . . According to the Warren Report, one of Oswald's three shots had missed. Yet investigators supposedly hadn't been able to determine which one it was or exactly where it had gone. Could this unreported fragment be evidence of that miss?

And what about the newly revised locations of entrance and exit wounds? Donahue quickly visualized the apparent trajectory of the head shot based on Fisher's information and the position of Kennedy's head at impact (hanging forward and turned slightly to the left.) Apparently, the shot had come in on a shallow downward trajectory; originating from behind, slightly above and . . . from the left.

No way Oswald could have fired this shot.

What else was back there along the bullet's plane of flight? In his mind's eye, reviewing the films and photographs of what was behind, to the left, and slightly higher than Kennedy's head, Donahue saw something.

After a long pause, Donahue took a deep breath and spoke.*

"Dr. Fisher, I've spent a lot of time studying this, and after what you've just told me about the location of the entrance wound, I just don't see how Kennedy's head wound could have been caused by a bullet from Oswald's gun. It seems like a physical impossibility.

"I know this sounds crazy, but is it possible that the head shot may have been an accident? Could it have come from someone in the Secret Service car? They were right behind the presidential limousine."

Fisher looked down momentarily, carefully weighing an answer. "Well, you know more about guns than I do," he said. "But that would certainly explain the strange antics of the government."

Though he didn't go into much detail, Fisher revealed that while the panel had initially received Clark's full backing and support in their work, the doctors' requests to view additional evidence—specifically the President's brain as well as edge scrapings, or tissue samples from the entrance hole in the skull—had been denied.

Like the brain, the edge scrapings were significant. Minute particles of metal from the bullet's jacket would have been deposited as the slug passed through the scalp and skull wall. To identify the metallic makeup of these deposits would be to identify the type of

---

*The following conversation was reconstructed from the recollections of Howard Donahue.

bullet that caused them, since different bullets use different types of
metal for the jacket material.

As Donahue listened, he could see Fisher was being extremely
cautious with his words, and consequently Donahue didn't push for
details. In time, Fisher went on to intimate that at the conclusion of
the panel's two days of study, there had been more than a little
resentment among panel members about the Justice Department's
refusal to provide the autopsy materials in question.

Then it occurred to Donahue: If appointment of the panel had been
designed to reassure the public and corroborate the Warren Commission findings once and for all, why had he not heard of its work
before running into Fisher? Why hadn't there been an announcement
by the attorney general or press release by the Justice Department or
news conference?

To Donahue, the answer seemed clear. Though the panel had
agreed to sign a document stating the evidence they'd observed was
consistent with the Warren Report's conclusions, the fact was, the
evidence wasn't consistent at all. Not by a long shot.

Donahue thanked Fisher very much and headed home.

7
KENNEDY'S UNKNOWN WOUND

EVEN AS DONAHUE MARVELED AT HIS MONUMENTAL good luck in linking up with Fisher, his mind raced as he labored to assimilate the information at hand. He worked in his basement by lamplight late into the night in a worn La-Z-Boy chair amid benches covered with guns, tools, and notes on the assassination, and he focused first on the curious fragment the panel found on the outer table of the Kennedy's skull—the fragment Fisher believed came from a ricochet. To Donahue, it seemed remarkable that the Bethesda autopsy team, the ones who'd actually taken the skull X rays, had missed this. Here was one more example of shoddy work by Humes and his crew.

Fisher had given Donahue a copy of the panel's sixteen-page report, and now Donahue scanned it for mention of the puzzling fragment. He found a brief description of the bullet remnant on page 11:

> Also there is, embedded in the outer table of the skull close to the lower edge of the [entrance] hole, a large metallic fragment which on the anteroposterior film (#1) lies 25 mm. to the right of the midline. This fragment as seen in the latter film is round and measures 6.5 mm. in diameter.

That was it. Even though Fisher said the panel believed the fragment looked like a ricochet fragment, there was no mention of this conjecture in the written report. In fact, there was no explanation for the fragment at all.

But if it didn't come from a ricochet, Donahue wondered, what else could it have been? The fragment was imbedded in the *outer* table of the skull just beneath the entrance wound. This meant it had to have penetrated the scalp from the outside. Dozens of smaller fragments were identified inside the skull—in the brain cavity—and had this one been there too, it would have obviously come from the disintegration of the bullet. Such was not the case.

Some years later, J. K. Lattimer, the New York urologist, would suggest in his book *Kennedy and Lincoln: Medical and Ballistic Comparisons of Their Assassinations,* that the fragment found by Fisher's panel—by virtue of its close proximity to the entrance wound—was actually a piece of the fatal bullet that sheared off as the slug impacted the skull.[1]

Donahue considered this in 1968. But never in his experience had he heard of a hard metal–jacketed military bullet "shearing" on impact; a soft lead bullet, yes. But not the type of military round Oswald fired.

Furthermore, even if the bullet could have performed in such an unlikely manner, physics would seem to require that the fragment be deposited above the entrance wound, not below it: The top side of the entrance hole would have acted like a chisel, scraping off a piece of the jacket as the bullet came down at an angle and in.

Much later, Donahue called Fisher to get his opinion about whether a shearing effect could have created the fragment. The two had only briefly touched on this possibility when they met at B. T. Smith's house. Fisher wasn't available, but Donahue did speak with another pathologist and associate of Fisher's, Dr. Thomas Smith. Like Donahue, Smith said he had never seen a fragment shear off a hard military jacketed bullet and deposit itself on the outer table of the skull.

Donahue would repeat his question about the likelihood of a hard metal–jacketed bullet shearing to every forensic pathologist he came in contact with in the years that followed. The answer was always the same: The experts had never seen or heard of such a phenomenon and considered it highly unlikely.

The fact that Fisher and his panel thought the fragment looked like it came from a ricochet was good enough for Donahue in 1968. He was convinced. That the fragment was located just beneath the entrance wound was, apparently, a coincidence.

A ricochet then . . . a missed shot. Donahue pondered the implications.

According to the Warren Commission, one of Oswald's three shots missed. The Commission couldn't say exactly which one it was, but they nevertheless asserted the miss in all likelihood was the second shot fired, since the Zapruder film suggested Oswald's first bullet penetrated Kennedy's neck and since most witnesses were in agreement that the head shot was the last one.

But now, suddenly, here was material proof that Kennedy was struck by a ricochet fragment. This wound had never been disclosed by the Warren Commission or anywhere else, except for the oblique reference in Fisher's panel report. Maybe, Donahue thought, this fragment was the result of Oswald's true first shot.

The implication began to sink in: If Oswald's first shot missed but peppered Kennedy with a ricochet fragment and it was in fact the second shot that struck the President's neck . . . Donahue tried to visualize the picture. The bullet must have smashed into the pavement fifteen or twenty feet behind and to the right of the limousine—nearly at the sidewalk—and exploded in a shower of fragments. It was justifiable to conjecture that Oswald's line of fire was reasonably in Kennedy's direction (his next shot hit Kennedy squarely in the back), albeit too low. The fanning of the shower increased the likelihood that one of these fragments then flew up and caught Kennedy in the head. The hot metal must have stung like a BB or pellet as it penetrated Kennedy's scalp.

A wound like that would explain Secret Service agent Kellerman's testimony about hearing the President cry out, "My God! I'm hit!" just after the first shot echoed through Dealey Plaza.

Virtually everyone who'd ever studied Zapruder's home movie—Warren Commission supporters and critics alike—had taken it as an article of faith that Kennedy's clenched fists and raised arms showed he was reacting to the wound through his neck as the limousine emerged from behind the Stemmons Freeway sign that momentarily blocked Zapruder's view. But what if Kennedy was actually reacting to the scalp wound? What if the shot that hit him in the neck and Connally in the chest didn't strike until a few seconds later?

Donahue quickly realized that if this was the case, the scalp wound—in addition to explaining Kellerman's testimony—would also resolve the problematic questions raised by the testimony of Connally, who adamantly asserted he was hit by the second shot. More importantly, it would explain the curious time lag on the Zapruder film between when Kennedy and Connally responded to being hit.

Fascinated with this emerging possibility, Donahue pulled out still photographs of the Zapruder movie and studied the frames taken as the limousine appeared from behind the highway sign. Conventional wisdom assumed otherwise, but Donahue's scrutiny revealed Kennedy wasn't necessarily grabbing his throat as he came into view. The President's hands were balled into fists and his arms were coming up, almost as if he was trying to protect his face, or, perhaps, reach for the back of his head. He even managed to bring his right fist in front of his mouth, above his neck. (See illustration 17.)

Certainly the President's actions were open to a number of interpretations, but one thing was clear: The argument could just as well be made that Kennedy was attempting to cover his face with his hands, not grab his throat.

Donahue then examined the frame taken just before Connally's violent reaction to his wounds. Here again was something he'd never noticed before. At frame 237, the instant before Connally begins to react, Kennedy's body pitches forward and his elbows shoot up dramatically. The President then pulls his still-closed fists up tightly toward his neck. (See illustration 18.)

Perhaps this motion marked the actual instant the bullet pierced Kennedy's neck. Donahue soon spotted a second detail that greatly strengthened this scenario. At frame 237, Connally's torso is twisted slightly to the right and his right shoulder is dropping. This attitude put the governor in an ideal position to receive from Kennedy's neck a bullet under his right armpit and through his chest to his thigh.

In fact, as far as Donahue could tell, the one-sixth of a second interval captured in frames 235–237 was the only time during the entire Zapruder film that the governor's body was in this position. Insofar as Connally begins to crumple from his wounds one-eighteenth of a second later, the conclusion that 237–238 marked the single bullet's true moment of impact seemed inescapable.

Therefore, if the single bullet struck both men at that point, then the first shot—the ricochet—must have come at least two seconds earlier. Oswald wouldn't have been able to work the bolt action on his rifle much quicker than that.

Donahue did some quick calculations and determined that a two-second interval would back-date the impact time for the ricochet to somewhere before frame 201, given each frame was one-eighteenth of a second. Frame 201 was taken a good distance before the car passed behind the sign.

The Commission, in its wisdom, had concluded Kennedy could not possibly have been hit (through the neck, of course) until the limousine was obscured from Zapruder by the freeway sign, between frames 210 and 224. Commission investigators used two assumptions to support this: Kennedy does not appear to respond to his wound until after the car begins to emerge from behind the sign (frame 225) and Oswald's view of the limousine, before frame 210, would have been blocked by an oak tree that stood in front of the book depository.[2]

Donahue disregarded the Commission's analysis and began scouring the earliest Zapruder frames for any evidence of Kennedy reacting to the ricochet wound in the frames before 200. The film's first frames show two motorcycles making the corner from Houston onto Elm. Then the limousine comes into view—flags on the fenders popping in the breeze and Kennedy waving to the crowds on the right.

Donahue stared at the pictures over and over again. In time, he saw that well before the car passed behind the sign, in the frames immediately after 189, a perceptible change occurred in Kennedy's manner: The quality of the photographs was poor through Zapruder's zoom lens but Kennedy nonetheless suddenly seemed to freeze, his waving hand halting abruptly.

If this movement showed Kennedy was beginning to react to the ricochet around frame 189, then it fit perfectly, since both he and Connally were seemingly struck by the second shot at frames 237–238—two and a half seconds later.

Donahue knew Oswald could have easily ejected the spent shell, slammed another round into the chamber, taken aim, and pulled the trigger within two and a half seconds. The Commission figured the minimum possible time between Carcano shots at 2.3 seconds,[3] and Donahue himself, though hardly an average marksman, had fired two rounds from a Carcano in about two and a half seconds each during the CBS reenactment.

The fact that Oswald's vision was obscured by the tree during this interval only strengthened Donahue's emerging understanding of the ricochet wound. Oswald must have been nervous as he crouched near the sixth-floor window. It was reasonable to imagine a rattled, shaking Oswald firing prematurely or firing as Kennedy appeared briefly through a hole in the foliage. It was, after all, the point where Kennedy was the closest, presenting the largest target. As well, Warren Commission marksmen had determined that the sight on Oswald's gun was badly out of line and probably wouldn't have resulted in an accurate shot. Ergo, Donahue thought, Oswald may have fired his first shot using the sight and then, realizing the scope was off, fired the second shot using the traditional iron notch sight at the end of the gun's barrel.

Strangely, the Warren Commission did not raise this possibility in their discussion of the shooting. Nor did they make any mention of the ricochet fragment on Kennedy's skull. The Commission did, however, consider—and reject—the possibility that Oswald's nerves caused the first shot to miss. According to the Report: ". . . the greatest cause for doubt that the first shot missed is the improbability that the same marksman who twice hit a moving target would be so inaccurate on the first and closest of his shots as to miss completely, not only the target, but the large automobile."[4]

The Report did acknowledge the testimony of Secret Service agent Glen Bennett in its brief discussion about the possibility of the first shot going wide. Bennett sat in the right-rear seat of the Secret Service follow-up car. After hearing the first shot, Bennett said, "I looked at the back of the President. I heard another firecracker noise and saw that shot hit the President four inches down from the right shoulder."[5] The Commission all but dismissed his statement by raising the possibility that the bullet hole was already there when Bennett saw it.[6]

Donahue, however, was inclined to believe Bennett. He knew impressions reported soon after an event are generally the most accurate, and Bennett's statement had been recorded on the evening of November 22.[7]

For Donahue, the evidence seemed to be converging around the probability that Oswald's first shot missed and struck Kennedy with a ricochet fragment. Still, he needed additional corroboration—someone who actually saw the bullet strike the pavement behind the car.

As the weeks flew past, Donahue periodically headed for the National Archives in Washington to dig through the volumes of Commission

evidence and testimony. Weekends came and weekends went as
Donahue pored over the testimony in search of the key witness.
Finally, one afternoon in the smoldering summer of 1968—not long
after Robert Kennedy was shot down in Los Angeles—Donahue
found what he was looking for. Her name was Virgie Rachley.

Rachley married some months after the assassination and became
Mrs. Donald Baker. She was working as a bookkeeper in the Texas
School Book Depository on November 22, 1963, and was deposed at
the U.S. Attorney's offices in Dallas on July 22, 1964, by Wesley
Liebeler, the bearded and rotund assistant counsel to the Commission. Donahue found the transcript of this deposition on pages 507–
515 in Volume VII of the Commission's exhibits.

Baker told Liebeler she'd seen Oswald around the warehouse in
the weeks before the assassination but had never spoken with him.
Her only impression was that he was "awful quiet." On November
22, Baker and several coworkers left the book depository shortly
after noon to watch the presidential motorcade come by.

LIEBELER: So, you were standing directly in front of the Texas
           School Book Depository Building and on the same side
           of Elm Street that the Texas School Book Depository is
           located?
BAKER: Yes.
LIEBELER: Tell me what you saw?
BAKER: Well, after he passed us, then we heard a noise and I
           thought it was firecrackers, because I saw a shot or
           something hit the pavement.

There was initially some confusion between Baker and Liebeler
over where Baker saw the "firecracker" strike, but the bookkeeper
pinpointed the location as behind and to the right of the presidential
limousine as the car pulled nearly even with the R. L. Thornton
Freeway sign, the first highway sign on the north side of Elm Street
and fifty feet or so closer to the book depository than the Stemmons
Freeway sign that momentarily obscured Zapruder's view.

LIEBELER: As you went down Elm Street that [sic] you saw this
           thing hit the street—what did it look like when you saw
           it?
BAKER: Well, as I said, I thought it was a firecracker. It looked
           just like you could see the sparks from it and I just
           thought it was a firecracker and I was thinking that there
           was somebody was fixing to get in a lot of trouble . . .

Liebeler pressed Baker on when the shot hit.

LIEBELER: You saw this thing hit the street before you heard the
             second shot, is that correct?
BAKER: Yes, sir; yes.
LIEBELER: Are you absolutely sure of that?
BAKER: I hope I am—I know I am.

Later, Liebeler again focused on the question of timing.

LIEBELER: In any event, you are quite clear in your mind that you
             saw this thing hit before you heard the second shot?
BAKER: Yes.[8]

Baker's description of the miss was just where Donahue had thought it might be, based on the estimated angle of deflection required to strike Kennedy with the fragment at or about frame 189. And Baker seemed certain about what she had seen.

Not long after he found Baker's testimony, Donahue discovered the statement of Royce Skelton, a railroad mail clerk who watched the motorcade come down Elm Street from atop the triple overpass. Skelton, too, thought he saw something strike the pavement near the President's car. He told investigators he saw the third or fourth shot kick up a puff of concrete dust off the car's right front fender.[9] The location and timing didn't add up for Donahue, but maybe Skelton was mistaken. (See also, in Appendix A to this book, agent Warren Taylor's statement that, as the first shot sounded, "out of the corner of my eye . . . I noticed what . . . might have been a short piece flying close to the ground.")

Later, he read the account of Harry D. Holmes. Holmes was a postal inspector who'd watched the motorcade through binoculars from an office window overlooking Dealey Plaza.

"I had my binoculars on this car, on the Presidential car all the time," Holmes told the Commission. "I realized something was wrong, but I thought they were dodging somebody throwing things at the car like firecrackers or something, but I did see dust fly up like a firecracker had burst up in the air."

Asked where he saw the dust fly, Holmes said, "Off of President Kennedy . . ."[10]

In the years that followed, other witnesses would emerge who said they thought they saw a bullet hitting the pavement near the limousine. Starvis Ellis was a motorcycle police officer who was riding alongside Dallas County Sheriff Bill Decker's lead car in the motorcade. He told the 1978 Select Committee on Assassinations he saw a bullet hit the pavement.[11]

And in 1989, Jim Marrs, author of *Crossfire,* a comprehensive book on assassination conspiracy theories, reported that Sheriff Decker himself thought he saw a bullet strike the street.[12] Here then, were five witnesses who believed they saw a bullet hit the pavement.

Donahue didn't know about Decker and Ellis in 1968. But as he reread Baker's testimony, the thing that seemed strangest of all was the fact that the Warren Commission had completely ignored the bookkeeper's deposition in its final report. Not a word. The information was available only by digging deep in the Commission's evidence volumes. Surely Baker's vivid and detailed recollections about what she saw and when she saw it were worth noting, particularly in view of the fragment found on the exterior of Kennedy's skull.

As far as that went, why on earth would the Commission ignore the evidence of Kennedy's ricochet wound? What could possibly be gained by disregarding information that suggested Oswald's first shot missed? If anything, the ricochet strengthened the single bullet theory, since it reconciled both Connally's testimony about being hit by the second shot as well as the time lag between when Kennedy and Connally reacted to their wounds. It would certainly seem to be worth pointing out. But the Commission did not.

Donahue didn't have a clue. It subsequently occurred to him that there was one last area of evidence that might shed some light on these questions and the mystery of the ricochet: the bullet fragments from the scene of the crime.

The presidential limousine was flown back to Washington on the night of the twenty-second and examined over the next several days by Secret Service and FBI agents. The car turned out to be a veritable lead mine of evidence. Donahue looked up the information in the Warren Report:

"One fragment, found on the seat beside the driver, weighed 44.6 grains and consisted of the nose portion of a bullet. The other fragment, found along the right side of the front seat, weighed 21 grains and consisted of the base portion of the bullet," Commission investigators wrote.[13]

A day later, FBI investigators found three small lead particles, each weighing between seven-tenths and nine-tenths of a grain, on the rug underneath the left jump seat Mrs. Connally had occupied.[14]

"The agents also noted a small residue of lead on the inside surface of the laminated windshield and a very small pattern of cracks on the outer layer of the windshield immediately behind the lead residue," the Report stated. "There was a minute particle of glass missing from the outside surface, but no penetration."[15] (See illustration 11.)

The agents also spotted a dent in the chrome molding across the inside top of the windshield, just to the left of the rearview mirror support.[16]

The Warren Commission concluded the fragments and the damage to the inside of the car were probably the result of lead that fanned out after the third shot hit Kennedy in the head.[17]

Maybe so, Donahue thought. But he was already highly suspicious of anything the Commission said about the head wound. And he was increasingly perplexed and troubled by the Commission's statements regarding fragments or shots that may have missed.

He decided the best thing to do was examine the bullet fragments himself at the National Archives. Donahue drove to Washington and was granted permission by the chief archivist to study the two large fragments found on and beside the front seat. As he stared into the folds and fissures of the twisted gray forms through a 30-power jeweler's loupe, two telling facts emerged. First, there was no cranial debris on either fragment. Had the slugs passed through the President's brain, they would have necessarily been coated with brain tissue, fluid, and blood. This material would have dried and hardened deep in the tiniest cracks of the fragments and been extremely difficult to remove.

The second oddity was that one of the fragments—part of the rear section of the broken bullet—had the jacket peeled backward 180 degrees and folded almost flat. One edge of this folded section literally formed a razor edge. It seemed improbable that such a sharp edge could have been fashioned as the bullet traveled through the skull and cranial tissue. Much more likely was the possibility that the razor edge and 180-degree fold were created by the bullet's impact with an immovable object—like concrete, for instance.

Like Elm Street.

Donahue retreated to Towson. He did various calculations about where the bullet would have to strike the pavement to reflect up over the trunk of the car and hit Kennedy. From his own experience he knew the angle of reflection would be less than the angle of incidence because the relative softness of surface and projectile make it impossible for a bullet to bounce up at exactly the angle it came down. Without tests, the precise reflecting angle could not be fixed, which meant there was a long line on the pavement defining possible points of impact. Using an aerial photograph of Dealey Plaza, he sketched the trajectory of what he was now fairly certain had been Oswald's first shot, the ricochet, based on all that he'd learned, and based on the location of the limousine at frame 189. This straight line passed from the book depository window down through the oak tree to the street, back up, through and past where the President was sitting and then straight on toward the middle tunnel of the triple overpass.

The middle tunnel of the triple overpass . . . Donahue recalled that James Tague, a witness to the assassination, had been standing in this area when he was struck in the face by what was apparently a bullet fragment. There was a nick in the curb near where Tague was standing.

Donahue once more turned to his by now dog-eared copy of the Warren Report. Tague, he read, was standing on the traffic island between Commerce Street and Main, on the south side of the middle tunnel portal.[18] Remarkably, Donahue's straight-arrow, three-dimensional ricochet line from the depository passed directly over this point.

Perhaps, Donahue thought, Tague's wound was caused by a piece of the fractured bullet that sailed over the presidential limousine at a diminished velocity, struck the curb, then ricocheted back up again. This scenario made sense, particularly since a chemical analysis of the gash on the curb by the FBI revealed traces of lead and antimony, but no copper. The absence of copper, according to the Commission, precluded the possibility that the curb mark was made by an unmutilated, full metal–jacketed Carcano round, since the Carcano's jacket was made of copper.[19]

However, the Commission said nothing about the possibility of the curb mark being made by a mutilated Carcano round. One of the two fragments found in the front seat consisted of a bullet base and its shredded copper jacket. Therefore, it seemed plausible to Donahue that the piece that flew over the car consisted only of a portion of the lead core. This would explain the absence of copper on the concrete.

In contrast to the simple logic of Donahue's view, the Commission's own interpretation of Tague's wound was vague and convoluted at best. They at first suggested that the one, never-identified shot that missed may have struck the curb in front of Tague and caught him with a fragment. On the other hand, they noted the lack of copper and hence alternatively proposed a scenario somewhat closer to Donahue's, i.e., that Tague's wound "might have been a product of the fragmentation of the missed shot upon hitting some other object in the area."

Yet at no point did the Commission explore the possibility that the missed shot was the first Oswald fired and the "other object in the area" was Elm Street, behind and to the right of the presidential limo and on a straightaway trajectory from the book depository.

Weeks had passed since Donahue had met with Fisher in B. T. Smith's den. Thanks to Fisher's information and the analysis it compelled, Donahue was confident that Oswald's first shot missed, ricocheted, and caught Kennedy with a lead fragment in the head. No one had ever suggested anything like this before, as far as Donahue knew. Then again, he figured apparently no one with any ballistics experience had studied the assassination in depth. And very few people knew about the metal fragment Fisher had discovered on the X rays of Kennedy's skull.

Yet if Donahue's understanding of the ricochet wound resolved a number of questions, it also raised a major one in their place. This difficulty came swinging around periodically in Donahue's mind: Why would the Commission ignore or, worse yet, suppress information that strongly indicated Oswald's first shot missed? They themselves said one of his shots had missed and there was ample enough evidence to conclude that this shot was the first. The Commission, of course, believed that Oswald wouldn't have missed his first shot because his target was closest to him then. But such conjecture didn't hold much water alongside physical evidence that proved otherwise.

There was something else, too.

As Donahue searched the Warren Commission depositions and other books for witnesses who might have seen the first shot miss, he'd come across a number of people who'd smelled gunpowder in Dealey Plaza. Mrs. Earle Cabell, wife of Dallas Mayor Earle Cabell, rode with her husband four cars back from the presidential limousine: "I was acutely aware of the odor of gunpowder."[20]

Tom Dillard, a photographer for the *Dallas Morning News,* rode five cars back in a press car, a Chevy convertible: "I might add that I very definitely smelled gunpowder when the car moved up at the corner."

Investigator: "You did?"

Dillard: "I very definitely smelled it."[21]

Mrs. Donald Baker, the bookkeeper and key witness who'd pinpointed the ricochet strike, said she too had smelled gunpowder.[22]

Likewise, Officer Earle Brown, a Dallas patrolman stationed atop the railroad bridge over Stemmons Freeway, about one hundred yards from the triple overpass on Elm, said he "heard these shots and then I smelled this gunpowder."[23]

Finally, there was Congressman Ralph Yarborough, who rode with Vice President Johnson in an open Lincoln directly behind the Secret Service follow-up car. Yarborough said he thought he smelled gunpowder.[24] How on earth, Donahue wondered, could all these people in all these different locations have smelled gunpowder? Oswald was sixty feet above the street and most of the windows in the book depository were closed. Bullets don't emit or trail gun smoke. And what about Officer Brown on the highway overpass? He was a considerable distance *upwind* from Dealey Plaza, and the wind was blowing briskly that day. Any gun smoke produced in Dealey Plaza could never have reached him.

It was very strange. . . .

Yet if Donahue was baffled about the source of the acrid odor and couldn't conceive of why the Commission would ignore evidence that suggested Oswald's first shot missed, he was still elated. In a few short months, he'd resolved in his own mind the last of the questions about the single bullet theory, the doctrine that Kennedy and Connally were wounded by the same bullet. At the same time, he'd discovered an entirely unknown wound suffered by the President. And more curious behavior by the Commission.

As the summer of 1968 faded, Donahue turned his attention back to Kennedy's head wound. Again thanks to Fisher, he was armed now with the actual location of the entrance wound and a better idea of the area of the exit wound in Kennedy's skull. Now a more accurate picture could be made of the bullet's trajectory.

Once more Donahue headed for the medical supply store to purchase a plaster skull. Once more he made measurements—this time based on Fisher's data on the head wound's location as well as his own estimate of where on the wound the bullet, had it remained intact, would have exited—and drilled.

Donahue positioned the skull as Kennedy's head had been just before the fatal bullet struck, and then inserted the wooden dowel. (See drawing 3.) This time, it was clear the bullet hadn't come from the limousine trunk. Rather, the trajectory came from left to right, on a shallow, nearly flat declination. Donahue's long-held suspicions were confirmed. Oswald's shot would have had to come from right to left. In his mind, the trajectory required by Fisher's location of the wounds categorically eliminated Oswald as the source of the fatal bullet.

Donahue went back to his drawing of Dealey Plaza and, based on the trajectory dictated by the wooden dowel, traced the line of the bullet from Kennedy back toward the Dallas County Records Building at the corner of Houston and Elm Streets.

He stared at the picture.

What disturbed him was not where the line terminated, near a midlevel window on the west side of the building, but an intervening object along the bullet's flight.

There it was. Again. The line passed directly over the Secret Service follow-up car.

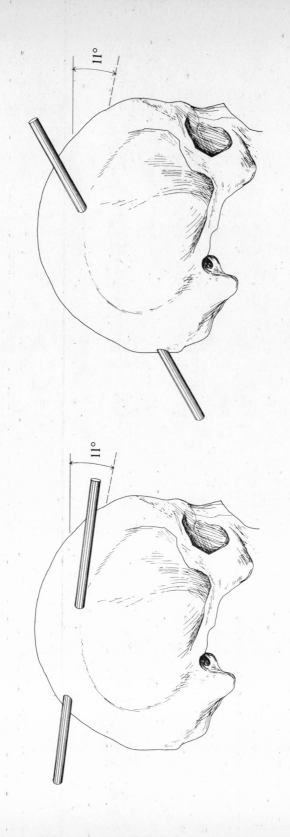

3. Donahue's skull models showing the trajectory based on Fisher's new information (left) vs. the erroneous Warren Commission–based trajectory (right).

8
MURPHY'S LAW

DONAHUE PICKED UP HIS SKETCHBOOK AND CAREFULLY drew two pictures—a top view and a side view—of the presidential limousine and the follow-up car just behind it.

Finding a top-view diagram of the limousines had been easy enough, but positioning the cars correctly pushed him to study carefully as many photographs as he could find. Comparing pictures, he noticed how almost simultaneous photos seemed to suggest different stories. One picture had the follow-up car looking slightly to the left; in another one it appeared to be slightly to the right. Eventually Donahue decided to place the Secret Service vehicle in his sketch directly behind the President's limousine. It couldn't be to the left, because agent Paul Landis had reported in his statement to the Warren Commission that he could see the right front wheel of Kennedy's car from his position on the right running board of the follow-up car.[1] And in none of the photos was there convincing enough evidence to place it markedly to the right. The distance between the cars could also be questioned, but strong consensus among witnesses and pictures suggested a five-foot gap.

Donahue reconfirmed his earlier judgments about the position of Kennedy's head at the moment of impact. Where to place the trajectory of the bullet through the skull was still a problem. The 1968 panel report was immensely helpful in fixing the correct point of entry, but it did not pinpoint the exit. The panel did emphasize the disintegration of the bullet, citing small and larger fragments of metal throughout the right side (none on the left side) with the heaviest concentration seen on the front half of the right side. (The report provided only a verbal description of what the panel had seen; there were no photographs or X rays.) This spray of fragments on the front half of the inside of the skull prompted Donahue to move his primary "exit point" farther forward than in his first sketches. It seemed sensible to keep it in the center of the spray. Taking this not as an actual "exit point," but where it was most reasonable to judge the bullet *would* have come out if it had gone through the skull intact and undeviated, and using the corrected entrance hole, Donahue now had a new "dowel line." From Zapruder 312 he recalculated the position of Kennedy's head at the moment of impact. This done, Donahue was able to deduce that the bullet was coming downward at an angle of roughly 7 degrees as it approached Kennedy.

Turning to his side-view sketch, Donahue drew a gradually rising 7-degree line backward from the President.

If his trajectory was correct, the bullet had apparently passed less than a foot above the windshield of the Secret Service car. The line continued on and passed over the rear seat of the convertible at a height of a little over five and a half feet above street level, then headed gradually up and away toward the Records Building.

He turned next to his top-view picture. Using the left-to-right trajectory dictated by aligning Kennedy's entrance and exit wounds, Donahue drew a line backward from the President. Viewed from above, the line headed back and diagonally over the passenger compartment of the follow-up car, then straight across the car's left-rear seat.

Donahue looked again at photographs of the Secret Service convertible. Scanning an old magazine from the time of the assassination, he found a picture taken by bystander Phil Willis. Willis was across the street from the book depository as the limousine made its turn onto Elm. After the President's car and the Secret Service convertible passed him, Willis swung his camera around to follow the receding motorcade and snapped the shutter. The picture captured a rear view of the limousine as it approached the Stemmons Freeway sign. Willis had said he heard the first shot and instantly took the picture. In the distance, Abraham Zapruder can be seen atop the grassy knoll, his Bell & Howell camera held steady to his eye. (See illustrations 12 and 13.)

The Secret Service car dominates the foreground. The lumbering '56 Cadillac is following the President's car closely. Two Secret Service agents are standing on each running board on either side of the car. Two more agents are in the back seat. The one on the right is gazing toward the crowds along the north side of Elm. The one on the left is looking in the same direction, but he is sitting up much higher, his whole back visible above the Cadillac's trunk. Apparently, the agent was riding on top of the seat back to gain a better view of the crowds.

Donahue then scanned a picture taken by Hugh Betzner, Jr. Betzner was standing on the same side of the street as Willis, but fifteen feet or so farther toward the west. He'd snapped his picture within a second or two of the Willis photo. Betzner's picture also clearly showed the agent sitting high up on the trunk deck of the car. (See illustration 14.)

Intrigued and perplexed, Donahue dug up the famous picture taken by veteran AP photographer James Altgens. Like Willis and Betzner, Altgens was on the south side of Elm Street, but farther down toward the triple underpass. Altgens told the Commission he heard what he thought was a firecracker as the motorcade came toward him and immediately snapped the shutter.[2] In remarkable detail, his picture compressed the motorcade scene just after the first bullet struck. (See illustration 15.)

Although Kennedy is all but obscured by both Governor Connally and the limousine's rearview mirror, his left hand can be seen coming up toward his face. The First Lady's white-gloved hand is visible extending toward her husband's arm.

In the Secret Service car, meanwhile, the two agents standing on the right running board have snapped their heads to the right and are looking back toward the book depository. The agents on the left running board are just beginning to react to the crack of the shot; just beginning to turn.

And the agent sitting up high on the left-rear seat . . . he has already spun completely around. Only the back of his head is visible as he stares up, directly it would seem, toward the oak tree and Oswald's roost on the sixth floor of the depository.

Donahue was astonished: Wouldn't a shot from the Records Building, with the trajectory of the one that struck Kennedy's head, have struck this man? He went back to his side-view drawing and sketched in the agent sitting up high on the rear seat. Sure enough, Donahue's estimated trajectory line from Kennedy's head passed directly through the agent. Donahue then drew the agent in on the top-view drawing. Once again, the bullet's line of flight passed through him.

Donahue stared at the drawings and the photographs. The trajectory had profound implications. So did the photographs showing the agent on the cusp of the seat. If the bullet came from the Records Building, this man would have been hit.

No Secret Service agent had been shot in Dealey Plaza, at least as far as Donahue knew. That left, then, only one other possibility.

The agent must have fired the shot.

How else could the trajectory be explained?

Donahue repeated his calculations of the bullet's flight and made sure he'd placed the agent in his proper place in the follow-up car. The results were unchanged.

An accident . . . Could it be?

Donahue thought back to the letter he'd written the Secret Service months earlier when the possibility of an accident had briefly crossed his mind. No agent had fired his weapon in Dealey Plaza, the answering letter said. Except for standard issue .38 caliber revolvers, the letter stated, the Secret Service did not disclose the types of weapons agents carried.

He recalled mentioning the possibility of an accident to Fisher. What was it Fisher had said?

"That would certainly explain the strange antics of the government."

But if the shooting really had been an accident, Donahue wondered, where was the weapon that had fired the shot? He scoured the Willis, Betzner, and Altgens pictures for signs of a rifle. He dug up other pictures of the Secret Service car taken before the motorcade reached Dealey Plaza. He studied the Zapruder stills for the thousandth time. He looked back into books critical of the Warren Commission.

Nothing. Anywhere.

Nonetheless, as he brooded on the implications of his findings, it occurred to Donahue that if the agent did fire the bullet, it would explain why so many people in the motorcade smelled gunpowder as their vehicles passed through Dealey Plaza. And why the police officer upwind from Dealey Plaza also smelled gunpowder. The odor would have lingered in the follow-up car and been effused during the high-speed race to Parkland. It would also explain one mystery that had dogged Donahue for months: The explosive, disintegrating characteristics of the bullet that hit Kennedy in the head.

Bodyguard ammunition.

Donahue needed more data. He'd already concluded that the slug—by virtue of its disintegration on impact—showed all the characteristics of a small-caliber, high-velocity, soft-nosed round. But what about the Warren Commission's test firings? Did the Carcano test bullets disintegrate in a similar fashion? Donahue didn't think so. The doctor who'd conducted the flawed analysis of the single bullet theory—the shots through goat meat and cadavers—Dr. Alfred Olivier up at the Army's Edgewood Arsenal, he'd done the head-shot tests as well.

What could be learned from Olivier?

In the spring of 1969, Donahue made a phone call to Edgewood. Luckily, Olivier was still employed there. Donahue got Olivier on the line and, without going into detail, explained that he was a weapons expert who'd been investigating the assassination. He said he'd be very interested in seeing the results of Olivier's head-shot test firings firsthand. Would it be possible to come and visit him? Olivier said he didn't see why not, and the two set an appointment for the following week.

Edgewood Arsenal is located an hour or so north of Baltimore on the shores of the Chesapeake Bay. The compound is part of the Army's Aberdeen Proving Grounds, a sprawling facility where in the 1960s the instruments of war—everything from artillery rounds to napalm—were tested and refined. Olivier was a veterinarian by training and responsible for studying the effects of gunshots on animals in the arsenal's wound ballistics lab.[3] Donahue found Olivier to be a friendly man with graying hair and wire-rimmed glasses. The men exchanged pleasantries. Donahue asked about the doctor's attempts to duplicate the President's head wound. Olivier explained he had test-fired Carcano rounds into ten human skulls filled with gelatin. The gelatin simulated the human brain.*

"Did the bullets break up?" Donahue asked.

"Yes, they did," Olivier replied.

"How big were the fragments? I mean . . . How many were there?"

"Well, in each case, I could find only two or three large fragments, but together they seemed to account for the bulk of the bullet's mass."

"So, the bullets didn't disintegrate or explode, as far as you could see?" Donahue asked.

"No," Olivier replied, "they did not."

Donahue asked if any of these fragments had somehow been deposited on the outside table of the skull. The ricochet wound . . .

"No," Olivier said. "Actually, I have the skulls here. I brought them out in anticipation of your visit. Would you like to see them?"

Olivier began pulling human skulls out of two plastic bags. Donahue quickly made a mental note. Olivier had obviously fired his shots into the skulls slightly above and to the right of the occipital protuberance—the spot Humes had misidentified as the entrance wound in Kennedy's skull.

Predictably, the resulting exit wounds were nowhere close to where Kennedy's exit wound was located. Most were in the face of the skull; shattering the bones in the forehead area. Olivier went on to state that of the ten test skulls only one had fallen off the podium he'd placed them on when he fired. Donahue quickly thought back to the violent movement of Kennedy's head on the Zapruder film.

After Olivier finished speaking, Donahue looked at him. "Dr. Olivier, I recently had the opportunity to speak with Dr. Russell Fisher, the Maryland state medical examiner. Do you know him? Fisher was on a panel put together last February by Attorney General Clark to examine the X rays and photographs from the Kennedy autopsy."

"No, I don't know him," Olivier said. "I think I heard about that panel, though. Had something to do with the Garrison case, didn't it?"

"Yes, I believe it did," Donahue said. "At any rate, Fisher's group uncovered some rather interesting information. It seems Humes misplaced the location of the entrance wound. Actually, it was one hundred millimeters above the occipital protuberance. They also found a fragment on the exterior of the skull which they concluded could have only come from a ricochet."

"Really?" Olivier said. His friendly manner began to fade like sunlight on a winter afternoon.

*The following conversation has been reconstructed from the recollections of Howard Donahue.

Donahue continued: "I've extrapolated the trajectory of the bullet based on Fisher's locations of the wounds, and . . . ah, I know this sounds incredible, but I believe there is a distinct possibility the head shot may have been fired accidentally by a Secret Service agent in the left-rear seat of the follow-up car. The trajectory leads right to that point."

Olivier stared at Donahue for a moment. Then he spoke.

"Did you discuss this possibility with Dr. Fisher?"

"Yes, I did," Donahue replied. "And you know what he said? He said, 'That would certainly explain the strange antics of the government.' "

Olivier remained expressionless. He said nothing.

As far as Donahue was concerned, there was nothing left to say. Or nothing left to learn from Olivier. He thanked the doctor for his time, feigned a pressing commitment in Baltimore, and departed.

The meeting with Olivier had been revealing, Donahue thought as he drove home. Just as he'd suspected, the Carcano bullet would not have disintegrated or sheared a fragment onto the outer table of the skull. And the bit about only one skull falling off the podium was equally telling. Olivier had fired from the same distance Oswald supposedly had. Yet clearly the Carcano round did not transmit as much energy to the skull as the shot that had hit Kennedy. Otherwise, Olivier's skulls would have gone flying.

As the weeks and months passed, the astonishing possibility that Kennedy's head wound may have been an accident was never far from Donahue's thoughts. And when he had time, he continued to search for additional evidence.

For the gun.

But life was becoming increasingly complicated for Donahue by 1969. He had given up a fifteen-plus-year career as a pharmaceutical salesman to go to work as a salesman for Diecraft Inc., a giant missile and rocket subcontractor based in Baltimore. By dint of hard work he'd become the company's sales representative for the southeastern United States. The firm supplied Donahue with a private plane and a pilot, Herman Krickler, and together the two men flew all over the South. Donahue would make sales calls at the General Electric or Westinghouse facility in Huntsville, Alabama, then fly to Pascagoula, Mississippi, to talk to the prime missile contractors for the Navy's nuclear submarine program. Then on to Florida to pitch the contractors huddled around NASA's Cape Kennedy launch facility.

The job paid well, but the hours, days, and weeks on the road took a toll. Howard barely saw his family. He'd arrive home in Towson on a Friday, collapse, then push out again on Monday morning and do it all over again. There was uncertainty, too, about the future. Contracts had poured into Diecraft through the sixties as the U.S. military geared up for the dual commitments of the Vietnam War and the spiraling arms race with the Soviets. Times were lush. By 1969, however, the strains of President Johnson's simultaneous attempts to build the Great Society and fight the Vietnam War had pushed the government's coffers to the breaking point.

Johnson was reluctant to raise taxes to pay for his guns and butter and, as a result, the government was fast running out of money. Even as the Vietnam War was reaching its peak, massive cutbacks were ordered in the defense budget. Donahue—on the front lines of the military-industrial complex—could see the effects of these cuts first-hand as 1969 progressed. Contract victories for Diecraft were fewer and farther between. One by one, Donahue saw his fellow salesmen let go. These layoffs were a mixed blessing for Donahue. On the one hand, he became increasingly worried the ax would fall on him. He hadn't worked at the company that long. On the other, he had earned the reputation as one of Diecraft's most effective salesmen, and with the departure of a growing number of his fellows Donahue found more and more of their territory being dumped on him. This translated into larger paychecks, but the already difficult life on the road became even tougher. Howard was home one weekend in the summer of 1969 talking the situation over with his wife.

"What are you going to do if you get laid off?" Katie asked.

"I don't know," Howard replied, perplexed and annoyed by the thought.

"You've always wanted to open a gun shop. Maybe now is the time to do it," she said.

"Maybe."

It was true Howard had long dreamed of merging his avocation with his vocation. He had developed a considerable array of skills as a gunsmith and owned a fair number of tools. And he'd put by more than enough money to cover start-up and inventory costs. But starting a business at age forty-five, or any age, is no swing in the park, especially when you have a wife and daughter to support. And while Howard had already showed entrepreneurial talent with his shotgun modification business, he knew that jumping in full-time was a completely different affair.

Husband and wife continued to discuss the possibility as summer progressed. But Howard demurred. Then one day the news came. Howard was laid off.

Katie didn't think twice. A few days later, after her husband had gone fishing to take his mind off the eternal quandary of having to work for a living, Katie headed up to the new shopping center under construction on Dulaney Valley Road, less than half a mile from the Donahues' row house.

With the manager in tow, she scouted a couple of the stores and found a size she figured would work. She wrote a check, signed a lease and met Howard at the door when he returned that evening.

"You'd better get busy," Katie said. "I rented a store for you today up at that new shopping center. You're going into the gun business.''

Howard was dumbstruck. He tried to get mad. But he couldn't. He went to work. And work he did in the weeks that followed—'round the clock, it seemed. He got in touch with gun wholesalers and ordered an inventory of rifles, shotguns, handguns, and ammunition. He found a bargain on five large glass display cases. He bought an old cash register. He had invoices and business cards printed up. He needed machinery, too, and after a lot of looking, he found a used Bridgeport milling machine and the tools to go with it: a ten-inch Southbend lathe, a drill press, and an industrial circular saw for woodworking.

On September 1, 1969, the big day finally arrived. Donahue's Gun Specialties opened in the rear court of the Dulaney Valley Shopping Center in Towson. Customers came. They bought ammo. They purchased handguns and brought rifles in for repair. They shot the breeze. They asked his advice. Donahue was proud. He was running his own gun shop.

But if he thought he'd worked getting the store off the ground, Donahue knew he'd have to push even harder to keep it flying. It seemed he lived at the store—opening the doors at 10:00 A.M. and not closing until 9:00 in the evening. Luckily, he'd gone into business at a most opportune time; the autumn hunting season was just beginning. Business boomed through the fall and winter. Before long, Donahue was well on the way toward recovering his $20,000 start-up investment. He was able to take a modest salary out of the business and he was happier than he'd ever been working for someone else.

Still, sacrifices had to be made, priorities realigned, and Donahue's probe of the assassination was first to go. Though his instincts told him he was onto something extraordinary in his investigation, there were not enough hours in the day. The business took precedence. As the months tumbled by, Donahue's assassination files gathered dust.

He still kept track of any information that emerged on Kennedy's killing. If an article appeared in the paper, he clipped it. With a little more than passing interest, he'd followed the increasingly twisted course of the Garrison case in New Orleans through 1968 and into 1969. He'd paid particular attention back in January of '69, when, much to his amazement, the results of Fisher's panel were finally released by the Justice Department. The move came as part of a Justice effort to block Garrison's subpoena of the Kennedy autopsy photos.

The New York Times ran the story of the '68 panel's findings in the lower right-hand corner of page 1 on January 17, 1969. The headline read: INQUIRY UPHOLDS WARREN REPORT—FINDS AUTOPSY PHOTOS SHOW 2 SHOTS KILLED PRESIDENT.

Fred Graham, the laconic southerner who would later go on to become legal reporter for CBS News, wrote the story. Graham was undoubtedly a good journalist, but he didn't seem to be in a very curious or skeptical frame of mind the day he wrote this article. The story might as well have been a press release written by the attorney general himself.

The lead read:

WASHINGTON, Jan. 16—A panel of four medical experts appointed by Attorney General Ramsey Clark to examine the secret autopsy photographs of President Kennedy's body has confirmed the Warren Commission's conclusion that the President was killed by two shots from behind.

The year-old report was released tonight by the Justice Department.

Graham made no mention of the fragment found on the outside of Kennedy's skull. He also missed the panel's even more revealing discovery: the mislocation of the entrance wound in Kennedy's head. Up to a point, this seemed understandable. The report was written in the driest of medical and technical language and Graham certainly was no pathologist.

Nevertheless, the answers were there. The report noted that Humes had placed the entrance wound near the occipital protuberance and then went on to state that the wound had been identified by the panel as being 100 millimeters above this fixed anatomical landmark. Certainly a physician-consultant employed by *The New York Times* would have been able to spot this discrepancy instantly. Had Graham bothered to call Fisher to confirm his understanding of the report, he might have knocked loose one of the bigger stories of his career. Then again, Fisher probably wouldn't have said much. But there was no comment in the article from any of the doctors who'd actually performed the study. This seemed an odd omission, given all the doubts that had been raised about the assassination. And no explanation was offered about why the Justice Department had waited a year to release the panel's results.

In defense of Graham, the reporter did come back three years later and break the news that President Kennedy's brain was missing from the National Archives. According to Graham's August 27, 1972, front-page story, Allegheny County, Pennsylvania, coroner and Warren Commission critic Cyril H. Wecht had been granted permission to examine the autopsy photos and X rays. But when he asked to see the brain as well as the all-important tissue samples of the President's wounds, as Fisher's group had, Wecht discovered the evidence was nowhere to be found.

Burke Marshall, a Yale University law professor and Kennedy family attorney, told Graham that he had no knowledge of the brain's whereabouts, but condemned Wecht for "chasing after parts of the President's body because he hasn't found any evidence that anything else was wrong."[4]

In any event, the Justice Department's release of the '68 panel report in early 1969 did exactly what Ramsey Clark intended it to do. Garrison's subpoena for the autopsy pictures was squelched[5] and the public was presumably reassured that the Warren Commission's explanation of Kennedy's killing was correct.

Notwithstanding Clark's repeated statements throughout 1968 aimed at discrediting Garrison's probe, the D.A.'s case had lurched along in its particular fashion that year. Garrison continued to collect evidence that he said pointed toward a right-wing/anti-Castro/intelligence conspiracy to kill the President. According to Garrison, the conspirators had killed Kennedy because they feared JFK planned a rapprochement with Castro and the Soviets and because of lingering and extreme bitterness over Kennedy's decision to withhold air support from the ill-fated Bay of Pigs invasion in 1961.[6]

Yet the public and press were no longer paying much attention. A *Chicago Tribune* report in December 1967 reflected the level to which Garrison's credibility had descended in the popular press and, at the same time, offered some telling insight into the D.A.'s past.[7] The story cited an old Army Medical Board Report that revealed that for four and a half years between 1950 and 1955 Garrison had undergone treatment for a "severe and disabling psychoneurosis" that had "interfered with his social and professional adjustment to a marked degree. He is considered totally incapacitated from the standpoint of military duty and moderately incapacitated in civilian adaptability."

In response to the story, Garrison claimed that he'd suffered from amoebic dysentery and that the Army had misdiagnosed this ailment as an "anxiety reaction" in the early fifties.[8]

In any event, the article further weakened Garrison's credibility, as did a statement he made in March of 1968. Commenting on the progress—or lack thereof—in his probe, Garrison asserted that President Johnson "should be hanged for suppressing evidence" relating to the assassination.[9]

This opinion undoubtedly did little to endear Garrison to federal officials, and in May a federal judge issued a temporary restraining order preventing the embattled D.A. from prosecuting Clay Shaw.[10] Shaw was the wealthy and respected New Orleans real estate developer Garrison had indicted in early 1967 in connection with the alleged conspiracy.

In December, however, the Supreme Court overturned the judge and Shaw's long-awaited trial was set to begin.[11] It was at this point Attorney General Clark played his trump card by releasing the results of Fisher's panel. The move blocked Garrison's subpoena for the autopsy material but could not stop the case from going forward. On January 29, 1969, the trial opened.[12]

For two years straight, Garrison had talked a good game. But when it came time to make his case against Shaw, he failed miserably. The credibility of a number of his witnesses was repeatedly called into question and his evidence was weak. On March 1, 1969, after less than an hour of deliberation, the jury returned a verdict of not guilty.[13]

Like the man himself, the Garrison case remains an enigma to this day. There is no doubt Garrison uncovered some curious and fascinating information over the course of his two-and-a-half-year probe, as Jim Marrs demonstrated in his 1989 book *Crossfire*. Among the details emerging from the Garrison case that seemed to point toward a conspiracy are these:

- Garrison was able to link Oswald to a shadowy group of former intelligence agents and Cubans active in supplying arms to anti-Castro forces inside Cuba. This group operated out of the New Orleans office of Guy Bannister, a close associate of Ferrie and a former FBI agent with ties to the intelligence community. Bannister died of a reported heart attack the year after the assassination.[14]
- The D.A. also brought to light the fact that a New Orleans attorney, Dean Andrews, had been approached the day after the assassination by one "Clay Bertrand," an alias commonly used by Shaw in his New Orleans homosexual liaisons. Bertrand reportedly asked Andrews to fly to Dallas to represent Oswald.[15]
- Several key people—including David Ferrie, the chief suspect in the alleged conspiracy—died mysteriously or violently as the Garrison case progressed.

Ferrie himself phoned Garrison's office soon after the story of the investigation broke in early 1967 and told one of the D.A.'s associates: "You know what this news story does to me, don't you? I'm a dead man. From here on, believe me, I'm a dead man."[16]

Less than a day after Ferrie's prophecy came true, another man under investigation by Garrison—a Ferrie associate involved in anti-Castro activities named Eladio del Valle—also turned up dead in a Florida parking lot: tortured, shot, and his skull split with an ax.[17]

Yet even with these ominous events and at least one witness who claimed to have seen Shaw discussing the assassination with Ferrie and Oswald, the D.A. could establish no direct motive for Shaw's involvement in the case and the information Garrison did have seemed badly mismanaged. On top of that, Garrison appeared to embrace the notoriety the investigation brought him. Many of his statements seemed outlandish and flat-out ridiculous.

To Donahue, the possibility that a conspiracy did exist was becoming increasingly irrelevant as the 1960s drew to a close. He'd always been inclined to dismiss such theories. But even if they were true, it changed nothing about his emerging understanding of what may have happened in Dealey Plaza.

Months stacked into years. For better or worse, the 1970s arrived.

Donahue's gun shop continued to do well. Howard employed several assistants, and Katie helped out behind the counter and with the books whenever she could.

Katie was a brave woman. When Howard was away at gun dealer conventions or hunting, Katie often ran the store by herself. At one point, a rash of holdups occurred at gun shops around Baltimore. One gun shop employee across town was shot dead. Katie continued working alone at the store, but always with a loaded .38 revolver in a holster at her side. Thankfully, the bandits never hit the Donahues' shop. Still, more than once five-foot-four-inch, one-hundred-pound Katie ordered suspicious characters out of the shop—the holster unsnapped and her hand resting easy on the gun.

By 1973, Katie herself was bitten by the entrepreneurial bug. After her daughter graduated from college, Katie decided it was her turn. On her fiftieth birthday, she opened her own business, a specialty fabric store known as Katie's Korner that catered to the well-heeled women of Towson. Like the gun shop, the business took off, but both husband and wife were run nearly ragged by the demands of their respective operations. Many nights Katie would wait alone at the Baltimore-Washington Airport to pick up the latest bolts of fancy European fabric she'd ordered from Paris.

Still, the Donahues were making some money and were in control of their destinies. It was worth the effort. And for Howard, an unexpected bonus from his gun shop business soon emerged. One day as he worked at his desk writing ammunition orders, two well-dressed men carrying briefcases came through the door.

"Lawyers . . ." Donahue thought.

Sure enough, the men were attorneys. One, in fact, was a state prosecutor. They made Howard an interesting proposition. Would he be willing to examine the evidence from a particular shooting incident and provide expert testimony when the case came to trial? The attorneys assured Donahue he would be remunerated adequately for his time.

Donahue agreed. The case in question involved a young man who'd been arrested on a deadly weapons charge. The man had pointed a small handgun at two people during an attempted holdup. The case seemed open and shut until it was revealed the gun was actually a cheap starter's pistol capable of firing only blanks. The question the attorneys had for Donahue was this: Could the gun have been easily converted to fire live ammunition? The key word was easily: It spelled the difference between a deadly weapons charge and a much less severe assault rap.

As Donahue examined the pistol, he initially figured the answer was yes. Each chamber in the pistol was partially obstructed by a ventilation baffle. Donahue assumed these baffles could be quickly removed. But when he tried to drill them out, he was surprised to find that the metal was extremely hard and caused the drill bit to deflect and emerge out the side of the chamber, thus rendering the chamber inoperable.

Next he put the pistol in his milling vise and attempted to mill the obstructions away. He met with only limited success, and in any case, it was unnecessary for him to carry his experiments any further. He'd shown that while the gun could conceivably be modified, it was by no means an easy or foolproof process. Donahue testified to his efforts in court and the deadly weapons charge against the young man was thrown out, although he was convicted of a lesser charge.

Word circulated about Donahue's expertise and availability as a firearms examiner and another case soon followed. This one involved an accidental shooting that left one young man dead. The parents of the dead man had filed a lawsuit against the owner of the gun. Donahue familiarized himself with the facts in the case and examined the autopsy photos and report.

The victim, it seemed, had been killed by a single gunshot wound to the head fired from a Remington model 11-48, 20-gauge semiautomatic shotgun. The projectile, a heavy rifled slug, had passed through the victim's temples in a straight line. Beyond that, not much else was certain. There was considerable conflicting testimony in the case and it became Donahue's job to figure out what had happened.

Apparently a few friends had gathered at the home of the gun owner. One of the friends was examining the gun. He testified that he opened the action, looked inside, and, seeing the weapon was empty, pressed the release button—allowing the bolt to slam forward. The friend then returned the weapon to rest on two pegs reserved for it on the wall at about eye level beside a doorway.

Instead of hanging the weapon so that one peg went behind the trigger guard, however, the man placed the weapon so the rear peg passed *through* the gun's trigger guard. As soon as he let go, the gun slid forward far enough to pull the trigger. Tragically, the victim was just walking through the door when the gun discharged.

Donahue quickly unraveled the mystery of how the gun, presumably empty, had in fact been loaded. He asked the gun owner if the weapon had ever been loaned out. The owner replied that yes, the gun had been loaned to a friend for use during the previous deer season. Deer season, Donahue thought. That explained the lead slug.

Being a deer hunter himself, Donahue knew that under state law, shotguns could be used on deer only if they fired a solid lead slug, not the typical buckshot shotguns usually fire. This is the sole restriction placed on deer hunting with a shotgun, and the weapon— semiautomatic or not—can carry as many shells as the magazine will hold. For bird hunting, though, shotguns are restricted by law to carrying just three shells: two in the magazine and one in the chamber.

This conservation ordinance limits the number of shots hunters can fire at migratory birds and presumably keeps hunters from blasting away indiscriminately at anything in sight. The shell limit is accomplished by placing a plug in the magazine that reduces the magazine's capacity to two shells. Donahue figured the friend who borrowed the gun to go deer hunting logically removed the plug and put four slugs into the gun, one in the chamber and three in the magazine.

Forgetting that there were four slugs in the gun when he unloaded it, the man—accustomed to the restrictions placed on bird-hunting shotguns—then ejected three shells and unwittingly left one in the gun. The weapon was returned to the owner and promptly hung back on the wall with the rear supporting peg behind the trigger guard. And there it sat, waiting only for an unfortunate series of events to culminate in the fatal accident.

A third, even more baffling shooting case came Donahue's way. Another attorney called the gunsmith. Apparently one of the lawyer's clients had been charged with first-degree murder as a result of a shooting death in South Baltimore. The facts were these: The defendant was throwing a party in his tiny row house when an uninvited guest barged in. The man was huge. He was a nasty, abrasive, quarrelsome drunk and he quickly began insulting women and picking fights.

In desperation, the host of the party ran up the narrow steps of his row house and grabbed a 12-gauge shotgun. Standing at the top of the stairs, he ordered the belligerent man from the house. Instead of leaving, the man began screaming profanities and advanced toward the host. Suddenly there was an ear-shattering blast and the drunk dropped to the floor, apparently dead.

Donahue obtained a copy of the autopsy report and found that the drunk had in fact lived for five days after being shot. He also read that the cause of death was a deep, depressed fracture on the top of the skull. What surprised Donahue most, however, was that the X rays showed no sign whatsoever of lead pellets in the brain, or, for that matter, lead skid marks on the skull. Donahue checked the police report. No lead pellets had been found at the scene of the shooting, the report said. He then looked at photos from the scene. No marks or depressions were visible on the walls or floors that could have conceivably been caused by a shotgun blast.

He then talked to the police officers who'd investigated the case. Did they find a shotgun wad at the scene? Shotgun wads are plastic or fiber partitions that hold the powder together and also keep it separate from the shotgun pellets as the shot moves out of the barrel.

Yes, the police officers said, they did find a coarse fabric wad. Donahue began to suspect what may have happened. He spoke with a witness to the shooting, a longshoreman, and asked him to describe what he'd seen.*

*The following conversation has been reconstructed from the recollections of Howard Donahue.

"[The defendant] is really getting pissed at that big son-of-a-bitch, and runs up the steps and comes back with his gun," the longshoreman said. "Standin' on the steps, he tells him he is going to blow his head off if he doesn't get the hell out. He aims this gun at him—I figured he's got to be bullshitting—when the gun goes off."

Donahue pressed on: "What happened next?"

"The room was full of this white smoke," the man said.

"What did this smoke smell like?" Donahue asked.

"A fart, it smelled like a fart."

That clinched it. The thick white smoke and obnoxious sulfuric odor were characteristic of a black-powder load, a blank. The man had apparently fired a blank shell at the drunk. But the black powder, at extremely close range, had turned the felt wadding in the shell into a lethal missile.

Donahue interviewed the defendant in the case and learned that when the man had gone upstairs to grab his gun, he opened his dresser drawer and removed a blank cartridge. There were also numerous lethal lead-loaded shells in the drawer. But the man grabbed what he thought was a blank. He said he'd only wanted to scare the drunk, and in any case he intended to shoot over his head.

Unfortunately, the bully raised his head unexpectedly as the homeowner pulled the trigger and the heavy felt wadding caught the man on top of the skull and caused the depressed fracture.

Donahue's determination of how the man had died—as well as the fact that the homeowner had grabbed a blank cartridge and not a live one—led the district attorney to reduce the charge from premeditated murder to accidental death.

Donahue found expert testimony work fascinating as well as lucrative, and he began to realize he had a knack for spotting relationships between apparently unrelated subjects, particularly when guns and ballistics were involved. These skills had already served him well in his investigation of the Kennedy assassination; they would prove invaluable in the years ahead.

9
THE DISCOVERY

IF DONAHUE SUSPECTED THE SHOT THAT HAD hit Kennedy in the head may have been an accident, it seemed fate was conspiring to remind him how easily mishaps occur when guns are found. One of the more frightening incidents took place the day an acquaintance, Pierce Lake, came by Donahue's gun shop to pick up his new Mauser .380 semiautomatic pistol. Lake was filling out the necessary forms to take possession of the gun when another customer sagely remarked that this particular type of pistol had a rather scratchy trigger pull.

Donahue figured he'd check it out. He noticed Lake's pistol lying nearby; its magazine partially inserted in the grip. The Mauser .380 was unusual in that by pushing the clip in all the way, the pistol's slide was released. This, in turn, loaded the chamber. Unfortunately, Donahue forgot about this feature as he picked up the gun and carelessly slammed the clip home. He then pointed the pistol toward a clock high on the wall. About the time he was thinking that, yes, the trigger was a little scratchy, an ear-shattering report rang out.

The bullet left the barrel at 900 feet per second and drilled the clock near dead center. With smoking gun in his hand and feeling like the world's biggest idiot, Donahue could only lamely remark: "Shoots a little to the right." A uniformed Maryland state trooper friend who happened to be in the store at the time took one look at the clock, one look at Donahue, and made for the door.

"I'm getting out of here before the cops arrive!" the state policeman said.

After he'd recovered from the initial shock of the blast, Donahue realized he'd better check next door. An H&R Block tax preparation office was adjacent to the gun shop, and Donahue was prepared for the worst as he entered the neighboring office. Seeing no one bleeding or sprawled on the floor, Donahue nonchalantly inquired, "Did a bullet come in here?"

Apparently more annoyed than frightened, a female accountant replied: "Why, yes, it did."

Luckily, the shot penetrated high up behind the clock and crossed the tax office near the ceiling. It then hit the far wall and dropped to the floor. Donahue picked up the slug, apologized profusely, and beat a hasty retreat.

Another time, a Baltimore city policeman named Jim (not his real name) stopped in to check out the latest guns and equipment. This was not unusual; Donahue had many friends who worked in law enforcement and they often came by to pass the time. The policeman spotted a new safety holster on the wall. The holster was designed specifically for police use. It was unique in that it allowed the pistol to be drawn only in a certain direction. This presumably reduced the chances of a criminal grabbing an officer's weapon during a scuffle.

The policeman put the holster on his gun belt, unloaded his Smith & Wesson .38, and did a number of quick draws and dry firings, or empty-chamber trigger pulls. He liked the holster so much he bought it and then reloaded his gun and put it back in the holster.

Katie happened to be in the store at the time with four Canadian junior high school wrestlers. The young men were in town for a tournament at nearby Towson State University, and Katie had befriended them and was leading the group on an impromptu tour of the town. Her husband's gun shop was to be the high point on the excursion. About then, a county sheriff's deputy walked in. Seeing his fellow officer sporting the new holster, the sheriff's deputy cheerfully called out, "Say, Jim, how fast can you get your gun out of that new holster?"

Jim made a lightning draw. Instantly the store echoed with the sharp pop of a .38, and from the rear of the shop came a loud crash. The bullet had slammed into a large storage case in the back room and hit some replacement gun stocks, sending them clattering to the floor.

The patrolmen stood paralyzed. The county cop shook his head and remarked, "On that note, I think I will leave."

The Canadians, who had watched the incident unfold in shocked silence, were quickly ushered from the store by a thoroughly mortified Katie. One of the wrestlers asked earnestly as he climbed back into the car: "Did he mean to do that?" Katie assured the young man that he did not.

Donahue, meanwhile, having had the experience himself, couldn't keep from laughing.

"You just won the distinguished asshole award!" he said.

"I already have that," the officer replied. "I ought to get a bird-turd cluster for this."

Seems this was the second time Jim had experienced an accidental discharge. On guard duty in the military years before, he'd just missed blowing his sergeant off an outhouse john with a shotgun.

An alarming number of Donahue's friends and customers had similar stories to tell. One acquaintance—a tall, skinny man—sent a group of shop regulars into hysterics one afternoon with his tale of near disaster.

"I had been married a little over three weeks," the man recounted. "It was a Sunday. My wife and I were lying on the couch watching a Western. We began kissing and petting, and well, you know, one thing led to another and we got undressed.

"Just for a joke, I went into the bedroom and strapped on my Western gunslinger belt with my Ruger .44 Magnum in the holster. I came back into the living room wearing the gun belt and nothing else and, seeing a stagecoach under attack by Indians on TV, I thought I'd be a wiseguy and come to the rescue. I pulled the Ruger and KA-BAM! The son-of-a-bitch was loaded!

"I hit the TV dead center. First the thing started to smoke and then it caught fire. If you can imagine me running back and forth to the kitchen with glasses full of water . . . all six-foot-five of me . . . wearing nothing but a gun belt!"

Howling uncontrollably, Donahue barely got his question out.

"What did your wife do?" he said.

"Nothing," the friend replied acidly. "She didn't do anything for a long time. . . . I didn't get any lovin' for two months!"

Thankfully, no one was hurt in these incidents and they seemed amusing in retrospect. But Donahue realized it could have easily been otherwise. If one of the Canadian wrestlers had been shot . . . Howard and Katie shuddered at the thought.

Taken together, the accidents graphically illustrated the old axiom: "If you are involved with firearms long enough, it is not if you will or will not have an accidental discharge, it is when."

By 1975, Donahue had picked up a new hobby that would, indirectly, lead him back onto the trail of the Kennedy assassination. He began collecting Civil War weapons.

Specifically, he collected Spencer repeating rifles, the state-of-the-art firearm from that war. The guns were revolutionary in their day because of their extremely rapid rate of fire. Due to the Spencer's seven-shot magazine and unique lever-action repeating design, the gun fired up to ten times as fast as the muzzle-loaders carried by the vast majority of Northern and Southern troops.

The gun's inventor, Christopher Spencer of Manchester, Connecticut, filed a patent for his weapon in 1860, the year before the war began.[1] For all the carbine's advantages, however, bureaucrats in the War Department and some generals were reluctant to adopt the weapon. One of their qualms was the absurd notion that soldiers might be inclined to "waste ammunition" if they could fire faster.[2]

Spencer nonetheless persevered and took his case directly to the field. His demonstrations of the gun immediately won converts and customers among combat officers and Union privates. The troops were so impressed that many bought Spencers with their own money.[3] The guns proved particularly valuable to cavalry troops, in part because of their shorter, compact design and, of course, because of their deadly firepower. In the spring of 1863, Spencers were issued to the several thousand veteran horsemen under the command of Union General John Buford.[4]

A few months later, Buford's men found themselves facing Confederates four times their number swarming across the fields and ridges west of Gettysburg, Pennsylvania. Thanks to the Spencer, Buford's men stalled the Confederate advance all through the long and bloody morning of July 1, 1863. The troopers' holding action bought Union commanders time and allowed them to bring up reinforcements to entrench on the high ground beyond Gettysburg. This position proved impregnable over the next two days. In the end, the Spencer helped the Federals win the decisive victory of the war.

Abraham Lincoln was so impressed with the Spencer's performance at Gettysburg that he asked the gun's inventor to bring the gun to the White House for a demonstration. Spencer and Lincoln headed for the fields where the Washington Monument was being built. The President, an old hunter himself, fired the gun a number of times. He was awed by the carbine's rate of fire.[5]

With Lincoln behind the Spencer, the War Department quickly dropped its opposition to the gun. The weapons flowed to Northern regiments in ever-increasing numbers as the war progressed. Not surprisingly, the guns were as destructive to the morale of the Confederate Army as they were to its ranks. Rebel soldiers called the guns "Yankee 7 Devils," for the seven-shot magazine, and bitterly cursed this deadly innovation of war.[6]

Huge numbers of the guns were eventually manufactured and many Spencers survived into the twentieth century. Production of the special cartridges used in the carbines, however, was halted in the 1920s. Hence, no ammunition was available to fire from the repeaters, though many of the guns were in mint condition.

Donahue was particularly frustrated by this. He'd acquired several Spencers, including one that had actually been owned by one of Buford's sturdy troopers. With typical ingenuity, Donahue decided the best way to solve the problem was to modify the carbine's breech so the guns could fire modern center-fire ammunition. Word spread quickly among Spencer owners that a gunsmith in Maryland was adapting the guns to fire modern ammo. Before long, Donahue was deluged with requests to perform the work.

With well-deserved pride, the gunsmith was quoted in a *Gun Week* magazine article on the repeater's resurgence: "The Spencers will speak again!"[7]

It was this involvement with the Spencer that led to a call in the fall of 1976 from Lieutenant Bill Welsh, then the Maryland state police firearms examiner. Welsh, an old friend of Donahue's, told the gunsmith he'd been talking to a journalist from the *Baltimore Sun* who was working on a story about Civil War guns. Would it be all right to send the guy over, Welsh asked?

A day or so later, the door of Donahue's gun shop swung open and in walked a towering man with a thick, bulldog face and the alert, roving eyes of a reporter. He wore a topcoat and carried a battered briefcase. Drawing hard on a cigarette, he pulled a worn, checkered cap from his broad forehead. Donahue figured him to be about sixty. He noticed the man walked with a severe limp.*

"You must be Mr. Howard Donahue!" the stranger boomed in a deep, sonorous voice. "I'm Ralph Reppert with the *Baltimore Sun*. Lieutenant Welsh tells me you're an expert on Civil War weapons."

Donahue put down his work and began chatting with the stranger. He showed Reppert his Spencers as well as several muzzle-loading Civil War rifles, and he pulled out ammunition for the guns. The men had talked for twenty minutes or so when the reporter glanced at a shelf behind Donahue's desk. He noticed a battered copy of the Warren Report.

"You're not interested in the Kennedy assassination too, are you?" Reppert asked.

Donahue, a little startled, replied that he was.

"Well, that's a coincidence! So am I. Read everything I can about it. A terrible day . . ." Reppert's voice trailed off, then his eyes perked up. "So . . . who killed him?"

"I wish I knew," Donahue said. "But I have my suspicions."

The discussion on Civil War guns was abruptly sidetracked. Over the next hour, Reppert listened in rapt fascination as Donahue told his story: How he became involved with the CBS reenactment and later decided to focus on the ballistic and medical evidence from Dealey Plaza, how he'd uncovered discrepancies in both the trajectory and nature of the head wound, and finally, his startling suspicion about the origin of the third shot.

Reppert was silent for some time after Donahue finished speaking. Finally he spoke. "Jesus . . ." Reppert said, "That is one helluva story."

"It would be if I could find the gun that fired the shot," Donahue replied. "But I can't find the damn thing anywhere."

"Well, even if you can't find it," Reppert said, "it seems to me like this would still be worth a story. I mean, you're a gunsmith, a firearms examiner; here's something people have never heard before. Nobody is going to question your credentials, that's for sure."

The men talked a while longer. As he left, Reppert turned and

---

*The following conversation has been reconstructed from the recollections of Howard Donahue.

grinned broadly. "I'll talk to my editor and see what he thinks about all this. Hell, maybe we can do something, eh?"

Maybe so, Donahue thought.

A lot of years had come and gone since he'd done much on the assassination. The gun store was Howard's number one priority and Katie's fabric shop number two. And after he'd been unable to find a weapon that could have fired the last shot, Donahue hadn't lost interest, but he had lost the scent. Now here was a reporter from the most prestigious paper in Maryland who seemed interested in his work. The reporter seemed like a friendly, trustworthy, outgoing man. Maybe there was a way to do something, break something loose, get back in the hunt.

Reppert called several days later. He said he'd talked to his Sunday magazine editor, Hal Williams. Williams wasn't exactly enthralled with the idea of an assassination story.

Years later, Williams recalled his conversation with Reppert.

"Ralph came to me and said, 'How about a story on the Kennedy assassination?' and I said, 'For Christ's sake, I'm not interested.'

"I'd had a friend who had a particular theory on the assassination and he bugged the hell out of me; he wanted me to talk to my friends in New York about getting a magazine article done," Williams remembered. "I told him to forget about it, and in the end it broke up our friendship. So when Ralph came to me with the idea, I thought, oh no, not another crackpot theory."

But Reppert was bound and determined. He told Williams he was going to write the story anyway.

" 'Fine,' I told him, 'go ahead.' But I was never going to run it," Williams recalled.

Donahue and Reppert met periodically in the weeks that followed. In a renewed attempt to find the gun, they dug back into the old files and looked again at every picture taken in and around Dealey Plaza. They used a magnifying glass to study the follow-up car.

Still nothing. Anywhere.

And then one Friday afternoon, several months later—as if on cue—the epiphany arrived. It came in the unlikely form of Warner Minetree, a lanky, middle-aged, independently wealthy friend of Donahue's who spent much of his time hunting or skeet-shooting. Minetree (pronounced Mina-tree) often came by the gun shop to chat or buy a new gun for his collection.

On this day he carried a thick book under his arm.*

"Hello, Howard," he said. "Say, I found this book on the assassination. You've probably read it, but I thought you might want it anyway for your collection; if you don't have it already, that is."

The book was William Manchester's 647-page semiofficial account of the assassination: *The Death of a President*. Actually, Donahue

*The following conversation was reconstructed from the recollections of Howard Donahue.

had never read the book, though it had come out in 1967 amid
considerable fanfare and controversy. Manchester had been retained
by the Kennedy family after the assassination to write a detailed
account of the events in Dallas. While the writer hadn't deviated from
the Warren Commission's explanation of the killing, he did manage
to get crossways with the Kennedys over certain details in his
narrative that the family deemed inappropriate. Lawsuits and charges
flew but the dispute in the end was resolved.

Donahue had long figured the book for what it was—a glorified,
albeit well-done rendering of the Warren Report—and consequently,
he'd never bothered to buy it. But he thanked Minetree, picked up
the heavy tome and began flipping through the pages. Not finding any
pictures, Donahue turned by chance to the opening page of chapter
three. The chapter, titled "Market," described the chaotic scene in
Dealey Plaza immediately after the shooting.

He froze. The hairs flew up on his neck. Right in the middle of the
page, right in front of his eyes, was what he'd been looking for for so
many years: *"From the rear of the follow-up car Agent Hickey raises
the barrel of the AR-15 and points it about aimlessly."*[8]

The gun . . .

The Colt AR-15 is the civilian version of the M-16, the automatic
rifle that was used as the primary American infantry weapon in
Vietnam. The gun is well known for the extremely lethal, explosive
nature of the bullets it fires. Due to its high velocity and the bullet's
relatively light weight, the slug disintegrates on impact.

Donahue quickly turned to the index. Henderson. Hendrix, Henry,
Henslee . . . Hickey. There was one other reference to the agent in
the book, on page 134. Donahue turned to it. Manchester was
describing the vehicles in the motorcade and the passengers they
contained. (See drawing 4.)

Halfback, the follow-up convertible, District license number GG 678.
Agent Sam Kinney, at the wheel, kept his eyes on the back of the
President's head. Emory Roberts, Halfback's commander, was next to
Kinney. Clint Hill stood on the left front running board. Agent Bill
McIntyre was behind him. John Ready was on the right front running
board, Agent Landis behind him. Dave Powers was in the right jump
seat, Ken O'Donnell in the left. Agent George Hickey sat in the left
rear, Agent Glen Bennett in the right rear, and on the seat between
them lay an AR-15 .223 automatic rifle, with a muzzle velocity so
powerful that should a bullet strike a man's chest it would blow his
head off."[9]

God, Donahue thought. The left-rear seat! Here was the missing
piece. . . .

"Find something interesting?" Minetree asked as he browsed amid
the gun cases.

"Yeah, I did," Donahue replied, numb inside. "Thanks a lot, Warner. This looks like a really good book."

Donahue's thoughts flashed back to the letter he'd written the Secret Service in 1968. The Service would confirm only that there were .38 revolvers present in the follow-up car. Now here was mention of an AR-15 in a national best-seller. Why had they withheld this information?

In the days that followed, Donahue poured himself back into his assassination probe with an intensity Katie hadn't seen in some time. After he'd closed the gun store and had dinner, Howard would once again retreat to his La-Z-Boy in the basement and work deep into the night. On days that he could, Donahue headed south to the National Archives in Washington. Sure enough, before long he'd discovered numerous confirmations of Manchester's account. The overriding question was: How had he missed the gun for so many years? He felt like a fool. There had been more than one sighting of the AR-15 that day, but in all his digging Donahue had never noticed any of them.

First, he found the Commission testimony of Dallas Mayor Earle Cabell, describing the immediate aftermath of the shooting:

INVESTIGATOR: You didn't in fact know who had been hit, I take it?
CABELL: No; we couldn't tell. We could tell, of course, there was confusion in the presidential car—activity. The Secret Service men ran to that car. From out of nowhere appeared one Secret Service man with a submachine gun. His attention seemed to be focused up toward the building.[10]

Then there was Senator Ralph Yarborough's affidavit. Yarborough had been riding directly behind the Secret Service car. Donahue had read in one of the assassination books that Yarborough smelled gunpowder in the motorcade. But Donahue had never looked at his deposition:

After the shooting, one of the Secret Service men sitting down in the car in front of us pulled out an automatic rifle or weapon and looked backward. However, all of the Secret Service men seemed to me to respond very slowly, with no more than a puzzled look. In fact, until the automatic weapon was uncovered, I had been lulled into a sense of false hope for the President's safety. . . .[11]

Finally, Donahue discovered a statement made by S. M. Holland. Holland was a rail traffic supervisor with the Union Terminal Co. He had watched the motorcade come down Elm Street from atop the triple overpass, and he'd received considerable attention due to his claim that he'd seen a puff of smoke on the grassy knoll at the time of the shooting. Holland's observations about the Secret Service

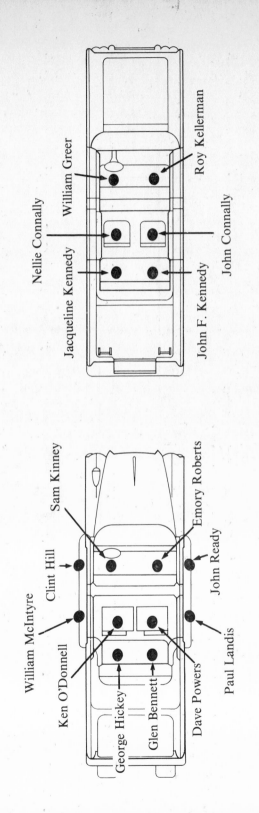

4. The location of everyone in the presidential limousine (right) and the Secret Service follow-up car (left).

agent appeared in *The Scavengers and Critics of the Warren Report,*
a 1967 book Donahue had read some years before:

INTERVIEWER: After the second time he was hit, what did the Secret
               Service men do?
HOLLAND: Well, I noticed that this Secret Service man stood up
               in the car, in the President's car.
INTERVIEWER: When did he stand up in the car?
HOLLAND: Just about the same time the President was shot the
               second time. He jumped up in the seat and was
               standing up in the, on the seat. Now I actually
               thought when they started up, I actually thought he
               was shot, too, because he fell backwards just like he
               was shot, but it jerked him down when they started
               off.
INTERVIEWER: What did he do when he stood up?
HOLLAND: He pointed this machine gun right towards that
               grassy knoll behind that picket fence.[12]

Donahue was transfixed. Holland had put the gun in the agent's
hands at the moment the last shot was fired and said the agent then
fell over.

Reading over Holland's comments again, Donahue realized that
Holland had said he saw the agent in the President's car, not the
follow-up car. This was impossible. There were only two agents in
the presidential limousine. One was driving and the other didn't stand
up with a rifle or pistol or anything else. Photographs of the assassination proved this.

Donahue wondered whether Holland had confused the two vehicles
as they came toward him down Elm. The Secret Service car was very
close behind the President's limousine. Although the Lincoln was a
sleeker, newer car, the convertibles bore more than a passing resemblance to one another.

Donahue next began searching for the testimony of the Secret
Service agents themselves. Rufus Youngblood, an agent who had
ridden with Vice President Johnson a few cars back from the follow-
up vehicle, had said he recalled seeing "Hickey in the Presidential
follow-up car poised on the car with the AR-15 rifle looking toward
the buildings."[13]

Special agent Winston Lawson had ridden with Dallas Police Chief
Jesse Curry and Dallas County Sheriff William Decker in the lead car
of the motorcade. Lawson's job had been to look backward constantly and maintain visual contact with the President.

Donahue scanned Lawson's five-page typed statement, dated December 1, 1963.

As the Lead Car was passing under this bridge I heard the first loud,
sharp report and in more rapid succession two more sounds like

gunfire. I could see persons to the left of the motorcade vehicles running away. I noticed Agent Hickey standing up in the follow-up car with the automatic weapon and first thought he had fired at someone.[14]

Christ, Donahue thought.

Next he dug up agent Glen Bennett's statement. Bennett had sat beside Hickey in the back seat. He was among the witnesses who believed Oswald's first shot missed. On the subject of the gun, Bennett had said, "A second shot followed immediately and hit the right rear high of the President's head. I immediately hollered 'he's hit' and reached for the AR-15 located on the floor of the rear seat. Special Agent Hickey had already picked up the AR-15."[15]

Emory Roberts, the agent in charge of the detail in the follow-up car, had reported that just after the shooting he turned and saw Hickey in the back seat with the rifle "and asked him to be careful with it."[16]

Likewise, agent William McIntyre had reported that immediately after the shots were fired, "agent Hickey was handling the AR-15."[17] McIntyre rode the left-rear running board of the follow-up car, directly beside Hickey.

Finally, Donahue found the testimony of Hickey himself. It was among the written statements of other agents in the Warren Commission Report, Volume 18, pages 761–765. According to Hickey: "At the end of the last report I reached to the bottom of the car and picked up the AR-15 rifle, cocked and loaded it, and turned to the rear."

Donahue scanned the testimony. Hickey had made no mention of falling over backward as S. M. Holland had remembered. And his statement about picking up the gun after the last shot was contradicted by Holland, who had seen him with the gun at the time of the last shot. Agent Bennett, meanwhile, said he had seen the shot strike Kennedy in the head and that he had then reached for the AR-15, only to find Hickey had already picked the gun up.

Hickey's comment about cocking and loading the gun after the shots were fired was also seemingly at odds with the testimony of Secret Service agent Roy Kellerman. When asked by the Warren Commission about the weapons available in the follow-up car, Kellerman had said that the AR-15 in the back seat was always "ready to go." Donahue took this to mean that the gun was stored cocked and loaded, with the safety on.[18]

Donahue reorganized his data. He ruminated, speculated. What did he have? Nine witnesses—including Hickey himself—had put the gun in Hickey's hands just after the last shot. More important, two of the witnesses had put the gun in Hickey's hands the instant the shot was fired. And one had seen the agent stand up and fall over about the time the shot hit home.

Donahue once more pulled out the Willis, Betzner, and Altgens pictures. Altgens had snapped this picture about five seconds before the head shot. Now . . . Based on that picture, Hickey had clearly heard the first shot. Sitting on top of the seat back, he had already spun completely around and was staring up toward the book depository. The other agents were just starting to turn. So, Hickey hears the first shot and looks back up to where he thought it came from. And in a second or two, the follow-up car goes a little farther and the oak tree that had obscured his view is cleared. At that point, Hickey must have seen the barrel of Oswald's gun. He had to. He was looking right at it. And Oswald fires again.

So Hickey reaches down and grabs the AR-15 off the floor, flips off the safety and stands up on the seat, preparing to return fire. But his footing is precarious. The follow-up car hits the brakes or speeds up. Hickey begins to swing the gun around to draw a bead on Oswald, but he loses his balance. He begins to fall.

And the barrel happens to be pointing toward Kennedy's head. And the gun happens to go off. And the bullet strikes with the "sickening sound of a grapefruit splattering against the side of the wall," according to Dave Powers, a Kennedy aide who rode in the jump seat of the Secret Service car.[19] (See illustrations 12–24.)

Plausible, Donahue thought. It was plausible.

But how plausible? If this was true, how come no one saw the accident? After looking over the pictures, Donahue thought he knew. There were ten men in the follow-up car. Two agents each were standing on running boards on both sides of "Halfback." Hence, when Hickey stood up, he must have been partially obscured from view by agents on either side—much like a quarterback dropping back to pass behind his blockers. In the pocket, so to speak.

Furthermore, it was reasonable to assume that after the President had been hit by the second bullet—and he was obviously hit at that point—everyone who wasn't diving for cover was watching the presidential limo, not the Secret Service follow-up car. Then, when people such as Yarborough and Lawson realized what was happening, they glanced up to see Hickey with the gun. After the shot was fired. After he'd gotten back on his feet.

But what about the dozen or so people on the overpass? They were looking straight down at Hickey. Wouldn't they have seen the muzzle flash if the AR-15 had fired? Donahue knew the answer was no. AR's and M-16s are equipped with a flash suppressor on the tip of the barrel. A bluish flame from the gun would have only been visible at night or twilight. It was high noon in Dealey Plaza. The sun was blazing.

Surely, though, someone would have heard the AR go off.

They did hear it, Donahue realized. They just couldn't pinpoint the location of the shot in the terror and confusion of the moment. Donahue remembered: What was it that the Warren Commission memo contained about the sounds of gunfire?

A shot actually makes three noises: the muzzle blast, caused by the smashing of the hot gases which propel the bullet into the relatively stable air at the gun's muzzle, the noise of the bullet, caused by the shock wave build up ahead of the bullet's nose as it travels through air, and the noise of the bullet's impact on the target.

Likewise, the memo said, not much credence should be placed in where witnesses believe the shots had come from, since "if a bullet travels faster than the speed of sound, the acoustics are such that an observer at right angles to the path of the bullet may perceive the shot to have been fired from a site *somewhere opposite to him*."[20]

A phenomenon like that might explain why some witnesses on the south side of Elm Street thought the bullet came from the grassy knoll. And too, the siren in the follow-up car was turned on immediately after the head shot.[21] The siren's wail may have had a disorienting effect on bystanders and made it harder to pinpoint the origin of the shot. In any case, the buildings on three sides of Dealey Plaza undoubtedly made the area one vast echo chamber.

Donahue returned once again to the archives. He found the testimony of Austin Miller, a railroad employee who had watched the motorcade from the triple overpass.

Investigator: "Where did the shots sound like they came from?"

Miller: "Well, the way it sounded like, it came from the, I would say from right there in the car."[22]

Royce Skelton, another witness who had watched from the overpass and among those who saw a ricochet strike, had told the Warren Commission he believed the shots came from around the President's car.[23] Rereading Mark Lane's *Rush to Judgment,* Donahue paused at the recollection of Mary Elizabeth Woodward. Woodward was standing on the north side of Elm Street, in front of the grassy knoll and nearly adjacent to where Kennedy was when the final shot hit. "There was a horrible ear-shattering noise coming from behind us and a little to the right," Woodward had said.[24]

Woodward's location of the shot may have been off, but if she had heard an AR-15, her description was right on target. An AR-15 .223 round, by virtue of its high velocity and high muzzle pressure, does make an extraordinarily loud crack; louder and sharper than the report from a gun like Oswald's.

Donahue wondered.

Did Hickey do it?

It wasn't as if he wanted to believe an accident had taken place in Dealey Plaza. He would have much preferred to find some piece of evidence that would have made it impossible. But that was just the point. So far, he'd found nothing of the sort.

What did he know?

He knew Hickey was seen with an AR-15 the instant the final shot hit home. He knew one witness saw him fall over. He knew the

AR-15 fired rounds encased in a thin copper jacket that upon impact ruptured to allow the bullet to disintegrate for maximum lethality, the Geneva Convention notwithstanding. He knew the bullet that hit Kennedy's head had shattered in exactly this fashion. Likewise, he knew Oswald's bullet could have never performed in such a manner. He also knew that numerous people in the motorcade smelled gunpowder as they passed through Dealey Plaza. And he knew that two witnesses thought the shots came from around the President's car.

Finally, he knew the bullet's trajectory led straight to Hickey and his gun. As far as he was concerned, this was an unshakable ballistic fact. The bullet that hit Kennedy in the head came from the left rear. From the follow-up car. From the AR-15.

Donahue was virtually certain.

Still, to accuse someone of accidentally killing the President of the United States was a hell of a thing to do. A bodyguard, no less. Donahue shuddered as he thought of the emotional torture the man must have endured. Then again, he thought, there were a couple of hundred million Americans and countless others around the world who had suffered, too. Who had wondered. Who had never known. Nothing Donahue or anyone else could do would change what happened that day. The deed was done. Now, it seemed to him, the only thing left was to be out with it.

Donahue called the *Sun* reporter.

"Ralph," he said. "Howard here. You're not going to believe this, and God help me if I'm wrong, but I think we can do the story. I found the gun."

10
BREAKING NEWS

REPPERT CALLED SEVERAL DAYS LATER. WILLIAMS, HIS editor, was still against the story—gun or no gun. But Reppert wasn't worried.*

"I'll just have to do a good job on it," the reporter said. "That way he won't have any choice but to run it. Anyway, I've got a couple of stories I'm in the middle of right now and I need to get them wrapped up first. There's no need to rush this, though. We'll take our time and do it right."

For his part, Donahue continued to sift the evidence for anything that might strengthen his case. A puzzling comment he'd read years before came to mind. In early February 1964 Earl Warren had told reporters that ". . . because of security precautions, some of the [Warren Commission] testimony might not be released to the public within their lifetimes."[1]

Donahue wondered: Why the secrecy? Had Warren known about the possibility of an accident? Had the Commission known? Or had they simply relied on information presented by the FBI and Secret Service, and in their ignorance reached the only logical conclusion they could have? Had they, in effect, been duped? It was impossible to say. Still, Warren's remark about restricting testimony because of "security precautions" seemed curious.

In any event, Donahue surmised the true cause of Kennedy's head wound must have been known at the very least among the President's top advisors and the Secret Service agents in the motorcade within minutes of the shooting. Several incidents at Parkland Hospital seemed to bear this out and offered a glimpse into how news of the accident may have been suppressed.

Veteran journalist Jim Bishop recounted one of these episodes in a single paragraph on page 225 of *The Day Kennedy Was Shot,* his lengthy, detailed account of the assassination published in 1968:

---

*This quote has been reconstructed from the recollections of Howard Donahue.

In the little corridor between trauma rooms, [Secret Service agent] William Greer stood guard over Mrs. Kennedy as [Secret Service agent] Clint Hill phoned the White House. He held the wire open. The operator cut in. "The Attorney General wants to speak with you." A small, tense voice came on. "What happened, Clint?" "There has been an accident." "How is the president?" Hill knew the President was dead. "The situation is bad." he said. "We'll get back to you."[2]

*"There's been an accident."*Bishop hadn't footnoted his source, nor was it clear Bishop had actually interviewed Hill for his book. Maybe the writer had simply extrapolated the quote from the general comments Hill made to the Commission. On the other hand, if the quote was accurate, it was odd Hill hadn't stated the obvious: There had been an assassination attempt and the President was mortally wounded.

Much more intriguing to Donahue, though, was the manner in which Kennedy's body had been removed from Parkland Hospital— firmly, quickly and illegally—by members of the Secret Service and the Kennedy entourage. Texas law requires an autopsy be conducted in a murder or violent death before the body can be shipped out of the state. Dr. Earl Rose, Dallas County medical examiner, was well aware of this, and he was prepared to make no exceptions for Kennedy or anyone else. But the President's close advisors and the Secret Service had other ideas.

In *Death of a President,* William Manchester reported the follow- ing conversation after Rose informed the presidential cadre the body would not be leaving the hospital until an autopsy had been con- ducted:

[Secret Service agent] Kellerman blocked the way. In his most delib- erate drawl Roy said, "My friend, this is the body of the President of the United States, and we are going to take it back to Washington."

"No, that's not the way things are." Rose wagged his finger. "When there's a homicide, we must have an autopsy."

"He is the President. He is going with us."

Rose lashed back. "The body stays."

"My friend, my name is Roy Kellerman. I am Special Agent in Charge of the White House Detail of the Secret Service. We are taking President Kennedy back to the capital."

"You're not taking *the body* anywhere. There's a law here. We're going to enforce it."

[Kennedy's personal doctor Admiral George] Burkley argued with Dr. Rose, physician to physician. It was useless. Kellerman, who hadn't moved from the doorway, gathered his million muscles and loomed forward.

"My friend, this part of the law can be waived."

Rose, stonewalling, shook his head.[3]

The confrontation escalated to the point of near physical violence over the next half hour.[4] Godfrey McHugh, Kennedy's Air Force aide, appealed to the mayor of Dallas to intervene. Mayor Cabell, however, said he had no authority to do so.[5] At the climactic moment, Kellerman, with the help of Kennedy advisors Larry O'Brien, Kenny O'Donnell, and others, rolled the casket down the long corridor from trauma room one toward the doors of the hospital and a waiting hearse outside. Rose blocked their path.[6]

According to Russell Fisher, the Secret Service agents reportedly had their hands on their guns when they (probably Kellerman) said to the doctor: "Either you move or we run it [the casket] over you."[7]

And Rose was shoved aside.[8]

This determination to circumvent local medical authorities didn't abate once the group made good their exit from Parkland. After the casket was loaded aboard *Air Force One* at Love Field, the Kennedy people repeatedly pressed the pilot to take off immediately.[9] According to Manchester, Kennedy advisor O'Brien was beset by the vision of Earl Rose storming aboard with the Dallas police department and carrying off the dead President's body at gunpoint.[10]

"We've got to go; we've got to get out of here; we can't wait," Kennedy advisor O'Donnell told Lyndon Johnson. But Johnson wouldn't budge.[11] He wanted to send a clear signal to the American people and the world that power had been transferred smoothly. He was determined to be sworn in as President before the plane took off.[12] It was an hour and fifteen minutes before a judge arrived to administer the oath. Only then did *Air Force One* roll out to the tarmac and throttle up and out of that black Texas day.

Donahue brooded over Hill's alleged comment about "an accident" and the high-handed behavior of the Secret Service and Kennedy people in removing the body from Dallas. Perhaps, he thought, it wasn't so much a deliberate decision to cover up what had occurred, but simply a panicked reaction to the chaos of the moment. After all, what could possibly be gained by telling the truth? Someone had clearly tried to kill the President. To disclose the accident might render one man's life intolerable and could stain the Secret Service forever. There was also the danger that some people might never accept the fact that the agent's shot had been an accident. That could lead to wild and unfounded speculation that the Secret Service intentionally murdered the President as part of a larger conspiracy.

Most importantly—from Attorney General Robert Kennedy's perspective—to reveal the truth might tarnish the image of his brother. That JFK was dead was ruinous enough. But at least he would be seen as a martyr now; forever ensconced in the minds of millions as the young prince cut down in his prime. The idea of divulging the dreadful irony, the mortifying absurdity of an accident, must have been too much for his brother to bear. Such an end was not worthy of a man like Jack Kennedy.

Consequently, when Hill had informed the attorney general of the "accident" during the Parkland phone conversation—and it was reasonable to believe that Hill or someone else had told Kennedy the specifics that afternoon—Bobby may well have, understandably, codified the cover-up: instructing that word of the misadventure go no further and that the President's body be brought back to Washington as rapidly as possible, Texas law be damned.

If Robert Kennedy had made such a decision, it was completely in keeping with his character. He was an aggressive man used to having things his own way. For three years he'd served as his brother's shield and cutlass. Now, with Jack dead, Bobby perhaps saw his cover-up as his final task in that role—an arguably humane decision that would serve primarily to protect the memory of JFK. Certainly Kennedy's position as attorney general put him in the ideal spot to execute such a cover-up. He was the nation's top law enforcement official and held authority over the FBI as well as considerable influence over the federal and state agencies involved in the preliminary investigations of the assassination.

The gunsmith's instincts that a cover-up may have developed in the minutes after the assassination would be supported by additional evidence accumulated in the years ahead—evidence that would continue to point to Bobby Kennedy as the key player in this fateful decision.

The weeks rolled on. Donahue relayed his latest findings to Reppert and the two were soon meeting weekly to work on the story. Reppert would interview Donahue with a tape recorder and call frequently with follow-up questions. He borrowed books on the assassination to fill in the background. He sent away for a transcript of the 1967 CBS television special Donahue had participated in.

And on March 21, 1977, he wrote Hickey.

Not knowing where Hickey lived or whether he was even still alive, Reppert wrote him on *Sun* stationery in care of the U.S. Secret Service at the Department of the Treasury. The reporter's tone was casual, and he camouflaged his motive in the broadest of terms. Reppert mentioned he was working on an article on the assassination and was attempting to contact a number of people who'd been present at the shooting. He asked if Hickey would be willing to talk.

Meanwhile, Reppert decided the article would work best if presented in two parts: Part one would recount Donahue's chance involvement and remarkable performance in the CBS reenactment and emphasize his credibility as a gunsmith and ballistics expert. Part two would build on this foundation with the story of Donahue's investigation and the stunning conclusions he eventually reached.

The days galloped by as Reppert wrote and Donahue continued to dig. The gunsmith had an interesting, if somewhat tangential, encounter in late March. A federal agent and longtime friend came into the gun store. The agent was aware of Donahue's theory, and when he heard the *Sun* was working on a story he volunteered to run the thesis up the chain of command at his agency, just to see how the brass would react. Several days later, the agent stopped by and said that when he told his supervisor about it, the supervisor had responded: "This is too big for me to handle." His boss then sent a written report on Donahue's theory to headquarters in Washington.

Later, the agent said, his superior called him back and asked, "What kind of guy is Donahue?"

"He's a firearms expert who has testified in federal cases," the agent replied.

"Oh shit!" the supervisor said, and hung up.

Donahue's research soon uncovered an intriguing piece of evidence that seemed to show—albeit obliquely—that President Johnson may have been among those who were aware of the accident. He ran across the item in *LBJ: The Way He Was*, a book written by longtime White House correspondent Frank Cormier. In the book, Cormier had recounted a visit LBJ made to Texas the Christmas after he had become President, a trip that included a visit to his ranch by an old friend of Johnson's, A. W. Moursund, for some deer hunting.

Moursund was driving and Johnson watching for deer in the scrub growth along the road when the President suddenly became irritated by his Secret Service guard following in a station wagon close behind. Johnson directed Moursund to stop the car. An agent ran forward to see what was wrong.

"Dammit," Johnson snapped. "I don't want you tailgatin' me! Now you keep that wagon back outta sight or I'm gonna shoot out your tires!"[13]

Cormier went on to say that while Johnson demonstrated genuine, if somewhat sporadic affection for some agents, he could also be pointlessly cruel toward them. "In an off-the-record talk at the White House, a few weeks earlier," Cormier wrote, "Johnson had shocked me by exploding: 'If I ever get killed, it won't be because of an assassin. It'll be some Secret Service agent who trips himself up and his gun goes off. They're worse than trigger-happy Texas sheriffs.'"[14]

Johnson's comments were obviously less than conclusive, but they were relevant. If nothing else, the words demonstrated Johnson had an aversion to the Secret Service and for this perhaps he had a reason.

As Donahue pondered the impending story and the weight of facts he had to back it up, two significant, unresolved questions lingered in his mind. The first was: Why didn't the Commission acknowledge that all available evidence strongly indicated Oswald's first shot had missed and ricocheted?

According to the Commission, the fragments found in the presidential limousine were remnants of the bullet that hit Kennedy in the head. Donahue's research, however, suggested this claim was not supported by the facts. The fragments appeared to be free of blood, bone, brain tissue, and hair, indicating they probably did not pass through the President's skull, and one was deformed in such a fashion as to show it likely hit something very hard, such as the pavement of Elm Street.

Perhaps it was only investigative ineptitude that allowed the Commission to ignore these facts, as they had the numerous eyewitness reports that suggested the first shot had missed. Because Humes never identified the ricochet fragment on Kennedy's skull in his autopsy report, investigators may well have been unaware of it and as a result unable to interpret the other clues that suggested the first shot went wide. If this were the case, it would logically follow that the Commission would have no reason to suspect that Kennedy was actually reacting to a superficial wound in his scalp and not the bullet through his neck when he first appeared from behind the sign in the Zapruder film.

Then again, Donahue found it difficult to accept that trained investigators could fail to interpret and integrate the other evidence pointing toward the first shot missing, even if they were unaware of Kennedy's ricochet wound. After all, Connally's position at Zapruder frame 237 (see illustration 18), the instant before he began to react to his wounds, was exactly as it needed to be to make the single bullet trajectory work. This alone should have caught investigators' attention and signaled a logical starting point in determining when the President and governor were hit by the single bullet.

Donahue, therefore, could not rule out the possibility that the Commission did know that the first shot had missed and struck Kennedy with a ricochet fragment, but suppressed the information in order to strengthen their claim that Oswald fired the final, fatal shot. Maintaining that the fragments found in the car came from the head wound accomplished this, since the bullet pieces were ballistically matched to Oswald's rifle. Undoubtedly the FBI and/or the Commission—if they were involved in a cover-up—were anxious for anything that would shift attention away from the actual source of the fatal bullet and hang the blame back onto Oswald.

As he mulled this mystery, the second question on Donahue's mind was whether Oswald fired three shots or two. There could be no way to answer it conclusively, but to Donahue, the evidence suggested Oswald fired just two—the ricochet and the neck shot.

It was true that three spent Carcano shells were found on the floor of the book depository near Oswald's sixth-floor roost. The Commission pointed to this as proof positive that Oswald had fired three times. Yet one of the shells was dented and showed numerous marks from the carrier, the large spring in the Carcano clip that pushed the bullets up to the chamber.[15] Donahue did not believe this dented shell could have been used to fire a bullet that day. The gun would not have functioned properly. Instead, he theorized that dent and the markings may have been made by Oswald inserting and reinserting a spent shell into the magazine to repeatedly dry-fire, or practice the Carcano's bolt and trigger action, without damaging the firing pin. As a Marine, Oswald would have known how to do this.

There was also the possibility the third shell had remained in Oswald's gun after his hurried shot at Major General Edwin Walker back in April of '63, and that Oswald had finally ejected it as he prepared for Kennedy's motorcade to appear on Houston Street. This, to Donahue, seemed like a reasonable explanation. On April 10, 1963, Oswald had written a note to his wife instructing her on what steps to take if he was captured, killed, or imprisoned. He then returned later that night, visibly shaken, and confessed he'd tried to kill Walker, a controversial right-wing activist.[16]

Because the bullet recovered from the wall in Walker's home was badly mangled, FBI ballistics experts could not positively identify it as coming from Oswald's rifle. But they did say that the slug had the "general rifling characteristics of (Oswald's) rifle."[17] By calculating the trajectory of the bullet based on alignment of the holes in Walker's window and wall, police were able to pinpoint the location the shot had been fired from. This position matched the vantage point of several photographs taken of Walker's house; photos found amid Oswald's possessions months later, after the assassination.[18]

Most significantly, no spent shell was found in the area from whence the shot at Walker had come. To Donahue, this supported his belief that Oswald had simply pulled the trigger and run, stashed the gun, then ejected the shell much later as he prepared to shoot Kennedy. In fact, Marina Oswald testified that her husband told her he hid the rifle in some bushes after firing at Walker and returned several days later to pick up the gun.[19]

If Oswald had fired three shots, Donahue figured, two of them must have missed. He certainly didn't shoot the bullet that hit Kennedy in the head. Perhaps Oswald's miss was the ricochet that wounded bystander Tague down by the triple underpass. And maybe the crack of Oswald's last shot blended with the report from Hickey's gun.

Then again, several witnesses inside the book depository had claimed to hear only one or two shots.[20] And Bonnie Ray Williams, who had watched the parade from the window just beneath Oswald, initially told the FBI he heard only two shots fired just above him.[21] To Donahue, these accounts, along with the dent in the third shell, seemed to point toward two shots from Oswald. And one from Hickey.

It was April 1977 now. Reppert was getting close. He'd worked through several drafts and was happy with the way the story had come together. It was time to take it to Williams and hope for the best.

* * *

In an interview years later, Williams recalled that "Ralph came to me and said, 'Hal, I don't care if you don't want to run it, but would you just do me the personal favor of reading it?'

"Well," Williams said. "I read the thing and the hair stood up on the back of my neck. It was one hell of a story."

Williams was soon the story's biggest backer. He discussed with other editors the possibility of jumping it off the front page. But that would have required that the article be cut significantly, and in the end the decision was to run it over two successive weeks inside the Sunday magazine.

A graphic artist at the *Sun* worked up some sketches of the bullets' trajectories as conceived by Donahue, and Reppert combed the *Sun* photo files for prints of the Altgens or Willis photos or anything else that might help the story. He was stunned by what he found, and immediately telephoned Howard.

"Howard, Ralph here. I found a picture of Hickey with the gun this afternoon in the photo morgue! No kidding! I'll bring it by. It's incredible."

Sure enough, Reppert's digging had turned up a gem. Like the witnesses' references to Hickey pulling out the AR-15, the Associated Press picture had no doubt been around, but once again Donahue had somehow missed it in all his years of research.

The photographer was unknown. He or she stood on the shoulder of the Stemmons Freeway, a half mile or so beyond Dealey Plaza. The picture's background shows the railroad embankment leading up to the triple overpass and, beyond the embankment, the shadowy form of the book depository. In the photo's immediate foreground is the presidential limousine. The car's image is blurred by its speed; by now the desperate race to Parkland is well underway. Judging by the location of the limousine, the photo was taken within a minute or two of the shooting.

Clint Hill, the agent who jumped aboard the limo after the final shot, is the only individual visible inside the presidential car. Still wearing his Ray-Ban shades, he is bent and braced against the wind— poised above the fallen President and First Lady in the back seat.

Less than twenty feet behind is the Secret Service follow-up car. Driver Sam Kinney is visible through the windshield. Behind and beside him a jumble of other human forms can be seen. Nine men were in the Cadillac at this point, including three of the agents who had stood outside on the running boards seconds before. One of them is now sitting higher than the rest. Like Hill, he is slightly hunched and stiff against the wind. The agent was probably Bill McIntyre, who had earlier been standing on the left-rear running board.

Behind McIntyre, in the left-rear seat, is Hickey. Only the top half of his head, his right shoulder, and his right hand are visible. In his hand is the gun. The AR-15's barrel, a portion of its plastic stock, and the gun's strap are clearly discernible. Hickey is holding the rifle to his right side with the barrel pointed up at a 45-degree angle. (See illustration 25).

Donahue and Reppert were thrilled. It was one thing to rely on the verbal recollections of witnesses who put the gun in Hickey's hands. It was quite another to have a picture taken within minutes of the shooting that showed him with the gun.

The discovery was fortuitous, for D day loomed. There was, however, one final question that needed to be resolved before the story ran. Should Hickey be named? Donahue didn't see much point in it, particularly since they now had a picture of him with the gun. As far as he was concerned, that was enough. Besides, anyone who really wanted to find out the agent's name could look it up easily enough in *The Death of a President*.

Reppert agreed. There was always the possibility that Donahue had somehow reached his conclusions in error, though it seemed unlikely at this point. Still, why risk it? If Reppert could find additional corroboration for later articles, there would be time enough to name Hickey publicly. Furthermore, the letter sent to Hickey had gone unanswered. It didn't seem fair to name the agent without speaking to him first.

And so . . . the artwork was finished, the story laid out and proofread. The day had come. On Sunday, May 1, 1977—almost ten years to the day after Donahue's long journey had begun with the CBS reenactment—part one of Reppert's story ran under the headlines KENNEDY ASSASSINATION: A DIFFERENT VIEW and AFTER TEST-FIRING, MARYLAND MAN HAS DOUBTS ABOUT OSWALD.

In the background, across the first two pages of the story, was a detailed ink drawing of the CBS reenactment tower with Donahue atop, firing down on the electric trolley moving on the temporary rails. The article told of the reenactment and Donahue's three-shot, three-hit performance, emphasizing his long experience with firearms and ballistics. The story also explained how Donahue had subsequently started his investigation and how he'd been surprised by the lack of firearms expertise displayed by so many who'd written about the killing. The closing paragraphs were guaranteed to draw readers back for part two the following week:

> In his nine-year study Mr. Donahue has sought not to discredit the Warren Report, but to support it. He still believes the report to have been put together honestly—on the basis of the information given to the commission. He believes, however, that its members did not have evidence which would have changed the report.
>
> Mr. Donahue believes today that no premeditated murder was committed in Dealey Plaza in Dallas on November 22, 1963.
>
> He believes that for a freakish, once-in-a-million turn of events, John F. Kennedy might be alive today, with Lee Harvey Oswald serving a

prison sentence for his *attempted* murder. And he believes he knows how President Kennedy was killed.

To be continued next week

Photos accompanying the piece included the Altgens picture taken just after the first bullet hit, showing Hickey turned completely around and looking back up at the book depository, a photo of Donahue sighting down the Carcano, and stills from the Zapruder film.

Part two rolled the following Sunday under the headline GUN EXPERT REASONS OSWALD DIDN'T FIRE FATAL SHOT. A full-page ink drawing was included showing Dealey Plaza with the presidential limousine and the Secret Service follow-up car making their way down Elm Street. The cutline read, "Dashes indicate path of bullets, according to the Warren Report. Dots show bullet paths, according to Donahue theory." Also pictured were the two plaster skulls Donahue had drilled and inserted with dowels to demonstrate the mislocation of Kennedy's head wound as described by Humes, as well as the actual wound location as described by Fisher and the 1968 panel.

And then there was the picture of Hickey with the gun.

The story itself recounted the inconsistencies Donahue had uncovered in connection with the head wound, his chance meeting with Fisher and the evidence the gunsmith had assembled pointing toward the accident. Taken together, the articles worked exceptionally well in conveying the substance of Donahue's work. In concise fashion, Reppert had presented more than enough facts to support both Donahue's credibility and the logic behind his conclusions. And he'd managed a difficult balance: Though the piece read like a detective thriller, Reppert had nonetheless avoided the lurid, sensationalistic tone that had characterized so much of the writing about the assassination.

Howard and Katie were elated. Donahue's theory, like a genie, was out of the bottle at last. Nothing anyone could do would get it back in now. Meanwhile, public reaction to the story was swift. A nerve had been struck. The day after the second part of the article ran, the *Sun* published the following editorial:

ACCIDENTAL DEATH?

Howard Donahue's reconstruction of the scene at Dealey Plaza in Dallas, that day in 1963, leads him to the conclusion that Lee H. Oswald did indeed fire upon John F. Kennedy—and wound him. But the cause of the fatal head wound immediately afterward, which came from another direction than Oswald's and another kind of bullet, may well have been a shot fired by a member of the detail assigned to guard the President, as the sound of gunfire induced him hurriedly to stand

and raise his weapon. If so, here is the grimmest example yet of Murphy's Law: the tendency of the worst to happen, at the worst time and in the worst possible way.

Given the expertness and the plausibility of Mr. Donahue's reconstruction, as set forth by Ralph Reppert these past two Sundays in *The Sun Magazine*, the Secret Service now owes the public more than just another no-comment reaction.

Information should be forthcoming from or about the individual special agent in question. Should there be no credible refutation of Mr. Donahue's startling hypothesis, an incidental consequence will be the deflation of one of our times' more curious psychological phenomena— the Dallas conspiracy nuts, or demonologists; that is, the persons who cannot believe that the killing was effected by anything less than a national or international plot. If Mr. Donahue is right, these theorists are left without even an assassination, just an accidental homicide.

But a new issue arises, of formidable solidity. Again if Mr. Donahue is right, then the true version of what happened that November noontime has been deliberately and skillfully and wrongly withheld from public knowledge. We would be faced, that is to say, with one more reprehensible example of cover-up.[22]

The Associated Press picked up Reppert's story that Monday morning and ran it on its "A, All-Points" wire. In typical wire service fashion, the reporter artfully condensed Donahue's theory to a succinct eighteen column-inches. The lead paragraph read:

BALTIMORE (AP)—A Maryland gunsmith who has spent years studying the assassination of President John F. Kennedy believes that a Secret Service agent accidentally fired the fatal bullet, panicking after hearing Lee Harvey Oswald's first shot.

At the gun shop, meanwhile, calls were pouring in. Most were from friends and neighbors congratulating Donahue on the story. There was also a call from a woman who did not identify herself. "She was sobbing," Donahue recalled. "I remember, she said, 'I can't tell you how relieved I was to find that the government was not involved in any conspiracy to kill our President.'

"I was startled, and then it swept over me that a lot of people must have felt the same way," Donahue said.

Later that afternoon, Donahue received queries from reporters with radio stations in both Toronto and south Florida. The Canadian reporter, Judy Webb, interviewed Howard for ten minutes and called several days later to say the broadcast had generated enormous interest in the Toronto area. By Wednesday, May 11, Donahue's story had jumped the Atlantic. A German-language version appeared as the lead story in the Zurich, Switzerland–based daily *Blick*. The headline read SENSATIONAL THESIS OF WEAPONS EXPERT: JOHN F.

KENNEDY SHOT TO DEATH BY BODYGUARDS. Unfortunately, the article was slightly mangled in translation; it had Donahue claiming that the single bullet theory was impossible from a ballistics standpoint. Nonetheless, the story did convey the essence of his conclusions reasonably well.

At the same time, letters to the editor were pouring in at the *Sun*. Almost all were complimentary, even laudatory, and between the lines, each seemed to convey the same relief the anonymous woman caller had expressed: As bad as the accident was, it was better than the nagging suspicions of a conspiracy involving elements of the U.S. government.

Reppert, meanwhile, reported that the story was the talk of the newsroom and that for the first time in memory, the Sunday paper had sold out of extra copies.

There was no official response from the Secret Service or any other government agency in the weeks following publication of the story. Donahue did, however, have two encounters that seemed to offer some oblique corroboration of his thesis. Once again, the information arrived via word of mouth at the gun shop.

An acquaintance who'd often done business with Donahue stopped by the shop not long after the article appeared. He told Howard of a relative who had recently retired from the National Security Agency, the super-secret intelligence outfit based at nearby Fort Meade, Maryland. The agency is so clandestine that in Washington parlance NSA is said to stand for "No Such Agency."

According to the man, his relative, upon reading the article, had said that "it was common knowledge among higher echelon officials at the NSA during the time of the assassination that Kennedy had been killed by his bodyguards."

It was certainly plausible that officials at the NSA would have been aware of an accident in Dallas in 1963. Like the CIA, very little escaped the NSA. Years later, in a lengthy article in *The Washington Post* documenting the means and methods of the agency, Nicholas Rostow, a former legal advisor to the NSA, was quoted as saying: "My experience with the National Security Agency is never, never— we don't exist, we don't collect, we don't know, nobody knows anything—and if there is a bullet coming right at the head of [the President of] the United States, then we can tell you precisely what time it is going to arrive.

"God forbid," Rostow added sarcastically, "if we should use this information in any way that might suggest that we know that this is going to happen because then we wouldn't know that it was going to happen again."[23]

Rostow's startling choice of words was surely coincidental, but they nonetheless conveyed the precision of knowledge the NSA was able to gather and the extent to which the agency was and is inclined to keep its information under wraps.

Donahue's second encounter involved another customer whose brother happened to be close friends with a Secret Service agent. Some time before the *Sun* story ran, the man said, the agent had attended a party at the brother's home. After getting very drunk, the agent had, without prompting and totally out of left field, blandly asserted that Kennedy was shot by one of his bodyguards. The man's brother dismissed the comment as meaningless, until he read Reppert's stories in the *Sun*.

Donahue realized these cryptic substantiations would never hold up in a court of law, not that it would come to that. But they were interesting. And they were unsolicited.

After the clamor following publication began to abate somewhat, Reppert and Donahue agreed the next logical step would be to write a book. To that end, Reppert mailed out a series of letters to publishing houses seeking a taker on the project, enclosing copies of the *Sun* articles and a rough outline of the book's proposed contents.

As the days drifted by, Donahue and Reppert remained confident that it would only be a matter of time before the story was picked up, fleshed out, and nailed down by the national news media. The public's reaction to Donahue's theory had been so dramatic that in those heady days of late May 1977 the idea that the story could somehow die stillborn seemed impossible. In any event, Donahue and Reppert had a book project underway, and to that end they continued to work.

Some weeks after Reppert's story appeared, Donahue's federal agent friend stopped back by the gun shop. He had a message. It seemed one of his fellow workers was a Secret Service agent who was a good friend of Hickey's. Hickey, his friend said, had seen the story.*

"Hickey said to tell you that if you ever mention his name, he'll sue," the agent said. "I don't know, Howard. I guess he's pretty upset. Maybe you might just want to back off, you know?"

---

*The following quote has been reconstructed from the recollections of Howard Donahue.

11

THE HOUSE SELECT COMMITTEE

THE NEWS THAT HICKEY WAS OUT THERE somewhere was encouraging. Presumably he was in the Baltimore-Washington area. Maybe there was a way to get his address. Reppert made a note to check with his police sources on the off chance they could locate the agent's home.

As far as the alleged legal threat went, neither Donahue nor Reppert gave it much thought. If Hickey was serious about setting the record straight, he knew where to find them. Until and unless the evidence surfaced that conclusively destroyed the theory, Donahue and Reppert were in full agreement. Work on the book would continue.

In fact, Donahue had long believed there might just be that kind of evidence—evidence that would instantly wreck his conclusions or, alternatively, prove them beyond a reasonable doubt—if he could only get his hands on it. For years he'd seen references to spectrographic tests conducted by the FBI on the bullet fragments recovered from the scene of the crime.[1] Spectrography is a process that involves incinerating tiny samples of the specimen in question and then comparing the color of the flames produced to those of known chemical/metallic standards.[2]

Since there were very likely significant differences in the metallic composition of the 6.5 Carcano and .223 AR-15 bullet jackets, Donahue reasoned that spectrographic comparison of the jacket material from Kennedy's brain would show conclusively whether the bullet that had killed the President came from a Carcano or an AR-15.

The curious thing was, the spectrographic results were not included anywhere in the Warren Report or in the Commission's volumes of evidence. And FBI spectrographer John Gallagher, although he testified about tests done on the President's clothes, was never questioned about tests done on the bullet fragments.[3] To Donahue, these omissions seemed bizarre, given the importance of the information to the Commission's lone-gunman thesis.

Reppert figured there had to be a way to get at the test data and to that end he contacted noted Warren Commission critic and assassination investigator Harold Weisberg, the Frederick, Maryland–based author of the *Whitewash* series. Weisberg had some startling news. Beginning in 1967, he said, he'd peppered the Justice Department with requests for a number of assassination-related documents, including the spectrographic analysis results.[4] Weisberg eventually filed a lawsuit under the newly instituted Freedom of Information Act aimed at recovering the test data. Government attorneys responded by arguing that revelation of the test results was not in the "national interest," though they never explained why.[5]

Eventually, though, the Justice Department relented and released several documents that they asserted were responsive to Weisberg's demands. Unfortunately, the only information from the spectrographic tests included in these papers were unidentified, partial, and therefore meaningless numerical notations made during the procedure.[6]

Then in 1973 a bombshell detonated in the form of a previously unknown letter from J. Edgar Hoover to J. Lee Rankin, chief counsel for the Warren Commission.[7] The letter, dated July 8, 1964, revealed that in addition to spectrographic analysis, another kind of test had been conducted on the bullet fragments. This was an extraordinarily precise and, at the time, relatively new procedure known as neutron activation.[8] The process involved irradiating organic or inorganic materials—in this case the bullet fragments—with nuclear particles. The specimens would then emit gamma rays, which could be counted, compared, and analyzed to reveal the exact composition of the substance down to parts per billion. The process was and remains vastly superior to spectrographic analysis and is so accurate it is often referred to as "nuclear fingerprinting."

Today, neutron activation has found applications in a wide range of areas. Among other things, it is used in agriculture for detecting pesticide residues on crops, in electronics for measuring impurities in silicon semiconductors, in medicine for tracing metals in metabolism, in geology for analyzing minerals, and in law enforcement for analyzing physical evidence from the scene of a crime.

Using the process, police can identify poisons administered to a victim by analysis of the victim's hair, compare tiny flecks of paint from hit-and-run automobile accidents and contrast minuscule spots of dirt or grease, among a host of other applications. Neutron activation conducted on a strand of Napoleon's hair and on hair removed from the exhumed body of Sweden's King Eric XIV has shown both men were probably poisoned with arsenic.

Hoover's 1964 letter blandly noted that "minor variations" were found in some of the Dealey Plaza bullet fragments, including those recovered from the limousine as well as those removed from Kennedy's brain, but that the differences were not sufficient to permit positive differentiation and or identification. In the years that followed, a number of assassination researchers jumped on this statement as proof of misrepresentation by the FBI director, since, they said, variations of any kind revealed in the precise neutron activation process unequivocally demonstrated the samples originated from different sources.

Donahue agreed it seemed odd that the process was reportedly inconclusive, given the supposed precision of the testing methodology. Then again, he knew that lead used in military bullets is there strictly for weight. As such, bullet manufacturers often use the cheapest lead available, usually waste lead generated in other industrial applications. This means that bullet lead is a nonhomogeneous substance that, when poured in a semiliquid state, can contain random pockets of various substances, including silver and arsenic and any number of impurities.

Donahue therefore reasoned that samples of lead taken from bullets manufactured in the same lot might appear to be exactly the same, or possibly, completely different. A bullet dug up at Gettysburg might not significantly differ in makeup from the lead found in the presidential limo. In other words, it might well be that neutron activation comparison of lead could be considerably less than conclusive.

On the other hand, Donahue believed that neutron activation tests of the jacket materials—the metal that encased the bullets—could reveal a great deal.

With this in mind, Reppert wrote Remington Arms Co., manufacturer of the AR-15 .223 round, and Winchester Western Cartridge Co., makers of the 6.5 millimeter Carcano round, asking for the specific metallic composition of the metal that encased the respective bullets. In time, he received replies. According to Winchester, the 6.5 millimeter Carcano jacket was made of 90 percent copper, 8 percent zinc and 2 percent impurities. Remington, meanwhile, reported the .223 hollow-point bullet jacket was made of 99 percent copper and 1 percent impurities.

No zinc.

So there it was.

If there were jacket fragments recovered from Kennedy's skull and they were shown to contain zinc, then the bullet must have somehow come from Oswald's gun. But if the jacket shards contained only copper and trace amounts of impurities, the bullet could not have come from Oswald's gun. And the only other high-powered rifle known to be present at the time of the fatal shot was Hickey's.

As he pondered this, Donahue realized there was a second proof that could be conducted on the jacket pieces: the width of the respective jacket materials. The AR-15 round has a very thin jacket.

The Carcano jacket is extremely thick; almost twice as thick as the AR-15 .223 skin. Microscopic analysis of the jacket pieces found in Kennedy's skull could quickly reveal the jacket width and therefore the type of the fatal bullet.

If there was ever evidence that would categorically prove Donahue right or wrong, it was the jacket material found in Kennedy's skull. Indeed, the fact that the government had only inadvertently revealed that neutron activation tests had been conducted, that they had never disclosed the results of these tests, that they hadn't even revealed the results of the less sophisticated spectrographic tests—all this, to Donahue, seemed odd. After all, if neutron activation had been done on the jacket material, and if the results had strengthened the Warren Commission's case, why wouldn't the government tout those results? Certainly they'd incorporated far less conclusive evidence in their case against Oswald.

There was something else.

According to Dr. Fisher's 1968 examination of Kennedy's skull X rays, close to forty tiny fragments were embedded in the brain. Yet when Fisher's panel asked to see the brain, they were told it was "not available." Likewise, when they'd sought to see a number of tissue samples taken from the President's brain and edge scrapings made from the bone and tissue around the entrance wound to the skull, the requests were again denied.

In fact, the brain, the tissue samples, and the scrapings seemed to vanish in the wake of the autopsy, according to Cyril Wecht, the Allegheny County coroner who'd looked at the photos and X rays in 1972. The brain and slides were not available at the National Archives in the years that followed and no one seemed to have any clue where they'd gone.

To Donahue, that this critical evidence was missing was highly suspect. The telling fact was that the missing materials were probably the only physical evidence that would have contained residue from—and in the case of the brain—pieces of the all-important .223 jacket material.

Donahue and Reppert realized it was imperative to get a look at the neutron activation test data to determine if the bullet jacket fragments were, in fact, tested. Reppert convinced his editors that the *Sun* should file a Freedom of Information lawsuit to recover the test results. Though it would undoubtedly take time, perhaps the *Sun*'s attorneys could pry the information out of the FBI.

Encouraged by revelation of the neutron activation tests and motivated by the prospect of a lawsuit to recover the results, Reppert continued to probe. He contacted a back-door governmental source and asked if the source might be able to run Hickey's name and pull up his address.

Bingo.

The source reported back that records did indeed show a George

Warren Hickey, Jr., date of birth April 24, 1923, living in a middle-class suburb outside Washington. Reppert immediately cranked out another letter, similar in content to his first, mailed it to the agent's home address, and waited.

Waiting, unfortunately, was something Donahue and Reppert were growing increasingly accustomed to in the weeks following publication of the article. For months, both had taken it as a matter of faith that once the article came out, the big guns of American journalism at *The New York Times, The Wall Street Journal, The Washington Post,* and other national dailies would level their sights on the theory and nail it down. This was probably a reasonable expectation, given the nature of what Donahue was suggesting. It failed, however, to take into account one of the dirty little secrets of big-time journalism: All too often, unless a reporter breaks a story, he or she is loath to acknowledge its existence, let alone follow it.

Reppert encountered this phenomenon firsthand when he sent a *Washington Post* reporter copies of his article with the suggestion the *Post* go after the story. When Reppert made a follow-up call several days later, the reporter asserted that neither he nor anyone else at the paper had any intention of working on the story since obviously it had been "covered adequately" in the *Sun.*

Perhaps it was this jaded arrogance, replicated in news rooms across the nation, that allowed Reppert's story to slip back toward oblivion in that early summer of 1977. Because that is exactly what happened. For all the story's compelling logic and promising leads, not one halfway curious reporter bothered to pick up the trail Donahue had blazed.

It was admittedly possible that the way Reppert wrote his article contributed to the stillbirth of Donahue's theory. As good as the piece was, it nonetheless presented the information in feature format, almost as if Donahue was some kind of fascinating eccentric and the conclusions he'd reached secondary to the man himself. This human interest approach made for good reading, but its conversational tone and lack of urgency no doubt prompted many to dismiss Donahue's work out-of-hand as just one more harebrained assassination theory and not worthy of serious consideration.

The fact that Reppert failed to pound on doors to get the story—he hadn't called the surviving members of the '68 panel, he hadn't called Warren Commission members, he hadn't talked to anyone who might have been able to confirm or refute Donahue's conclusions; in fact, it wasn't clear he'd talked to anyone at all other than Donahue—undoubtedly contributed to this perception. Perhaps if Reppert had written the article in hard news fashion with numerous attempts at confirmation and bannered high on the front page, exposé fashion, the story might have taken hold. But he hadn't. And it didn't. And as the weeks rolled past, it became painfully clear Donahue's theory had sunk back to the bottom of the pond; ignored, dismissed, and soon to be forgotten.

1. This picture, known as CE 697, gives the false impression that Kennedy and Connally were perfectly aligned along the right side of the vehicle.

2. Typical critic's "magic bullet" trajectory, erroneously showing Kennedy and Connally sitting in a straight line.

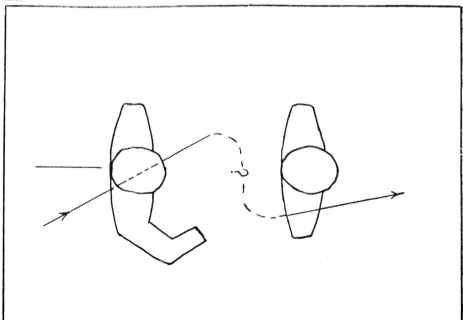

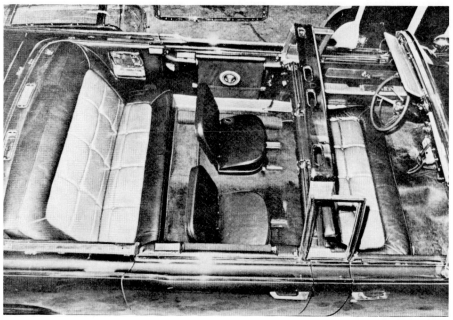

3. View of limousine interior shows jump seats much lower and farther inboard than rear seat on which Kennedy rode.

4. Overhead photo, CE 698, clearly shows Connally sitting farther inboard than Kennedy.

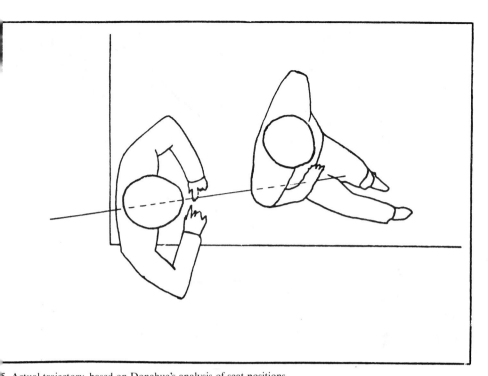

5. Actual trajectory, based on Donahue's analysis of seat positions.

6. Incorrect locations of Kennedy's back wound, as shown in Dr. Boswell's autopsy sketch.

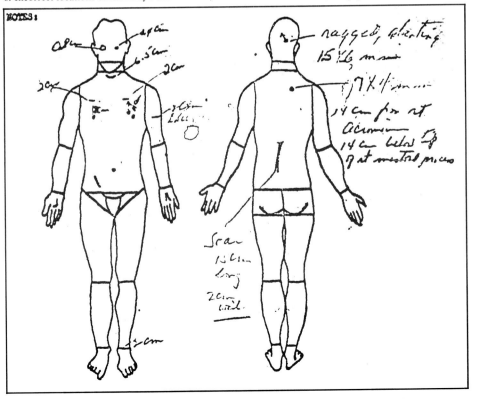

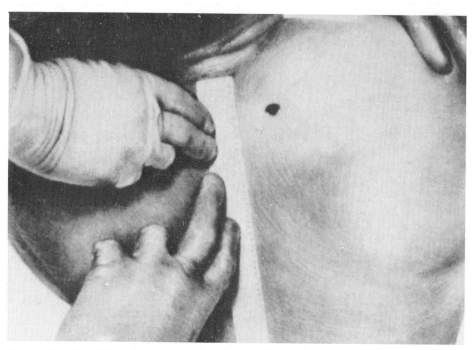

7. Actual location of Kennedy's back wound, as shown in House Select Committee drawing made from autopsy photograph.

8. CE 399, the "magic bullet." Faint curvature from right to left reveals the bullet was by no means in pristine condition.

9. Base of CE 399 shows slug was severely flattened and bent. Note extreme thickness of full-metal jacket surrounding lead core.

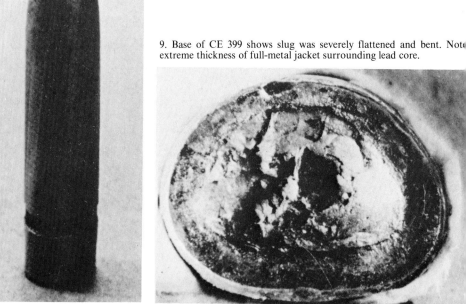

10. 6.5 Mannlicher-Carcano

11. Ricochet damage to windshield of presidential limousine.

12. Willis slide #3, showing limousine and follow-up car on Houston Street, taken seconds before both cars turned onto Elm Street. Note location of Hickey, high on left-rear seat back. *(© 1963 by Phil Willis)*

13. Willis slide #5, taken at or just before first shot. Arrow points to Kennedy's head. *(© 1963 by Phil Willis)*

14. Photo by Hugh Betzner, Jr., taken fifteen feet west of Willis at approximately the same time.

AP photographer James Altgens snapped this picture just after the first shot. Kennedy's left hand is coming up toward ace just behind the limo's rearview mirror. Hickey, seen behind follow-up car driver Sam Kinney, has already turned pletely around in response to the shot. *(AP/ Wide World Photos)*

16. Zapruder frame 183—Hickey visible sitting up on seat back of follow-up car just before the first shot.

17. Z-230—Kennedy reacting to first shot ricochet. Fragment from the broken bullet at this point has embedded in the outer table of the skull, causing Kennedy to exclaim, "My God, I'm hit!" Note hand is raised toward face, above the neck.

18. Z-237—Kennedy is now struck by bullet through the neck. Fists close up tightly toward Adam's apple, elbows splay out, and torso pitches forward, one-eighteenth of a second before Connally begins to react. Note Connally in position to receive wounds under right armpit, through right wrist, and into left thigh.

19. Z-312—Kennedy's position just as bullet was about to impact his skull. Note forward and slight left tilt of head.

20. Z-313—Kennedy's head is bursting after impact. *(© 1967 by LMH Co. All rights reserved. © 1991 by LMH Co. All rights reserved.)*

21. Z-316—massive destruction to front right area of head visible. *(© 1967 by LMH Co. All rights reserved. © 1991 by LMH Co. All rights reserved.)*

22. Z-321—back of Kennedy's head shows no exit wound, despite claims of some critics.

23. Mary Moorman photo, generally accepted to be taken just after impact, likewise reveals no exit portal on rear of skull. *(UPI/Bettman)*

24. Agent Clint Hill climbs aboard the limousine, just after the last shot. *(AP/Wide World Photos)*

25. Motorcade racing to Parkland Hospital along Stemmons Freeway. Hickey with AR-15 identified and visible in left-rear seat of follow-up car. *(AP/Wide World Photos)*

26. Using a mirror, House Select Committee gelatin block test showing explosive disintegration of AR-15 .223 (M-16) round from two angles. This test, although virtually replicating massive damage done to Kennedy's skull, was omitted from the committee's final report. No. 113 on the adjacent list of exhibits from committee's ballistics hearing, Sept. 8, 1978, identifies it as AR-15, .223 (M-16).

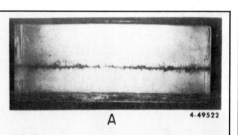

A   4-49522

B   4-40416

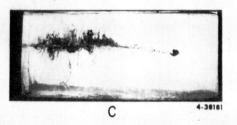

C   4-38181

MANENT CAVITIES LEFT IN GELATIN TISSUE MODELS BY BULLETS

6.5-mm Mannlicher-Carcano ball at 60-yd range
7.62-mm M80 ball at 55-yd range
Cal .257 Winchester-Roberts soft-nosed hunting bullet at 55-yd range

27. Gelatin block tests published in the House Select Committee's final report. Compare relatively narrow wound channel of full-metal jacket 6.5mm Carcano round in block A to photo of .223 round test (illus. 26 above).

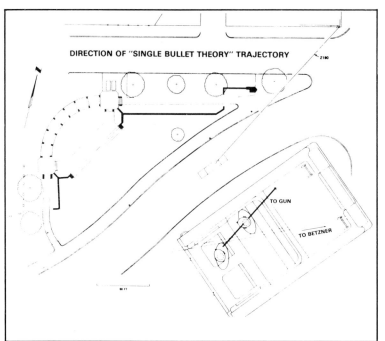

DIRECTION OF "SINGLE BULLET THEORY" TRAJECTORY

Z190

TO GUN

TO BETZNER

28. Committee draw showing trajectory of sin bullet correctly pla Kennedy at extreme ri of seat.

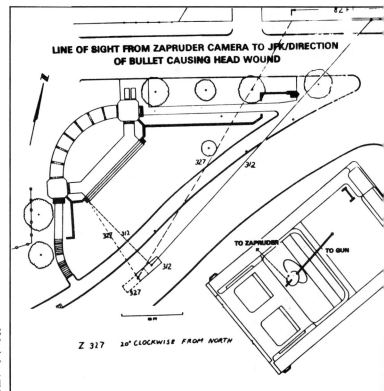

LINE OF SIGHT FROM ZAPRUDER CAMERA TO JFK/DIRECTION OF BULLET CAUSING HEAD WOUND

82 FT

327   3/2

327   3/2

3/2

327

TO ZAPRUDER   TO GUN

Z 327   20° CLOCKWISE FROM NORTH

29. Committee drawing purporting to show head shot trajectory incorrectly moves Kennedy two feet to the left. Position of head and head wound channel also incorrect.

30. Colt AR-15

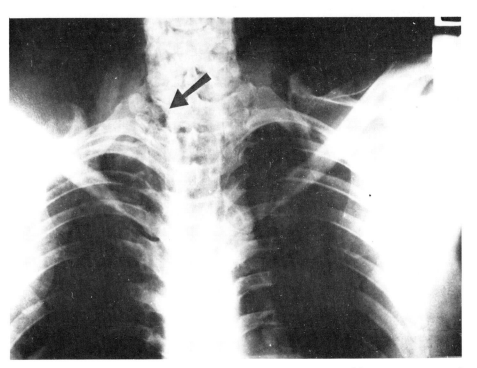

31. Autopsy X ray shows massive destruction from Oswald's second bullet to right transverse process of first thoracic vertebra. This wound would have severely damaged spinal cord and very likely proved fatal.

32. Hickey driving follow-up car during Warren Commission reenactment of assassination in summer of 1964.

* * *

Disheartening as this was, Donahue knew there was one more avenue along which his conclusions might be conveyed to a wider world. This route led through the U.S. House of Representatives; specifically, through the Select Committee on Assassinations.

In one sense, the timing of the *Baltimore Sun* article couldn't have been better, for the Kennedy assassination was back in the news that spring in a way it hadn't been since the heyday of Jim Garrison's New Orleans investigation in 1967 and 1968. The previous September, the House of Representatives had reopened investigations into the assassination of both President Kennedy and Martin Luther King, Jr. These efforts were triggered primarily by evidence of widespread government lawlessness emerging from the Watergate scandal.

It was probably inevitable that Watergate would resurrect old questions and beg new ones about the Kennedy assassination. With the collapse of the Garrison case in 1969, Warren Commission critics had been discredited and the rising tide of uncertainty surrounding the events in Dallas pushed back. But Watergate reversed this trend and proved that blind trust in government was not necessarily well placed. After the revelation of the Nixon Administration's crimes, even the most naive citizen was forced to admit that the government would and could break the law, lie, cheat, and generally abuse the public trust for political ends.

Consequently, a spirit of avenging cynicism swept the land, and with it came a haunted feeling that the government had, in presumably burying the facts surrounding the Kennedy assassination, somehow gotten away with the biggest cover-up of all. More concretely, evidence and allegations were coming out of a direct if unsubstantiated link between crimes of Watergate and the assassination. As far back as Garrison's probe, charges were raised that the CIA was somehow involved in Kennedy's killing. Now the gamey scent of the agency was turning up everywhere as the Watergate drama unfolded.

Two of the five burglars arrested in the break-in of the Democratic National Committee headquarters had some connection to the CIA.[9] By September 1974, the story had broke that the Nixon Administration had authorized $8 million between 1970 and 1973 for covert CIA activities designed to destabilize the rule of Chilean Marxist President Salvador Allende.[10] Allende was murdered in a coup in 1973 and many believed the CIA had a hand in Allende's death.

Growing suspicions about the magnitude and malignancy of the CIA's operations were confirmed by *New York Times* investigative reporter Seymour Hersh in December 1974. Under a banner headline, Hersh reported that the CIA had conducted a massive, illegal domestic intelligence operation during the Nixon Administration against the antiwar movement and other dissident groups active in the U.S.[11]

President Gerald Ford three months earlier had suggested that the CIA operations in Chile were just one more necessary operation in the Cold War's twilight struggle, and thus could be justified.[12] But it became slightly more problematic to explain away a KGB-like spying apparatus directed against at least ten thousand American citizens. As a result, Ford appointed a "blue-ribbon" panel two weeks after Hersh's article broke to investigate the domestic operations of the CIA.[13] The group, headed by Vice President Nelson Rockefeller, quickly became known as the Rockefeller Commission. It forged ahead with a mandate to examine the breadth of the CIA's activities against American citizens and report its findings within three months.

As the commission neared the end of its investigation in March, word filtered out that the panel was probing the long-standing rumor of CIA involvement in the Kennedy assassination.[14] This charge had been most recently raised by civil rights activist and comedian Dick Gregory. Gregory claimed photographs taken of three vagrants detained in Dealey Plaza shortly after the assassination showed two of the men to be Watergate conspirators and former CIA agents E. Howard Hunt and Frank Sturgis.[15]

The allegation was followed two days later by another Seymour Hersh bombshell claiming that the CIA, with the assistance of organized crime, had been instrumental in planning an aborted assassination attempt on the life of Cuban Premier Fidel Castro in the early 1960s. The same week Hersh's story appeared, *Time* magazine quoted "credible sources" as saying that in addition to one or more plots on Castro's life, the CIA had been involved in assassination conspiracies directed at two other Caribbean leaders, Rafael Trujillo of the Dominican Republic and Francois Duvalier of Haiti.[16]

Suspicions about CIA assassination activities escalated again in April. Syndicated columnist Marianne Means and Walter Cronkite of CBS News both revealed that in separate conversations, former President Johnson had suggested that the assassination of Kennedy may have been ordered by Castro in retaliation for the plots against the Cuban dictator.[17]

By now, the Rockefeller Commission's hand was forced to address both the issue of CIA assassinations in general as well as possible agency involvement in Kennedy's death. Consequently, the commission ordered a reexamination of the Kennedy autopsy material in late April. The purpose was to determine whether the fatal head shot could have been fired from the front and not the rear, as the Warren Commission concluded.[18]

On June 10, 1975, two months behind schedule, the Rockefeller Commission presented its final report to the President. As Seymour Hersh had reported, the panel confirmed that the CIA had indeed engaged in a massive, illegal domestic surveillance operation. On the subject of political assassinations, the commission was silent. Ford ordered this portion of the commission's report kept secret and its contents turned over to the attorney general for further investigation.

As for the Kennedy assassination, the commission reported that investigators found no credible proof linking the CIA or anyone else (other than Lee Harvey Oswald) to the killing.[19]

Any comfort this may have offered those who suspected the worst about the killing, however, was chilled considerably the day after the report was released. Cyril Wecht, the forensic pathologist and outspoken Warren Commission critic who'd studied the autopsy material three years before, claimed his testimony about the President's wounds had been "seriously" misrepresented in the Rockefeller panel's final report.[20]

According to Wecht, the commission was "perpetrating a fraud upon the public" by publicizing a secondary part of his testimony— that he'd found no evidence of a gunman firing from the grassy knoll—while simultaneously ignoring his primary conclusion: that the single bullet theory was not supported by the evidence and therefore, two gunmen must have fired on the President from the rear.[21]

"Obviously it is a distortion to suggest, on the basis of a selected portion of my testimony, that I concur with the Commission's implied defense of the Warren Report when the great bulk of my testimony was directly to the opposite effect," Wecht said.

In any event, skepticism about how deeply the Rockefeller Commission would dig into the Kennedy assassination had been widespread from the start; to many die-hard critics, Wecht's assertions simply confirmed the investigation was just one more whitewash. These doubts were driven in large part by the fact that former Warren Commission assistant counsel David Belin had been made executive director of the commission. With Belin's appointment to the second official government probe into Kennedy's slaying, cynics once again saw the black hand of conspiracy at work.

In fact, the drumbeat for a new investigation into the Kennedy assassination began even before the Rockefeller Commission finished its report. In February 1975, Texas Congressman Henry Gonzalez introduced a resolution calling for congressional investigations into the deaths of both Kennedy brothers and Martin Luther King, Jr., as well as the attack on George Wallace.

Gonzalez told fellow lawmakers:

> I have introduced this resolution after much consideration. It has not been a decision I have made hastily. . . . I was at Dallas the day that President Kennedy was killed and I suspended judgment on the questions that arose then and shortly thereafter until Watergate, August 1972, revealed possibilities heretofore considered not possible.
>
> We must settle once and for all, in the interest of the welfare of our country and the future of its people, the truth of what happened in Dallas on November 22, 1963, and what Lee Harvey Oswald carried to his grave. . . . There are many more disquieting questions to be resolved . . . but they must be answered with calmness, objectivity, dispassion and fairness.[22]

Gonzalez was soon joined in his appeal by Congressman Thomas Downing of Virginia. Downing's suspicions about the assassination were kindled after viewing an optically enhanced version of the Zapruder film in April 1975. The violent backward movement of Kennedy's head apparently convinced the congressman Kennedy had been shot from the front.[23]

By July 1975, Senator Richard Schweiker of Pennsylvania had taken up the cause. Schweiker was member of a Senate committee that picked up the CIA probe where the Rockefeller Commission left off. The Senate investigative group was known as the Church Committee, named for its chairman, Senator Frank Church of Idaho. Although the Church Committee at that point had uncovered nothing to indicate CIA culpability in the killing, Schweiker was apparently far from convinced. According to the senator, the committee received CIA documents "where minutes were erased, where blanks were made, where all kind of cover-up procedures were involved." All this led Schweiker to believe that "the more you dig into government secrecy and the so-called national interest, the more you have to conclude that government secrecy is invoked as a cover-up for bad deeds."[24]

Down this deepening river of skepticism came a *Houston Chronicle* story in early September 1975. The article reported the Dallas police and FBI had covered up a conversation showing the Bureau knew Lee Harvey Oswald could have posed a threat to President Kennedy before the assassination.[25] Three hours after the shooting, according to the article, Lieutenant Jack Revill of the Dallas police was told by FBI agent James Hosty that the Bureau had been aware Oswald posed a danger to the President. When Dallas Police Chief J. E. Curry subsequently reported this information to the press, however, he received a telephone call from the FBI agent-in-charge in Dallas, Gordon Shanklin, saying that "the bureau was extremely desirous that I retract my statement to the press. I then appeared before the press again and retracted my statement."[26]

For his part, Shanklin denied ever having made such a request.[27] Hosty, still with the FBI in 1975 as a special agent in Kansas City, told the Houston paper: "I like my job. I can't say anything about anything."[28]

Additional details emerged several weeks later. According to *The New York Times,* top officials of the FBI two days after the killing ordered the destruction of a note in which Oswald conveyed violent threats against the Dallas police. The note was received by Hosty about ten days before Oswald fired from the book depository.[29]

Oswald was apparently upset by the FBI's continued attempts to interview his wife in connection with his aborted defection to the Soviet Union. If nothing else, the note's existence showed that FBI Director Hoover perjured himself by claiming to the Warren Commission that the FBI had no reason to believe Oswald was capable of violence.

This disclosure begged the obvious question about what else Hoover may have suppressed. Two other facts leaked out in the fall of '75 that seemed to offer a partial answer. Jack Ruby, Oswald's killer, had reportedly been on the Bureau's payroll as an informant in the 1950s.[30] And a former code clerk at the FBI field office in New Orleans claimed the Bureau's southern offices were warned there would be an assassination attempt against Kennedy in Dallas. The warning came five days before the President was killed.[31]

These disclosures deepened suspicions about the FBI role in the assassination and intensified calls for a new investigation. As a result, on October 13, 1975, the House Civil and Constitutional Rights Subcommittee announced it was launching a limited probe into the FBI's relationship with both Oswald and Ruby.[32]

Senator Schweiker added a note of foreboding urgency two days later when he predicted the Warren Report was about to collapse "like a house of cards" as a result of evidence accumulating at the Church Committee. He added, somewhat equivocally, "The only thing I'm certain about is that we don't know the truth about the Kennedy assassination."[33]

The public clamor to get to the bottom of the assassination was by now reaching a fever pitch. Schweiker's assertions coincided with the first "national convention" on the assassination, held at the University of Hartford in mid-October.[34] The three-day event was presided over by Mark Lane, the former New York State assemblyman who'd written *Rush to Judgment,* one of the earliest books critical of the Warren Commission. Jim Garrison, the embattled former New Orleans district attorney who'd conducted the Ferrie-Shaw investigation, told upward of two thousand cheering college students that the CIA, with help from the FBI, plotted and carried out the assassination. He received a standing ovation.[35]

Meanwhile, George and Priscilla Macmillin, a husband and wife team of assassination authors, noted in *The New York Times* that "the extraordinary vitality of the rumors about the Dallas assassination is one of the astonishing phenomena of American life in the past decade." These various theories, the couple somberly concluded, "have become a permanent enclave of irrationality in our national consciousness."[36]

Irrational or not, former Warren Commission attorney Belin stunned Commission critics on the twelfth anniversary of the assassination by joining the chorus calling for a new investigation. "The primary reason for this request is that I believe it would greatly contribute toward a rebirth of confidence and trust in government," Belin asserted. He added he was confident a new inquiry would uphold the Warren Commission's findings.[37]

But he nonetheless condemned as "inexcusable" the CIA's failure to disclose to the Warren Commission the plots against Castro's life and he was equally critical of the FBI's secret destruction of the threatening Oswald note.

"The Warren Commission found [no evidence of foreign involve-
ment]," Belin said. "but the Warren Commission did not have any
information concerning the CIA assassination plots."[38]

Belin's appeal caught the ear of at least one former Commission
member: President Gerald Ford. Ford had previously warned against
reopening the Kennedy case, saying it would be "unwise."[39] Less
than a week after Belin's statement, however, the President reversed
himself and cautiously endorsed the idea of a "responsible group or
organization" investigating the "new developments" in the assassination.[40]

By this time, revelations were tumbling out of the Church Committee that, along with growing evidence of possible Kennedy culpability
in the CIA assassination plots, exposed the dark underside of the
Kennedy Administration and helped propel the late President's slide
from virtual deity status toward the flawed realm inhabited by mere
mortal men.

From the late 1950s through 1962, it seemed, Kennedy had maintained a sexual liaison with Judith Campbell Exner. Exner was a onetime Hollywood hanger-on who'd been the mistress of mobster Sam
Giancana and a close friend to crime boss John Rosselli. Infidelity
was destructive enough to Kennedy's lingering golden image. But the
prospect of the king of Camelot cavorting with a mob moll and
opening himself to the possibility of blackmail begged even more
questions about Kennedy's judgment and self-control.

This reassessment of Kennedy as a leader and a man reached
something of a nadir in January 1976 when radical attorney William
Kunstler called John and Robert Kennedy "two of the most dangerous leaders in the country" and added he was "not entirely upset"
by their assassinations.[41] Kunstler's statements were roundly condemned and the attorney later claimed his words were taken "totally
out of context."[42] Still, a school in the Midwest debated whether to
remove a portrait of Kennedy due to revelations of the late President's sexual antics,[43] and self-righteous citizens around the country
bristled with moral outrage over news of the President's nocturnal
activities.

The Church Committee finally finished its work in June of 1976.
The committee's final subreport dealt specifically with the Kennedy
assassination. (Previous reports addressed other intelligence-related
issues.) Although the senators said they could find no new evidence
"sufficient to justify a conclusion that there was a conspiracy to
assassinate President Kennedy," they were nonetheless sharply critical of both the FBI and CIA investigations into the murder.[44] In the
case of the CIA, the senators castigated Warren Commission member
and former CIA Director Allen Dulles for his failure to inform the
Commission of the plots against Castro. As for the FBI, the committee wrote:

The FBI conducted its investigations in an atmosphere of concern among senior bureau officials that it would be criticized and its reputation tarnished. Rather than addressing its investigation to all significant circumstances, including all possibilities of conspiracy, the FBI investigation focused narrowly on Lee Harvey Oswald.[45]

Due to these deficiencies, the committee determined, the Warren Commission had been unable to perform a thorough investigation or reach definitive conclusions. Yet the Warren Commission's conclusions had not collapsed like a house of cards, as Senator Schweiker had so boldly predicted some months earlier. In the end, the vocal Pennsylvanian would nonetheless accuse both the CIA and FBI of a "cover-up" in connection with the assassination and say the entire case remained a "jigsaw puzzle" with pieces still missing.[46]

Other committee members declined to endorse Schweiker's claims, but all were in agreement a new investigation was warranted. Such a prospect finally seemed at hand on September 14, 1976, when Speaker of the House Carl Albert told the press he expected the House of Representatives to vote for new investigations into both the JFK and King murders in the near future.

"It's reaching the point where there is so much interest that Congress will probably have to do something about it," Albert lamely remarked.[47]

The vote came three days later and the House Select Committee on Assassinations was officially born. Congressman Downing was appointed chairman. Downing's colleague and the earliest congressional advocate for a new investigation, Henry Gonzalez of Texas, was penciled for the chairmanship when Downing retired at year's end.

Instrumental in the ultimate success of Gonzalez's and Downing's long-standing call for a new investigation was the Congressional Black Caucus. Among the many ugly revelations of 1975 and 1976 were disclosures that the FBI had for years conducted a systematic campaign of harassment against Martin Luther King. The Bureau's activities, including surveillance, wiretapping, and attempts at blackmail, were apparently sanctioned by Hoover himself.[48] As a result, black leaders understandably questioned whether the FBI investigation into King's death was as complete as it might have been. Some even wondered if the Bureau played a role in the Memphis killing. These concerns dovetailed nicely with the efforts aimed at establishing a new investigation into the Kennedy murder. Presumably a committee looking at both assassinations would answer the questions of FBI culpability in the King case and lay to rest the many mysteries surrounding Kennedy's death.

The prospect of final resolution for these notorious murders was reinforced in October when Downing tapped Richard Sprague, a former Philadelphia assistant district attorney, to be the committee's chief counsel and head investigator. Sprague had earned a reputation as a razor-sharp investigator in Philadelphia, in large part by obtaining a conviction of W. A. "Tony" Boyle in the 1969 triple murder of Boyle's union rival Joseph Yablonski, his wife, and daughter.[49]

Reviewing Sprague's record and his role in the Boyle case, *The New York Times* cooed approvingly, if somewhat incoherently: "In tracking the Yablonski killers, hired gunmen who did not know their principal but whose Appalachian fears and loyalties the prosecutor was able to play off against one another, Mr. Sprague sent Mr. Boyle to prison for life."[50]

The hard-boiled Sprague vowed to attack the King and Kennedy inquiries as separate homicide investigations and seemed to offer the guarantee of a no-holds-barred, lead-where-it-may probe.[51] Commission critic Mark Lane hailed Sprague's appointment as "the best possible choice."[52]

Sprague, in fact, had been Downing's second choice. The congressman had initially sought Washington attorney Bernard Fensterwald for the post. But Congressman Gonzalez was already seething about being passed by for the committee chairmanship and he balked at the Fensterwald pick. The attorney was forced to withdraw.[53]

Trouble immediately broke out on another front. Sprague, obviously enjoying the limelight, went before Congress in early December and informed lawmakers he would need $13 million to do his job. The amount was far in excess of the money spent on the Warren Commission and double the cost of the Senate Watergate investigation.[54]

Sprague justified his request by stating that a staff of 170 was required to do competent investigations of both murders since, for obvious reasons, the committee would be unable to rely on "in-house" FBI and CIA investigators, as the Warren Commission had done.

Congress was stunned by the size of Sprague's request, but seemed initially willing to go along with it, particularly in view of Sprague's tantalizing assertion that the committee had uncovered "new and disturbing" questions about both the King and Kennedy murders. But then on January 2, 1977, a brickbat came flying Sprague's way in the form of a *New York Times* article headlined COUNSEL IN ASSASSINATION INQUIRY OFTEN TARGET OF CRITICISM. Reporter David Burnham's exposé outlined a series of controversies associated with Sprague's tenure as an assistant district attorney in Philadelphia.

Of *The New York Times* article's impact in 1976, former committee investigator Gaeton Fonzi wrote several years later: "There is no doubt that Sprague's record had points worthy of valid criticism, but the *Times'* piece left out the grays and painted Sprague a heavy black. Intended or not, the piece had the effect of a well-placed torpedo. It almost sank the Assassinations Committee."[55]

An attempt to fund the assassination panel through a voice vote failed several days after the story appeared. Consequently, the funding issue was for all practical purposes forced back to its procedural starting point. With no money, the committee drifted deeper into legislative limbo and disarray.[56]

Critics quickly pounced. California Democrat Don Edwards asserted Sprague's proposed investigative techniques—including the use of wiretaps and lie detectors—were "wrong, immoral and very likely illegal." Edwards further questioned the committee's plan to hold public hearings and attacked the highly public role Sprague had played in the nascent committee's activities.[57]

Jumping on next was Colorado Congressman Timothy Wirth. Wirth demanded to know how the committee came to choose Sprague as its chief counsel and suggested that since Sprague was a congressional appointee, he should be required to make a full financial disclosure to the Congress.[58]

Gonzalez, having finally ascended to his much-coveted chairmanship with the retirement of Downing, suddenly found the committee crumbling beneath him. Lashing out, he said he "felt like a guy who has been slugged before he has a chance to get into the ring and fight" and he called the fateful *New York Times* article "a journalistic vendetta dredged from the turgid and murky waters of big-city politics."[59]

Gonzalez's picturesque counterattack, however, did little to blunt the growing armada of committee critics, who continued to pour broadsides into Sprague and his "grandiose" budget requests.[60] As January ended, there seemed a very real possibility the committee would be dead and buried before real work could begin. In early February, however, the House voted to keep the committee alive at least until the end of March. At that point a new budget would be presented and the matter reconsidered.[61]

Yet just when it appeared a degree of normalcy might be returning to the committee, another ugly political fight came crashing out of the House chambers into the public eye. The adversaries this time were Gonzalez and Sprague and, very quickly, Gonzalez and the rest of the committee. A clash between the power-hungry chairman and his gruff and egotistical subordinate was probably inevitable, but few could have predicted the extent of the bloodletting.

Gonzalez attacked on February 10 when he moved to fire Sprague on grounds the former prosecutor had "engaged in a course of conduct that is wholly intolerable for any employee of the House." Specifically, Gonzalez complained that Sprague was "making a consistent attempt to undermine my chairmanship and malign me personally with the members of the committee staff."[62]

But if Gonzalez figured his colleagues would back him up, he figured dead wrong. The eleven other committee members told Sprague to ignore Gonzalez. The committee staff issued a statement saying Sprague had "been directed by the committee to disregard the orders of Henry B. Gonzalez, committee chairman, on the basis that he does not have the power unilaterally to discharge Mr. Sprague. It is only the committee which has this power."[63]

The dispute quickly became an all-out political melee as Gonzalez assailed Sprague with new charges. This time, he claimed the former assistant district attorney had refused to file a financial disclosure statement, had continued to work as a private attorney while on the committee payroll and had "stated to the committee staff that neither he nor they can be subject to the control of any member, either myself or anyone of you."[64]

Other committee members reacted by predicting the investigation's demise. "I think the struggle that has occurred makes the continued existence of the committee very doubtful," said Illinois Congressman John Anderson. Connecticut Congressman Christopher Dodd said the committee was "in intensive care," and added, "I don't believe the committee will ever get on its feet again, and I think that is a tragedy."[65]

The committee did not get to its feet, but it did not die either. Rather, the investigation lay in a bloody heap, still breathing spasmodically and spitting up teeth as the impasse between Gonzalez, Sprague and the rest of the committee members dragged on. It was soon apparent, however, that Gonzalez's position was untenable. He'd alienated the committee members with his unilateral attempt to fire Sprague and at the same time he'd been humiliated by the committee's refusal to back him.

On March 6 Gonzalez bailed out. The embattled Texan slashed all the way down—criticizing committee members for trying to usurp his powers, attacking the Democratic leadership for failing to come to his rescue and for the last time hacking away at Sprague.[66]

Numerous congressmen again dictated the committee's obituary, but once more the assassination investigation stayed alive. On March 30, the House voted 230 to 181 to fund the committee for another year. The trade-off: Sprague had to go.

"With Sprague resigning, they claim it means 40 more votes," crowed House Speaker Thomas "Tip" O'Neill.[67]

Congressman Louis Stokes of Ohio became the new committee chairman and a search for Sprague's successor began. For his part, Sprague leveled his own parting volley in early April, saying Gonzalez was guilty of "McCarthyism" and that O'Neill and other Congressional leaders had failed to support the committee's effort.[68] All in all, the spring of '77 wasn't kind to the former assistant district attorney. Earlier, the Pennsylvania Supreme Court had overturned Sprague's much-heralded conviction of Tony Boyle. Following his departure from the committee, Sprague retreated to Philadelphia to try the case all over again.[69]

By early June, Stokes had settled on G. Robert Blakey as Sprague's replacement. Blakey, a professor at Cornell University Law School, was named to the post after what Stokes termed an "exhaustive" search.''[70] Exhausting might have been a better word, since two of Stokes's earlier choices—former Supreme Court Justice Goldberg and former Watergate special prosecutor Archibald Cox—understandably wanted no part of what had become, in the eyes of many, an unmitigated fiasco.[71]

And then *The New York Times* struck again, citing a confidential source who asserted the committee had come up with virtually no new information in its eight months of work, and much of what the committee did have had been spoon-fed to investigators by none other than Mark Lane, the perennial Warren Commission critic and author of *Rush to Judgment*.[72]

"We certainly have come up with nothing earthshaking," the source told the *Times*, "and much that witnesses tell us is in conflict with what they supposedly told people who have written books about the assassinations and who have provided the basic leads for the committee to pursue."[73]

It was into this environment—still reeling from the power struggles between Gonzalez and Sprague, facing a new and untested leader in Blakey and under attack once again from the press—that Howard Donahue dealt his wild card on June 7, 1977.

Donahue wrote to Robert Tannenbaum, the deputy chief counsel in charge of the Kennedy investigation and a Sprague appointee who'd survived the purges of March. In his letter, Donahue noted that *Sun* editor Hal Williams had already forwarded copies of Reppert's story and he politely asked for the opportunity to present his information publicly before the committee.

Then he sat back and waited for a reply.

12
KATIE DONAHUE FORCES THE ISSUE

MUCH TO DONAHUE'S SATISFACTION AND SOMEWHAT TO his surprise, he received a call several weeks later from James Wolf, an assistant counsel to the committee staff. Wolf said the committee was very interested in what he had to say and asked if Donahue could come down to Washington on the twelfth day of July for an informal meeting with several staff members. Donahue assured the attorney he'd be there. Evidently, the powers that be at the committee were taking his conclusions seriously. It didn't matter as much now that the press had ignored the story. The committee had more probing powers than a newsroom full of reporters. If anybody could get to the bottom of what had happened in the presidential motorcade that day, they could.

Donahue and Reppert in fact realized the committee probably stood a better chance of obtaining the results of the neutron activation tests than did the *Baltimore Sun*. Donahue would certainly ask them about it. Consequently, both men agreed it made sense to hold off on the Freedom of Information suit at least until it was clear what the committee would or wouldn't do. There didn't seem much point in spending the newspaper's money if the test results could be obtained faster and more easily through the committee.

The meeting day arrived. Howard and Katie headed for Washington in the sweltering heat of high summer. Arriving at the committee offices, the couple was greeted by Jack Moriarty, a former District of Columbia Police Department homicide investigator, Kenneth D. Klein, assistant deputy chief counsel on the Kennedy side of the investigation and Jim Conzelman, a staff researcher.

The investigator listened intently as Donahue explained how he believed the fatal bullet's left-to-right trajectory and explosive, disintegrating impact ruled out Oswald as the triggerman. The gunsmith used photos, drawings, and eyewitness accounts to highlight his belief that Hickey's bullet had been the killing one. He emphasized the importance of obtaining the neutron activation results, and, if possible, the brain, tissue samples, and bone scrapings from the autopsy. He also suggested the committee try to gain access to Warren Commission exhibit 843: three small irregular pieces of bullet removed from Kennedy's brain during the autopsy. The fragments, like the brain and the tissue samples, could be critical pieces of medical evidence—if any of the fragments were from the jacket rather than the core of the bullet, they could show conclusively whether the jacket material came from an AR-15 or a Carcano.

Donahue went on to explain why he believed the single bullet theory was correct; how so much of the information surrounding that subject had been misconstrued and mangled by both the Commission and the critics. Finally, Donahue urged the committee staffers to interview Hickey himself.*

The investigators listened quietly. Finally Moriarty asked: "If you really believe Hickey did it and you know where he lives, why don't you go talk to him?"

"Because I don't think that's my job, Mr. Moriarty," Donahue replied. "I think that's your job. Or the job of law enforcement. We've already written him a couple of times and he hasn't responded. If I went over there, he'd slam the door in my face. He's already threatened to sue me. I'm not afraid of him, but I just don't see what I could do by going to see him. The only way he's going to talk is if you people call him to testify under oath."

The investigators assured Donahue they would do their best. Finding the missing autopsy material was already a priority for the committee, they said, and getting a look at the neutron activation results was something they'd previously discussed as well.

"There's a good possibility you'll be called to testify when our public hearings are held," Moriarty said. "Right now, I don't know when that will be, but we'll definitely be in touch."

The meeting ended with handshakes and warm words all around. Howard and Katie were much encouraged as they drove back to Baltimore. In the months since he'd discovered the existence of Hickey's AR-15, Donahue's conviction about the origin of the fatal shot had never wavered. Now that the committee was apparently pursuing the case, he figured it was only a matter of time before the truth would be out.

The fact that the committee was taking Howard seriously was confirmed for Katie when she received a call the next day from Conzelman, one of the investigators who'd been present at the meeting. Howard was working, so Katie spoke with the staffer at length and tried to answer the follow-up questions he had. Although

*The following conversation has been reconstructed from the recollections of Howard and Katie Donahue.

the researcher seemed eager to learn more, one of his queries gave
Katie considerable pause.*

"Now, Mrs. Donahue, can you tell me who manufactures the
Pristine bullets?" Conzelman asked matter-of-factly.

"Well . . . ah," Katie hesitated. "There isn't really a bullet with
the brand name Pristine. That's just a term, a derogatory term, really,
that the Warren Commission critics have used to describe the bullet
found at Parkland Hospital because of its undamaged condition,
which of course the critics don't believe would have been possible
given the wounds the bullet caused to Kennedy and Connally. They
also call it the 'magic bullet.' It's the same thing, really."

"Ah yes. Of course. I see," Conzelman said quickly. He thanked
Katie for her time and assured her the committee would be in contact
as the investigation progressed.

Howard had a good laugh when he heard about Conzelman's
question.

"Well, it is funny," Katie said, "but I just hope it's not an
indication of the knowledge level we're dealing with down there."

"Yeah," Howard replied, "but don't forget: Moriarty is a former
homicide detective. He knows exactly what I'm talking about. Conzelman no doubt means well, but he's just a puppy. It doesn't matter
how knowledgeable he is."

Flagged by Reppert, the *Baltimore Sun*'s Washington correspondent reported Donahue's meeting with the congressional investigators in a twelve-inch story on page A-5 the next day. The article
noted that Donahue had urged the committee to obtain the neutron
activation tests and quoted him as saying it was now up to the
committee to find the facts.[1]

"If they want to get the information, they can prove whether I'm
right or not," Donahue said. Once again, Hickey's name was not
mentioned in the newspaper.

But as summer advanced and the prospect of public hearings drew
closer, the idea of revealing Hickey's name to the world loomed large
for Katie and Howard. They talked of it often. Like Moriarty, Katie
believed Howard had a responsibility to confront Hickey face-to-face
and she repeatedly urged her husband to drive down to Washington
and get it done. But Howard resisted. What was the point, he'd ask?
Hickey wasn't going to talk to him, not after the *Sun* article. Reppert
had written him twice now; no replies each time. They'd made an
effort to reach him. Furthermore, even though Hickey's name wasn't
mentioned in the *Sun* stories, the agent had to know it was just a
matter of time before Donahue would tie him publicly to the accident.

Therefore, if Hickey felt he was about to be grievously wronged,
he could come forward and demonstrate why Donahue's conclusions

---

*The following conversations have been reconstructed from the recollections of Howard and
Katie Donahue.

were in error. He could instruct his attorney to write the *Sun* and Donahue threatening a libel suit. He could ask the Secret Service to publicly come to his defense.

He'd done none of that. If Hickey had been badgered repeatedly to address a string of groundless theories involving him, it would be understandable if he stopped responding to inquiries. But as far as Donahue knew, Hickey had never been approached by anyone since the Warren Commission, and certainly not by anyone suggesting that Hickey himself was the answer to the mystery. Hickey's silence further convinced Donahue that his theory was worth pursuing.

But Katie knew there was probably a more fundamental reason why her husband was unlikely to force a showdown with the agent. Confrontation just wasn't Howard's style. He was an investigator unsurpassed in sifting the physical evidence from the scene of the crime, as his long and remarkable assassination probe had shown. He was not, however, by nature a prosecutor. Whatever it took to face a man down and accuse him of inadvertently shooting the President . . . for better or worse, Howard didn't have it. He was fundamentally a deferential man who avoided criticizing others, a person who instinctively liked others and wanted very much to be liked in turn.

In fact, from the moment Donahue concluded Hickey fired the fatal shot, he'd been determined, come what may, to treat the agent with the respect he believed Hickey deserved. And he didn't believe Hickey needed to be harassed in his home. Not by him, anyway.

Colleen Donahue remembered her father's reluctance to confront Hickey.

"He didn't want to call him up or drive down to his house or send him letters because he felt the man was a victim," Colleen said. "I think his biggest fear was that Hickey would freak out and kill himself and my father would feel responsible."

Given the extent to which questions about the assassination had gnawed away at the country for so many years, a less compassionate person might have responded differently and couched his or her arguments in cries of anger against those who covered up the accident and even against Hickey himself. But that wasn't Howard. In fact, the more he thought about it, the more he was inclined to believe the government had probably made the right decision in keeping the truth from the American public in 1963. The trauma of the assassination had been terrible enough. There could have been no way of knowing how the American people would have reacted to news that Kennedy had been killed accidentally.

Of course, as time advanced, this lack of candor had spawned many demons. Despite the empathy Donahue felt for Hickey, and it was considerable, he realized revelation of the truth was imperative now and long overdue. The American people deserved no less. Katie felt much the same way. But she still thought it important to try to reach Hickey one more time. And so, one summer evening in 1977, she sat down with a tape recorder and started to talk.

Addressing the Secret Service agent, she introduced herself and explained that her husband had studied the assassination for many years and had concluded that Hickey had fired the fatal shot.*

"I realize you're probably aware of Howard's conclusions from the article in the *Baltimore Sun* in May, and I could certainly understand that you'd be very angry at him for bringing this out.

"But I want you to know that Howard is not a vindictive man and feels, as I do, a great deal of compassion for you and all you've been through. I can't pretend to understand how you must have felt when you realized what you'd done. To me, it seems like the kind of thing that would be almost too much for one person to bear."

Katie added she assumed Hickey must have been instructed never to reveal what had happened that day, but soon Howard would go before the Assassinations Committee hearings and tell all he knew to the world. She wanted Hickey to know that, she said, and she asked him again if he'd be willing to meet with Howard or Ralph to set the record straight. In closing, Katie earnestly, if somewhat naively, assured Hickey that both she and Howard would do all they could to help him obtain good legal representation and would fight to prevent the government from stripping him of his pension, if it came to that.

Then she mailed the tape by certified mail. A receipt came back with Hickey's heavy, sharply scrawled signature on it a few days later, indicating he'd received the package. Only time would tell whether the agent would respond. But Katie slept a little easier. She'd done what she could.

The summer of 1977 was all but gone as Howard labored to reestablish his work routine from the days before publication of the *Sun* article. This was not easy, due to a deluge of requests to provide expert ballistics testimony. After reading of Howard's knowledge of weapons and bullet behavior, lawyers from all over Baltimore began calling to ask if he could help in this or that gunshot case. Although the courtroom responsibilities stretched him ever thinner, Donahue took on as much of the work as he could. The money was good and he enjoyed the challenges each case posed.

One of these cases demonstrated again how easily accidental discharges happened when guns were around and, as far as Donahue was concerned, bore a telling resemblance to the tragedy he believed had taken place in the back seat of the Secret Service car.

The police department called Donahue in to investigate the shooting of a motorcyclist by a policeman. The police department presented Donahue with the physical evidence but didn't allow him to interview any of the parties involved. There was considerable contro-

*The following quotes have been reconstructed from the recollections of Howard and Katie Donahue.

versy surrounding the case, and police officials were anxious to see what kind of conclusions an independent investigator might reach.

The facts were these: A policeman pulled over a young motorcyclist for speeding. The youth was a known troublemaker. Consequently, the cop drew his revolver as he approached the suspect. When it was over, the kid was shot through the head.

Donahue eventually deduced that the officer must have lost his footing on a particularly steep highway embankment as he was putting the young man up against the cruiser to search him. Although the patrolman had his pistol pointed into the air, the gun apparently tilted forward slightly when he slipped and a convulsive muscular reaction caused him to accidentally pull the trigger. The bullet pierced the young man's helmet, entered his skull, exited near the top of his head, and went back out through the helmet. Mercifully and remarkably, the bullet passed directly between both cerebral hemispheres and caused no mortal damage. The young man, in fact, made a full recovery.

Donahue's understanding of the episode confirmed the story told by the police officer, who was not charged in the shooting, and demonstrated the kind of involuntary physical reaction Donahue believed Hickey must have experienced when he fell over backward with the AR-15.

In addition to the expert testimony work, Donahue began to receive requests to make presentations on his theory to civic groups and schools in the Baltimore area. The first of these came through Reppert. A Rotary Club member from Havre de Grace, Maryland, called to say he'd been intrigued by Reppert's article and asked if Mr. Donahue would be willing to present his theory at the group's monthly dinner meeting. Reppert told Donahue of the offer and the latter quickly accepted. Not much later, both men found themselves facing a room full of attentive listeners at the Rotary Club hall.

Donahue took the podium after dinner and delivered a forty-minute presentation outlining his theory. He used photographs and a hand-drawn chart of the bullet trajectories for visual aids. When he'd finished, the club members, mostly businessmen and their wives, responded with sustained applause and immediately began peppering the gunsmith with questions. One young woman stood up and said that while she was no ballistics expert, Donahue's evidence seemed to her logical and compelling. For all that, the woman wondered, if this scenario was really true, how was it that the real facts surrounding the President's death had never come out in the fourteen years since the assassination?*

"Look at it this way," the woman said. "If you were a Secret Service agent, one of ten or twelve who saw it, wouldn't you go home

---

*The following conversation has been reconstructed from the recollections of Howard and Katie Donahue.

and, after a couple of tossing-and-turning nights, finally break down
and tell your wife? And about five years after that, wouldn't she in a
moment of weakness mention it to a friend or a relative? And a
couple of years later, wouldn't that person break their promise of
secrecy and tell somebody else? It seems like the truth would have
gotten out, even if all those with firsthand knowledge gave blood
oaths of secrecy.''

The question was well taken and went to the weakest link in
Donahue's theory.

''Well, I agree it seems unlikely,'' Donahue responded. ''But very
big secrets have been kept before. Take, for instance the British effort
that cracked the German communication codes in World War II. This
was an extremely important project that helped turn the tide of the
war. Hundreds of people were involved, yet the facts didn't come out
until long after the war was over. Even then, a number of top
intelligence officials were extremely upset that the information had
been revealed.

''There was also the construction and operation of the *Glomar
Explorer,* the ship Howard Hughes built for the CIA to recover a
sunken Soviet sub. Thousands of people were involved in building
and operating this ship, yet the truth remained buried for years.

''And of course there was Kennedy's philandering. His romps were
many and widely known, not just by the presidential staff and the
Secret Service, but also among the Washington press corps. But no
one spilled the beans until Judith Exner, a mistress to the mob, broke
the silence long after Kennedy's death.''

Donahue added that it was a predictable, if perilous, logical trap to
assume that since the facts surrounding the accident had never come
out, the accident therefore must never have occurred. The fundamental and inescapable fact was, he said, that a rigorous analysis of the
evidence pointed to no other conclusion.

On this central question of why the facts have apparently remained
hidden for so long, perhaps future generations will possess insight or
information not available at present. It does seem remarkable that
such a startling event, if true, would not have been revealed, particularly in view of the fact that no murder in American history had been
more thoroughly probed, analyzed, dissected, scrutinized, and pondered as Kennedy's.

Then again, much of that analysis was flawed and a number of
critically important facts were missed. Consequently, the many theories born from these efforts in the end served only to submerge the
possibility of an accident that much deeper. This colossal diversion-
ary effect was perhaps quietly welcomed by those who may have
actually understood what had occurred.

It is also true that there is no telling how many of the received and
accepted explanations of major events of the past are in fact not the
way things happened at all. It is perhaps naive to think that if two

dozen people know the truth, the truth must come out; obviously, if successful multiperson cover-ups *have* prevailed in history, we would, by definition, be unaware of it.

But all of this thinking assumed that many people did know about Hickey's role, and Donahue was not at all sure that had to be the case. For years to come he would even reflect on the possibility that Hickey himself was unsure about what had happened.

If there *were* people in the know, they obviously would have had little incentive for disclosing the facts themselves. Unlike the *Glomar Explorer* or cracking the Axis codes in World War II, the accident that killed Kennedy was a very different kind of secret. It was not a crime but a mistake; something no one could ever be proud of. It was a stain on Kennedy's legacy, a stain on the Secret Service, and a terrible stain on one unfortunate man. Hence, there would be no kudos or congratulations for anyone even remotely connected with the events in Dallas if the facts were to emerge. Yet beyond those who were involved, directly or indirectly, virtually no one else was in a position to know what had happened.

The facts, then, were self-limiting and restricted to a small but powerful constellation of people whose interest was well served by continued suppression of the truth. The Secret Service wasn't going to tell. The Kennedys weren't going to tell. And Earl Warren, if he knew, wasn't going to tell. For him to reveal the truth after the Warren Commission's investigation had concluded—assuming he knew it—would have been to link his name forever to a massive and artfully constructed fraud.

On the other hand, Warren might have become a hero by blowing the whistle before the Commission's work had finished. But again, to have done so would have been to admit the government had lied about the assassination from the start. Such an admission was clearly untenable. It is not hard to imagine the nation's top judge gravely weighing the cost and benefits of revealing the accident and deciding that, at least in this case, truth could justifiably be sacrificed for the good of all. The fact of the matter was, Lee Harvey Oswald had tried to kill the President. That he didn't succeed, that the fatal shot was accidentally fired by someone else, changed nothing. Indeed, the whole sorry scenario would never have unfolded if Oswald hadn't pulled the trigger in the first place. In that sense, Oswald bore complete responsibility for what happened.

If Warren had rationalized the cover-up, of course, he probably hadn't foreseen the conflagration of doubt the Warren Report would ignite. Had he been able to, maybe he would have chosen a different path, if for no other reason than to protect his good name. Yet by the time the public skepticism and indignation raged around him, it was too late for Earl Warren. He was trapped by his decision and had no choice but to live with its results.

Finally, the kind of hearsay confirmation the young woman alluded to in her question had indeed trickled out, at least as far as Donahue was concerned. It seemed unlikely the man who reported that his relative heard Kennedy was killed by his bodyguards when the relative worked at the National Security Agency had made that up. Likewise, why would the drunken Secret Service agent have nonchalantly said that Kennedy was killed by his own bodyguard unless he had some reason to believe it was true? At the time he'd said it, Reppert's story had not yet appeared.

The question and answer session at the Rotary Club that evening went on for some time until club leaders finally shut it down around midnight. Like the letters to the editor that poured into the *Sun* following Reppert's article, the intense interest shown by the dinner guests confirmed there was something very appealing in the stark, scientific simplicity of what Donahue was saying. Once again, the overriding emotional response seemed to be one of relief. Like the crying woman who called the day after the *Sun* article ran, the Rotary audience appeared thankful to learn the shooting was probably an accident; grateful the government wasn't covering up something far worse.

Of course, Donahue's understanding of the fatal shot in no way precluded the possibility that Oswald was involved in some kind of conspiracy; that larger, darker forces were indeed at work in Dealey Plaza. But at the same time, that possibility and all that went with it was unarguably diminished if one believed that only Oswald and Hickey fired guns that day, and that the final shot was an accident.

More lectures followed. To better make his case, Donahue assembled a slide show of pertinent photos and diagrams and polished and expanded his talk. After each lecture, the audience response was very much the same; astonishment, acceptance, and relief characterized the average person's reaction. Younger audiences seemed particularly interested in what Donahue had to say. More than once a college-age person would stand up and ask whether the agent— Donahue still was not naming him publicly—perhaps hadn't pulled the trigger on purpose.

Donahue would reiterate that he did not and could not believe that, that everything pointed toward a freak accident, that experience had taught him accidents happened too often when guns were around, particularly in the chaos of combat-type situations. Few apparently doubted Donahue on this point. But the question reflected the abiding cynicism of the times and showed how deeply the assassination conspiracy theories had taken hold.

So it went through summer and fall. Donahue's fees for the talks was one hundred dollars and up, depending on the resources of the audience. He spoke at civic clubs, area universities, junior colleges, radio talk shows, and later, local television programs. He enjoyed the appearances; they were an opportunity to make some extra money and a chance to get the story out as he waited for word back from the Assassinations Committee.

That word still hadn't come by the end of 1977, but Donahue remained optimistic. He was heartened that at least the committee's investigation was finally moving forward under the new and presumably effective leadership of G. Robert Blakey.

Blakey, the new chief counsel, came to the investigation in July from Cornell University Law School, where he'd taught law and been director of the school's Institute on Organized Crime. The latter post reflected Blakey's long-standing interest in the Mafia. In 1959, Blakey served as counsel to the McClellan Committee, the congressional probe into mob racketeering that put the Kennedy brothers' duels with Jimmy Hoffa in the national spotlight. From there he went on to Bobby Kennedy's Justice Department in 1961 and served as a prosecutor in the department's antiracketeering division until after the assassination. Blakey then retreated to academia, where he played a major role in authoring the so-called RICO statute, a prosecutory tool that has proven highly effective in nailing mobsters, fraud artists and con men. Blakey also penned several books on the mob.

Now that he'd returned to Washington, the attorney wasted little time in making his presence known. He quickly seized complete control of the committee's activities. Blakey decided whom the committee would interview and whom they would skip, which leads would be pursued and which would not, who would be hired, who would be fired, and what the overall investigative agenda would be.[2]

No doubt the committee needed strong guidance after so many months adrift on the political rip tides of Washington. But Blakey's tactics nonetheless alienated some and raised questions about how rigorous his investigation was going to be.[3] Early on, in fact, Blakey announced that henceforth the committee would not look at any new evidence in the assassinations of King and Kennedy, but would rely instead on the old evidence assembled by law enforcement agencies over the years.[4] This was an astonishing statement, given that presumably the purpose of the congressional investigation was to uncover exactly the kind of new data Blakey now said was not needed. Blakey must have had his reasons for this dramatic, some would say inexplicable, reduction in the scope of the investigations, but they were not apparent to those who still believed the committee would make an all-out effort to ferret out the truth.

The new chief counsel further estranged many both inside and outside the committee by consolidating his authority behind a shroud of secrecy. This curtain began to descend with his first announcement to the press: "The purpose of this news conference is to announce there will be no more news conferences."[5] Blakey tightened his grip on the committee's information flow by requiring that all staff members sign nondisclosure agreements as a condition of employment. The agreements barred staffers from revealing anything about the committee's work; in fact they prohibited employees from even disclosing that they worked for the committee. And if the secrecy order was ever violated, the committee could come after the offender in the courts, even long after the committee's work was finished.[6] This emphasis on secrecy seemed to critics wrongheaded and, like the decision to ignore new evidence, completely at odds with the idea and spirit behind the committee's formation in the first place.

Nonetheless, the committee did exist and it was working; no small accomplishments considering all that had gone before. At least Blakey managed to avoid the kind of political pungee sticks that had impaled his predecessor. A key House procedural vote in October 1977 reflected surprisingly broad support for the committee and seemed to signal the investigation finally had the kind of congressional mandate needed to effectively pursue the twin probes.[7] *The New York Times* proclaimed this overwhelming 290–112 vote, which essentially gave the committee unrestricted subpoena power, "the most significant recent development" in the committee's yearlong history.[8]

And if some of Blakey's tactical decisions arguably undermined the scope and methods of the investigation and perhaps damaged morale, he did double the committee's staff from 56 to 114 and he boosted the number of field investigators from five to 28. At the very least, it seemed the committee would have the resources to do the job.[9]

Donahue was willing to give Blakey and the committee the benefit of the doubt. There was still no word by late 1977 about when the public hearings would be, but Howard was hopeful he'd be among the first to testify when that day finally arrived. Even now, he thought, the investigators were probably collecting evidence and interviews to corroborate his theory. Maybe they'd even spoken with Hickey.

Meanwhile, Donahue stayed busy. During that fall of 1977, he was contacted by Blaine Taylor, editor of the *Maryland State Medical Journal,* with a proposition. Taylor had penned a laudatory letter to the *Baltimore Sun* after seeing Reppert's article and he was very much impressed with Donahue's analytical skills and ballistic expertise. As a result, Taylor asked if the gunsmith would be willing to write an article for the journal that would rebut a study published a few months earlier attacking the Commission's single bullet theory. Donahue agreed and the piece ran in February 1978 under the title "Was the Magic Bullet Really Magic?" Donahue's article laid out succinct evidence that he believed supported the conclusion that a single bullet fired by Oswald did in fact wound both Kennedy and Connally. The gunsmith's theory about the origin of the fatal head shot was only obliquely addressed, though Taylor did mention it and the *Sun* article in the introduction.

The months were racing past now. Like Howard, Katie had been hopeful about the prospect of action by the House committee after the meeting the previous July with Moriarty, the former homicide detective. But by the spring of 1978, Katie was starting to sense something was not right. Her suspicions stemmed primarily from the fact that neither she nor Howard had had any further contact with the committee after Conzelman's call and his goofy question about the pristine bullet. And the several times Howard had left messages for staffers, the calls were not returned. It seemed reasonable to Katie that if the committee were actually pursuing Howard's conclusions, they would get back in touch to confer on particular details. At the very least they should have returned Howard's calls. That was just common courtesy.

Although Katie would occasionally express these concerns to Howard, he'd tell her not to worry. The committee was busy, he'd say. We'll hear back from them soon enough. But the days kept folding into months and months into seasons and still no word came. Katie was becoming ever more agitated. Even Howard's faith was starting to fade. Consequently, in April of 1978, nine months after the meeting in Washington, Katie did what most people do when they have a problem with the federal government.

She called her congressman.

Clarence D. Long was a Democratic representative for the Second District of Maryland and his office had helped Katie before. Katie called a woman she knew there and explained the situation. The staffer listened sympathetically and agreed to set up an appointment for the Donahues to meet with Long the following week in Washington. Katie informed Howard of her plan when he returned home from work that evening.*

"Howard, I'm going to Washington to see Clarence Long about the committee next week. You can come with me, or you can stay here. But I'm going to talk to him. I just feel like the committee is jerking you around and I intend to do something about it."

This was the first Howard knew of the scheme, but he wasn't surprised. Katie was a stubborn woman once her ire was up. She wouldn't back down from anyone. Howard knew that, and he knew that if Katie thought something was wrong, well, it probably was. So he didn't need much convincing to go with her to the meeting in Washington. If nothing else, perhaps Long could give them some idea of what the committee was up to.

Congressman Long was a tall, white-haired man who'd been an economics professor before winning his congressional seat in the early 1960s. Now he greeted the Donahues with a gentle charm and warmly ushered them into his office. Howard briefly explained his involvement in the CBS reenactment, his subsequent investigation and his eventual conclusions about the fatal bullet's explosive effect, its trajectory, and its origin. He emphasized the importance of the

---

*The following conversation has been reconstructed from the recollections of Howard and Katie Donahue.

neutron activation results and the samples of the brain tissue; how they could quickly prove him right or wrong, and he showed Long a copy of the *Sun* article.

Then Katie explained how they'd met with committee investigators the previous July, how at the time she and Howard had thought the investigators would make a sincere effort to pursue Howard's theory; that Howard would be called to testify.*

"However now," she said, "I have my doubts."

Long listened, then scanned Reppert's story. A few minutes later, the congressman gazed up over his reading glasses and said, "Well, this is certainly a very compelling case you've constructed here, Mr. Donahue. Very compelling indeed. Now tell me, what is it you want me to do?"

Katie pressed on. "Congressman Long, we'd appreciate it very much if you could turn up the heat on the committee. We want to know if they're pursuing this, if they plan to let Howard testify. The American people aren't paying however many millions for this investigation just so the truth can be hidden one more time."

Long listened intently, nodded gravely, then buzzed one of his aides and asked the young man to get him the number of the committee. The staffer returned and Long promptly dialed and asked for Tannenbaum, the head of the committee team conducting the Kennedy side of the investigation. The investigator wasn't available, but Gary Cornwell, deputy chief counsel on the Kennedy side, was. Presently Long had him on the line.

"Mr. Cornwell, Congressman Clarence Long. How do you do, sir. Ah . . . Mr. Cornwell, I have two of my constituents, Mr. and Mrs. Howard Donahue of Towson, Maryland, in the office here and they've informed me of the work Mr. Donahue has done investigating the Kennedy assassination. And I must say, his conclusions are quite remarkable. Now, they've told me they've been in contact with your people, but unfortunately I think they've gotten the impression that this matter is not being actively pursued by your staff.

"Therefore, I'd like very much for you to meet with them and apprise them of your investigation. It seems Mr. Donahue's work could potentially be of great service to this country. . . . No . . . No, I don't think that will do. They've come down from Baltimore today and I would like you to meet with them today, if possible. . . . Fine, I'll send them over with one of my staff members. Thank you, Mr. Cornwell. This is a matter of considerable interest to me, and I trust I'll be kept abreast of developments."

The Donahues were dazzled at Long's prompt intervention on their behalf and delighted to gain instant access to one of the top administrators in the committee. Thanking the congressman, they left with

---

*The following conversation has been reconstructed from the recollections of Howard and Katie Donahue.

his press secretary, Jerry Ruden, and within the hour were in Cornwell's office nearby.

Cornwell was a top man in the Kennedy probe and a Blakey recruit. He'd come to the committee from the Justice Department's Organized Crime Strike Force in Kansas City. Blakey described him as a "tough, hard-driving investigative prosecutor."[10] Long's press secretary made introductions, and once again Donahue briefly explained his work and his meeting with committee investigators that previous July.*

"The fact is, I'm wondering if you people are pursuing this," Donahue said. "I'm starting to get the impression that you're not. I've tried to call Mr. Moriarty, Mr. Conzelman and Mr. Klein several times but received no response. What's going on, Mr. Cornwell?"

Cornwell assured Donahue that many different theories were being pursued simultaneously and that while committee investigators were quite busy, they undoubtedly would be back in touch. To Howard and Katie, however, it appeared Cornwell didn't really take Donahue, Congressman Long, or this encounter very seriously at all.

Donahue persisted. He asked what progress the committee was making in obtaining the neutron activation tests. Cornwell responded by saying that, unfortunately, he was prohibited by the rules of the committee from disclosing what the committee had or hadn't found.

"I wish I could tell you more, but honestly my hands are tied," Cornwell said as he sucked his pipe and leaned back in his chair.

"Well," Donahue said, "at least tell me if you've found the edge scrapings, the tissue samples taken from around the entrance wound. They're extremely important. The bullet jacket would have left tiny flakes of metal as it entered the scalp and if you subjected those flakes to neutron activation, it would show immediately what kind of bullet it was. You could prove me right or wrong that quickly, Mr. Cornwell."

Cornwell demurred. He said he'd never heard of any edge scrapings and didn't know where they might be.

Katie had stayed quiet long enough.

"Mr. Cornwell. I really don't feel you're taking Howard seriously. You say you can't do this, you don't know that. I think Howard should be given the opportunity to testify. The American people have every right to hear what he has to say. If his conclusions are wrong, you should be able to destroy him on the stand with any number of experts. But I'm getting tired of—"

Howard kicked her under the table.

"—of you people giving him the short shrift, which is exactly what is going on here today."

Cornwell was inert, vaguely distracted.

---

*The following conversation has been reconstructed based on the recollections of Howard and Katie Donahue.

"Believe me, Mrs. Donahue, we're doing all we can to establish what actually happened in Dallas," he said. "We appreciate your husband's interest and input very much, and, as I say, the field investigators will no doubt be in contact as soon as they can. Now, unless there's anything else . . ."

So there it was. The Donahues retreated. As they drove home, Howard pondered the look on Cornwell's face, the vacant, expressionless eyes.

"It was the exact same look Olivier gave me up at Edgewood Arsenal when I told him the shooting was probably an accident," he said ruefully. "It's the government mask; it's the way they all respond. Devoid of expression. Nothing that would reveal anything. Complete camouflage."

Several gloomy days later, the Donahues received a letter from Long. The congressman informed them that Cornwell had looked into it and reported he could find no edge scrapings made during the autopsy. The letter went on to say that:

> Mr. Cornwell suggests that you send him the articles that mention the edge sections at the Assassinations Committee office.
>
> I personally will be inspecting the files on Agent George Hickey this week, and will bring up any questions I have directly with Mr. Cornwell.
>
> If I can ever be of any further assistance, please let me know.

The article noting the existence of the edge scrapings appeared in the November 27, 1972, issue of *Modern Medicine* magazine and was written by Cyril Wecht, the coroner who'd testified before the Rockefeller Commission and who was now one of the physicians on the committee's eight-member medical panel. Donahue sent the article to Cornwell and pointed out that the edge scrapings were also referenced in the supplemental autopsy report included in Volume 16 of the Warren Report.

Long's press secretary, Jerry Ruden, called a week or so later to report that while the edge scrapings had obviously been made, Cornwell had looked once more and could find no record of them anywhere. Ruden said Cornwell suspected the samples may have been destroyed by the FBI. The press secretary didn't say why Cornwell thought the FBI might have done this. And he didn't say anything about what Long found when he looked in Hickey's file.

In fact, the only other communication from Long's office came about a month later, when the congressman forwarded a copy of the following letter written by Blakey himself.

Dear Congressman Long:

The letter of your constituent, Howard Donahue, dated April 7, 1978,

which you forwarded to the Committee, and the article enclosed
with his correspondence of April 17, 1978 inquire as to the present
whereabouts of ". . . flesh and bone wound edge tissues . . ." and
bullet fragments taken from President Kennedy's skull because
of their reported relevance for Neutron Activation Analysis (N.A.A.)
testing to identify ". . . the fatal bullet . . ."

Although the Committee is generally restricted from commenting
on the substance or procedure of its investigation you may feel free to
report to Mr. Donahue that the Select Committee is aware of the
importance of Neutron Activation Analysis, is cognizant of the
materials which can be tested by procedure, and will subject all such
relevant materials to appropriate analysis. The Select Committee
has obtained from the FBI all material in their possession which is
relevant to this testing.

With respect to the tissue materials which are mentioned in Mr.
Donahue's correspondence, they were not included in the October 26,
1966 inventory of items turned over to the United States by Mrs.
Kennedy, as noted in the very article Mr. Donahue enclosed. There-
fore, these materials were not turned over to the United States
(National Archives) at that time, nor is there any evidence that the
FBI ever obtained possession of them.

You may inform Mr. Donahue that the Select Committee appreci-
ates the importance of these materials and does not consider the
matter closed, and that we are grateful for his input and continued
interest in this matter.

Sincerely,
G. Robert Blakey

To Donahue, the letter was significant as much for what it didn't
say as for what it did. Nowhere did Blakey suggest, as Cornwell
apparently did, that the FBI had destroyed the evidence. In fact,
Blakey made a point of saying that as far as he knew, the FBI never
had possession of the all-important tissue samples. Even more telling
to Donahue was the fact that at no point did Blakey acknowledge the
idea that Donahue was putting forward, namely, that Hickey had
shot the President. It seemed unlikely that this was an oversight; the
letter's language was too carefully crafted for that. Perhaps, Donahue
figured, Blakey wanted nothing on the record that would show he
was aware of what Donahue was suggesting.

Yet Blakey must have known. The idea that the chief counsel of
the investigation would have taken the time to write Long without
understanding just who Donahue was and why he was so interested
in the edge samples and the neutron activation results simply didn't
wash. Not when one took into account the Donahues' previous
meetings with Cornwell and Moriarty and Blakey's penchant for
micromanaging the investigation.

As far as Long went, Donahue didn't know what to think. The congressman's sudden and unexplained disengagement from the issue seemed odd. It was, of course, quite possible that Long simply assumed the committee was now taking Howard's conclusions seriously and hence quickly forgot about the matter altogether.

Alternatively, perhaps Long was told by committee investigators that Donahue was some kind of kook; that his theory was ridiculous. Or maybe the investigators simply ducked behind their familiar veil of secrecy and informed Long that, while they appreciated his interest, they really could say no more about the matter.

Not for the last time, the Donahues were left feeling abandoned and misled. There was still a chance Howard would be called to testify at the public hearings. But it was a remote chance. Again time passed, and again and not surprisingly, no word came.

And so it was that Howard and Katie headed for Washington in September of 1978 for the committee's public hearings. They were determined to make one final attempt to present publicly the information Howard had assembled.

The hearings were held in one of the massive, block-square House Office Buildings near the Capitol. Arriving early, the Donahues managed to get seats near the front of the room. The day progressed as witnesses took the stand, one by one, to testify on the vast minutia of assassination facts and rumors the committee was sifting through. Finally, at a break in the action, Donahue flagged a passing staff member and, identifying himself, suggested that perhaps his request to testify had been misplaced. The young staffer said he'd look into it and report back. But the staffer never returned and the day's hearings drew to a close. Just maybe, Donahue thought, his chance to testify would come when the hearings continued the following day.

The Capitol Hill traffic was horrendous the next morning as Katie searched for a place to park. Ever resourceful, she simply pulled up behind a line of orange cones in an area reserved for congressmen adjacent to the side entrance of the building.

"Mr. Donahue here for the Kennedy hearings," she announced to a policeman stationed on the curb. Apparently mistaking the white-haired, sharply dressed Donahue for a congressman, the officer promptly opened the car door on Howard's side and, ignoring Katie, escorted Donahue into the building.

The couple again found their seats near the front of room. Again Howard spoke to a staff member and questioned whether his written requests to testify had been misplaced. But the day wore on and no one made any effort to inform Donahue when, or if, he would be testifying.

Back in Baltimore that evening, an increasingly agitated Katie managed to put through a call to Moriarty. At their first meeting, Moriarty was the one member of the committee's staff who'd seemed most supportive of Donahue's work. What's more, he was a former homicide detective with the District of Columbia police force. If anyone on the committee staff had the background to grasp the ballistic and forensic evidence Donahue had assembled, he did.

Moriarty agreed to have breakfast with the Donahues the next day. The couple met him and two subcommittee staff researchers, Jim Conzelman and a man named Williams, early in the morning at a bustling Capitol Hill cafeteria. Conzelman had also been present at that first encounter months earlier; he was the one who'd called Katie a day or so later with the question about the pristine bullet.

Donahue again outlined the evidence he'd assembled and, as emphatically as he could, reiterated what he believed to be the ballistic irrefutability of his conclusions. When he'd finished, Moriarty looked him straight in the eye.*

"Mr. Donahue," Moriarty said. "I have to tell you . . . I was talking about your work with Bob Blakey, the committee's chief counsel, and frankly, it's my opinion that he's never going to allow you to testify. I don't know what his problem is. But I don't think he's going to let you testify."

Donahue leaned forward in his chair. "Why is he against letting me speak?" he said. "It's not like I don't have some qualifications."

Moriarty's reply seemed desultory and evasive. As the meeting broke up, Moriarty said he would talk to Congressman Louis Stokes, the Ohio Democrat who chaired the subcommittee, tell him of the meeting, and do what he could.

Howard and Katie made their way to the hearing room. About midmorning, Williams, one of the researchers who'd been present at the breakfast meeting, came up, leaned over, and told Howard that the possibility of testifying was looking doubtful. He didn't say why, but added: "You should pass a note up to Stokes and ask him directly if you can speak. I'm serious. You have some valuable information and the committee ought to hear it."

Katie promptly scribbled a note to Stokes. "Howard Donahue is seated down on the floor, he has information pertinent to the hearings and requests permission to testify."

She beckoned a page and instructed the young woman to take the note to the representative. Stokes sat with other congressmen on a raised podium area at the front of the room. Katie watched as the page made her way to the front and presented the note. Stokes studied it briefly, said something, then handed it back. The page returned to Katie and reported that Congressman Stokes would not allow Mr. Donahue to testify.

"On what grounds?" Katie asked. When the page said she did not know, Katie told her to go find out.

---

*The following conversations have been reconstructed from the recollections of Howard and Katie Donahue.

"Because he has not been scheduled to testify," the page said upon her return.

Katie was furious. After the hearings ended, she found a pay phone and dialed the subcommittee offices. Moriarty and Williams were not available, so she asked for Conzelman.

"Mr. Conzelman, this is ridiculous," Katie announced, her voice unsteady with rage. "Howard is the only one here with any information that makes any sense, and you people are refusing to even listen to him. He is a qualified firearms expert. You can't simply ignore what he says.

"Now, I want you to understand that we will not be muzzled and that we are not leaving Washington until Howard has been heard. We are prepared to come over there and sit in the lobby of your office and I will create a disturbance unless we get to talk to someone. You can lock me up if you want, but Howard is going to have his say."

Conzelman said he would try to round up some investigators for Howard to talk with. He told Katie to stand by and he would call her right back. A few minutes later, Conzelman reported that he'd found several investigators who would listen to Donahue.

"Fine," Katie snapped. "We'll go to the car to get Howard's slide projector and we'll be right up."

The couple was waiting at a bank of elevators a few minutes later when G. Robert Blakey walked past. Blakey was the balding, heavy-eyed Cornell law professor who served as the committee's chief counsel and, according to Moriarty, the official who would not let Donahue speak publicly.

"Professor Blakey, I'm Katie Donahue. This is my husband, Howard. May we speak with you for a moment?" Katie offered as she approached the attorney.

Blakey shot her an icy, imperious stare, glanced at Howard, and then, without so much as a word, turned his back, stepped into the crowded elevator, and was gone. The Donahues were mystified by the encounter, but it only redoubled their resolve to make the most of the upcoming audience with the staff investigators. If Blakey wouldn't listen, perhaps his people would.

At the committee offices, Conzelman ushered the Donahues into a small room. Moriarty and several other investigators appeared moments later.*

"Okay, what is it you're so eager to show us, Mr. Donahue?" one of the newcomers asked. His tone was brusque and condescending.

Howard set up his slide projector, turned down the lights, and quickly got to the heart of his thesis. He explained each photograph and diagram and described in detail how the pictures related to the ballistic and forensic evidence he'd assembled. He spoke for twenty

---

*The following conversations have been reconstructed from the recollections of Howard and Katie Donahue.

minutes. When he turned up the lights, the investigators stared at him in silence. Finally, one of the men said he needed to get something and walked out of the room. A few moments later, the man returned with a large, blown-up photograph of Zapruder frame 312, the frame that recorded the instant before Kennedy was hit by the bullet that destroyed a large part of his skull.

"Mr. Donahue," the investigator said in that officious, self-important voice so common in Washington. "Obviously, you have reached your conclusions as a result of erroneous information."

According to the expert, Kennedy's head was actually turned much farther to the left than frame 312 seemed to indicate. Ergo, the investigator said, the gunsmith's conclusions about the bullet's trajectory were wrong.

But Howard had studied the Zapruder film as long and hard as any man alive. He was incredulous that this "expert" could actually claim Kennedy was turned nearly 90 degrees to the left when the photograph clearly showed this was not the case at all. "Hell . . . that's absurd," Donahue erupted. "His head was nearly profile when the bullet hit; turned just slightly to the left. For Christ's sake, look at him!" (See illustration 19.)

Another awkward silence followed. The expert picked up his photograph and left the room. The meeting broke up. As the group filed out into the hall, Donahue pulled Moriarty aside and asked him what was going on.

"Listen, I've got to run now," the investigator said. "But I'll give you a call and we can talk about this, okay?"

The Donahues made their way back to the car. Katie fought back tears as they drove out of Washington.

"What are we going to do now, Howard?" she asked. "Did what that man said about the picture make any sense? Why won't they give us the time of day? They treated us like we were a couple of idiots."

Howard assured his wife the investigator's explanation of the Zapruder picture was absurd. But if the experience with Blakey's committee had been distressing, he said, it was also instructive. Donahue was, after all, a qualified firearms expert. For that reason, it would be difficult for congressional investigators to dismiss him as yet one more assassination oddball. Yet that was exactly what they had done. Obviously, they had no intention of examining the evidence he had assembled.

As the couple made their way north along Interstate 95 in the gathering darkness, Howard's resolve to pursue his investigation was unshaken.

"Sooner or later," he reassured Katie, "the truth on this thing will come out."

13
BLAKEY'S $5 MILLION FOLLY

DONAHUE FOUND IT DIFFICULT TO FATHOM THE apparent bad faith the House Select Committee showed toward him and his theory, particularly in view of the flawed conclusions the committee eventually reached on its own. Had Donahue been a lawyer or a poultry farmer or a professor of philosophy, it might be a little easier to understand how his conclusions could have been so readily dismissed. Undoubtedly the assassination nuts were coming out of the woodwork through 1977 and 1978 and besieging investigators with one wild-eyed scheme after another.

But Donahue was not irresponsible. He was not an assassination gadfly. He was a veteran weapons examiner and firearms expert. His conclusions were grounded in that expertise. Furthermore, irrespective of Donahue's qualifications, the publication of the *Baltimore Sun* article made his theory a matter of public record and would seem to call for some sort of response from the committee.

There seems no justifiable explanation for why the committee responded to Donahue the way it did. The whole reason for the panel's existence was to get at the truth of what had happened in Dealey Plaza. And here the committee had been presented with a highly plausible scenario, developed carefully over a long period of time by an expert with excellent qualifications, which seemed to account for details not explained by any other reconstruction.

And yet they did nothing.

At the same time, there was one alternative theory they did choose to pursue that showed just how distorted their judgment had become.

In photos of the assassination, a man can be seen twirling a black umbrella along the curb of Elm Street just as the shots rang out. Given the man's presence at the murder scene, skeptics found his actions strange, particularly since the morning rain of November twenty-second had passed hours earlier. A Manchester, Massachusetts–based architect by the name of R. B. Cutler consequently came up with the notion that the "umbrella man" was in fact the assassin; that his umbrella was actually a sophisticated weapon that fired a rocket-powered, biodegradable dart into the President's neck.

Cutler's theory was a textbook example of the kind of absurd conjecture that for years had eclipsed the real facts of the case, yet the committee went to considerable lengths to identify the mystery man and prove or disprove Cutler's hypothesis. Admittedly, investigators were also looking into the slightly less inane theory that the man's umbrella represented some kind of signal to the assassin or assassins.

Newspaper advertisements seeking information about the umbrella man ran in the Dallas papers, and eventually a warehouse manager named Louie Steven Witt stepped forward. Witt was subpoenaed by the committee and testified publicly in late September 1978. He told the committee he had held up the umbrella as the President's limousine drove past in an obscure attempt to heckle Kennedy. Apparently a friend had informed Witt before the President's visit that the umbrella had been a "sore spot" with the Kennedy family ever since Joseph Kennedy, the President's father, had served as ambassador to Great Britain in the years before World War II. The umbrella was thought to symbolize the elder Kennedy's support for the appeasement policies of British Prime Minister Neville Chamberlain.[1]

With the infamous umbrella at his side, Witt admitted that his idea was a foolish one. He said he wished he'd never taken the thing to Dealey Plaza, whereupon committee chairman Louis Stokes insisted the umbrella be opened to prove it was not a weapon.

"Maybe you ought to turn it the other way," Stokes joked.[2]

That the committee could rationalize devoting time and resources to the umbrella man theory while ignoring the ballistic conclusions of a qualified firearms expert revealed at best a woefully incompetent and incomplete investigation.

In any event, when the committee's public hearings finally did get under way that September, it appeared at first that the investigation's conclusions would not differ significantly from those reached by the Warren Commission.

"You may get new insights into old problems," a committee spokesman told the press on September 5, 1978. "You will not necessarily get new results."[3]

The first witnesses to testify publicly were Governor Connally and his wife, Nellie. For nearly three hours on September 6, the Connallys recounted their vivid impressions of the shooting.

"There was no screaming in that horrible car," Mrs. Connally recalled. "It was just a silent, terrible ride. Our husbands were dying in our arms."[4]

For his part, the governor continued to maintain—as he had since the day after the shooting, the Warren Commission's conclusions notwithstanding—that the first shot Oswald had fired did not wound

both him and the President. Connally admitted it was possible a
single bullet had hit them both, but he reiterated he didn't think it
was the first.[5]

Donahue was convinced Connally's understanding of what had
happened was exactly correct. Oswald's first shot had missed, ricocheted, and struck Kennedy in the back of the head with the fragment
Dr. Fisher's panel had identified on the skull X rays in 1968. It was
Oswald's second bullet that had pierced the President's neck and
struck Connally. Although this first-miss scenario resolved a number
of long-standing controversies and strengthened the much maligned
single bullet theory, committee investigators never bothered to raise
the possibility during the governor's testimony. Apparently they were
as oblivious as the Warren Commission to the numerous Dealey
Plaza witnesses who had reported seeing a bullet hit the pavement
near the limousine.

It was more problematic, however, for the committee to ignore the
fragment Fisher had found on Kennedy's skull, and a second opportunity to explore the implications of the ricochet emerged the next
day when Michael Baden, chief medical examiner for New York City,
presented the findings of the committee's medical panel. Baden,
however, reported the fragment to be a one-dimensional metallic
smear that he claimed separated from the fatal bullet as the slug
impacted the skull.

Donahue heard this and shook his head. He'd looked into the shear
possibility in 1968 and he'd discussed it with several pathologists.
Each believed it virtually impossible for a tough, full metal–jacketed
round to perform in this manner. In any case, the question of the
fragment did not come up again during the hearings and was quickly
forgotten amid the torrent of medical evidence Baden presented. Nor
was it mentioned in the committee's final report.

Yet months later several details surfaced in the committee's own
documents that indicated Kennedy very likely was hit by not one,
but rather a barrage of ricochet fragments.

The medical evidence appendix published in early 1979 contained
reports from two radiologists who'd independently examined the
President's skull X rays. One of these physicians, Dr. G. M. Mc-
Donnel of Los Angeles, wrote that in addition to the Fisher fragment,
he'd identified a second bullet piece on the exterior of Kennedy's
skull. McDonnel's fragment was smaller than Fisher's and located
slightly to its left. Unlike the Fisher fragment, this new shard was not
attached to the bone but embedded in the galea, the tough, rubbery
membrane between the scalp and the skull.[6]

The presence of this second bullet piece obviously strengthened
Donahue's conclusions about the first-shot ricochet. So too did
information provided by the second outside expert, Dr. David O.
Davis, chairman of the radiology department at the George Washington University Hospital. Davis wrote that his examination of the

X rays revealed a number of small fragments that appeared to be dispersed across the right side of Kennedy's head in such a way as to suggest they were located not inside the skull, but outside it, embedded in the scalp.[7]

Davis said he was at a loss to explain where these fragments might have come from and his startling suggestion that the right side of Kennedy's scalp may have been peppered with lead did not make it into the medical panel's final report. As for the fragment discovered by McDonnel, the panel asserted that this fragment, like Fisher's, had probably sheared off the fatal bullet on impact.[8]

McDonnel, however, apparently was not totally in accord with this explanation. Instead, he proposed the two fragments may have somehow worked their way back out through the entrance wound and attached themselves to the outside of the skull and galea during the transport and handling of the President's body.[9]

To Donahue, this explanation was even more absurd than Baden's shear interpretation, since it would have been virtually impossible for the pieces to migrate from the point of the bullet's disintegration through the shredded, semisolid brain mass all the way back to the entrance wound, then pass through the small hole to affix themselves finally outside the skull. It was clear to Donahue that the experts never considered the possibility of a ricochet and hence were casting about for some way to explain the fragments' presence. This befuddlement was reflected in a transcript of the panel's interview with Dr. Humes. (See Appendix C.) As the group pondered how the Fisher fragment could have ended up where it did, panelist Dr. Joseph H. Davis gamely suggested that perhaps the piece punched back out through the scalp after the bullet began to break up.[10] Like McDonnel's explanation, this scenario defied the laws of physics and it was not embraced by Davis's colleagues. In the end, the panel had no choice but to fall back on the equally implausible explanation; that a full metal–jacketed round had sheared off two pieces of metal on impact.

Donahue, however, believed that the location of the fragments on both the rear and now the side of Kennedy's head precluded any possibility except a ricochet. This understanding was reinforced when he reexamined Zapruder frames 189–191, the interval he believed marked the moment Kennedy was struck by the ricochet fragments.

In the pictures, Kennedy's head is turned at a shallow angle to the right as the President waves to the crowds along Elm. This attitude put him in a perfect position to receive a hail of fragments in the top-rear and right side of the scalp, sprayed up and out after the first bullet struck the pavement to the right and rear of the limousine. Undoubtedly, the sting of these multiple penetrating wounds would have been extremely painful—painful enough to cause the President to cry out, "My God, I'm hit!"

As for the medical panel's findings regarding the whole of the medical evidence, predictably, in Donahue's opinion, they too suffered from a dearth of imagination and insight. According to Baden's committee testimony of September 7, 1978, the available evidence showed Kennedy was hit by two shots fired from above and behind.[11]

This was certainly true, but the doctor failed to mention anything about the direction of the wound channel across the President's brain, relative to the position of Kennedy's head at the moment the bullet hit. As far as Donahue was concerned, had this basic question been addressed, it would have become clear that Oswald could never have fired the last shot.

Likewise, Baden and the medical panel offered no explanation for how one of Oswald's bullets penetrated two men and remained virtually intact, while a second shot fired a few seconds later disintegrated into more than forty minute fragments. This inconsistency, like the trajectory, begged some kind of explanation. Yet neither question was confronted even obliquely in testimony or in the committee's final report.

No doubt the committee's pathologists reached their conclusions in good faith, Donahue figured. And certainly they were experienced, reportedly having been responsible for some 100,000 autopsies between them.[12] But it seemed doubtful this experience involved wounds inflicted by the highly destructive M-16. Fisher, himself one of the giants of American pathology, had acknowledged his own lack of ballistic expertise to Donahue back in 1968. "Well, you know more about guns than I do," Fisher said when Donahue first suggested the possibility of an accident. Apparently, a sophisticated understanding of weapons and bullet behavior was not a prerequisite with pathologists, even one so eminent as Fisher.

The cult of expertise—the nearly mystical and unassailable powers conferred upon those who claim vast knowledge in esoteric fields—may make it difficult to accept the idea that the medical and ballistic authorities relied upon in the congressional investigation of JFK's murder apparently had little more than an average understanding of weapons and ballistics. Yet the group's blindness to basic flaws in their own work clearly demonstrates this fact. The only other possibility is that the medical panel knowingly suppressed the evidence, and Donahue did not believe the physicians could have been so thoroughly compromised.

For him, though, it was a helpless, embittering experience to watch from the audience that day as Baden squandered a singular opportunity to set the record straight. Here was final proof that Donahue's repeated attempts to enlighten the committee had failed. His disappointment, however, was assuaged somewhat by a series of intriguing revelations that soon surfaced.

The first came the same day Baden testified about the conclusions of the medical panel. Commander James Humes, the much maligned

naval pathologist who'd performed the original autopsy, had been
called to testify. Plainly ill at ease, Humes took the stand and was
quickly confronted by staff attorney Cornwell over the most egre-
gious error in the autopsy—the four-inch mislocation of the entrance
wound on the skull.

Pressed for an explanation, Humes equivocated, hemmed, and
finally stated unconvincingly that although there may have been some
semantic difficulty or misunderstanding, he'd really meant to describe the wound's location correctly. Then, almost as an after-
thought, Humes admitted he had not been allowed to see either the
photos or the X rays from the autopsy until 1966.

Donahue was thunderstruck. Humes never had access to the very
materials that would have allowed him to describe accurately and
locate the President's wounds! No wonder he had gotten the entrance
wound wrong. Incredibly, this meant that the entire Warren Report
was written without the benefit of this most vital and unimpeachable
information.

Apparently it was Secret Service agent Roy Kellerman who had
taken control of the autopsy material that night at Bethesda.[13] Kellerman wasn't called to testify by the committee, and it was unclear
from Humes's testimony why the agent did what he did. Donahue
knew, however, that Kellerman was head of the President's protection detail in Dallas and among the group who'd successfully bullied
their way past Dr. Rose at Parkland Hospital to get the President's
body out of town. And Kellerman was probably in contact with
Bobby Kennedy as that grim day wore on. It didn't seem farfetched
to believe that it may have been Bobby Kennedy who'd ordered
Kellerman to get control of the material and keep it under wraps. The
fact that the very X rays and photos in question turned up in the legal
possession of the Kennedy family shortly after the assassination and
were not returned to the National Archives until 1966,[14] in Donahue's
view, further implicated the attorney general in this crucial decision.

More important, the committee's subsequent conclusion that
Bobby Kennedy was likely responsible for the mysterious disappearance of the President's brain and key tissue samples during 1965–
1966[15] suggested to Donahue that RFK was instrumental, purposely
or not, in thwarting a competent, thorough analysis of the medical
evidence. The committee asserted that RFK's decision to dispose of
the brain was probably motivated by his fears that the brain would be
put on unseemly public display in future years.

Donahue, however, knew the brain and the edge scrapings that
disappeared with it would have contained shards of the AR-15 jacket
and could have been identified as such. Whoever had made this
material disappear had sharply reduced the odds that the true origin
of the shot would ever be revealed.

The handling of the entire body of medical evidence—from the
disappearance of the brain to the restriction of the autopsy photos

and X rays—had the apparently intended effect. The brain was out of the picture forever, Humes's autopsy report was fuzzy and inaccurate and outside scrutiny of the photos and X rays was delayed for years. Humes, of course, paid the highest price when this shroud descended. For decades he was vilified and ridiculed in the controversy that swirled around the assassination. He could rightly be blamed for his failures in the autopsy room. But it seemed harder to criticize Humes for the shortcomings in his report, since he was never allowed to compare the observations he made during the autopsy with the X rays and photos.

At the committee's ballistics hearings—the proceedings Donahue had tried so mightily to be a part of—additional information surfaced that, to Donahue, again fit a pattern of elimination or obfuscation of any evidence that pointed to the actual origin of the bullet.

The testimony by various experts focused primarily on the single bullet theory. This shopworn controversy was seemingly put to rest thanks to the neutron activation work of Vincent Guinn, a University of California professor of radiochemistry. Guinn reported that neutron activation tests showed the lead fragments removed from Connally's wrist were indeed pieces of the "pristine bullet" recovered at Parkland Hospital,[16] although Guinn never explained how this conclusion could have been reached with any degree of certainty through the analysis of lead, since lead is nonhomogeneous and hence subject to wide variances in composition from sample to sample.

Turning to the head wound, Guinn said tests of the lead fragments removed from Kennedy's brain showed they too were probably from a Carcano bullet. But he quickly added a curious qualifier. According to the professor, the fragments tested—represented by the National Archives as having come from Kennedy's brain—were not the same brain fragments the FBI tested when the agency did its own neutron activation analysis back in 1964.[17]

Guinn explained to reporters that a small container represented by the National Archives as holding all the metal recovered from the President's brain contained only two fragments, one weighing 41.9 milligrams and the other 5.4 milligrams. Yet FBI records from the original testing in 1964 showed a total of four samples were removed from the President's brain, and none had weights corresponding with the pieces at the National Archives.

"The pieces brought out by the archives did not include any of the specific pieces the FBI analyzed," Guinn said. "Where [the originals] are, I have no idea."[18]

This revelation received scant notice in the press and only passing mention in the committee's final report. But again, to Donahue, it was easy to surmise what might have taken place if someone knew the original metal fragments from the brain were verifiably from the AR-15. It was likely, he thought, that the original brain fragments were simply switched with pieces from Oswald's ricocheted bullet, a number of which he believed had ended up on the floor of the President's limo. This swap allowed the "brain fragments" stored at the National Archives to be traced to Oswald's rifle, and at the same time, covered the disappearance of the four genuine fragments taken from Kennedy's brain. If, for example, among those original pieces were shards of zincless copper jacket, the Carcano could be eliminated as the source of the bullet and suspicion would turn to the AR-15.

Significantly, the documentation released in support of Guinn's testimony showed he did not test any pieces of copper jacket material and instead analyzed only the lead from the bullet core.

As for the long-sought-after results of the FBI's own neutron activation testing, Guinn said that he had access to this data during his testing and that "I initially could not make any sense of it," but that, after completing his work, he reviewed the FBI data and found the numbers fit substantially with his findings. Once again, however, no mention was made as to whether copper from the bullet's jacket was tested and if so, what the conclusions were. Nor were the FBI's original test results released by the committee.

Yet another clue surfaced that day that further strengthened Donahue's belief that his conclusions were correct. A press package containing reams of ballistic test data and charts was made available to those who attended the ballistic hearings. Included in the package were photographs of gelatin blocks shot with various caliber bullets. The gelatin simulated the human brain. The tests were designed to mimic the President's head wound.

Among the bullets tested by the committee were a 6.5 mm Carcano round, a .30 caliber rifle bullet and a .223 M-16 (which is the same as an AR-15) round. Side-view photos showed both the 6.5 mm and the .30 caliber full metal–jacketed bullets punched straight, relatively narrow channels through the gelatin, wounds in no way consistent with the damage done to the President's brain.

The M-16 bullet, however, tumbled, disintegrated, and gouged a huge, gaping portion from the gelatin, leaving tiny fragments near the front of the block in a carbon copy of the wound Kennedy suffered. (See illustrations 26 and 27.)

No explanation was offered at the committee hearings for why the Carcano bullet failed to replicate the President's head wound, why the M-16 bullet did, or for that matter, why an M-16 round was tested at all. Nor was the picture of the M-16 bullet test block reprinted in the committee's final report, although photos of the other bullet test blocks were.

Although the congressional hearings dragged on for most of that September, Donahue never returned after his thwarted attempt to testify. He didn't miss much. The increasingly wooden atmosphere of the proceedings—made worse each day by interminable introductory remarks offered up by Blakey—contributed to the impression that the investigators were moving inexorably through a replay of the Warren Report.

For Donahue, this sensation was driven home in spades when he read about the testimony of an expert in flight trajectories from NASA, and later when he studied in detail the final appendix section on bullet trajectories. The NASA expert, Thomas Canning, testified that analysis of the bullet wound channels, combined with a precise understanding of Kennedy's and Connally's positions at the time they were hit, showed all bullets fired came from the book depository.

In reaching his conclusions, Canning worked in part from two scale drawings made from maps of Dealey Plaza and photographs taken at the time of the shooting. Donahue found reproductions of these renderings when Canning's report was published in 1979.[19]

Although the top-view drawing demonstrating how the "magic bullet" had penetrated both Kennedy and Connally accurately showed the President sitting at the extreme right of the limousine's rear seat (see illustration 28), Canning's drawing meant to illustrate the trajectory of the fatal head shot, also a top view, inexplicably placed Kennedy two feet farther inboard, almost in the middle of the seat (see illustration 29). This, despite the fact that every photograph of the assassination showed Kennedy had remained on the right side of the seat until after the last shot hit home. Donahue shook his head but decided to assume that Canning had not used this erroneous placement in tracking this trajectory. Such discrepancies aside—and there turned out to be a number of them—the committee's trajectory analysis was the first detailed study by an official body of this critically important element in the shooting, and after the text of the hearings was released in 1979, Donahue eagerly pored over the committee's conclusions and compared them with his own.

In Donahue's view, given the now precisely designed entry point, the entire question of the trajectory back to the gun source hinged on two key variables: the position of Kennedy's head at impact, and the point on Kennedy's massive exit wound that was to be designated "the exit point," that is, the outshoot point if the bullet *had* continued intact and undeviated from its path prior to striking the skull.

The essential elements in the head position were its tilt forward and its rotation to the left. Donahue had long ago concluded that Kennedy's head was turned only moderately to the left: 15 degrees at most. The committee asserted it was turned much more: 25 degrees.[20]

As for tilt, the committee said it was 11 degrees. Donahue decided to work with this because he could do no calibrations that conclusively persuaded him it was wrong. This was in part because the head was also tilted *left*, toward Kennedy's shoulder, clouding somewhat any attempts to fix the *forward* tilt with surety. (He determined that this leftward tilt had, by itself, a minimal effect on trajectory because as the exit point went left, so did the entry point.)

With the head turned 25 degrees and tilted 11 degrees, Canning was able to line up two bullet holes—the precise entry and the most convenient choice of exit points—to project a trajectory line coming down from the book depository to Kennedy.

But, obviously, key to this reconstruction was the acceptance of *the* "exit point." The committee's medical panel had found a point that they suggested was the most probable candidate. According to the panel, a small defect, or hole, on a piece of bone from the area above Kennedy's right temple (the "Harper bone fragment") could represent the point where the bullet passed out of the skull. The hole was termed "semicircular" several times, but Donahue found it hard to discern anything like a curved arc there.[21] (See drawing 5.)

The more he looked at the committee's reasons for selecting this point, the more doubtful Donahue became. For one thing, Donahue had over the years reinforced his convictions that the designation of a single exit point was not just problematic but unjustifiable. The bullet, everyone agreed, had disintegrated and sprayed a multitude of fragments across the right side of the brain. In one of the appendices the committee said: ". . . the anterior-posterior and lateral X-rays of the skull indicate that the vast majority of missile fragments moved in a cylindrical, slightly coned, pathway, in the same direction as the bullet's path prior to striking the skull."[22]

To Donahue, this description was inherently inconsistent with the stance that "the bullet" had a single exit point. Indeed, in another passage in the committee's text, the medical panel openly acknowledged that the exit point might well be at any one of several such "defects" detectable in the X rays, or it could even be at some other point where the skull was so damaged that there were portions of it altogether missing, either blown out onto Dealey Plaza or pulverized entirely.[23]

The 1968 panel had cited "relatively large fragments, more or less randomly distributed . . . in the right cerebral hemisphere."[24] They also noted a trail of tinier fragments 1.8 inches long that lined up with the entry hole and that the committee was ready to infer indicated "the bullet's" course, except that it petered out before reaching a point up front . . . where there was no defect in the skull.

Donahue looked still closer at the committee's argument. The committee's chosen exit location was at the extreme forward edge of the wound. This was untenable, he felt. If *the* bullet had exited there, why was the skull shattered for five inches above and behind that location, and why could metal fragments be seen embedded in the inner table of the top of the skull all across those five inches? It was hard to believe that "the bullet" would smash to pieces skull four and five inches above and behind its point of exit-impact and yet not extend the portal even a centimeter below and in front of it.

Still more conclusive grounds for rejecting the committee's exit point came to Donahue when he observed where the fragments were.

If the bullet was chaotically disintegrating, and if, in the committee's own words, the fragments had moved in a *cylindrical, slightly coned, pathway, in the same direction as the bullet's path,* how was it that virtually all the fragments appeared to be above the committee's chosen exit point? (See drawing 6.)

All of these vague, ambiguous, and inconsistent observations in the committee report—coupled with the almost riotous disputes and ramblings revealed by the transcript of "experts" studying the X rays in 1978 (see Appendix C)—combined to confirm Donahue's skepticism. It seemed to him the final drafters and illustrators of the 1978 report had unwarrantably seized on a definite, single, pinpointed exit hole. No doubt it was intolerable to them, who were supposed to be issuing the definitive report on factual matters, to write, from a platform of doubt, an honest admission that they couldn't be sure. Besides, they *needed* a precise exit to do any trajectory plotting at all; and they needed *this* exit point to make their trajectories work. By "work" Donahue meant "fit," because his impression now was that the whole business smacked of expediency; they had a preconceived scenario of what had happened in Dallas that day, and now they were choosing points and rotations that fit their story.

So when Donahue sat down yet again with his drafting tools and sketchbook he was determined, to the extent he could humanly avoid it, not to err in the same ways he thought the committee had. This meant first that he had to avoid being sucked into a search for *the* exit hole, because it was misleading and by now he honestly didn't believe there was one. He *would* turn his mind to determining the location of the theoretical exit hole—that is, where the bullet would have come out if it hadn't disintegrated into a shower of fragments.

Then, after fixing such a point, he would list a range of other possibilities. He wanted to come up with a better argument for *his* point selection, but, in response to potential challenges, he wanted to be able to show his argument did not live or die dependent on the acceptance of one precise point—as he was beginning to suspect the committee's argument might.

He would then do the same thing with the degree of rotation—the other major datum on which he disagreed with the committee.

Studying exhibits now available purporting to show the skull damage and the pattern of metal fragments, Donahue estimated from a variety of viewpoints the center of the portal and the central axis of the forward-moving "cone" of metal debris. He marked his spot on the skull. It was, he noted, just about where he'd put it ten years ago in his work after reading the 1968 panel report.

This now allowed him to produce his equivalents of figures II6 and II7 in the committee's Appendix on Photographic Evidence (see drawing 7)—i.e., a side view and a frontal view diagram of the skull showing inshoot, outshoot, and angles of trajectory. Donahue also produced something not available anywhere in the entire committee report, either in X ray, sketch, or diagram: a top view of the skull.

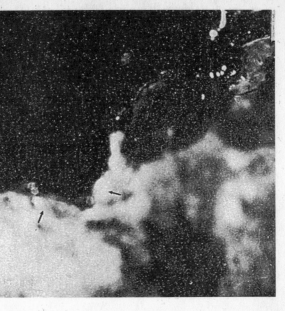

B.

FIGURE 25.—Closeup photograph of the semicircular exit defect in the margin of the fracture fragment in the right parietal region.

A.

FIGURE 28.—Photograph of the exterior surface of the Harper bone fragment.

5. House Select Committee photographs showing the "Harper bone fragment" (A) and the "semicircular exit defect" (B) in Kennedy's skull. The Forensic Pathology Panel believed they saw a semicircular notch in both photographs, which is not readily apparent to the viewer in either.

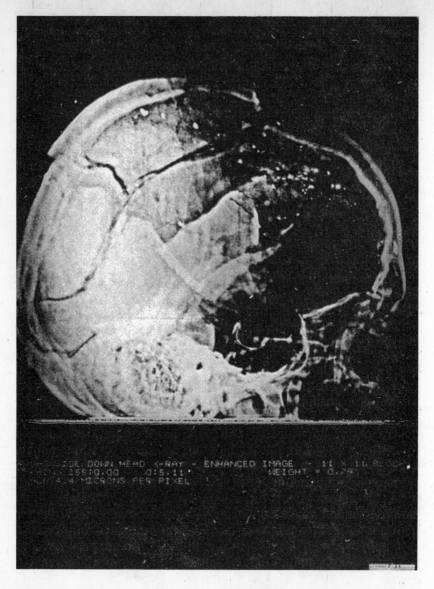

FIGURE 20.—Photograph of a computer-assisted image enhancement of a lateral X-ray of the skull (autopsy X-ray No. 2).

6. House Select Committee X ray of Kennedy's skull seems to indicate that most of the bullet fragments in the skull are high up and toward the back. The committee never published a top view of Kennedy's skull in either X ray or drawing.

LOCATION OF HEAD WOUNDS IN PRESIDENT KENNEDY

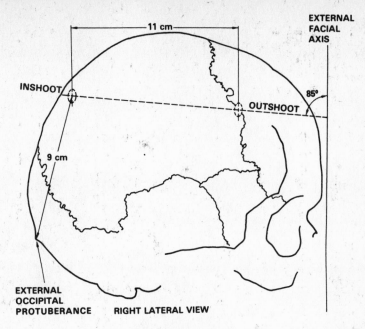

FIGURE II-6

LOCATION OF HEAD WOUNDS IN PRESIDENT KENNEDY

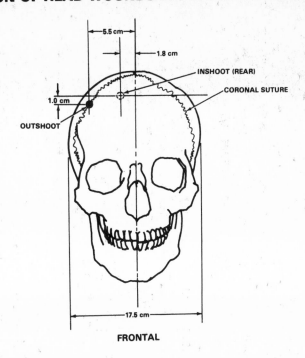

FIGURE II-7

7. House Select Committee drawings indicate the inshoot, outshoot, and bullet path through Kennedy's skull according to their analysis.

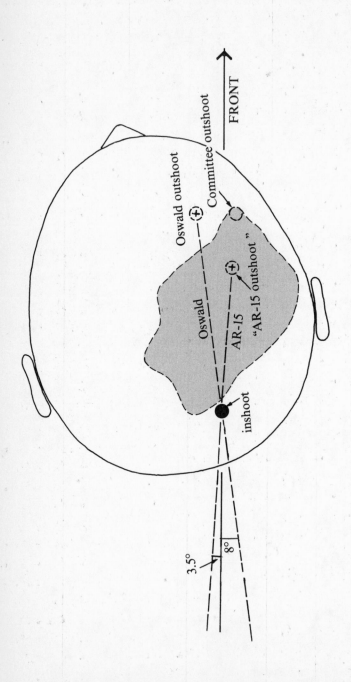

8. Overhead of Kennedy's skull rotated 15° to the left as Donahue believed it was. At this rotation, a shot from Oswald's line of fire would miss the exit portal whereas a shot from the AR-15 would have exited, if it had not disintegrated in the skull, somewhere near the center of the portal.

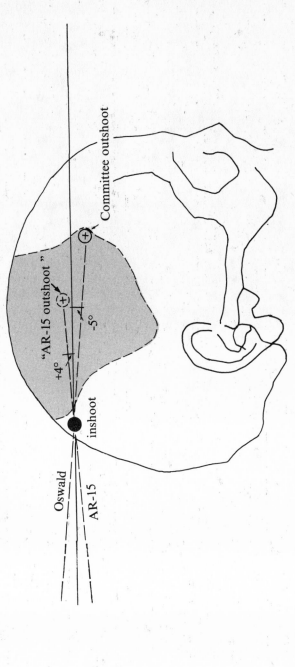

9. Upright side view of Kennedy's skull. Donahue's analysis led him to believe the head shot bullet rose at about 4° through the skull on a line that would have exited near the center of the portal. Donahue believed there was no single outshoot since the bullet had disintegrated in the skull. The House Select Committee concluded the bullet passed through on a 5° downward slope.

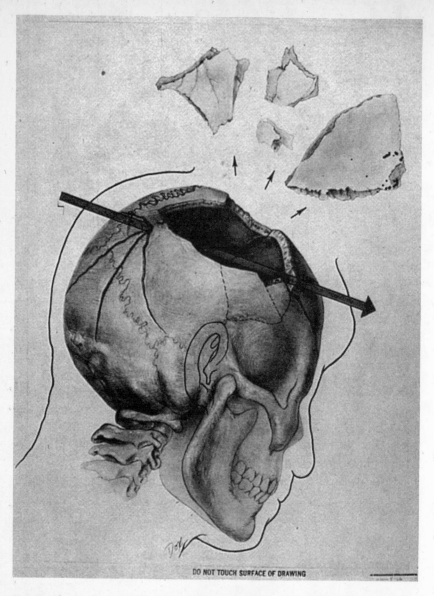

DO NOT TOUCH SURFACE OF DRAWING

FIGURE 29.—Scale drawing of the frontal and right side of a human skull, which depicts the displaced bone fragments and the extensive fragmentation of the skull.

10. The House Select Committee's own rendering of the skull shot. When the mind's eye rearranges this skull to the vertical, the line of fire does not appear to be falling 5°; most viewers would judge it *rising* to exit some few degrees higher than it entered.

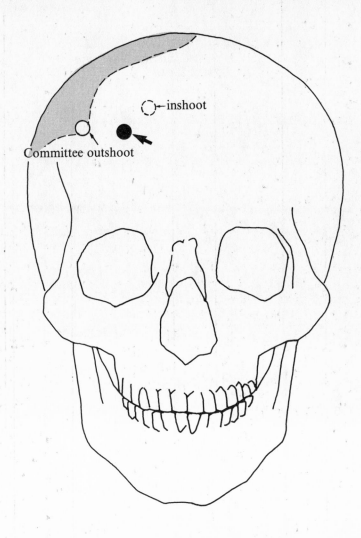

11. Front view of Kennedy's skull showing the committee's inshoot and outshoot points. Using Donahue's 15° head rotation to the left, the outshoot (see arrow) of an Oswald bullet would be over 2 centimeters from the closest point on the exit portal.

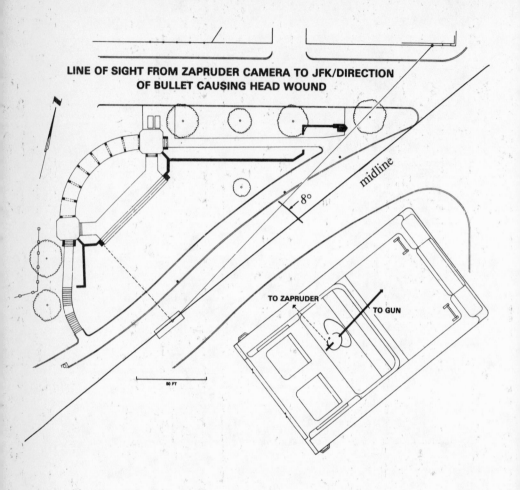

LINE OF SIGHT FROM ZAPRUDER CAMERA TO JFK/DIRECTION OF BULLET CAUSING HEAD WOUND

8°

midline

TO ZAPRUDER

TO GUN

50 FT

12. Committee overhead drawing of Dealey Plaza showing the right-to-left angle of fire from Oswald to Kennedy. Adding a midline to the limousine and measuring the angle of fire reveals an 8° angle rather than the 6° most people have assumed.

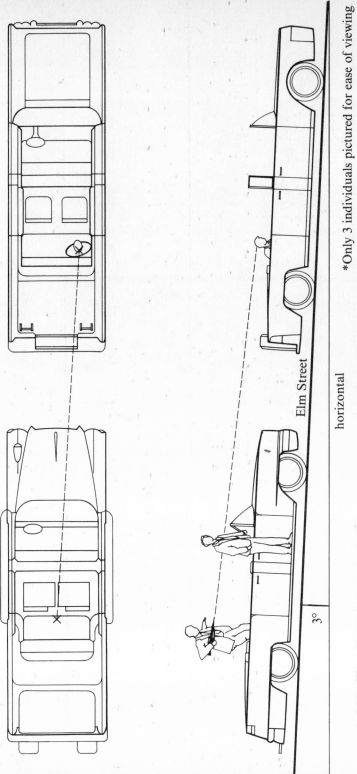

Elm Street

horizontal

3°

*Only 3 individuals pictured for ease of viewing

13. The line of fire from the AR-15 to Kennedy's head, according to Donahue's analysis.

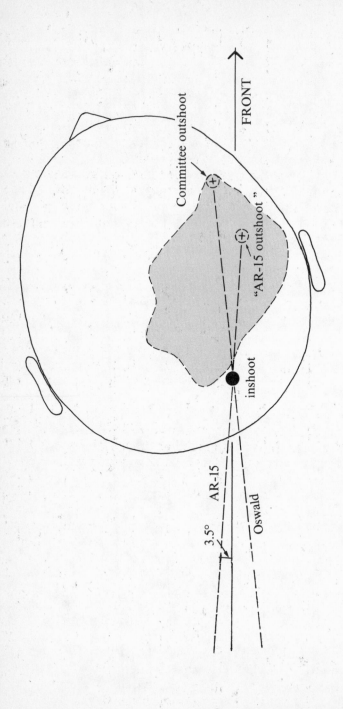

14. Overhead of Kennedy's skull rotated 25° to the left as the House Select Committee claimed. The line of fire from the AR-15 would still leave the skull within the exit portal.

He measured the angle from left to right of his inshoot-outshoot line. The committee's text stated this angle was 18.6 degrees from the inshoot to their chosen outshoot, though it is shown on none of their illustrations. In other words, if you looked straight down on the skull diagram and drew a line straight forward from the inshoot (a parallel to the midline of the skull), the line would indicate the path of fire if the bullet had gone directly forward in the direction Kennedy was "looking." But, instead, the committee said it went almost 19 degrees to the right, relative to that straight forward line.

Donahue was interested to see his own projection was also between 18 and 19 degrees (about 3.5° from the AR-15 to Kennedy plus the 15° leftward rotation of the head). (See drawing 8.)

However, when he did the side view he found a large disagreement with the committee. Measured on an upright skull, their chosen outshoot entailed that the bullet had gone *down* 5 degrees, while Donahue's entailed a *rise* of 4 degrees.[25] (See drawing 9.) In sum, the committee said that the bullet, from the instant it entered, went to the right and down; Donahue figured to the right and up. (See drawing 10.)

Well, what was the trajectory of the bullet as it *approached* the skull? That is, what gun source did it track back to?

Donahue believed the head was rotated 15 degrees; the committee said 25.

Donahue redid the calculations he'd first done ten years earlier. At 15 degrees rotation, and 18½ degrees left to right through the head, the angle to Kennedy from behind was 3½ degrees left to right. That line still passed over the left-rear seat of the Secret Service car. Obviously it tracked back to nowhere near Oswald at the depository.

To make it track back to the depository, you had to turn the head more than 15 degrees. In fact, it looked as though 25 degrees did the trick. At 15 degrees' rotation, a shot from Oswald came out almost at the center of the frontal bone—two centimeters or more from the nearest known defect or bone loss. (See drawing 11.)

As he studied this result, it became clearer what a tight corner the committee trajectory analysts were in. Given what they had accepted as the exit point—the farthest forward and farthest down notch in the entire portal—the only head position assumptions that worked for them were a 25-degree rotation and 11-degree tilt. Because the committee announced that the bullet came down from Oswald's area at 16 degrees, and in from the side at a fixed angle they never stipulated, the committee was locked in. (See drawing 12.) They could not choose an outshoot higher than the notch without changing either the 11-degree tilt angle or the 16-degree downward angle. They could not rotate the head any less than 25 degrees without moving the outshoot to a place on the skull where there was no hole.

Donahue decided it was time to do as precise a side view of the two cars as he could. When he was done he was satisfied that the

drawing corroborated his thesis. It showed the distance between the
AR-15 and Kennedy to be about twenty-four feet. He knew the
11-degree tilt of Kennedy's head was relative to the horizon and not
to Elm Street, which was sloped downward at 3 degrees at this point.
Thus, to find the angle downward from the AR-15 to Kennedy, he
had to measure on his drawing the height of the muzzle and the height
of the head. It turned out that the back of the follow-up car was one
foot higher than the back of Kennedy's car because of the 3 degrees.
Donahue pictured the agent in the left-rear seat rising to stand on
that seat, losing his balance as his heels sank into the soft seat
cushion, and accidentally discharging the gun. (Donahue put himself
through a test by jumping to his feet on the back seat of an available
convertible. He fell over backward every time, even when he placed
a small wooden platform on the seat to help steady him.) He did a
sketch and estimated the AR-15 muzzle at about two feet nine inches
above Kennedy's head. The angle downward was 7 degrees. (See
drawing 13.) When the line of fire struck the head tilted forward at 11
degrees, its continuation, while still going down at 7 degrees relative
to the horizon, went *up* 4 degrees relative to the level plane of the
skull.

He realized that in his own calculation—and everyone else's—
there were premises that amounted to rough estimates. For example,
the committee stated that Kennedy's head was four feet above Elm
Street. If in fact it was less than four feet, then the angle down from
the AR-15 was greater than 7 degrees, and so the line of fire through
the skull would be less than 4 degrees upward.

So Donahue tried various different angles—suppose the follow-up
car *was* to the left, and Landis saw the President's front tire only by
leaning way out? Suppose his choice of exit point should have been
farther back? More to the left . . . et cetera. He determined that his
thesis survived a far greater number of changed premises than the
committee's. For example, the AR-15 shot still exited within the
perimeter of the portal if he accepted the committee's 25-degree
rotation (see drawing 14), but if they accepted his 15-degree rotation,
their exit point couldn't fit.

Yes, there *were* premises that, if insisted on, would imply rejection
of Donahue's *and* of the committee's thesis, but this was not going
to shake Donahue unless someone were to cite such a premise that
was also something Donahue could believe, and he'd never encountered such a disqualifying fact. In the end, Donahue's reexamination
of the trajectory question strengthened his conviction about the origin
of the fatal shot.

Nonetheless, as the committee's two-year mandate was set to
expire January 3, 1979, the conclusion that Oswald had acted alone
seemed secure. Consequently, few were prepared for the intellectual
hand grenade that detonated December 20 and rained the committee
with controversy.

On a radio talk show in Grand Rapids, Michigan, committee member Congressman Harold Sawyer let it slip that expert acoustical analysis of a police recording made during the assassination revealed with 95 percent certainty that a fourth shot was fired at the President from a gunman on the grassy knoll.[26] Apparently a microphone on one of the motorcycles in the presidential motorcade had stuck open and accidentally transmitted the sounds of the Dealey Plaza back to the dispatcher's office, where they were recorded as a matter of course on a dictabelt.[27]

This recording, later transferred to tape, languished for years in the private possession of a Dallas police officer. After committee investigators learned of its existence, however, acoustics expert James Barger was called in to study the sounds on the recording. But none of the noises on the tape could even be remotely construed as gunshots. Only sporadic police chatter, sirens, and the steady, monotonous thump of the policeman's Harley-Davidson were audible to the human ear.

Barger nonetheless was able to filter out the motorcycle sounds and other white noise until he arrived at four "audible events" on the tape that he concluded might be gunshots. If true, this contradicted the Warren Commission's findings that only three shots were fired and by definition required that a conspiracy had taken place.[28]

Barger then suggested an elaborate acoustical reconstruction be done to compare the echo patterns of gunshots fired at Dealey Plaza with the impulses identified on the dictabelt, the goal being to confirm the presence and identify the origins of the shots.[29] Microphones were placed all around Dealey Plaza and for several hours one hot summer morning in 1978, police marksmen, firing from the book depository and grassy knoll, drilled sandbags along Elm Street with rifle fire fifty-six times.[30]

Despite the effort, the "acoustic fingerprint" revealed by the test was inconclusive. In the end Barger could only assert that there was a "50–50 chance" a fourth shot had been fired by a gunman on the grassy knoll.[31] Blakey, however, had spent considerable time and money chasing the secrets of the audiotape and he was determined to obtain something that would bolster his apparently emerging view that a conspiracy was responsible for the President's death. Blakey admitted as much in his 1981 book *The Plot to Kill the President*, written with journalist Richard Billings:

> By this time, we could not help feeling competitive and thinking in terms of winning or losing. We had been led by the evidence to date to suspect an event that we had come to want to prove. Using the inevitable football analogy (inevitable, certainly, if you had gone to Notre Dame, as Blakey had), we had reached the goal line, owing to Barger's brilliant effort, but we had not scored.[32]

In an attempt to get across that goal line, then, Blakey called in two more acoustics experts to review Barger's work and make their own assessment about the probability of a fourth shot and a gunman on the knoll. No doubt much to Blakey's satisfaction, studies by Mark Weiss and Ernest Aschkenasy of Queens College in New York revealed that the chances a fourth shot was fired from the knoll were, in fact, nearly 100 percent.[33]

"It's a prima facie case of conspiracy," one committee source crowed to *The Washington Post*. "Everything must now be rethought."[34]

Barger and his associates, meanwhile, did a little rethinking of their own. Despite his earlier assessment that there was only a 50–50 chance of a fourth shot from the knoll, Barger and his experts examined the Weiss-Aschkenasy data and soon concurred with the new findings.[35]

Weiss and Aschkenasy testified at a specially scheduled hearing on December 29, less than a week before the committee was set to go out of existence. They reiterated their certainty about the shot from the knoll—from the front—and matter-of-factly asserted that their calculations "could not be refuted."[36]

But neither could they be corroborated, at least by any existing evidence from the scene of the crime. Certainly not the medical evidence. Baden, the head of the committee's medical panel, recalled in his 1989 book that, following the acoustics expert's revelations, Blakey

> asked me if I could say that my forensic evidence was consistent with the acoustical findings. "Consistent with" is one of those catch-all phrases that mean something could be possible. It is used a lot in our profession, especially on the witness stand when evidence can be interpreted in more than one way. All Blakey wanted me to say was that a grassy-knoll bullet might have struck the President. I didn't believe that. Forensically speaking, I was certain that absolutely nothing from that grassy knoll had hit the President.
>
> On the final day of the hearings, just before I was due to testify, Blakey decided we were running out of time and scratched me. I have always thought that there would have been enough time for me if I had been more in tune with the acoustics experts.[37]

Without Baden's acquiescence, Blakey and the grassy knoll truebelievers were forced to conclude that the gunman firing from the front must have missed. Given that the distance between the supposed gunman and the President was barely one hundred feet, this was a dubious proposition, particularly since the gunman had apparently missed not only the President, but also the limo, everyone else in the car, and the bystanders along both sides of Elm Street. Not exactly the performance one would expect from a professional "torpedo" working the most important job of his career. Likewise, there was the problematic, long-standing question of how a gunman on the knoll could have escaped without being spotted and captured by the several dozen witnesses who had run to the area immediately after the shooting.

Nonetheless, Blakey had "scientific evidence" of conspiracy in hand and evidently was not about to let the lack of substantiating evidence get in the way of history. As a result, at the eleventh hour in its tortured, two-year journey, when virtually all the hard evidence seemed to indicate otherwise, the committee hung the proposition that Kennedy was "probably" assassinated as the result of a conspiracy from the slender and solitary thread of the acoustics evidence.

Left begging were questions of the most fundamental sort: Who was behind this conspiracy? How was it carried out? Why? The committee was unable to provide even speculative possibilities. Instead, they threw the entire muddle into the lap of the Justice Department and claimed it was now the responsibility of that agency to flesh out the details.[38]

And then they disbanded.

Those who had hoped more responsible and complete answers from the $5.5 million investigation would be forthcoming with the committee's final report were disappointed when the document appeared in the summer of 1979. In the introduction, Blakey marveled that "on the issue of conspiracy, we have, I believe, drastically altered the verdict of history," but he quickly qualified the statement with an disingenuously deflective admission of the committee's central failure:

> . . . we stopped short of that climactic point in the mystery novels when the murderer is named. I do not apologize. I believe the committee fulfilled its mandate to the letter, given the restrictions that are appropriate in a legislative proceeding. We did what we could and what it was proper for us to do.[39]

As to the central questions of who was behind the conspiracy and why, the report admitted the committee found insufficient evidence to conclude that the Soviet government, the Cuban government, anti-Castro Cuban groups, or organized crime played a role in the President's death. As a way out, the report added, "the committee could not preclude the possibility that individual members of anti-Castro Cuban groups or the national syndicate of organized crime were involved in the assassination."[40] But then, admitting the truth, the report authors swung back the other way: "There was insufficient evidence, however, to support a finding that any individual (anti-Castro Cuban, organized crime) members were involved."[41]

Reaction to Blakey's conclusions was swift. David Belin, the former assistant counsel to the Warren Commission and one of the

first to call for a new investigation into the assassination in the mid-
1970s, ripped into the committee's findings in a lengthy article in *The
New York Times Magazine* in July 1979. Predicting the conspiracy
conclusions "will not stand the test of history," Belin called the last-
minute acceptance of the acoustic evidence "one of the biggest flip-
flops in recent Congressional history" and said that once the committee's failures come to light, "the folly of the multimillion-dollar
supersecret investigation will become clear to all."[42]

Even some committee members could not abide by Blakey's conspiracy findings. In a joint dissent published as an appendix to the
committee's final report, Congressmen Samuel Devine and Robert
Edgar wrote:

> Standing alone, the opinion of the acoustics expert that a third shot
> came from the grassy knoll is simply their opinion. Unless supported
> by other evidence, it is not sufficient to establish conclusively there
> was indeed another shot, another shooter, or a conspiracy.[43]
>
> Officer H.B. McLain of the Dallas Police Department was identified
> by the acoustics expert as being the operator of the motorcycle with
> an open mike to the left and rear of the presidential limousine.
>
> But, apparently, the officer himself rejects the assumption, which
> led to the test and reenactments. He asks a very simple, but important,
> question: "If it was my motorcycle, why did it not record the revving
> up at high speed plus my siren when we immediately took off for
> Parkland Hospital?"[44]

Congressman Harold Sawyer also noted the inherent weakness of
the assumption that it was McLain's microphone that had stuck open,
an assumption upon which Blakey and the experts staked their entire
argument. Like McLain, Sawyer noted that there was no change in
the rhythm or intensity of the motorcycle engine noise and "there is
no audible sound even resembling sirens until a full two minutes"
after the experts' "shots" were said to have occurred.[45]

Sawyer further pointed out that chimes could faintly be heard on
the tape. An exhaustive search of Dealey Plaza and a wide-ranging
check with those familiar with the area in 1963 failed to reveal any
possible source for the mysterious music.[46]

Already listing dangerously, the acoustics conclusions took a hit
amidships when an Ohio rock drummer named Steve Barber uncovered evidence all the experts had missed. The same month the
committee's report came out, *Gallery* magazine produced a special
issue on the Kennedy assassination that included a record of the
controversial dictabelt recording. Playing the record over and over,
Barber was able to identify the barely audible words of Dallas County
Sheriff Bill Decker barking the order "Hold everything secure" on
radio channel 2 during the crucial ten-second interval that supposedly
contained the gunshot impulses.[47]

This discovery all but destroyed the acoustics theory, since it was an established fact that Decker didn't give his order until a full minute and a half after the assassination. Apparently, Decker's order on channel 2 bounced onto the motorcyclist's channel 1 through a radio wave phenomenon known as "cross-talk."[48]

The FBI in 1980 conducted its own analysis of the acoustics expert's work and concluded the expert had proved neither that the sounds on the recording had originated in Dealey Plaza, nor that they represented the sounds of gunfire. The expert's findings, the FBI said, were therefore "invalid."[49] Blakey responded by calling the FBI report "superficial, shoddy and shot full of holes" and "a sophomoric analysis."[50]

But the coup de grace came with a study by the National Academy of Sciences in 1982. The prestigious academy confirmed Barber's conclusions about the cross talk and the timing of Sheriff Decker's order, and likewise agreed that the committee's findings were totally in error.[51]

For his part, Blakey attempted to salvage his reputation and capitalize on his committee experience with his 1981 book *The Plot to Kill the President*. Apparently the chief counsel had never signed the nondisclosure agreement he had forced everyone else on the committee to ink as a condition of employment back in 1977. If he had, his book would have been a blatant violation of the agreement, since it made extensive use of committee evidence and closed-door testimony and was essentially a rewrite, albeit gussied up, of the committee's final report.

It also served as a showcase for Blakey's encyclopedic knowledge of organized crime. Yet establishing an even halfway credible link between the mob and the assassination was something Blakey could not do.

Indeed, as misleading titles go, Blakey's book is an all-time classic. The subtitle, "Organized Crime Assassinated J.F.K.—The Definitive Story," recedes like a mirage as the chapters progress. For the first 340 pages, Blakey goes back over well-trodden ground surrounding the assassination. He also includes a lengthy section on the history of the mob. Finally, in the last chapter, all of thirty-two pages long, Blakey outlines the "Plot to Kill the President."

This, too, is a travesty. Most of the chapter consists of pretentious and irrelevant filler on how the classical elements of Greek tragedy related to Kennedy's death. And about the only potentially plausible evidence Blakey can point to supporting his mob-hit assertion are the hearsay statements of mobster John Roselli. Roselli told columnist Jack Anderson in the early 1970s that the assassination was the work of Cubans connected to Santo Trafficante, the mobster who'd ruled in Cuba before Castro took over. According to Roselli, Oswald was recruited as a decoy. When he was captured, the mob arranged through Jack Ruby to have him killed.

Roselli later told a West Coast associate he'd made the story up and he denied the Trafficante hit scenario in testimony before the Church Committee in 1975. A year later, Roselli was murdered, a fact to which Blakey attached great significance.

But if the professor thought he'd presented "the definitive account of the most consequential assassination in twentieth-century America," as the jacket bragged, few others agreed. *The New York Times* didn't bother reviewing the book. In an extremely brief item, *The Washington Post* suggested the work came across "with all the excitement of a wheat market report."[52] The most succinct and damning synopsis of *The Plot to Kill the President* appeared in *Choice,* a scholarly journal of literary review used by librarians, educators and book buyers:

> Blakey's familiarity with the efforts of the congressional reinvestigation are manifest yet the work fails to deliver its advertised goal of providing the "definitive story" of the assassination. There is little new information here. The work of the House committee is rehashed; a great deal of previously known information about the history and modus operandi of organized crime is provided. The "reconsideration" of the roles of Oswald and Ruby is a rehash of previous speculation and of facts long known. The conclusion of an organized crime conspiracy to assassinate JFK may be valid, but the book does not come close to presenting a convincing case for that conclusion. No real evidence is presented that organized crime was responsible beyond the uncorroborated stories of a couple of witnesses of dubious credibility and the antipathy of mobsters toward the Kennedy brothers. The analysis is neither new nor compellingly articulated and is not a useful contribution to the literature of the assassination.[53]

The committee's long and tortured journey had come to an end. Though Blakey's findings were discredited, the facts surrounding the President's death had nonetheless been submerged ever deeper in a morass of disinformation and clutter.

For Donahue, there was one final revelation involving the committee's work that surfaced in 1983 when he interviewed Harold A. Rose, a former Baltimore homicide detective who'd worked as an investigator for the committee. Rose had been responsible for interviewing Secret Service agents and police officers who'd been present in Dallas.

At their meeting, Rose informed Donahue that he'd traveled extensively around the country to question a number of Secret Service agents and police officers about what happened in Dallas.*

"So did you interview Hickey?" Donahue asked. "He was right there in Washington."

---

*The following conversation has been reconstructed from the recollections of Howard Donahue.

"No. I did not," Rose replied.

"Why not?" Donahue asked.

"I really don't know," Rose said finally.

Transcripts of the interviews Rose did conduct never appeared in the committee's final report, appendices, or anywhere else.

14
THE AR-15

DONAHUE RUMINATED AS THE DAYS PASSED. It was clear by now that no one of consequence was taking his conclusions seriously. Not the government, and with the exception of Ralph Reppert at the *Baltimore Sun,* not the press. Still, abandoning the investigation didn't cross his mind. He was sure he was right. One way or another he was going to prove it to the world. The only real question now was, which way should he turn?

In theory, at least, there was still the possibility of the book collaboration with Reppert. In those heady days following publication of the *Sun* article, both men had been in full, excited agreement that a book would be the next logical step. But the prospect seemed to be fading by 1979. Reppert's obligations at home and on the job left him time for little else, and his health was not good.

For years, Reppert had been a "wheelhorse" at the *Baltimore Sun,* according to former editorial writer James H. Bready, a longtime friend. Reppert was a versatile newsman who covered the big stories, wrote almost every Sunday for the magazine and regularly cranked out a humor column entitled "Reppert's People," which featured amusing anecdotes about Reppert's mythical home life and his zany, imaginary wife, Harriet.

But Reppert's funnyman facade masked an existence shadowed by tragedy and pain. In the 1950s, Reppert's young daughter returned from a party, complained of not feeling well, lay down on the couch, and died within an hour or two of a mysterious viral ailment, according to Hal Williams, Reppert's Sunday editor. After their daughter died, Ralph's first wife, Ruth, became increasingly despondent, and eventually took her own life. The couple's son, Peter, meanwhile, was legally blind and his well-being was a constant source of concern for his father.

And if all that was not enough, Reppert battled almost constant physical pain. He'd been on a boat once doing a story about fishermen in the Chesapeake Bay when the vessel pitched and sent him crashing down on his back. The fall damaged several vertebrae, left Reppert permanently disabled, and eventually triggered serious pain in his leg. Reppert never complained about his ailments, friends said, but his belabored movements and the painkillers he routinely gulped made it clear he was seldom free from suffering.

The reporter's spirits were lifted somewhat in the spring of '78 when his story on Donahue won first place in the Don Feitel Memorial Award journalism competition: best Sunday magazine article in the country for 1977. The judges wrote that Reppert's "impeccably written" piece rang with "an arresting irony," and aptly noted Donahue's theory contained "that element of coincidence and human blunder that is the essence of true tragedy."

But the recognition did nothing to alter the increasingly bleak reality of Reppert's life, and so the book project languished. Then one morning in the autumn of 1979 Katie Donahue received a call from Ralph. This was not unusual; he liked Katie and often rung up to talk. Ralph was calling from the hospital. He'd gone in for some tests, he said.*

"It's been hard these past months, Katie," Reppert said. "Sometimes, when I think about it, I wonder if my life has amounted to a damn thing, frankly.

"I just wish I'd gotten onto Howard's story ten years earlier. My life might have been different. But I'm too old and too sick and I don't have the physical energy to pursue it anymore."

Katie scolded Reppert. She told him his career had amounted to a great deal. He was highly respected by his colleagues and by people in the community, and in any case, his working days weren't over.

"You and Howard will write that book yet," she said.

"I doubt it," Reppert replied. He chuckled. A nurse was giving him a sedative by injection.

"I told the nurse I don't drop my drawers for anyone," Reppert quipped. A few minutes later the drug began to take effect.

"I have to go to sleep now," he said. "Just promise me, Katie, that you won't let Howard's theory die with me. I am convinced he is right. I know he is."

Reppert's words were slurred as the drug enveloped him. "Don't quit, Katie. Don't let Howard quit."

"We won't, Ralph," Katie said. She was crying now. "We'll see it through."

Reppert went home from the hospital the next day and spent an hour on his bad leg cleaning paint cans, ladders and heavy boxes out of the garage. When he'd finished, he pulled his car inside. He left the motor running, closed the garage door, and took a piece of hose

---

*The following conversation has been reconstructed from the recollections of Katie Donahue.

off the wall. He put one end over the exhaust pipe and one end in his mouth.

And his pain finally ended.

Howard learned of Reppert's suicide through an ambulance attendant who'd gone out on the call. What Katie told Reppert about how much his colleagues and readers admired him was borne out at the memorial service: The church was packed, standing room only. And so Reppert was laid to rest as the seventies drew to a close.

Aside from the occasional speech, Donahue did little with his theory in the weeks and months that followed. Reppert's death was a serious blow. The reporter had been an important ally and a faithful friend. Perhaps another break would come, Donahue thought. He'd always gotten breaks before. All he could do now was bide his time and keep an eye out for anything new that surfaced on the assassination.

Since that day in 1977 when he'd first identified the AR-15 as the weapon that fired the fatal shot, it had intermittently occurred to Donahue that he ought to learn more about the gun. (See illustration 30.) As it turned out, a coincidental encounter following a talk he'd given at a Baltimore civic club helped in this task.

The gunsmith had just finished addressing the Merchant's Club, a well-respected Baltimore institution whose membership included the old guard of the business community. The crowd was heading for the door when a lean, middle-aged man with an angular face approached the podium. He introduced himself as William Mullen, a principal with the Baltimore-based export firm of Cooper-Macdonald Inc.

Donahue listened as Mullen quietly explained the central role Cooper-Macdonald had played in the Army's begrudging acceptance of the M-16 as its standard infantry weapon in the early to mid-1960s. In connection with this effort, Mullen said, the company's president, Robert Macdonald, had successfully sold the Secret Service on the AR-15, the prototype of the gun. It was one of these newly issued rifles that had accompanied the presidential protection detail to Dallas on November 22, 1963.

The information was eerie, but what chilled Donahue's spirit that night was the tale Mullen went on to tell of the rifle's development and the Army's subsequent attempts apparently aimed at sabotaging the weapon. This chicanery, driven by the kind of corrosive pettiness so often found in large bureaucracies, eventually led to an untold number of needless combat deaths in Vietnam and was well documented by congressional investigators in 1967.

The wretched saga of the M-16 nonetheless remains little known to this day, although writer James Fallows did report it in riveting and grim detail in the June 1981 edition of *Atlantic Monthly* magazine. According to Fallows, the machinations surrounding the Army's adoption of the M-16 were a "pure portrayal of the banality of the evil."[1]

Years later, Mullen recalled his version of events.

Development of the Vietnam-era M-16, according to Mullen, had its origins in the Korean War. American soldiers in Korea were armed with the M-1, a semiautomatic weapon that had done yeoman's work as the standard American infantry rifle of World War II. Semiautomatic meant the trigger had to be pulled separately for each of the eight shots in the gun's clip. Unfortunately for the Americans, some of the Chinese units fighting in Korea were equipped with the new Kalashnikov AK-47 assault rifle, a weapon that marked the same kind of technological departure that the Spencer repeater brought to the Civil War. Unlike the M-1, the AK-47 was capable of firing sustained bursts by simply holding down the trigger. This kind of continuous "hose effect" firepower was previously available only with heavy machine guns, or smaller submachine guns that fired a pistol round and hence were ineffective beyond one hundred yards or so.

Mikhail Kalashnikov, however, was able to incorporate in his weapon the best features of both the traditional infantry rifle and the machine gun: The AK-47 was easy to fire, its clip could hold up to thirty rounds, the bullet would shoot a considerable distance with great accuracy and penetrating power, and most important, the weapon could do it all with lethal automatic capability.

American troops on the ground were quick to grasp the disparity between their own weapons and those of the Chinese. Like the Confederate infantrymen in the Civil War who faced the unrelenting fury of the Spencer repeater, American GIs who came in contact with the AK-47 grew to loathe and respect the enemy's abundant firepower and the weapon that made it possible.

As a result, Mullen said, the Army decided in the mid-1950s to begin development of a new rifle that would incorporate the primary features of the AK-47, notably its full-auto capability and its ability to penetrate at great distance.

In keeping with Army tradition, work on the weapon was conducted by a clubby association of Army brass, weapons designers and companies known collectively as the Ordnance Corps.[2] In his 1981 *Atlantic Monthly* article, Fallows characterized the Ordnance Corps as "small-time, insular, old-fashioned. Historically, its first instinct, when presented with a new technical possibility, has been to reject it and stick to traditional solutions."

The result of the corps' development effort was the M-14 rifle, a .30 caliber weapon. The Army predictably sang the praises of the new rifle, but the full-sized .30 caliber round used in the gun drew immediate criticism in some quarters. According to Mullen, Pentagon studies had long shown that if infantry weapons were equipped to fire smaller rounds, there would be a dramatic increase in firepower for the individual soldier, since smaller bullets weighed less and the troopers could therefore carry more.

The studies also revealed that if fired at extremely high velocity, smaller bullets had the additional advantage of being considerably more lethal than larger ones. This paradox was due to the fact that smaller bullets were inherently less stable than larger rounds and thus were inclined to rupture and release all their energy immediately upon striking human flesh. The tumbling, explosive disintegration of the smaller bullet transferred the energy instantly through the semi-liquid tissue of the human body. The result was a wound channel much larger and more destructive than that caused by a heavier bullet. Because of its greater weight and stability, a larger caliber round often passed cleanly through the human body—leaving only small entrance and exit holes in its wake.[3]

Yet even with the advantages inherent in a small, high-velocity bullet, the Army favored the heavy .30 caliber round in the M-14—primarily because it was the same caliber as the slug used in the standard infantry machine gun. The prospect of being able to supply both weapons with the same type of ammunition held great appeal for military planners. Equally important was the fact that the Army had fought America's European allies long and hard to have the .30 caliber bullet adopted as the standard NATO round in the late 1940s. Apparently, a tacit admission that the Europeans might have been correct in their advocacy of a smaller caliber bullet would have been unacceptable to the Pentagon.

Yet because the M-14 had been designed with logistical concerns more than combat in mind, the new gun quickly proved a disaster in the field. When fired on full automatic, the M-14 became virtually uncontrollable. This was due to the heavy kick that resulted from the gunpowder charge needed to propel the big .30 caliber slug, according to Fallows.[4]

Still, the Army had spent $500 million[5] to develop the M-14 and there would be no turning back. Deficiencies or not, the weapon was formally adopted by the Army in January 1959.

In the meantime, Mullen recalled, a small Costa Mesa, California, company called Armalite had begun experimenting with the possibility of making weapons from lightweight aerospace materials. Eugene Stoner, a young inventor with an extraordinarily facile mind, was the driving force in this effort. In time Stoner produced a lightweight, semiautomatic 7.62mm (.30 caliber) rifle called the AR-10.

Army General William Wyman knew Stoner and was aware of the work Armalite was doing. Consequently, Wyman asked Stoner if he might be able to take what he'd learned from the AR-10 and develop a smaller caliber version with full automatic capability.

Stoner agreed and six months later came up with the AR-15. The gun fired a .223 round—essentially the same-sized bullet generations have used to plink away at tin cans and rabbits. But this particular

.22 bullet was propelled by a huge charge of powder that sent it flying at 3,200 feet per second; three times as fast as a standard .22 round and 400 feet per second faster than the M-14. And it could fire fully automatic.

Stoner's gun proved remarkable in more ways than one. Unlike the M-14, the AR-15 kicked hardly at all. Furthermore, because Stoner built the weapon's stock out of high-strength plastic, the gun weighed two and a half pounds less than the M-14. Yet it was every bit as durable as the heavier rifle. Most important, the AR-15's lighter weight and smaller bullets would allow soldiers to carry three times as much ammunition into combat as they could with the M-14. And Stoner had specifically designed the weapon so that many of its parts could be stamped out, thus reducing the cost and time required to mass-produce the rifle, Mullen said.

Since Armalite was little more than an inventor's workshop, the firm had already sold development rights on any weapons it produced to Fairchild Industries by the time Stoner finished the AR-15. Fairchild CEO Richard Boutelle, in turn, began searching for a manufacturer to actually produce the gun. He knew that Baltimore-based Cooper-Macdonald had exported thousands of Colt Industries firearms over the years. As a result, Boutelle asked Robert Macdonald to approach the nation's oldest arms maker about manufacturing Stoner's new gun.

At Macdonald's suggestion, Colt looked at the weapon and soon after agreed to manufacture it. By 1959, Hartford, Connecticut–based Colt was geared up and ready, willing, and able to go with manufacturing. If anyone was interested in buying it, that is.

In search of customers, then, Macdonald, Stoner, and Mullen headed for the Far East that year, drawing on the contacts Mullen had established in his role as Cooper-Macdonald's export representative in Asia through the 1950s. On the tour, the three men conducted hands-on demonstrations of the rifle's capabilities for military officials in the Philippines, Singapore, Indonesia, Thailand, Burma, and India. The response was overwhelming. The gun was extraordinarily reliable and relatively cheap, but what made it so appealing in Southeast Asia was its lightness and ease of use. Unlike their experiences with the unwieldy M-14, the physically slight Asians had no trouble firing the AR-15.

It was on this journey that Stoner discovered just how lethal the AR-15 really was. To pass the time, Stoner and Mullen would hang green coconuts from strings for target practice. A standard .30 caliber round passed cleanly through the target, leaving a neat hole. But when the men fired the thin-jacketed .223 round at the hanging target, the coconut literally exploded.

Stoner had planned the AR-15 around the .223 bullet to take advantage of the tumbling, explosive disintegration inherent when a small, high-velocity round strikes semiliquid material. But even he was surprised at how destructive the weapon proved to be, Mullen said. Indeed, the .223 slug demonstrated all the deadly characteristics of a soft-point or hollow-tipped bullet. Its full—albeit very thin—metal jacket, however, technically made the bullet legal under the Geneva Convention warfare rules. Like nearly every other military arms designer around the world, Stoner had sought to bypass the Geneva Convention restrictions and thereby increase the lethality of his weapon. Unlike many weapons engineers, he had succeeded well beyond his own expectations.

While Stoner and Mullen toured the Far East, back in the U.S. the Army and others had begun extensive testing of the rifle in simulated combat conditions. In every way possible, the gun proved exceptional. It fired with great rapidity, it was light and easy to shoot, it was accurate, and it was reliable. Even when subjected to the mud, dust, and rain of the field, the AR-15 almost never misfired or jammed.[6]

Still, the Army brass remained infatuated with the idea of a standard-sized bullet. And they weren't about to admit their M-14 project had been a massive and costly failure. So they demurred on Stoner's new weapon and chose instead to continue cranking out the inferior M-14. In any case, Mullen recalled, there was considerable prejudice against the AR-15 among Army officers, who, among other things, considered the .223 round "too puny" for infantry, test results notwithstanding.

By 1962, however, the Air Force had caught wind of the AR-15 and, having no similarly hidebound ideas about what a weapon should or shouldn't be, they tested the rifle thoroughly. The results convinced the Air Force brass that the gun was indeed a winner and they promptly ordered thousands of the rifles for Air Force sentries around the world.

For its part, the Army continued to test the weapon at a number of diverse locations worldwide. Their official verdict:

> The weapon was inferior in some respects to the M-14 and equal to it in others. Consequently, the gun in no way represented enough of an improvement in the "state of the art" to justify replacing the M-14.

But when Secretary of Defense Robert MacNamara's "whiz kids" began evaluating the reams of data from the numerous AR-15 tests that by then had been conducted by both the U.S. military and by foreign allies, they quickly saw the gun was in fact far superior to the M-14. As a result, President Kennedy was confronted with conflicting reports on the new gun: The Army said it was mediocre at best; the DOD said it was exceptional. The President asked MacNamara to find out who was telling the truth. This MacNamara did through an investigation by the Army's Inspector General's office.

The IG's probe revealed that hardliners in the Ordnance Corps had actually rigged a number of their tests by using a dry run to select "only those tests that will reflect adversely on the AR-15 rifle. . . ."[7]

Mullen recalled: "We saw so much duplicity, chicanery, and double dealing, Macdonald became evangelical about this. If it took him to the grave, he was going to get the Army to adopt this weapon because it was so superior."

With the revelations that emerged from the Inspector General's probe, the die was cast, and by 1963 the Army was compelled to begin buying the weapon in large quantities. But the Ordnance Corps was stung by the rebuke they'd received from the Inspector General, and they were apparently determined to even the score. Consequently, the command ordered three key modifications in the gun, now known as the M-16. First, a completely unnecessary manual bolt-closing device was installed. Second, the rifling, or grooves inside the gun's barrel, were altered. Finally, a new type of gunpowder was mandated for the .223 cartridge.[8]

Fallows reported that the bolt assist device was added for no other reason than that all previous Army rifles had used a manual bolt and therefore the AR-15 would have one, too. The belief was apparently that a soldier needed "something to push on, that this would be a comforting feeling for him," according to Stoner, who argued against the modification, since it would reduce reliability and add nothing but weight and cost to the gun.[9]

Mullen said Stoner also urged the Army not to change the rifling in the gun's barrel, as this would reduce the lethal tumbling effect of the bullet. Once again, however, the Army ignored him.

As for the final change, Stoner argued against it most strenuously of all. The ordnance brass proposed a switch from the DuPont gunpowder Stoner had incorporated in the weapon's original design to a cheaper, dirtier, recycled powder manufactured by Olin Mathieson. Stoner warned that the switch would be extremely detrimental to the gun's reliability, since the dirtier powder would burn slower and therefore increase the weapon's cyclic rate of fire. This would inevitably lead to metal fatigue, broken parts, jamming, and finally, an inoperable weapon.

Once again, however, it didn't really matter what Stoner said. The decision to switch powder had already been made by the time the Army got around to interviewing the designer of the weapon about the change, according to Fallow's *Atlantic Monthly* article.[10]

Stoner's dire predictions were soon borne out by a series of Army tests, which showed the AR-15 was six times more likely to jam when the Olin ball powder was used. Colt, the weapon's manufacturer, was increasingly panicked by the switch and informed the Army it could no longer guarantee the rifle's performance with the powder. Fallows wrote that the Army responded by telling Colt not to sweat it; the company could use whatever kind of powder it wanted for the weapon's acceptance tests, but the Army would continue using the Olin ball powder in the field.[11]

And so it was that when the Army began shipping large numbers of M-16s to American combat troops in Vietnam in 1966, the ammunition that accompanied the weapons contained the ill-suited, mismatched powder. The results were as predictable as they were horrendous. By the time the weapon had reached most fighting units in early 1967, reports were filtering back in letters to home of the gun's notorious unreliability. The first word that surfaced publicly came from an unidentified New Jersey Marine:

> Do you know what killed most of us? Our own rifles . . . the M-16. Practically everyone of our dead [in a recent battle] was found with his rifle torn down next to him where he had been trying to fix it."[12]

Fallows quoted another soldier's letter in his *Atlantic Monthly* article. According to a Marine officer from Wisconsin, the M-16 jammed at critical times in battle. Frequently, the officer reported, as many as half the rifles in his unit failed to work in battle. This led to several instances in which Marines were killed within a dozen feet of the enemy because their M-16s didn't work.[13]

The Army responded to the criticisms by claiming soldiers weren't cleaning the weapons properly.[14] But a congressional investigation headed by Congressman Richard Ichord of Missouri soon found otherwise. Testifying before Ichord's committee in the fall of 1967, representatives of the Ordnance Corps could offer no plausible justification for changing the powder.

To those who understood what had happened, people like Stoner and Mullen, it was clear the Army's actions had been primarily designed to discredit the weapon that had so thoroughly outperformed the M-14.

Ichord's committee issued a scathing report outlining the Army's malfeasance. According to the committee, the Army system of procuring new weapons "has built-in confusion, possibly to prevent pinpointing responsibility." The report charged that the decision to continue using the Olin powder, even after Stoner had warned against it, "bordered on criminal negligence."[15]

But no one went to jail. And even though the AR-15 was eventually modified to accommodate the Olin powder and the jamming problems were partially corrected, the Army never went back to the original DuPont powder that had helped make the gun such a smashing success. Nor were the changes the Army arbitrarily ordered in the rifling ever corrected. Consequently, the AR-15 lost forever the remarkable combination of performance and reliability that had so marked its dazzling debut.

Years later, Mullen could hardly speak about all that had happened in connection with the AR-15 without raw emotion boiling forth.

"When I write my book, I'll have to do it on asbestos paper," he said. "Because my words will burn."

15

THE FINAL BREAKTHROUGH

ASIDE FROM A CHILLING LOOK AT CRIMINAL malfeasance by an official government entity, the insight Mullen provided (and Fallows later brilliantly reported) about the AR-15 allowed Donahue to refine further his understanding of the President's head wound. For the first time, the gunsmith was able to create a detailed mental picture of the physics involved in the bullet's explosive impact with Kennedy's skull.

Because of its slower velocity and thick copper jacket, Donahue knew Oswald's 6.5mm Carcano bullet would have fractured mechanically, that is broken up as a result of the physical impact with the skull. Oliver's tests in 1964 proved this: When fired into a skull, his Carcano bullets separated into several large fragments consisting of the lead core and thick copper jacket.

But because the AR-15 .223 round traveled at a velocity one-third again as fast as the Carcano bullet, because it was lighter and because it had a much thinner jacket, the AR-15 bullet would have—and did—behave in a fundamentally different way.

When the .223 round struck the President's skull, the bullet was already hot from the friction created by its flight and by its movement out of the barrel of the gun. The slug's temperature increased even more from the friction created by penetration of the skull wall. As a result, the lead beneath the jacket melted, or liquefied. Then almost immediately, the lightweight, inherently unstable bullet began to tumble. This motion increased the bullet's cross-section profile and consequently intensified the drag on the projectile. The ensuing stress ruptured the thin copper jacket near the cannelure, the recessed imprint near the base of the bullet that clamps the round to the cartridge. The missile's tumbling motion, combined with its enormous centrifugal velocity, then shredded the already ruptured jacket and flung the now-molten lead core outward in a circular pattern near the front of the brain.

These minuscule droplets of lead quickly solidified after striking the much cooler brain fluid and tissue. Dr. Fisher, in his conversation with Donahue, had described the presence of exactly this kind of tiny, round lead fragments located throughout the front of Kennedy's brain and embedded in the top of Kennedy's skull.

To Donahue, this sharper picture of the .223's impact characteristics reinforced his belief that a bullet from Oswald's gun could not have caused the wound Kennedy suffered. Later, his conclusions about the differences between the AR-15 bullet and a full metal–jacketed military round were confirmed in a pathology textbook written by Dr. Vincent J. M. Di Maio, one of the nation's foremost authorities on gunshot wounds.

According to Di Maio's *Gunshot Wounds: Practical Aspects of Firearms, Ballistics and Forensic Techniques:*

> Military bullets, by virtue of their full metal jackets, tend to pass through the body intact, thus producing less extensive injuries than hunting ammunition. Military bullets usually do not fragment in the body or shed fragments of lead in their paths. Because of the high velocity of such military rounds as well as their tough construction, it is possible for such bullets to pass through more than one individual before coming to rest. These bullets may be almost virginal in appearance after recovery from the body.
>
> One exception to these observations is the 5.56-mm M-16 cartridge. This particular cartridge has gained widespread notoriety in both the lay press and the medical literature. The wounds inflicted often are described as explosive in nature. . . . The 5.56-mm round does not explode in the body; it does, however, have a tendency to tumble and fragment, with [the] lead core "squirted" out the base. Because it does fragment, it tends to lose considerable amounts of kinetic energy, thus producing relatively severe wounds for the amount of muzzle energy it possesses.[1]

Di Maio went on to describe the so-called "lead snowstorm" visible on X rays of .223 wounds, and included an example in the text. The X ray showed a hail of minute, irregular fragments embedded in tissue in a pattern nearly identical to the one seen in the Kennedy autopsy X rays. "Such a picture is not seen with pistol bullets, nor with one exception, with full metal–jacketed bullets. The sole exception is the 5.56-mm [.223] cartridge, whose propensity to fragment has been previously discussed."[2]

Donahue's review of the performance characteristics of the respective AR-15 and Carcano bullets was well timed, for in 1980, one of the most sophisticated ballistic investigations yet of the Kennedy assassination appeared. The book was entitled *Kennedy and Lincoln: Medical and Ballistic Comparisons of Their Assassinations* and was written by John K. Lattimer, a physician at Columbia University's

School of Medicine. Lattimer was a urologist by training, but he'd gained considerable experience with gunshot wounds as a combat surgeon in World War II.[3]

Most important, Lattimer was the first private citizen to view the Kennedy autopsy photographs and X rays after restrictions on the material were finally lifted in 1971. He'd accomplished this simply by making formal requests with the National Archives to view the evidence.[4] His requests were granted on three separate occasions in 1972, 1973, and 1975.[5]

Even with this unprecedented access, however, Lattimer failed to tumble to the inconsistencies surrounding the head wound. Like the majority of assassination researchers, Lattimer focused much of his attention on the single bullet theory and left the subtle but profound questions posed by the head bullet's left-to-right trajectory and its disintegration on impact unasked and unanswered.

Nonetheless, Lattimer did achieve breakthroughs in his research that Donahue found to be extremely important. The most startling of these was his conclusion that the bullet that had struck Kennedy's neck had cracked one of his vertebra, and in so doing, caused a grave, probably fatal concussive wound to the spinal cord.[6]

This claim flew in the face of the conventionally held view that Kennedy probably would have survived the neck wound. Indeed, Doctors Fisher and Morgan, following their review of the X rays for Ramsey Clark in 1968, had concluded the bullet had barely brushed the vertebra and broken no bones.

Lattimer, however, discerned that tiny splinters visible on the X rays in the vicinity of the first thoracic vertebra were in fact bone, not bullet, as Fisher's '68 panel had concluded. This meant the bullet cracked the vertebra and grazed, or at least brushed, alongside the spinal cord. Hence, if Kennedy would have survived the trauma at all—something Lattimer doubted—it probably would have been only as a vegetable quadriplegic.[7]

Lattimer pointed to a late-nineteenth-century medical article written by William Thorburn to bolster the contention that Kennedy's spinal cord had been seriously damaged by the bullet. The article noted that a neuromuscular reflex causes the elbows to fly up and out immediately after severe trauma is inflicted on the spine in the cervical area. Included in Thorburn's article was a drawing of a man who'd experienced just such an injury: His elbows and arms were high and wide and in virtually the same position as Kennedy's were immediately after Oswald's bullet struck his neck.[8] (See illustration 18.)

Donahue was able to confirm Lattimer's conclusions about the mortal nature of the neck wound when he obtained a slide of one of the X rays used as evidence during the House Select Committee investigation. The X ray was a front-view, or anterior-posterior, look at Kennedy's neck and chest. Studying it with a magnifying glass,

Donahue was startled by what he saw. The transverse process of the first thoracic vertebra was not only fractured, as Lattimer had suggested, but displaced in three directions. (See illustration 31.) Incredibly, the damage to Kennedy's spine was far greater than anyone had suggested before. In fact, the damage was so obvious that Donahue could only conclude that neither Fisher, Morgan, nor Lattimer had ever seen this particular X ray; they'd apparently only seen lateral, side-view pictures of the spine.

The realization that Kennedy's neck wound would have likely been fatal, by itself, had a profound effect on Donahue. Until Lattimer's book and his own subsequent examination of the unknown X ray, he'd believed Hickey's shot was the one that had killed the President. Now he realized the AR-15 round had struck a man already doomed. Obviously this fact reduced the catastrophic implications of the accident and, to Donahue's way of thinking, made the government's decision to continue covering up the event even less justified.

At the same time, Donahue's new understanding of the neck wound proved to be an unexpected but immense personal relief. In the years since he'd identified Hickey as the gunman, Donahue had developed considerable empathy toward the agent. Now it was almost as if, having set out to prove to the world that a well-intentioned man had been involved in a ghastly accident, he wanted to cushion the blow. Perhaps these goals were mutually exclusive. But the fact that the accident would ultimately have had no bearing on whether Kennedy lived or died was a great comfort to Donahue.

Lattimer, for his part, took his detailed approach to the neck wound one final step in his book. The doctor pointed out that even if the spinal cord damage had not proved fatal, the fact that the President suffered from Addison's disease would have, on its own, significantly reduced the President's chances of survival. Addison's disease involves a chronic insufficiency of cortisone and other steroidal hormones manufactured by the adrenal glands. Treatment became relatively routine in the late 1940s with the advent of synthetic cortisone, a substance capable of duplicating many of the regulatory functions performed by the naturally produced hormone. It is well known that Kennedy was regularly taking oral cortisone treatments at the time of his death. One by-product of long-term cortisone use, unfortunately, is that the body's ability to resist infection is significantly diminished.[9] Lattimer believed the wound through Kennedy's bacteria-laden trachea would have likely caused serious infection—infection the President's weakened immune system would have had great difficulty defeating.[10]

Interestingly, the fact that Kennedy suffered from Addison's disease was never publicly revealed while he was living. Robert Kennedy, in fact, had categorically denied rumors his brother suffered from the ailment during the 1960 presidential campaign.[11] Then in 1967, in a fine piece of medical detective work, University of Kansas oncologist John Nichols demonstrated that Kennedy's disease had actually been well documented in a medical journal article in 1955. The article in question appeared in the November 1955 issue of *The Archives of Surgery* and described the dangers and complications of back surgery performed a year earlier on an anonymous thirty-seven-year-old male patient with Addison's disease. According to Nichols, evidence conclusively showed the procedure was indeed the back operation performed on then–Senator Kennedy in October 1954. The physician who wrote the original article declined to confirm or deny Nichols's conclusions.[12]

To Donahue, the fact that Robert Kennedy had lied about the existence of JFK's Addison's disease showed that RFK was willing to misrepresent the truth in order to protect his brother politically. This further strengthened Donahue's belief that Bobby Kennedy would have had no qualms about covering up the accident in 1963.

The final, major contribution Lattimer made toward a clearer understanding of what had actually happened in Dallas was his refutation of conspiracy theorists' claim that the sharp, violent backward movement of Kennedy's head proved the final shot came from the front. The currency of this long-held view—first suggested by Josiah Thompson in 1967—increased dramatically in 1975 after the Zapruder film was shown for the first time on national television. Critics argued that if Kennedy really was shot from behind, physics would require that the President's head and shoulders be driven forward. Conversely, the backward movement shown on the film seemed to prove unequivocally that the shot had come from the front.

To anyone who'd ever watched a shoot-'em-up Western movie, this seemed like a logical argument. But as Lattimer and a University of California scientist were able to demonstrate, such a claim was based on an inaccurate and incomplete understanding of physics and physiology.

After the gruesome Zapruder film ran on a late-night talk show in early '75 and rekindled the controversy about shots from the front, Luis Alvarez, a Nobel Prize–winning physicist, became intrigued with the question of just how the human skull did respond when hit from behind with a high-velocity bullet. Alvarez made some quick calculations and speculated that perhaps the jet-propulsion effect of a large amount of liquid and semiliquid brain material pushing out of the exit wound would have enough force to drive the head and shoulders backward. If true, this would explain the seemingly inconsistent movement of the President's head.[13]

Alvarez designed an experiment to test his premise. He took appropriately sized melons and wrapped them in duct tape to simulate the human skull and the strong scalp fibers that surround it. He then suspended some of the melons in air with tape, placed some on pedestals, set up a remote camera and opened fire with a high-powered rifle.

The results of the test, according to Lattimer, were as dramatic as
they were illuminating. In every case, the melons were either hurtled
off the pedestals toward the gun—or, in the case of the suspended
melons, spun upward and toward the gun so violently that they tore
loose of their restraints.[14]

Lattimer conducted similar experiments and produced like results.
The doctor went on to suggest that a neuromuscular reflex triggered
by damage to the brain probably caused the muscles in the President's back and shoulders to tighten. Since Kennedy was leaning
slightly to the left when the shot hit, this sudden rigidity would have
further contributed to the President's movement backward and to the
left.[15]

Alvarez and Lattimer's efforts represented the most cogent analysis ever done on the mysterious backward movement of the President's head. To Donahue, their findings were conclusive, particularly
since the gunsmith had already determined there was no ballistic or
forensic evidence to support the idea that Kennedy had been shot
from the front.

All told, Lattimer's book—though flawed in the aggregate and
essentially an updated endorsement of the Warren Report—helped
Donahue refine his understanding of the shooting in several important
ways. It also served as a prelude to his discovery of one final piece
of evidence that, to him at least, again pointed inexorably to the
AR-15 as the origin of the last shot.

The path to this breakthrough began in the summer of 1980, nearly
a year after Reppert's death. Donahue returned from work one
evening and found a small public notice from the newspaper set out
on the dining room table.

"You have any interest in that?" Katie asked, sticking her head in
from the kitchen.

"Could be," Howard replied, reading the item.

Apparently George Washington University was sponsoring extension classes in the Baltimore area for a master's program in forensic
science. Registration was scheduled for later that month. Donahue
pondered the idea.

Once more, he'd reached a crossroads in his professional life. The
gun shop was still a going concern. But the economic picture had
changed considerably through the late 1970s. Large discount chains
were gobbling up an ever greater share of the firearms market, both
in Baltimore and nationwide, and increasingly, Donahue was having
a hard time competing. Almost every week, would-be buyers came
into the gun shop to price a particular firearm. Much to Donahue's
chagrin, the customers would then triumphantly announce that the
same gun could be bought for 10 or 20 percent less at a discount
store. It wasn't that Donahue's profits were excessive. On the contrary. Margins were cut to the bone. But he still couldn't match the
deep discounts of the large, volume-driven chains. At the same time,

cost pressure was building against the business on another front. Insurance premiums were skyrocketing. Part of the increase stemmed from the dramatic industry-wide price hikes of the last half of the seventies and the first half of the eighties. Part of the problem was the crime wave sweeping suburban Baltimore.

In any event, the fact was that Donahue did not possess the business skills necessary to adapt and survive in the increasingly harsh marketplace. As losses at the gun shop increased, Donahue was forced to think seriously about closing the business down. What he hoped to do instead was focus on his two highly profitable sidelines: gun appraising and expert witness work.

He knew the credentials gained from the George Washington University forensic science courses would increase his credibility as an expert witness and firearms examiner. He also wondered if perhaps he might not be able to learn something new about the Kennedy assassination if he had just a little more training. And so Donahue returned to school, at the seasoned age of fifty-eight. Two nights a week he drove to Ft. Meade, halfway between Baltimore and Washington, for classes.

The first course on the agenda that autumn, Physical Aspects of Forensic Science, focused on analysis and identification of the physical evidence, including paint fragments, broken glass, fabric, oil or dirt marks, or anything else that might provide a clue from the scene of the crime. Not surprisingly, most of those enrolled in the program were police officers or state and federal investigators. While Donahue found the sessions fascinating for the most part, at times he couldn't help but feel like a self-taught country lawyer who'd practiced law all his life and then finally decided to get a degree to make everything official. But Howard worked diligently and in the end passed the final exam in good shape.

One of the courses that soon followed was Firearms Identification. The class focused on standard ballistic analysis, including the various procedures used to determine the origin and capabilities of a particular bullet. Most of the material was familiar to him, but Donahue nonetheless found it beneficial to review and occasionally supplement his existing knowledge.

The instructor of the class was a man named Cortlandt Cunningham, formerly chief of the Firearms Identification Unit of the FBI. The name seemed vaguely familiar to Donahue, although he hadn't a clue as to why. In any event, he thought little more about it as the weeks passed.

In the spring of 1981, the gunsmith enrolled in the course he had looked forward to the most: Biological Aspects of Forensic Science. The class presented a generalized overview of the biology of forensic pathology—everything from wound identification to blood analysis. Again, Donahue was already familiar with much of the material, but a good deal of it was new.

For the final project in the class, students were given the choice of writing about the pathology of any one of a number of well-known murder cases. Among these was the Kennedy assassination. Donahue relished his good luck and jumped on the opportunity. The professor gave the students almost a year to complete their projects and Donahue worked on his steadily, carefully laying out the chronology of his investigation and the conclusions he'd eventually reached. In the course of double-checking his facts and reviewing sections of the Warren Report and other books, a name caught his attention. Cortlandt Cunningham, his former firearms identification instructor. That's where he'd seen the name before! Cunningham was one of the FBI firearms examiners who'd tested Oswald's Carcano and .38 special for the Warren Commission. He was also among the agents who'd removed broken bullet fragments from the Presidential limo on the night of November 22.[16]

Earlier, Donahue had visited the National Archives to examine the two largest bullet fragments found in the limo. Because of the absence of brain matter, blood, and hair in the cracks and folds of the lead, he'd concluded the bullet pieces had not passed through Kennedy's skull at all, as the Warren Commission claimed. Donahue instead believed the fragments originated from Oswald's true first shot—a miss that struck the pavement behind and to the right of the President and showered the limo with ricochet fragments. Several of these caused superficial wounds in Kennedy's scalp; another apparently cracked the car's windshield.

Donahue wondered if perhaps the two big fragments had been covered with blood and brain matter when they'd been recovered, and had simply been thoroughly cleaned before being sent to the National Archives. Cunningham, like all federal agents, was probably prohibited from discussing the specifics of any case he'd worked on, particularly one as notorious as the Kennedy assassination. But Donahue decided to call him anyway.*

"Mr. Cunningham. How do you do? . . . I'm Howard Donahue. I was in your firearms identification class last semester and ah, I'm working on a term paper on the Kennedy assassination for Biological Aspects. I had one question that maybe you could answer for me."

"I'll try," Cunningham replied, friendly enough.

"What I wanted to know is this: Do you remember if there was any cranial residue on the bullet fragments you picked up from the presidential limousine on the night of the twenty-second? You know, blood or hair or brain tissue or anything like that?"

"Well," Cunningham paused. "That's a good question. I sent the fragments up to Blood [the FBI's forensic serology lab], but never got an answer."

---

*The following conversation has been reconstructed from the recollections of Howard Donahue.

The response was less definitive than Donahue would have liked, but nonetheless it supported his suspicion that there probably had been no organic matter at all on the fragments. If there had been, it would likely have been visible to the naked eye and Cunningham would have remembered it. More important, the information would have been included in the Warren Report, since the presence of blood and bone on the lead would have strengthened the Commission's contention that the car fragments came from the head wound.

The fact was, no serological report was ever produced. Even Cunningham never received an answer. Once again, Donahue had uncovered an incongruity that he believed, indirectly at least, supported his conclusions about the origin of the shot.

The gunsmith toiled away on his term paper and finally completed it in April of 1982. The final product was a solid piece of work that conveyed precisely his conclusions and the manner in which they'd been reached. The professor, a notoriously tough grader, thought enough of the paper to give it an A.

Sometime later Donahue was browsing through his class materials and textbooks when a thought occurred to him. What, he wondered, was the diameter of the entrance wound in Kennedy's skull? Didn't he have that dimension somewhere? Wouldn't it show whether the last bullet had come from Oswald or Hickey?

Of course. Oswald's bullets were 6.5 millimeters in diameter. The AR-15 round was 5.56 millimeters in diameter. Therefore, if Oswald had fired the final shot, the hole in the skull should have been at least 6.5 millimeters in diameter. Donahue was fairly certain the dimensions of the entrance wound were in Dr. Humes's autopsy report. Thumbing through the document, he read that there was a "lacerated wound measuring 15 × 6 mm [in the scalp]. In the underlying bone is a corresponding wound through the skull. . . ."

The pathologist's language was maddeningly imprecise, but Humes seemed to be suggesting that the wound through the bone was six millimeters in diameter, half a millimeter smaller than the diameter of Oswald's Carcano bullets. Donahue hurriedly turned to the Warren Report's narrative description of the entrance wound. He found it on page 88: "The small hole on the back of the President's head measured one-forth of an inch by five-eighths of an inch (6 by 15 millimeters.)" Six millimeters . . . There it was again.

How, Donahue wondered, could Oswald's bullet have passed through a hole smaller than its diameter? And how would the Commission explain this apparent physical impossibility? He read on:

> The dimensions of that wound were consistent with having been caused by a 6.5 millimeter bullet fired from behind and above which struck at a tangent or an angle causing a 15-millimeter cut. The cut reflected a larger dimension of entry than the bullet's diameter of 6.5 millimeters, since the missile, in effect, sliced along the skull for a fractional

distance until it entered. The dimension of 6 millimeters, somewhat
smaller than the diameter of a 6.5 millimeter bullet, was caused by the
elastic recoil of the skull which shrinks the size of an opening after a
missile passes through it.[17]

Donahue was baffled. He could accept the explanation about the
fifteen-millimeter vertical axis of the wound, given Kennedy's head
had been tilted forward when the bullet hit. It was true the bullet
would have sliced, or "trenched," along the bone for a fraction of an
instant before penetrating. But to say the critical six-millimeter
horizontal dimension was caused by "the elastic recoil of the skull
which shrinks the size of an opening after a missile passes through
it . . ." Certainly the scalp tissue may have shrunk. But the underlying
bone? To Donahue, it was impossible. As far as he knew, bone was
an inflexible substance with the approximate consistency of masonite
or hard, dense plastic. After all, the skull would be worthless as a
container for the brain if it flexed or shrank. The whole purpose of
the skull is to stabilize and protect the delicate, nearly liquid tissue
of the brain.

The gunsmith then realized there was a way to test the Commission's claim about the size entrance wound a 6.5mm Carcano bullet
made. The packet of press information he'd picked up back in 1978
at the Assassinations Committee's ballistic hearings contained a
photograph of one of the Warren Commission's Carcano test skulls.
These were skulls the well-meaning but misinformed Dr. Olivier had
drilled with Carcano rounds in 1964 in an attempt to duplicate
Kennedy's exit wound. A rear-view photograph of the skull clearly
showed the entrance wound. Using a dial caliper, a precise measuring
instrument, and standard dimensions of a human skull, Donahue was
able to extrapolate the size of Olivier's entrance wound at between
eight and nine millimeters; considerably larger than the six-millimeter
wound the President apparently suffered.

Of course, this raised the question: Was the measurement of the
President's wound really accurate? It was hard to say. Humes's
language was predictably vague and Donahue realized that half a
millimeter was a very small increment. He knew that it was quite
possible the measurement had simply been made inaccurately. Then
again, the original skull hole measurement was made not by Humes,
but by Pierre Finck, the only pathologist experienced in gunshot
wounds present at the Bethesda autopsy.[18] It was reasonable, therefore, to assume that Finck had measured the hole correctly, even if
Humes had subsequently placed the wound four inches too low in his
final report.

Searching for additional information, Donahue next turned back to
the report produced by Dr. Russell Fisher's 1968 panel. Here he
found two seemingly contradictory references to the entrance hole's
diameter. In the first, based on an examination of photographs of

Kennedy's head, the panel concurred with the Commission's measurement of the scalp wound: 6 millimeters by 15 millimeters.

Further into the report, however, Fisher's group stated that the skull hole was judged to be eight—not six—millimeters in diameter. But looking closer, Donahue realized there was a basic contradiction here. According to the report, the sole basis for this assessment was an examination of one lateral, or profile, X ray of the President's skull. Reading this, Donahue realized it would have been physically impossible for the doctors to measure the hole's *horizontal* dimension (whether six or eight millimeters) through an examination of a *side-view* X ray. Fisher's panel had apparently measured the only thing they could see; namely, the hole's fifteen-millimeter vertical dimension distorted and truncated due to the hazy, obstructing effect of the cross-section of bone they necessarily would have had to peer through when viewing the hole from the side-view X ray.

Assuming, then, that the six-millimeter measurement was accurate and a measurement of the skull wound as well as the scalp wound, was there any validity to the Commission's claim regarding the elasticity of the skull? Was it actually possible for bone to shrink?

Donahue rang up a pathologist at the Baltimore city morgue, Dr. Gregory Kaufman, to get an expert's opinion. Without going into specifics, Donahue informed Kaufman that he was conducting a shooting investigation and was interested in the relationship between the size of an entry wound in the skull and the caliber of the bullet that inflicted it.

Kaufman's answer: "The size of the entry wound in the skull is always slightly larger than the caliber of the bullet causing it."

Donahue would put the question to a number of pathologists in the years ahead, and the answer was always the same. The skull, they said, does not shrink, although later Donahue did unearth at least one report that seemed to indicate otherwise. In the January-June 1964 issue of *Zacchia,* a German medical journal, Dr. Lorand Tamaska reported that tests with a variety of handguns fired into fresh cadaver skulls revealed the skull could in fact shrink by as much as one millimeter after a bullet passed through.

Reading this, Donahue realized that Tamaska's use of only handguns in his tests significantly diminished the information's relevance to the Kennedy case. The bullets Tamaska fired traveled at relatively low velocities of between 700 and 1,200 feet per second. The Carcano bullet, on the other hand, traveled at 2,200 feet per second, and the AR-15 round at 3,200 feet per second.

Due to their high speed, the rifle bullets would pulverize the area immediately adjacent to their point of penetration and thus create a hole slightly larger than their diameter, as Kaufman had reported. The pistol bullets, on the other hand, because of their slower velocity, would push through the bone without nearly the destructive peripheral damage.

So what did he have? Donahue reviewed his findings:

- It was highly doubtful that a 6.5mm, high-velocity bullet could create a six-millimeter hole.
- Oswald's bullets were 6.5mm in diameter. Kennedy's skull wound was apparently six millimeters in diameter.
- According to at least one pathologist, bullets always cause entrance wounds in the skull slightly larger than their diameter.
- The AR-15 round was 5.56mm in diameter. A six-millimeter entrance hole, therefore, was completely consistent with the AR-15 .223 bullet.
- The Warren Commission's own tests proved a Carcano round caused an entrance wound of at least eight millimeters in diameter.

Like the gold miner who pans for years and finally sifts out a sizable nugget, Donahue was at once ecstatic and relieved by his discovery. True, the entrance hole diameter proof was less than conclusive. But if Finck's measurement was correct, and there was no reason to think it was not, then the hole in Kennedy's skull was incompatible with a Carcano round and completely compatible with an AR-15 .223 bullet.

For Donahue, this new piece of evidence converged with the bullet's trajectory and disintegration to establish, in his mind at least, complete certainty about the origin of the shot.

And yet . . . the gunsmith could only laugh ruefully to himself as he sat alone in his basement late on that fateful night. For after all, what did it matter? Who really cared? Whom could he tell about his discovery now? He'd gone to the press before. He'd gone to Congress. Nothing had come of it. And now the world was rolling on. It was the 1980s. The Kennedy assassination was a long, long time ago.

So the days and weeks passed, and ever so gradually, a sense of dull frustration began to erode the optimism Donahue had felt for so long about his work. He was still excited about his latest discovery, but with each day that went by, the possibility that his conclusions would die with him loomed ever larger in his mind. With an edge of bitterness, the gunsmith wondered: What would it take to make people listen? Where were the journalists, the writers, the film makers? Surely someone must see the logic behind his conclusions and pursue the trail he'd blazed.

More than anything, Donahue simply wanted the American people to know what he knew; to see what he saw, to finally understand the tragedy that had lacerated the country so many years before. Because the wound had festered, never healed. The question "What really happened in Dallas?" still hung across the land like a pall.

He'd spent fifteen years of his life digging for the truth of the assassination. He was tired. He was getting old. Through 1982, Donahue struggled gamely to write something himself. But the effort was desultory. Howard lacked the discipline and the time necessary to write a book.

On the surface he remained, as always, unfailingly bright and cheerful, but Katie and their daughter, Colleen, could sense a deep sorrow creeping into Howard's heart as the months and years rushed past. At one point, Donahue's hopes were momentarily lifted when Katie in typically bold fashion approached CBS *60 Minutes* anchor Mike Wallace following a speech he'd made at a local university. Katie walked up to the podium and, introducing herself, handed the famous reporter an envelope containing the *Sun* articles and background information on Howard. Wallace took the envelope and graciously thanked her, but neither Howard nor Katie ever heard from Mike Wallace or *60 Minutes* again.

Donahue's spirits did improve again in November 1982 when a writer from the *Sun* magazine included a section on the gunsmith and his theory in a roundup story coinciding with the nineteenth anniversary of the Dallas shooting.

The article reviewed the theories of a handful of well-known assassination buffs and told of Donahue's involvement in the CBS reenactment, the long years of his probe, and conclusions he'd eventually reached. Once again, Hickey's name was not mentioned.

And although the article triggered a new wave of requests from civic groups seeking Donahue for lectures on the assassination, in time that subsided. Once again the gunsmith found himself, for all intents and purposes, alone. Meanwhile, the tough economic reality at the gun store showed no signs of improving. Katie was back helping out most of the time now. In 1980, she'd closed her fabric store after the landlord refused to renew the lease. Her seven-year run in business had been a prosperous one. But by 1983, the gun shop was losing money at a considerable rate. The deep recession of the early Reagan years exacerbated the situation, and with Katie's income gone now, times grew harder.

When the bottom line did not improve as Donahue had hoped with the autumn hunting season of 1983, the long-delayed decision to close the store was made. Howard shut the doors for good in February 1984. Luckily, he found no shortage of expert testimony and gun appraisal work and the transition to freelancer was relatively smooth.

A year earlier, Donahue had abandoned pursuit of his master's degree. Going to school cost money and time, two commodities in short supply as he'd struggled through 1983 to turn his business around. The classes had been moved to Washington, doubling his travel time, and in any event, he'd already taken the most important courses.

And if he didn't have a master's degree to display on his résumé, he was still able to cite the courses he'd attended. The new credentials, plus his already established reputation in Baltimore legal and law enforcement circles, combined to generate more than enough work to sustain the couple's modest lifestyle. And life went on well enough.

But just when it seemed the Donahues had reached a new equilibrium in their lives, catastrophe struck. In the autumn of 1984, Katie suffered a massive stroke. She was diagnosed as having a hypertensive bleed, a stroke affecting her entire left side. The trauma left her unable to talk or swallow, she could barely see and she could not move her left foot, leg, hand, or arm.

Howard found the best doctors he could and almost immediately Katie was started on an aggressive physical therapy program. In her head, Katie was overwhelmed and humiliated by what had happened. But through the fog she vowed she would never let the stroke defeat her.

Howard and Colleen visited the hospital every day. Within two weeks, Katie was showing marked improvement. Although she'd still not regained much function in her extremities, she was able to talk slowly and swallow, and her vision was improving. In time and with help, she was able to get into a wheelchair. Even so, the doctors privately told Howard that the chances of his wife recovering fully anytime soon—if at all—were extremely remote.

About a month into the rehabilitation, the director of the hospital's physical therapy program informed Katie that she'd placed her name on the waiting list for a bed at Baltimore's Good Samaritan Hospital.*

"They have an excellent program for stroke victims," the therapist said gently. "You'll be able to learn all the skills you'll need to function with your disability."

Katie struggled to sit upright in her wheelchair. She looked the woman straight in the eye as the weeks of frustration came to a head.

"Never mind about that," she said sharply. "You can just cancel that reservation, because I do not intend to be a stroke victim, and I do not plan on spending any more time in this Goddamn wheelchair."

The old blood was up now.

"I am going home this weekend and I'll work it out from there," she said finally.

The therapist was horrified. But Katie was adamant. She called Colleen and instructed her to make arrangements to rent a hospital bed forthwith. Several days later, Katie checked out, although only after agreeing to sign a release absolving her doctor and the hospital of any liability.

Katie's electric hospital bed was set up in the Donahues' family room, just off the kitchen. From her bed, Katie could watch TV, answer the telephone and supervise Howard's cooking, which improved steadily as the days wore on. Though initially uncertain and

---

*The following conversation has been reconstructed from the recollections of Katie Donahue.

apprehensive about caring for his invalid wife, Howard was soon managing admirably. He'd dragged a mattress down from the bedroom and every night either he or Colleen kept a vigil.

But that did little to make the nights much easier for Katie. Her mind was constantly whirring and if she was lucky, she might get an hour's sleep. So she passed the endless hours after midnight listening to the radio. One of her favorite programs was "The Larry King Show," the live, nationwide talk show that covered the waterfront of American life.

One night King's guest was an author named John Davis. Davis was a first cousin of Jackie Kennedy and had just written a book called *The Kennedys: Dynasty and Disaster*. As he talked of the Kennedys and the assassination, an idea occurred to Katie.*

"Howard," she hissed toward the dark, inert form sprawled on the mattress nearby. "Wake up. Listen to this guy."

Howard groggily pulled himself up.

"His name is John Davis," she said excitedly. "He might be worth trying to get a hold of to write the book on your theory. He knows all about the Kennedys and he's even related to Jackie."

Howard mumbled agreeably and fell back asleep.

The next morning, Katie reminded Howard of what she'd heard the night before.

"It probably wouldn't hurt to try to contact him," he mused. "Who knows, he might jump at the opportunity."

That afternoon Howard drafted a letter. He outlined his investigation and the conclusions he'd eventually reached and asked if Davis would have any interest in writing a book about it all. Then he mailed it off care of Davis's publisher and waited for a reply.

Thanksgiving passed and Katie continued to make remarkable progress. Though she still couldn't walk, she was routinely rolling out of bed and crawling up the stairs to her bedroom. By early January, the physical therapists and doctors were marveling at her recovery. They called it miraculous. But Katie wasn't surprised. She'd vowed to whip the stroke and she had.

Donahue received a letter from John Davis some weeks after Christmas. Davis apologized for being so slow in responding. Much to Howard's delight, Davis said he was very interested in the theory and the possibility of doing a book. He asked Howard to send the *Sun* article and any additional material he might have, and Donahue quickly obliged.

The early 1980s had not been kind to the Donahues. But now, just maybe, things were about to turn around.

---

*The following conversation has been reconstructed from the recollections of Howard and Katie Donahue.

16

HOPE DIES HARD

DONAHUE WAS THRILLED AT THE PROSPECT OF working with a successful author, and the two men corresponded frequently through the first half of 1985. Davis continued to express a great deal of interest in a collaboration and Donahue obligingly forwarded the writer a steady stream of the assassination material he'd assembled over the years.

Howard and Katie finally met Davis face-to-face that summer in Washington at a three-day convention on the Kennedy assassination. They found him to be charming and urbane and although a contractual relationship was not formalized, the Donahues were confident Davis was in earnest about pursuing the story.

But as the weeks went by and letters bounced back and forth, Donahue became increasingly mystified, then exasperated by Davis's seeming inability to focus on or comprehend the ballistic evidence the gunsmith had developed. Over and over, Davis would ask the same rudimentary questions. Over and over, Donahue would explain how the trajectory of the bullet, the slug's explosive disintegration, and the diameter of the entrance wound proved, to him anyway, that Hickey had fired the last shot.

To Donahue, it seemed Davis wasn't listening. Admittedly, part of the problem may have been in the way Donahue communicated the information. It was true the gunsmith could sometimes deluge the uninitiated with a flood of scientific nuance and detail. Conversely, Davis may have been distracted by the success of his Kennedy book or feeling the strain from the grueling publicity tours he undertook to promote it. For whatever reasons, the connection between the two men began to break down.

When Davis finally let it be known that he was under contract to write a new book detailing the apparent connections between organized crime and the Kennedy assassination, Donahue saw the writing on the wall. Contact between the two become increasingly strained and erratic.

Davis's "mob-hit" book would go on to become the 1988 best-seller *Mafia Kingfish—Carlos Marcello and the Assassination of John F. Kennedy*. The story detailed evidence suggesting that New Orleans mob boss Carlos Marcello had had Kennedy killed in retaliation for the Kennedy brothers' attempts to destroy the Marcello crime organization. Davis presented his scenario in compelling fashion and drew from a wide variety of sources, including evidence assembled by Jim Garrison over the course of his 1967–69 Ferrie-Shaw probe.

But aside from the habitual, vague suggestions of a gunman on the grassy knoll, the author made no attempt to present any ballistic evidence that could conceivably support the idea that more than one gunman had fired on the President. Adding insult to injury, from Donahue's perspective, was the fact that the only mention the gunsmith received in the book was in the back-page acknowledgments, where Davis thanked one "Harold Donahue" and a host of others for supplying "important documents and information on an informal, nonremunerative basis."[1]

And yet there was one revealing encounter that emerged as a result of Donahue's involvement with Davis. Early on, Davis had recommended Donahue pay a visit to Harold Weisberg, a fellow Marylander and the well-known shaman of assassination theorists. Davis figured the veteran Warren Commission critic might be able to offer some insight or evidence that could help substantiate Donahue's theory. But Howard was skeptical. He'd read several of Weisberg's books and had long marveled at the author's lack of knowledge about firearms and ballistics—ignorance that allowed Weisberg to conjure up a hail of bullets from the grassy knoll and elsewhere in Dealey Plaza. Donahue was likewise put off by the shrill, excoriating tone of Weisberg's writings. Weisberg spoke at nearly every turn about the black hand of a government conspiracy, yet he never seemed able to develop any logical arguments about who specifically was behind this treachery or why.

Even so, Donahue in late 1985 had been willing to do whatever he could to advance the book project with Davis. And he had to admit that Weisberg did provide key information to Ralph Reppert back in 1977 concerning the government's neutron activation testing of bullet fragments removed from Kennedy's brain. Just maybe the cantankerous critic had something else of value in his files. With nothing to lose, Donahue dropped Weisberg a note. Weisberg responded several days later and said he'd be happy to have lunch with the gunsmith and his wife.

He added that he was aware of Donahue's theory from the *Sun* article but didn't know of any evidence that justified the gunsmith's conclusions. Every photograph from Dealey Plaza appeared to disprove the accident scenario, Weisberg said.

This vote of no confidence notwithstanding, Howard and Katie drove to Weisberg's farm in western Maryland and spent the afternoon with the king of the critics. Through lunch, Weisberg complained bitterly about the University of Maryland's refusal to accept his donation of the thousands of assassination-related documents he'd collected over the years. When the subject of Donahue's theory finally came up, Weisberg dismissed it out of hand. But despite his earlier claim, he could provide no photographs that refuted the thesis. He did point out that in the Altgens picture, taken just after the first shot was fired, no crack was visible on the limousine windshield. Ergo, Weisberg said, Donahue's belief that the first shot had missed, ricocheted, and struck the windshield with a fragment was unsupported by the photographic record.

Donahue responded by noting that the bright sunlight that day may have made the crack invisible from the front. As well, a bystander wearing white was visible through the windshield at exactly the place where the crack was later found. This likely further masked the presence of the broken glass in the Altgens photo.

Weisberg nonetheless remained adamant in his belief that the head shot came from the front, from the grassy knoll. At one point he leaned forward conspiratorially and told Howard, "I have proof the bullet entered from the front. The wound was surrounded by fragments." Donahue smiled wanly to himself. Weisberg's understanding of the fragments was exactly backward. An M-16 bullet—or any thinjacketed, high-velocity round—enters the skull, disintegrates, and then deposits fragments on the side opposite from where it enters.

This was clearly demonstrated by the gelatin block tests the House Select Committee had conducted in 1977–78. Photos showed the M-16 round fired by committee marksmen shattered and tumbled after striking the gelatin and caused enormous "tissue" damage before spraying multiple, minute fragments forward, to the front of the block, opposite from the side the bullet entered on. (See illustration 26.)

In fact, the shattering, fragmenting "wound" in the gelatin nearly replicated exactly the one Kennedy suffered, although this was never acknowledged by the committee. Moreover, Donahue knew the only weapon capable of inflicting a frontal wound as massive as Kennedy's would have been a shotgun fired from a few feet away. No shotgun pellets were found in Kennedy's brain and, obviously, no one was seen with a shotgun along Elm Street.

Of course, the gunsmith mentioned none of these troublesome technicalities to Weisberg as the old man held court that afternoon. Donahue did point out that in his opinion, the bullet's trajectory, explosive disintegration and the size of the entrance wound proved Hickey had fired the last shot. He did not, however, belabor the point. It was obvious Weisberg knew absolutely nothing about firearms and ballistics. And it was equally obvious the critic had no desire to begin learning now.

And so the day faded and Howard and Katie bid the venerable critic good-bye. More than anything else, the Donahues felt sorry for Weisberg as they drove home that evening. Here was a man over seventy years old who'd given a good part of his life to studying the Kennedy assassination. Now his health was failing, the state university couldn't care less about his painstakingly amassed collection of assassination documents and, to top it off, his conclusions about how Kennedy died were flat wrong.

Following the encounter with Weisberg, Howard realized he would have to finish the investigation on his own. He knew there was an important subject that needed to be reexamined in greater detail: the Secret Service in general and, in particular, their actions in Dallas. What more could he learn?

Like many twentieth-century American institutions, the Secret Service was forged in the caldron of the Civil War. Originally, the Service was conceived as part of the Treasury Department and charged with investigating and combating currency counterfeiting, which was endemic in the war years. It was not until after the assassination of President William McKinley in 1901 that the agency picked up the additional duty of protecting the President.[2]

In time the Service would also be responsible for shielding the vice president, the President-elect, major presidential candidates, former Presidents and their wives, widows of former Presidents, presidential children and visiting heads of state.[3] The agency also developed a sophisticated research division that today undertakes the daunting task of identifying and monitoring potential assassins. As well, the Service continues to retain authority in cases involving counterfeiting.

But it remains the President's stoic, steadfast bodyguards who dominate the public's perception of the famous organization. The Secret Service agent has emerged as something of an archetypal American hero in recent decades: strong, courageous, and willing to lay down his or her life in the blink of an eye to defend the leader of a free and open society. This image is not exaggerated, for the job is dangerous, difficult and relentlessly stressful. Even in earlier, less violent times, the lot of an agent was a hard one.

Kentuckian Edmund Starling worked on the White House protection detail for thirty years, from 1914 to 1944. His biography, written by Thomas Sugrue in 1946, provides one of the most detailed glimpses of the day-to-day life of an agent. The book captures the atmosphere of grinding pressure agents face as they wrestle with the nearly incompatible goals of protecting the President and allowing the American people a degree of access to their leader.

In one of his many letters home, Starling recounts a typically enervating journey—accompanying President Wilson to Philadelphia for the second game of the World Series in 1915:

Well, we are back from another arduous trip full of hard work, loss of
sleep, nervous tension, and anxiety. . . .

We landed in Phila. about 1 p.m. and were met at the station by a
vast throng, which the policemen could hardly handle. At 1:25 p.m. we
rode out to the baseball game, 26 squares from the depot. I rode on
the running board of the automobile all of the way and literally pushed
the President and his crowd through the entrance of the ball park. The
police seemed to be powerless to keep them back.

[After the game] we hurried back to the depot, people yelling all the
way, and it was certainly with a sigh of relief that I felt the train move
forward in the direction of Washington, D.C.[4]

Former Secret Service agent Marty Venker would describe his
duties in similar terms more than seventy years later. For Venker,
protecting Presidents (in his case, Ford and Carter) was a grueling
mix of mind-numbing travel, fourteen- to eighteen-hour days, six
months straight without a day off, abject boredom and always the
lurking prospect of disaster. Venker told biographer George Rush in
the 1988 book *Confessions of an Ex-Secret Service Agent*:

You started to view crowds like excitable animals. They could stam-
pede at any moment. You never knew what would spook them. People
act differently together than they do as individuals. . . . Mostly you
relied on your sense of human character. You learn to look for the face
that doesn't belong. The guy who's grinning at some solemn event like
a memorial service. You can usually tell when someone's having a
psychotic episode.[5]

Of course there were times when I felt like a moving target. But you
just had to assume, "Hey, it won't happen to me." You couldn't get
morbid, or you'd be paralyzed. I wondered, and I'm sure every agent
wondered, if when the time came to take the bullet I'd go through with
it. But you know, heroism and self-preservation don't always conflict
with each other. If some nut pulls a gun, shrinking away from it is
what'll get you killed. You only have one chance to dive on it before it
goes off. Later, if you're still alive, you can shiver and say,
"Hoooooooly shit!"[6]

In time, the pressure cooker of guarding Presidents and former
Presidents—notably Richard Nixon—led Venker to a nervous break-
down. He rallied, recovered and found a new career in music. But
fatal heart attacks, alcoholism, and suicide were and are by no means
uncommon among the men responsible for shielding the President. A
study conducted in 1978 by the National Institutes of Health concluded that Secret Service agents aged two years for every year they
spent guarding the President.[7]

This ratio must have been considerably higher for the agents who
protected Kennedy. Unlike his predecessor, JFK was active, ener-

getic and constantly on the move. In 1963 alone, the President made eighty-three trips domestically and abroad.[8] Between October 1962, when *Air Force One* was commissioned and the flight to Dallas a little over a year later, Kennedy logged 75,000 miles on the presidential jet.[9] This schedule was punishing enough for the Secret Service, given the painstaking advance work and complicated police liaison procedures each trip demanded, not to mention the elements of danger and uncertainty that attended each new town or city.

In the case of Kennedy, however, the Service's difficulties were compounded by the fact that the President was at best cavalier and too often profoundly fatalistic when it came to his own safety. For Presidents to bridle under the intrusive embrace of the Secret Service was nothing new, but a combination of factors made Kennedy a particularly hard case. As a consummate politician, JFK naturally resented anything that interfered with his ability to get close to the people. He also viewed himself as a man's man and no doubt took exception to actions that he felt diminished his casual machismo in the eyes of the public.

More to the point, it had been a very near thing for twenty-seven-year-old Jack when a Japanese destroyer sliced his PT boat in half in World War II. Perhaps this event, along with the death of his older brother, Joe, marked the origins of Kennedy's abiding obsession with death. This bleak preoccupation was particularly evident in the President's oft-noted love for the poem "I Have a Rendezvous with Death," a mournful ode penned by American Alan Seeger shortly before he was killed in the service of the French Foreign Legion during World War I.

With his ascension to the presidency, JFK's fatalism translated into running gallows humor about the possibility of being killed in office. During a motorcade in California, an admirer tossed a small life jacket into the President's car. Kennedy joked to Dave Powers, who sat beside him, "If they wanted to kill you, you wouldn't be around."[10]

Not long before the trip to Texas, a speeding motorist flew past the presidential limousine on a road in Virginia. To Charles Bartlett, a reporter and family friend, Kennedy teased: "They shouldn't allow that. He could have shot you, Charlie."[11]

The President's disregard for his own safety reached a zenith in the fading days of autumn just before his assassination. Kennedy traveled to New York City a week before the trip to Dallas and was scheduled to cross Manhattan by motorcade at rush hour. He was concerned that the motorcade would cause a major traffic tie-up. As a result, the President decided to forgo the customary escort of thirty-five to fifty motorcycle policemen and likewise ordered the motorcade's drivers to obey all traffic lights.[12]

These decisions sparked tremendous anxiety among the Secret Service agents and New York police officials charged with ensuring

Kennedy's safety. Their concern was well founded. Kennedy's limo had just pulled up to a red light at Madison Avenue and 72nd Street when a sharp-eyed photographer spotted the President. The photographer promptly advanced nearly to the window, raised his camera, and released the shutter and flash.[13] Police officials no doubt cringed to think of what could have happened had the quick-thinking photographer been a gunman.

A second incident occurred the following day. Kennedy's limo was dutifully stopped for a light at Avenue of the Americas and 54th Street when a group of teenagers suddenly surrounded the car.[14] "It took several uniformed patrolmen, their clubs raised as a precaution, to free the car from the crowd, one of whom could have assassinated the President," *The New York Times* reported.

The President's scorn for caution culminated with a fateful decision made during his trip to Tampa on November 18, 1963, four days before the assassination. Apparently, Kennedy was growing increasingly annoyed by the presence of Secret Service agents riding on the back bumper of the presidential limousine. This was nothing new, as he had often expressed his unhappiness with the agents' presence. In Tampa, however, Kennedy specifically instructed special agent Floyd Boring to "keep those Ivy League charlatans off the back of the car."[15] This command may have cost John F. Kennedy his life, for if two agents had been riding on the back bumper in Dallas, there is a chance one or both would have had time to dive forward and shield the President's body with their own before the lethal wounds were inflicted.

It was clear to Donahue that Kennedy's actions and attitudes played a real, if not decisive, role in what happened in Dallas. Not surprisingly, though, the Secret Service were themselves subjected to considerable criticism in the aftermath of the shooting. Questions immediately arose about reports that nine agents—including four who rode in the follow-up car (Landis, Hill, Ready, and Bennett)[16]—had been drinking in the Fort Worth Press Club until after midnight on the twenty-second. (Hickey was not in the group.) Subsequently, seven of the agents went to a beatnik club called the Cellar and partied for several more hours. Though reportedly no liquor was served at the Cellar, critics suspected the night on the town may have hindered the agents' ability to react to the gunfire.[17]

Driver William Greer's failure to speed up or take evasive action until after the final shot was also viewed by many as a major failure. To Donahue, this criticism was justified, for had the fifty-four-year-old Greer floored it at the first sound of shots, Kennedy's life would probably have been saved. Then again, Greer and Roy Kellerman, his superior who rode beside him in the car, were likely concerned about overreacting. They knew how sensitive Kennedy was to such things.

One of the most astute critics of the Secret Service performance in

Dallas was none other than U. E. Baughman, a former Secret Service director who'd retired seven months into the Kennedy Administration after thirty-four years with the agency. In an interview in early December 1963, Baughman said "there are a lot of things to be explained" about the actions of the President's protection detail in Dallas. The former director wondered why the book depository had not been searched before the motorcade passed and how it was that Oswald had managed to escape the building after the shooting. Baughman also noted that witnesses saw the barrel of Oswald's rifle sticking out from the sixth-floor window. This prompted him to ask the question: "I am not critical of the Secret Service, but why didn't they use the machine gun to spray the window? . . . I don't know what happened in that follow-up car."

A spokesman for the Secret Service responded by stating the agency had instituted "a blanket policy" prohibiting any comment on the shooting until the Warren Commission investigation was complete.

Baughman's query about why the book depository window wasn't sprayed with machine-gun fire after the first shot raised two interesting questions: If Hickey really didn't fire the shot that hit Kennedy in the head, what was he doing in that interval between the time Kennedy was first struck and the time of the final head shot? And if he didn't fire the last bullet, why didn't he attempt to return fire at the window *after* the President was struck in the head?

As far as Donahue was concerned, the fact that Hickey had never fired back, that all the agents in the follow-up car, with the exception of Clint Hill, seemed paralyzed and dazed as the cars rolled down Elm Street, all fit his scenario that Hickey was attempting to return fire when the gun accidentally discharged. After that, Hickey, along with everyone else in the vehicle, was too shocked to do anything more.

Baughman's successor, Secret Service Director James Rowley, was questioned at length by the Warren Commission about the agents' reactions to the shots and particularly about the drinking incident the night before. Rowley acknowledged the agents had violated Secret Service regulations by drinking while technically still on duty. But he said the men had just finished their shift and were simply looking for something to eat and added that in any case he didn't believe the relatively small amount of alcohol consumed had impaired their ability to respond.[18]

He said he'd decided not to discipline the agents for their after-hours drinking because "formal punishment or disciplinary action would inevitably lead the public to conclude that they were responsible for the assassination of the President in Dallas. I did not think in the light of history that they should be stigmatized with something like that or their families and children."[19]

As for the agents' reactions to the shots, Rowley defended his men by saying that in fact agent Hill did react immediately. Before the last shot was fired, Hill had jumped from the follow-up car's running board and sprinted toward the presidential limo.[20] Yet at no point did Rowley volunteer that a second agent, in addition to Hill, did react almost instantly. Agent Hickey had picked up his automatic rifle and was preparing to return the sniper's fire. Numerous witnesses had seen him with the gun in his hands. Hickey's actions, in fact, showed remarkable presence of mind and considerable courage. Pointing this out would have certainty put the Secret Service in a better light. And though unsuccessful in his actions, Hickey could have been reasonably painted as something of a hero. More to the point, since the AR-15 was the primary defensive weapon in the follow-up car, it would have seemed necessary and appropriate for Rowley to discuss the disposition of the gun and the actions the man responsible for it had taken when the motorcade came under fire, particularly in view of Baughman's public criticism.

Unless Rowley had good reason for ignoring Hickey's actions. For ignore them he did.

In its narrative of the assassination, the Warren Commission did mention in passing that "Special Agent George W. Hickey Jr., in the rear seat of the Presidential follow-up car, picked up and cocked an automatic rifle as he heard the last shot."[21] The report went on to state: "At this point the cars were speeding through the underpass and had left the scene of the shooting, but Hickey kept the automatic weapon ready as the car raced to the hospital."[22]

Donahue spotted several inaccuracies and omissions in this statement.

First, Hickey had picked up the gun before—not after—the last shot, according to both Glen Bennett, the agent who sat beside him, and S. M. Holland, the railroader who had watched the motorcade from atop the triple overpass.

Similarly, the Warren Commission's statement that Hickey did not pick up the gun until the motorcade was speeding through the underpass was contradicted by no fewer than eight eyewitnesses. Holland, Yarborough, Dallas Mayor Cabell, plus agents Bennett, Lawson, Roberts, McIntyre, and Youngblood had all reported Hickey had the gun in hand at or just after the time of the shots, well before the cars disappeared into the underpass.

The Warren Report further asserted that Hickey had cocked the gun after he had picked it up. But Roy Kellerman had testified that the AR-15 was on the floor of the car and "ready to go," i.e., loaded and cocked.[23] Donahue figured Kellerman's version had to be correct. The Secret Service would have naturally been concerned that the gun could jam in an emergency and would therefore have required it to be cocked during a motorcade. Very likely all Hickey did was flip the safety off.

And nowhere in the Report's version of events was it mentioned that Hickey had apparently fallen over with the gun in his hand, as Holland had reported.

Beyond the Warren Report's passing reference to Hickey picking up the rifle, the agent was mentioned only a few other times in the Warren Report and Commission evidence volumes. There were the allusions to Hickey with the rifle in hand in the statements of the other agents. There was also the curious reference to Hickey that Donahue found on page 143 of Volume V. On May 24, 1964, FBI investigators conducted a photographic reenactment of the shooting in Dealey Plaza to understand better the timing and trajectory of the shots. (See illustration 32.) Ironically, the same Secret Service Cadillac that had trailed the presidential limo on November 22 was used to represent the President's car.

From 6:00 A.M. until 1:00 in the afternoon, pictures were taken from numerous vantage points as the lumbering convertible made repeated solo passes down Elm Street. The investigators' goal was to correlate the reenactment photos with the photographs taken during the assassination—particularly the Zapruder film—and in so doing determine the exact positions Kennedy's car had been in at each recorded interval.

In his testimony in Volume V, FBI photography expert Lyndal Shaneyfelt was being questioned by Warren Commission assistant counsel Arlen Specter about who had been present during the reenactment.

SPECTER: And were there representatives of the Secret Service participating in that onsite testing?

SHANEYFELT: Yes; there were. Inspector Kelly was present, Agent John Howlett was present, the driver of the car, or the Secret Service agent whose name I do not recall . . .

SPECTER: George Hickey?

SHANEYFELT: That is correct.

Donahue was amazed. What on earth was Hickey doing there?

Beyond the references to Hickey picking up the AR-15, the Warren Commission statements made by the agents provided little more than an intriguing if incomplete glimpse into the agents' activities prior to, during, and immediately after the shooting.

Kinney, the driver of the follow-up car, reported that he and Hickey had arrived in Dallas on the evening of November 21 aboard an Air Force C-130 that carried the President's limousine and the follow-up car, known as 100-X and 679-X respectively. The agents were met upon their arrival by Forrest Sorrels of the Dallas Secret Service field office and Winston Lawson, Secret Service advance man on the Dallas trip. The vehicles were unloaded and parked in a garage near the main terminal of the airport, and Hickey and Kinney made arrangements for several Dallas policemen to guard the cars through the night. Once that task was finished, the group made their way to the Dallas Sheraton Hotel.

Hickey and Kinney checked in, washed up, changed clothes, and then drove with Lawson to the Dallas Trade Mart, where Kennedy was scheduled to speak the next day. After checking the building out, the men went for a two-hour dinner and subsequently retired after 11:00 P.M.

The next morning, Hickey reported in his statement written several days after the assassination that he:

> Awoke about 7 a.m., washed, packed suitcase, checked out of hotel and had breakfast. About 8:30 a.m. Agent Sorrels met Agent Kinney and me outside the hotel and drove to the airport arriving about 9 a.m. We went directly to the garage and relieved the police of the security of the cars. Washed and cleaned both cars and checked outside, inside and underneath for security violations—none found. We drove the cars to the area where the President was to be met about 11:00. Cars were kept under close observation until arrival of the President, when Agent William Greer of the White House Detail took over control of 100X and Agent Kinney 697X.

Of the events in Dealey Plaza, Hickey wrote that the first shot sounded like a firecracker.

> I stood up and looked to my right and rear in an attempt to identify it. Nothing caught my attention except people shouting and cheering. . . . At the moment [Kennedy] was almost sitting erect I heard two reports which I thought were shots and appeared to me completely different in sound than the first report and were in such rapid succession that seemed to be practically no time element between them . . . the last shot seemed to hit his head and cause a noise at the point of impact which made him fall forward and to his left again.

After the shooting, Hickey said that agent Clint Hill

> looked into the rear of [the limousine] and turned toward [the follow-up car] and shook his head several times. I received the impression that the President at the least was very seriously injured. A few moments later shift leader Emory Roberts turned to the rest of us in the car and said words to the effect that when we arrive at the hospital some if us would have to give additional protection to the Vice President and take him to a place of safety. He assigned two of the agents in the car to this duty. I was told to have the AR 15 ready for use if needed.

Once at Parkland, Hickey went to the vice president's car with gun in hand and requested that Johnson come into the hospital immediately. Along with several other agents, Hickey escorted LBJ into the building and then returned the AR-15 to the follow-up car "as ordered by Agent Roberts." A little while later, Hickey wrote, he was asked by Dave Powers to find a priest, "which I did."

Hickey and Kinney were soon instructed to take 100-X and 679-X back to the airport and get the vehicles aboard the C-130. Hickey drove the presidential limo and both cars proceeded nonstop under a police escort. Once the vehicles were loaded, "we stood by until the plane took off," Hickey wrote.

The Warren Report's final conclusions regarding the Secret Service's performance in Dallas were circumspect, to say the least. The Report noted the difficulties inherent in protecting the President and acknowledged Kennedy's nearly constant travel and resistance to security precautions made matters worse.

Some of the Commission's more direct criticism was aimed at the Protective Research Section, the Service entity in charge of monitoring and investigating individuals who could conceivably pose a threat to the President.

As for the drinking incident the night before the assassination, the Commission wrote:

It is conceivable that those men who had little sleep, and who had consumed alcoholic beverages, even in limited quantities, might have been more alert in the Dallas motorcade if they had retired promptly in Fort Worth. However, there is no evidence that these men failed to take any action in Dallas within their power that would have averted the tragedy.[24]

Finishing his reexamination of the Secret Service and agent Hickey as discussed and revealed in the Warren Report, Donahue next turned back to review the conclusions about the Secret Service reached by the House Select Committee. For the most part, the committee criticisms of the Service echoed those of the Warren Commission. The committee did additionally point out that the Dallas protection detail had not been informed of two separate threats against Kennedy received by the Protective Research Division in the autumn of 1963. Regarding the performance of the agents in the motorcade, committee investigators downplayed the possible adverse impact the drinking incident may have had on the agents' ability to react. However, they did conclude that "Secret Service agents in the motorcade were inadequately prepared for an attack by a concealed sniper."[25]

The committee tempered its criticism in this area by mentioning the "positive, protective" performance of Clint Hill and also agent Thomas Johns, who left Johnson's follow-up car during the shooting in an effort to reach the vice president's vehicle.[26] Yet again—as had been the case in the Warren Report—there was no mention, let alone analysis, of the actions Hickey, as the gun man in the car, took, or might have taken, in response to the shots.

Donahue finished his review of the Secret Service, struck by the enormous difficulties inherent in protecting the President. At the same time the contradictions and omissions surrounding the AR-15 and the man responsible for it were stark.

And that's where it stood when the present arrived.

17
TODAY

BY THE SPRING OF 1991, FOURTEEN YEARS had passed since Ralph Reppert's article had appeared in the *Baltimore Sun*. Through all that time, no one had ever been able to shoot down Howard's conclusions. No one had even tried. The Secret Service never came forward to refute his findings. No one from the Warren Commission or House Select Committee ever took it upon themselves to challenge his work. He never heard from any of the Secret Service agents who rode with Hickey in the follow-up car that day. And he never heard from Hickey.

The silence was deafening.

So what about it? Was he right? Were Donahue's arguments coherent, consistent, and correct? Had he really solved the assassination of President Kennedy—at least a major piece of it—or had he simply deluded himself, convincing himself through years of selective analysis that his conclusions were accurate to the exclusion of everything else?

The body of evidence that Donahue did assemble over nearly a quarter-century suggesting that George Hickey accidentally shot John F. Kennedy is sizable. The bullet's trajectory, its fragmentation, the size of the entrance wound in Kennedy's skull, the fact that Hickey was seen to fall over with the gun at the time of the last shot, the gunpowder odor that drifted through Dealey Plaza, the absence of cranial debris on fragments purportedly from Kennedy's head wound, the dent in the empty shell found in the depository that would have precluded a third shot from that location, the disappearance of the brain and other crucial tissue samples that could have identified the final bullet, these facts—along with numerous anomalies and omissions in both official assassination investigations that arguably suggest the government may have been aware of an accident—all converge to create a powerful case that Donahue's conclusions are correct.

Admittedly, Donahue's case is built entirely on circumstantial evidence. No eyewitness ever suggested that Hickey's weapon went off, although several said the sound of the shots seemed to come from around the presidential limo. No one ever stepped forward to confirm Donahue's scenario. Then again, it is logical to assume that if Donahue is right, no one who knew about the accident would stand to gain anything by coming forward to confirm it.

And if Donahue is not to be believed, then the above-mentioned facts and many others need to be explained, and Donahue's interpretation of them refuted. Until and unless that happens, until evidence emerges that conclusively destroys his theory, to dismiss it out of hand would be irresponsible.

What about all the people Donahue had contact with over the course of his investigation? What did they think about what he'd found? What about the government's ballistic and forensic authorities? How would they explain the discrepancies Howard had unearthed? And what about Blakey? And Moriarty? And others on the '78 committee staff who had contact with Donahue? What would they say for themselves?

Russell Fisher, the pathologist who'd provided Donahue with key information about Kennedy's head wound in 1968, died in May of 1984. Fisher's fellow Marylander on the '68 medical panel, Russell Morgan, died in early 1986. The two other panelists, Alan Mortiz and William Carnes, have also died.

As for the Warren Commission, the three principals with the most direct knowledge of the evidence from and the investigation into the shooting—Commission general counsel J. Lee Rankin, his special assistant, Norman Redlich, and Arlen Specter, former assistant counsel and now a U.S. Senator from Pennsylvania—all declined to be interviewed for this book.

Repeated efforts to arrange an interview with Louis Stokes, the Congressman who'd chaired the 1978 House Committee investigation into Kennedy's death, were also unavailing.

G. Robert Blakey, chief counsel of the 1978 House Select Committee, responded to a written request for an interview by writing back to say that he no longer gave interviews on the assassination. He added that all he had to say had been said in his book *The Plot to Kill the President*. When subsequently contacted by telephone at his office at Notre Dame School of Law, Blakey declined to talk about any specific information, saying, "The only fair thing you can put in the book is Professor Blakey declined to be interviewed about the general subject."

Each of the four House Select Committee staff members Donahue met with face-to-face in 1977 and 1978—Jack Moriarty, Jim Conzelman, Gary Cornwell, and Kenneth Klein—all said they could not recall any memory of the meetings or of Howard Donahue, and only two expressed the vaguest recollection of the theory itself. None could say conclusively whether the committee had investigated Donahue's findings or not.

When each was subsequently mailed copies of correspondence and news articles documenting that the meetings with Donahue did indeed take place, none responded. Apparently, all four had blanked out any memory of their interactions with Donahue, including Cornwell, who'd been asked to meet with the gunsmith by Maryland Congressman Clarence Long, and Moriarty, who'd seemed most interested in what Donahue had come up with.

For his part, Moriarty categorically denied he would have ever told Donahue that he did not believe Blakey was going to allow the gunsmith to testify. "I'm sure that never happened, with me or anybody else," Moriarty said. "That couldn't have been."

Congressman Long, who'd arranged the meeting between Donahue and Cornwell, was in a retirement home by 1991 and reportedly semicomatose much of the time.

As for the neutron activation testing done by the House Committee, Dr. Vincent Guinn disputed Donahue's contention that testing of lead may sometimes be less than definitive due to the presence of random pockets of impurities in the metal.

Yet Guinn had himself reported in a technical paper in 1978[1] that, at least in the case of the 6.5mm Carcano round, comparative tests showed the bullet's lead to be "remarkably heterogeneous" with vastly differing amounts of assorted elements found throughout the test group.

In any event, Guinn went on to say that in his work for the House Select Committee, he did not test any copper jacket material from the bullet fragments allegedly recovered from Kennedy's brain, nor was he aware that the FBI had. Donahue had long believed tests of the jacket pieces could quickly prove his thesis right or wrong, since the copper Carcano jacket contained a significant percentage of zinc, while the AR-15 jacket did not.

According to Guinn, the tests were not conducted because the activation process is ineffective with copper.

"The copper jacket is pretty hard to do by activation analysis because the copper and zinc—of which those are made—get so highly radioactive that it obscures any little bit of other activity that would be there," he said. "I tried it years ago, and every time I had so much copper and zinc radioactivity that you couldn't see anything else."

However, Guinn's assertion that copper can't be effectively tested was disputed by another neutron activation expert, Dr. Frank Dyer of the Oak Ridge National Laboratory in Tennessee. It was Dyer and a colleague, Dr. Juel Emery, who did the original activation testing on the assassination bullet fragments for the FBI back in 1964.

"It gets highly radioactive in that you can't measure anything until

that copper itself decays," Dyer said. "But you could do it. Undoubtedly you could measure silver, zinc, gold, and other impurities. You
wait for three or four days and you could measure it. We do that all
the time. It's a common thing. We radiate things that become fairly
radioactive and then we wait until we can see traces of other things."

Dyer confirmed that he had not tested any copper jacket material
for the FBI in 1964. Asked why not, Dyer said: "Well, Juel and I just
did what the FBI wanted us to do, you know."

The neutron activation question aside, there is no evidence that a
second test of the jacket materials—microscopic examination of the
jacket width—was ever conducted by the Warren Commission, the
House Select Committee, or the FBI. Insofar as the .223 round's
jacket is considerably thinner than the full-metal jacket of the Carcano round, such a comparison would clearly reveal the type and
hence the origin of the bullet that had hit Kennedy in the head.

As for the House Select Committee's medical and ballistics experts, nearly all who were reached revealed a surprising lack of
sophistication, consistency, and imagination in their understanding
of Kennedy's head wound, at least as far as Donahue was concerned.

Werner Spitz, medical examiner for the city of Detroit in 1978 and
a committee medical panel member, suggested that the bullet's
impact with the skull would have caused the slug to disintegrate
explosively in the manner in which it did. When informed that tests
by Warren Commission's Alfred Olivier showed a Carcano round
actually broke up into only two or three pieces upon penetrating the
skull, Spitz responded by saying he was not familiar with the physician's tests.

He added, "I've done a lot of trying to duplicate gunshot wounds
in cadavers, and it is very difficult to get an exact duplication. To
shoot into a [gelatin-filled] skull is not exactly comparable to shooting
into a head that is covered with tissue and contains a brain and all
that."

Dr. Joseph H. Davis, chief medical examiner for Dade County,
Florida, and '78 committee panelist, likewise said he thought the
bullet's fragmentation was consistent with a Carcano round. He
added: "It's all a matter of happenstance. There is no rule of thumb
that says a jacketed bullet is going to behave in a certain specific way
and a nonjacketed bullet is going to behave in a totally different
way."

Earl Rose, the Dallas County coroner who'd battled the Kennedy
staff and Secret Service in a vain attempt to keep the President's
body in Dallas in 1963, was also a member of the '78 panel. In 1991
he said he could not remember whether the fragmentation issue had
even been discussed by the panel.

"I don't recall all the details," Rose said. "My memory is not
accurate."

Michael Baden, the chairman of the medical panel, argued that the
bullet that hit the President in the head hadn't disintegrated at all.

"No, that's wrong," Baden said. "There were two major pieces of the bullet [found in the car]. Most bullets, not all, when they hit bone, will cause some lead to come out sort of like fine sand on the X ray. It doesn't fragment."

Asked whether the fragments found in the car were covered with blood, bone, and hair, indicating they'd passed through the President's head, Baden responded, "I don't recall."

The committee's ballistic experts likewise revealed an apparent lack of precision in their memory concerning the bullet that had struck Kennedy in the head.

John Bates, Jr., was senior firearms examiner at the New York State Police Academy in 1978. Thirteen years later, he asserted that the bullet would have broken up in the manner that it did upon impact with Kennedy's skull. Two of Bates's colleagues on the committee's four-member ballistics panel, Donald E. Champagne of the Florida Department of Law Enforcement and Monty C. Lutz, a firearms examiner with the Wisconsin Regional Crime Laboratory, also asserted the bullet's fragmentation was not inconsistent with a Carcano round.

"You can't go by what you've seen before because, you see, there's no way of predicting what's going to happen to these bullets," Champagne said. "You can't say a particular type of bullet is going to do certain things, because once that bullet leaves the muzzle of the weapon, you have no idea what's going to happen with that bullet."

Champagne's assertion and Davis's similar claim that bullet behavior is too random to be analyzed are surprising statements coming from individuals whose professions presumably involve making those kinds of determinations. Unlike Bates, Champagne, Lutz, Davis, Baden, and Spitz, Donahue was convinced the Carcano round—by virtue of its thicker jacket and much slower velocity—would have fragmented in a manner fundamentally different than the .223 AR-15 round. This is not simply basic physics. It is common sense.

As to the question of the bullet's trajectory, again, the experts' claims that the head shot came from the book depository seemed anecdotal, ad-libbed, and uninformed, although that was perhaps the result of faded memories.

"It depends entirely on how he held his head," said Werner Spitz. "Sure, you can position the head in such a way to make it so [the bullet would have to make] a sharp angle. But I don't believe that is so. I don't think the pictures that were taken at the time illustrate the exact position . . . so you can derive exactly how his head was held at the time."

In fact, Zapruder frame 312 does show the position of Kennedy's head the instant before the bullet hit.

Baden, chairman of the medical panel, said, "The bullet went in a straight line. Well, it may not be clear to you, but it matched up. The bullet hit the President, continued in a straight line, and struck the windshield.''

Thomas Canning, the committee's trajectories expert who'd concluded in 1978 that all shots came from the book depository, was asked about the discrepancy between the drawings he'd done to illustrate the trajectories of the two bullets that hit Kennedy. (See illustrations 28 and 29.) When informed that his head shot drawing had inaccurately placed Kennedy two feet to the left of where he was actually sitting, Canning acknowledged a mistake may have been made.

"It's entirely possible," Canning said. "That kind of discrepancy can seep in because of subjective failure in examination of photographs. I don't remember any discussion of it, though."

Asked why the inaccurate picture had been left out of the committee's final report, an omission that seemed to show someone was aware of the discrepancy, Canning said he assumed the committee simply had had more visual aides than it could use.

As for his analysis of the head shot trajectory, Canning said he and others on the committee photo interpretation panel had concluded Kennedy's head was actually turned much farther to the left than one might initially suppose in looking at Zapruder frame 312, the frame taken an instant before the bullet hit. This, despite the fact that the frame clearly shows Kennedy's head nearly in profile and turned only slightly to the left, with his ear prominent in the center, and the cheek, right eye, and nose visible in the front.

Canning nevertheless asserted that what appeared to be the President's nose was actually "a little angle of the lapel of Mrs. Kennedy's jacket that was silhouetted against her pink blouse" and therefore, he said, Kennedy's head was turned much farther to the left. This reasoning ignores the fact that had Kennedy's head actually been turned more sharply to the left, his ear would have necessarily been much closer to the front, the back of his head much more visible, and the cheek and eye area nearly out of sight.

Canning's interpretation also missed the fact that in Zapruder frame 316, taken after the bullet hit, the object described as Mrs. Kennedy's lapel remained exactly where it had been before the bullet hit, relative to the rest of Kennedy's head, and exactly where the President's nose should logically have been. (See illustration 21.) More to the point, Mrs. Kennedy's position had changed by this time and her collar and lapel were clearly and completely visible well in front of the President. As well, Mrs. Kennedy's lapel was black, not white, the color of the object Canning claimed to be the lapel.

Oddly, Canning's comments were even seemingly inconsistent with his own trajectory conclusions in the committee's final report, namely that the head was not turned dramatically to the left but only turned by 25 degrees.

As for the six-millimeter diameter of the entrance hole in Kennedy's skull, the committee's experts offered similar opinions to explain this apparent discrepancy. Rose questioned whether the hole had been measured properly. He did acknowledge, however, that the skull could not have shrunk after the bullet passed through, a claim the Warren Commission had made to explain the incongruity.

Spitz's reply was similar. "If that is the correct measurement, I agree a [6.5 mm] bullet would not pass there. But I don't know how accurate that measurement is."

Davis likewise questioned whether the measurement was accurate.

"The measuring technique of a bullet hole is very difficult," Davis said. "You take a ruler and you hold it up there. Those measurements are approximations."

Baden asserted that "the size of bullet holes in bone varies a great deal. Sometimes it's approximately the size of the bullet, sometimes it's larger, depending on how it strikes.

"I think you're overreaching if you think that the difference between six millimeters and six point five millimeters is a significant difference when you're measuring from an X ray," he said. "It is not uncommon at all to have bullet [holes] going through bone measured slightly smaller than the bullets."

Donald E. Champagne, one of the committee's firearms experts, offered the peculiar explanation that the 6.5mm Carcano is a "nominal caliber. That doesn't necessarily mean that is the caliber of the bullet."

As for the committee's other experts, Dr. Charles S. Petty did not return calls. Panelist George S. Loquvam declined to comment on the record, although his statements differed little in substance from those of the other panelists. Dr. James Weston died in the early 1980s. Neither John I. Coe, medical panelist and formerly chief medical examiner of Hennepin County, Minnesota, nor Andrew M. Newquest of the ballistics panel could be reached for comment.

Only one medical panel member, Cyril Wecht, the Pennsylvania pathologist and longtime Warren Commission critic who'd dissented with the committee's final opinion about the plausibility of the single bullet theory, agreed that the apparent discrepancies identified by Donahue raised valid questions.

On the fragmentation question, Wecht said: "I tend to agree with you. . . . It is my experience, including bullets that are not as powerful and fully jacketed military ammunition like this, that they do not explode into dozens of pieces. They may break into two or three fragments or pieces, but they don't just disintegrate like that. And so when you say it behaved much more like a soft or hollow-point or so on, I agree with you. I've been saying that for a long time."

Regarding the diameter of the entrance hole, Wecht said, "That sure does raise an interesting question. . . . I can't answer why the measurement of the hole in the skull would be less than the diameter of the bullet. It should not be."

Wecht stressed that "there is no elasticity [in the skull]. There is no expansile quality of bone. If anything, the hole should be a little bigger, because the energy of the bullet is being dispersed. Of course, they would probably say, 'Well, these measurements were not taken that precisely.' But that's not really a very good answer. There's no reason why the measurements shouldn't have been precise."

It is worth noting that the measurement of the entrance wound was made by Pierre Finck, the only pathologist present at the autopsy who had any experience with gunshot wounds.

Finck, contacted at his home in Switzerland, declined to discuss the assassination or autopsy. Dr. James Humes, who was in charge of the autopsy that night, did not return calls.

As for Burke Marshall, the longtime Kennedy family attorney, he called Donahue's conclusions "preposterous."

"The President was killed twenty-eight years ago," Marshall said. "Virtually every year, there are a whole bunch of theories by people that try to explain how he was killed. But I've never heard of [Donahue] or this theory before."

Nicholas Katzenbach, a former deputy attorney general and close aide of Attorney General Robert Kennedy, said: "[Donahue's conclusion] sounds wild to me, but I don't know who Donahue is and I don't know who Hickey is, and I don't know what tests he's made. I know nothing about the subject." Asked if Robert Kennedy could conceivably have suppressed information about the errant shot, Katzenbach said, "That's crazy. I think that is so far out of character for the attorney general as to be crazy."

In response to a request for comment on Donahue's conclusions, the Secret Service said through deputy assistant director of public affairs David Holmes that "our position continues to be that as exactly expressed in the Warren Commission. All evidence that refutes [Donahue's theory] is established in the Warren Commission Report."

However, the Warren Report does not contain one important document that could go a long way toward casting doubt on Donahue's conclusions—if that document exists. This is an FBI shooting team report. Shooting teams consist of several agents specially trained in firearms. After a gunshot homicide, the teams routinely reconstruct the sequence of events in the shooting. As part of this process, all law enforcement officers present at the scene are interviewed. Also, all firearms present—including those of law enforcement officers—are collected and inspected to determine whether the weapons were fired.

When informed the Warren Report did not contain such a report, Holmes said, "Obviously they probably didn't have those procedures instituted at the time."

Donahue, however, had reason to believe that all the agents present in Dealey Plaza had been sequestered by the FBI, interviewed, and forbidden to talk to each other the day after the shooting. Donahue was told this by a man he met following a presentation he'd given on his theory at a Maryland civic club in the late 1970s, a man who asserted he was close friends with one of the agents who had ridden in the follow-up car. According to this story, a shooting team did investigate the agents present in Dallas. Presumably the team wrote a report based on their conclusions; yet no record of it was ever made public.

As well as the interviews conducted immediately after the assassination, Secret Service agents present in Dallas were also interviewed by investigators for the House Select Committee in 1977–78. Once again, the results of the interviews were never released.

Predictably, a handful of Secret Service agents from the Kennedy era angrily denounced Donahue's conclusions.

Winston G. Lawson, who'd ridden in the lead car in the motorcade and who'd reported he had initially thought Hickey had fired at someone, said: "That's about the biggest bunch of bullshit I have ever heard in my life. That's absolutely ridiculous. That's all I've got to say. Thank you for calling. Good-bye."

David B. Grant, an agent who'd been stationed at the Dallas Trade Mart at 12:30 on November 22, said, "Nonsense. Total and utter nonsense. Why? Because I was there. Nonsense. Good-bye."

Former agent Richard E. Johnsen, who was also at the Trade Mart on November 22, said: "Ha, ha, ha. That's way out. My God, that's way out. That's too far out to even think about. That is beyond my comprehension."

Is Donahue wrong?

"Oh, I'm sure of it. Because I just can't think how it could possibly happen. My God, someone had to turn up a stone to get that one."

Gerald A. Behn, a former supervisory agent of the White House Detail who did not make the trip to Texas, said: "That's a lot of bull, because none of our guns were fired. Nope, I don't believe that. Anything's possible, but I'm fairly positive sure that it did not happen. As far as I'm concerned, it did not happen. That's the first time I've heard that."

Floyd Boring, another former supervisory agent who'd worked the Tampa trip a week before the assassination but who'd also remained in Washington during the trip to Dallas, said: "I don't know who this guy [Donahue] is or what he does, but I would go with the Warren Commission's report. I think [Donahue's] just trying to make a name for himself. I don't think he's on the right path. I don't know, he might be."

Boring added that if Hickey's gun had been fired, it would have fired a burst of two or three shots, since the gun would likely have been stashed in the car with the selector in the full automatic position and the safety on.

Donahue, however, knew from studying the early-model AR-15s

that it would have been impossible to have the gun in the full auto position with the safety on. To turn the safety off and put the gun in semiautomatic mode, the selector level is pushed up a quarter turn. To put the gun in the full automatic position, the lever has to be pushed around 180 degrees. Since semiautomatic mode is the first position up from the safety and represents the fastest way to make the gun fire, Donahue believed Hickey had switched just to this point, and not to full auto, as he grabbed the gun.

James R. Rowley, the director of the Secret Service in 1963, said he could not remember why he didn't mention the fact that Hickey had grabbed the AR-15 in defending charges before the Warren Commission that the agents were slow to react in Dealey Plaza.

As for Donahue's theory, Rowley said: "That's the first information I had in that category. I'm saying I didn't hear of anything like that, and I'm quite sure there would have been a report on it. It would have been pursued if it did come up."

John Ready, an agent who rode on the running board of the follow-up car, declined to discuss the matter. None of the other agents who rode in the follow-up car with Hickey could be located, although a request was made through the Retired Secret Service Agents Association to have the agents contact this writer about Donahue's conclusions. None did.

Dave Powers, a top Kennedy aide who rode in the right jump seat of the follow-up car on November 22, was reached. The late Kenny O'Donnell once described Powers as President Kennedy's only close friend outside of Bobby. For many years, Powers has kept the Kennedy flame alive as chief curator of the Kennedy library in Boston.

When asked if he had any comment on Donahue's theory, Powers replied, "No. No. Agent Hickey was in the car I was in. You know, I never talk about that tragic day in Dallas. I gave testimony to the Warren Commission and then stopped talking about it. I admire you for the research you're doing and all that, but there's nothing I can say about, you know, the assassination. I'm awfully sorry. I admire the pursuit that you are doing."

Months later, Powers was asked again about Donahue's theory. This time, he denied it happened, and said Hickey would have shot him (Powers) if the gun had gone off, since he (Powers) stood up in the follow-up car at the time of the shooting to take pictures. When Powers was reminded that there is no photographic record of him standing in the follow-up car as the vehicle headed down Elm Street, nor had Powers ever mentioned standing up in his deposition to the Warren Commission or in the book he wrote about Kennedy, Powers said, "Well, I'm not certain. But the point is, whether I was standing or sitting, someone a foot away from me or two feet away from me couldn't fire the gun without me hearing it."

Asked if it was possible that in the chaos and confusion of the moment, he may not have been aware that a gun had discharged behind him, Powers said he would have known.

On March 12, 1991, George Warren Hickey, Jr., signed a certified letter receipt indicating he'd received a correspondence from this reporter. The letter stated that a book on Donahue's conclusions was in the works, that the deadline was April 30 and that the book would likely be published by the end of 1991. The letter went on to note the attempts Donahue and Ralph Reppert had made to contact Hickey in the 1970s, and said that while Hickey was within his rights in not responding, the imminent publication of the book required that another effort be made.

The letter further stated that it was a little-known fact that Kennedy would probably have died anyway from the wound through his neck, and suggested that setting the record straight about what happened in Dallas would be beneficial to all.

As of April 4, 1991, Hickey had not responded to the letter. On April 5, Hamilton Brown, executive secretary of the Former Agents of the Secret Service Association, was contacted in an attempt to reach Hickey and other agents who were in the follow-up car.

"I've heard of you," said Brown, who was working on the protection detail for Joseph Kennedy at Hyannis Port on November 22, 1963. "I understand the book that you're writing is the allegation that George Hickey was the fellow that actually shot the President."

Brown went on to question—if this scenario was correct—why Dave Powers or Kenny O'Donnell, who rode in the follow-up car, hadn't spoken up immediately about what had occurred. But at no point during the forty-minute conversation did Brown attempt to refute or even address the physical evidence Donahue had assembled. Instead, he threatened legal action on Hickey's behalf.

When informed that Hickey had not yet responded to a query from this writer, Brown said, "And he won't be." He went on to say that Hickey was extremely distressed by Donahue's investigation.

BROWN: [Donahue's] been harassing the hell out of him.
REPORTER: He hasn't been harassing him. I don't think that is a
            correct statement.
BROWN: Wouldn't your state of mind be kind of suspect if
            somebody accused you of assassinating the President of
            the United States?
REPORTER: First of all, I don't think he's accusing him of assassi-
            nating the President of the United States. Accuse is
            maybe too strong a word, but I think he's saying that
            there's a strong possibility that that gun discharged
            accidentally. There's a big difference there. Nobody's
            saying that Hickey did anything on purpose and
            nobody is more sympathetic to Hickey than Dona-
            hue. Furthermore, if I was Hickey, the minute I saw

that article in 1977, I'd have been right in Donahue's
face saying, "Listen, you sonofabitch, another
word about this and, you know, I'll hurt you." That's
what I'd do.

BROWN: I think Mr. Hickey talked to Mr. Donahue and referred
him to the Warren Commission.

REPORTER: That's not true. Donahue's never spoken with Hickey.
Never.

BROWN: Well, that's not what I hear from George.

REPORTER: I guess we've got a disagreement there.

Brown was repeatedly asked to contact the other agents who were
in the follow-up car to see if they would be willing to talk to the
author. Brown declined to give addresses or phone numbers for any
of the agents and would only say that if the book was published,
"then we'll produce everybody that is still alive that was on the
follow-up car and they will make statements, that 'No, he did not fire
the gun.' "

On Friday afternoon, April 12, 1991, Donahue and this writer drove
to Hickey's home and knocked on the door. No one answered. Two
days later, around 10:30 A.M. on a Sunday morning, a second visit
was made. Again no one answered.

The following note was left:

Mr. Donahue and I stopped by this morning. We also came by last
Friday afternoon. We're still interested in hearing your side of this,
but if you don't call in the next few days, we won't bother you any
more and we won't be back. Should you change your mind in the
months ahead, you have my phone number. Howard's number is xxx
xxx-xxxx.

[signed]
Bonar Menninger

Hickey never did respond.

If George Hickey didn't pull the trigger, why didn't he make an effort
to put an end to Donahue's speculation once and for all, particularly
when he knew a book on the subject was in the works? It's hard to
believe that any one of us, cited in a thesis like this, would not write
one word to try to halt the publication of the book. If he really didn't
want the story to be printed, and he'd figured for years that no
response was the best way to kill the story, wouldn't it have been
logical—indeed, imperative—for him to have abandoned this strategy
of silence in the face of an impending book? Hickey was not *required*
to make one phone call or write one line of denial, but what was
Donahue to think then? And what was he to *do*—refrain from making

public what he honestly believed was the explanation of Kennedy's death as long as Hickey refused to comment?

As for the few Secret Service agents who were asked about the merits of Donahue's theory, they denied it, often angrily and with derision. But no one refuted it. No one attacked the evidence, point by point. No one, with the exception of Brown, took it upon themselves to try to dissuade this writer from pursuing the story. And Brown's effort consisted primarily of making legal threats.

And what about the members of the House Select Committee, the government investigators most familiar with Donahue's work? Robert Blakey wouldn't even talk about Donahue. He hung up the phone. Jack Moriarty, Jim Conzelman, Gary Cornwell, and Kenneth Klein— all men Donahue had met with and briefed on his conclusions—each said they did not remember the gunsmith or his theory.

Not one of them remembered a firearms examiner who had suggested a Secret Service bullet killed the President?

As for Donahue, he never doubted that his conclusions were correct.

"I started out on my investigation with no preconceptions," Donahue said. "If anything, I was trying to prove the Warren Commission correct. And after I made my discovery, I tried very hard to prove it wrong. I wanted to be wrong. But I found nothing to indicate that I was.

"I do not believe George Hickey is to blame for what happened. He was a brave man trying to do his job. He was at the wrong place at the wrong time and fate stepped in, that's all. If we assume that someone in Washington knew what really happened—and it's hard for me personally to believe that no one knew—then I feel the government never should have kept this secret. It's always true that cover-up and deception breeds more deception. And then it breeds wilder and wilder scenarios by observers whose instincts tell them something isn't accounted for here, these stories we're being fed don't work. We should have put the Kennedy assassination to rest a long time ago.

"Now I've given twenty-five years of my life to this. It's up to the American people to decide who is right and who is wrong. I've done all that I can."

NOTE FROM
THE PUBLISHER

When *Mortal Error* was first submitted to St. Martin's Press, three issues arose.

The first was the publisher's usual question: Does the manuscript say something interesting to the point of being compelling, and does it say this in a way that is clear and stylistically palatable? We thought the answer to this was not difficult: yes, it does.

The second was: Is its argument cogent enough to merit dissemination? Arriving at an answer to this, we found, *was* difficult. Some of the reasons we decided it was cogent enough will be explained in the following pages.

The third was an adjunct to the second: Given that *Mortal Error* would publish the name of the man whom Howard Donahue honestly believes fired the bullet that killed John Kennedy, and the fact that that man is still alive, was the public airing of the argument's conclusion important enough to warrant subjecting that man to the kind of attention he would receive when Donahue's thesis became nationally known? This was the hardest question of all, and, again, this chapter will try to explain our decision.

Here is how we considered the cogency of the argument.

St. Martin's has, as of the moment of this writing, in the past few months declined to be the publisher of three other books containing theories about what happened in Dallas, and to be the paperback reprinter of four more. Each of them seemed to be marred throughout by either faulty reasoning or unwarranted assumption of fact. The minds behind the books, we felt, were either sincere but not analytically acute enough for the job; or insincere and meretriciously selective of the data; or simply uninformed. We decided that, in these cases, we did *not* want to be involved in these books' dissemination.

We were told the central conclusion of *Mortal Error* before we read it, and it seemed so at odds with anything we'd previously heard that our first reaction was probably exactly what would come to most people who were given a one-sentence summary of Donahue's thesis: exasperated skepticism. We expected another indefensible Dallas theory.

But as we turned the pages of the manuscript and its supporting illustrations, it became clear that Donahue—and his chronicler, Bonar Menninger—were both certainly sincere and perceptive enough. And Donahue's expertise about firearms and ballistics in general, and the Dallas-pertinent data in particular, seemed substantial.

We would, to verify this impression and to weigh the validity of his thesis, eventually read thousands of pages about guns, bullets, and the events in Dealey Plaza. We would study dozens of illustrations— photographs, movies, television videos, drawings, and diagrams. We would examine government reports and appendices, commentaries on them, and independent investigations. We brought Donahue and Menninger to New York twice for what amounted to interrogation, and called them repeatedly on the telephone with specific queries.

The aim in all of this was to prepare ourselves to understand certain facts essential to Donahue's thesis, and to test the reasoning with these facts. At the outset of the program, none of us on the team at St. Martin's was what is known as a Kennedy assassination buff. It is not hyperbole to say we had read "thousands" of pages; any student of the events in Dallas is able to show you a shelf with dozens of books. As our education increased we became able to discern disqualifying ignorance and wildly untenable assertions in many of these volumes.

We did not find such things in Donahue's thesis.

Inevitably our attention was at last focused on the three government tracts Donahue referred to constantly: the Warren Commission Report; the report of the 1968 panel of medical examiners of the autopsy text, the photographs, and the X rays; and, most especially, the Hearings Before the Select Committee on Assassinations of the U.S. House of Representatives (HSCA), published in March of 1979—in particular, on Volume II, and Volumes VI and VII of the Appendices, which addressed in detail the very matters that Donahue's thesis involved.

As you read a government technical report, there is—or at any rate there *was*, before the Warren Commission Report—a tendency to want just to embrace it as information, *the facts,* as you did textbooks in school. But the long record of justified skepticism about *any* assertion concerning the Kennedy assassination, government assertions certainly included, plus the nature of Donahue's conclusions, pushed us to question closely every line we read. We tried to do this with Bonar Menninger's manuscript describing the evolution of Howard Donahue's analysis, and, of necessity, we soon found ourselves doing it with the government's official volumes.

It is worth examining the results of applying what might be called

benevolent skepticism to one narrow aspect on which both the HSCA
and Donahue spent a lot of time. The comparison, we think, is
revealing not only about the complexity of these issues but about the
relative acuteness and dependability of judgment of the minds at
work. (Be prepared, alas, for a matted combination of the gripping
and the tedious. The questions of Dallas cannot be addressed respon-
sibly by anyone content with expansive pronunciamentos based not
on research but solely on quick impressions and hackneyed intuition.
No critic, including St. Martin's, can pretend to have combed every
conceivable source, but we have tried our best, and it involved such
tweezing detail as follows.)

The aspect we will focus on here is the trajectory analysis—how
the HSCA and Donahue tracked back to the spot from where the
head shot had to be fired. You have read Menninger's account of
Donahue's thinking on this. The HSCA explanation is given in
Volume VI of the Appendices to the Hearings.

The format of the Appendix to the Hearings is to give the conclusion of each section first, and follow it with the analysis that led to
that conclusion. Initially, the HSCA conclusion sounds succinct,
precise, and clear:

[Paragraph 123] The bullet that caused Kennedy's head wounds at
Zapruder frame 312 came from a point 29° to the right of true north
from the President. The bullet was descending at an angle of 16° below
horizontal as it approached him. This trajectory intercepted the plane
of the Texas Book Depository approximately 11 feet west of the
southeast corner of the building at a point 15 feet above the sixth floor
windowsills.

As we read this, the reference to "true north" gave us pause. In
his 1967 book, Josiah Thompson—with no documentation cited—
gave the directional angle of the head shot as 6 degrees right to left,
relative to the midline of President Kennedy's limousine.

(The nomenclature of the various commentators is a source of
much potential confusion. *Angle of direction* is meant to refer to the
route on the *horizontal plane*—i.e., as though you were looking down
from above; it tells you nothing about the angle of slope. *Angle of
slope* means the route on the *vertical plane*—the degree to which the
bullet is traveling up or down. It's important to keep in mind the
question of up or down *relative to what*. In the HSCA conclusion
give above, it stipulates "horizontal." This is distinguished, for
example, from the plane of Elm Street, which was sloped down 3
degrees from horizontal at Z-312. It is further distinguished from
what is sometimes termed the "horizontal midplane" of the skull.
This is the plane running fore and aft that is always perpendicular to
the "facial axis"—the line from brow to upper lip, which is taken to
be perpendicular to the horizon when the skull is erect. Thus when

the skull tips forward, the "horizontal midplane" is no longer parallel to true horizon. If the facial plane tilts 11 degrees from true horizon, so does the midplane. This entails that if the bullet's path through the skull were sloped 5 degrees downward from the midplane, and the whole skull was tilted 11 degrees forward, the path's angle remains − 5 degrees relative to the midplane but it is now − 16 degrees relative to true horizon. All of this was important for the House Select Committee to keep straight, and, as we shall see, they didn't.)

On our first reading of the HSCA conclusion, we put the question of "true north" on hold; no doubt its applications would be explained in the analysis. In fact, it is not. The citation "29° to the right of true north" has no utility whatever; it is never mentioned again in Volume VI. In discussing *the head shot,* the HCSA never gives any horizontal angle except the reference to true north. But since we are never told the angular relationship of anything else, either to true north or to Elm Street, Zapruder's line of sight, or Oswald's line of fire, we are reduced to taking the HSCA's word for it on numerous critical data, and we soon found we could not do that.

The Appendix did supply illustrations that, in testimony recorded in Volume II of the Hearings, were said to be drawn to scale. Working from the blowup of the HSCA diagram showing the horizontal angle of Oswald's shot, the St. Martin's team measured that angle at 8 degrees, rather than Thompson's 6 degrees. We then turned to a blowup of the committee's "orthogonal projection onto a vertical plane" showing the 16-degree downward slope. The conclusion distinctly says the 16 degrees is to horizontal. But in their own diagram the slope is incontrovertibly to *Elm Street.* But Elm Street itself is sloped 3 degrees at this point (said the HSCA; the Warren Commission said 3.9 degrees). So in that diagrammatic drawing the slope of the shot purporting to track back to Oswald is not 16 degrees to horizontal but 19 degrees. (See drawing 15.)

Was this simply an illustrator's error not noticed by the committee? It is hard to think so, given the scrutiny this illustration received before scores of officials at the oral hearings. An examination of the text reveals it was surely someone's error, and not solely the illustrator's.

We pursue this ostensibly tiny slipup because it eventually leads to enough confusion, inconsistency, and ostensible error on the HSCA's trajectory analysis to put their conclusions in fundamental doubt and heighten our respect for Donahue's contrasting view.

At this point we need to back up to explain how HSCA *did* the analysis of the trajectory. They retained an engineer from the Space Project Division of NASA, Thomas N. Canning, to do it for them. (Appendix D in this book is the extract of the trajectory section of Volume VI. However, the explanation of Canning's methodology is difficult to understand without the investment of long study, so the reader may be grateful for this summary, which is not to claim that *it* is easy reading either.)

LINE OF SIGHT FROM ZAPRUDER CAMERA TO JFK/SLOPE OF BULLET CAUSING HEAD WOUND

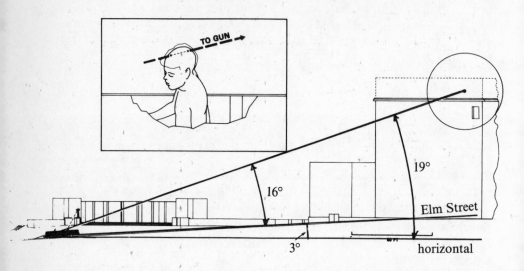

15.

Canning's basic method may be conveyed by likening it to the use of mirrors in telescopes or surveillance mechanisms. If you know exactly where your eye is, and where the mirror is, and what its angle to you is, you can figure out where you are "looking" when you peer at the mirror. From various sources Canning determined where the President's car was on Elm Street at Z-312. Then his job was to place his "mirror" correctly in that car. His mirror was Kennedy's head. By using a precise inshoot hole and outshoot hole he had two points that defined a straight line. If he could establish the head's exact position and orientation in space at the moment of impact, he could, so to speak, look into the exit hole, back through the entry, and see where the line led somewhere behind the President.

To establish the head orientation, Canning worked from Z-312. This meant that his basic starting datum was Zapruder's camera. If he could fix the position of the camera, the distance to Kennedy's head, and how his wound-determined straight line related to the straight line of sight from Zapruder, he could plot the backward course of the bullet—i.e., its trajectory.

For example, if by carefully examining Kennedy's features in Z-312 he could conclude that Kennedy was showing an exact profile to the camera, and that his head was perfectly erect, then Canning's job was all but done. The medical team had told him (*in effect,* it told him; in the end it was apparently Canning himself who finally provided the measurements and angle of the inshoot and outshoot, relative to the horizontal midplane of the skull) that "the bullet's" path was 5 degrees downward from back to front and 18.6 degrees from left to right—that is, if you looked at a top view of the skull and drew a line from inshoot to outshoot, that line would describe an angle 18.6 degrees off to the right of a line going straight forward through the head.

All Canning would then have had to do was attach to a stick representing Zapruder's line of vision another stick angled down 5 degrees and crossing at 18.6 degrees. Then he could sight backward on the second stick and see where the bullet had started.

In theory the method was fine. He could trace his bullet source without ever having to say or know anything about true north, the angle of Elm Street and the car, the angle of Oswald's shot relative to the midline of the car. But in practice the method was complicated; it could not escape the simple "eyeballing" estimates Canning abjured in oral testimony, and it was based on certain assumptions that Canning never spelled out or gave reason for believing.

The complications arose with the obvious fact that Kennedy was *not* showing an exact, erect profile to the camera. His head was rotated away from Zapruder, it was tilted away, and it was nodded forward.

Canning told the committee that he addressed this problem by constructing a model of Kennedy's head and torso and taking a series

of what he called "calibration photographs," a system that freed him
from more eyeball estimates. The system seems to have consisted of
putting the mannequin in various different attitudes, photographing
them, and comparing them to one another and to Z-312. (If the
comparison was done with more than a ruler, protractor, and eyeball,
we are never told about it.) In oral testimony when the committee
was shown the model photograph said to duplicate Kennedy in Z-
312, Senator Dodd of Connnecticut noted that it didn't look nearly
so tilted as Z-312. Canning replied, "I can assure you the images play
games with you." After further questioning he conceded "the interpretation of these features is a major source of potential error."
Before his testimony was done, Canning conceded that there was
enough potential error in his method for his radius of possible gun
source to extend not just beyond the book depository to the Dal Tech
building across the street, but beyond the Dal Tech to the Records
Building—the building behind the AR-15. (See pages 193 and 199,
HSCA Hearings, Vol. II.)

Now we must focus in further. To make the final estimate of the
degree of forward nod of Kennedy's head, the HSCA trajectory team
found the model photo they judged was the best Z-312 replica. It
shows the mannequin tilted toward a descending plumb bob. "The
essence of the reference system is shown by that vertical line"
delineated by the plumb, said the oral testimony.

One can only infer that the team drew a line indicating what they
judged to be the facial axis and measured its intersection with the
vertical line of the plumb. That meant, the 11-degree nod was 11
degrees toward true horizontal—not the slope of Elm Street. This is
reasonable, because consider: Zapruder was standing on a pedestal
well off to the side of Elm Street. We assume the pedestal was
horizontal, not tilted at 3 degrees. So to talk of Zapruder's line of
view is to posit a man and a camera that are vertical. And the text
seems to underline this by saying (paragraph 131), "nodding forward
by about 11° (clockwise, as viewed by Zapruder)." But then why
does it say ten paragraphs later (141), "establishing the relationship
of those elements critical in determining the degree to which Kennedy's head was nodding forward (for example, the line from his brow
to his upper lip relative to the slope of the street) also required careful
and repetitive measurements to minimize errors." To the slope of
the street? It has to mean the horizon. Who threw out "the essence
of the reference system"? And how *could* they measure relative to
the slope of the street? The quoted sentence begins to sound not only
wrong but hollow, describing a task never undertaken.

And yet four paragraphs later (145) in the analysis of Kennedy's
neck shot is a mention of his being "inclined forward at an approximate angle of 11° to 18° relative to a line drawn upward from
perpendicular to the road surface." But five paragraphs after that it
says, "Kennedy was inclined forward by approximately 11° to 18°

(from true vertical)." But true vertical is not perpendicular to the road surface.

Then in their examination of the neck shot we find constant reference to something never mentioned in the head shot section, the midline of the limousine; "the bullet was moving from right to left by 13° relative to the middle of the limousine . . . the direction of the trajectory was then determined by drawing a line on a scaled diagram of Dealey Plaza at a 13° angle relative to the car and extending it to the rear. . . ."

Why, we asked ourselves, would the HSCA use angles relative to the car in tracking the neck shot but not the head shot? Donahue used the car in both of his analyses.

It is not sufficient to argue that Z-312 was enough for their purposes. Canning himself told the committee, "It is really quite a difficult frame to work with." It might have been easier if he had worked with *all* of it, that is, if he had used the *car* as was done on the neck shot. Given the immense amount of time the report says was spent measuring and remeasuring, it seems it would have been possible to do a parallel tracking of the trajectory by fixing Kennedy's head relative to the midline of the car and measuring the angle backward from the known position of that car.

It's true that that system also depends on firm decisions about the tilt and rotation of Kennedy's head, but besides providing a second check on the trajectory it would have given the public something it could understand better, and in their eyeballing way, verify.

The best guess at this moment would have to say that the line on the committee's orthogonal projection showing a slope of 16 degrees to Elm Street is an artist's error. We have to believe that Canning, seeing an 11-degree nod to true horizontal, and a 5-degree slope within that nodding head, asked the artist to draw a line back at 16 degrees from true horizontal. What he got was a line rising 19 degrees.

But we cannot know with surety what happened. Not inconceivable, but doubtful, is the possibility that the artist truly depicted what Canning's "mirror" contraption implied, drew it up, and Canning pulled the 16-degree angle off the rendering. It is fairly certain he did not recognize the rendering was wrong. If that is what he did the HSCA scenario has a problem: "The bullet" came out 3 degrees below their chosen outshoot at a point where there is no hole in the skull. (For more minor but disturbing evidence of HSCA undependability, take a ruler and measure the dimensions cited on their front view rendering of Kennedy's skull in figure II-7. (See drawing 7.) You will find that if one measurement is 17.5, then another can't be 5.5. They have given us a physically improbable and mathematically impossible head. Small flaws like this repeatedly vex the earnest reader bent on tracing the path of the HSCA's thinking.)

A third advantage to working from the car, as the HSCA did on the

neck shot and Donahue did on both shots, is that the validity of their
trajectory would not hinge on the mystery of "Zapruder's line of
view." Zapruder was not shooting the exact profile of Kennedy, or
of the *car* either—but we are never told what the angle of his line of
view to that car was. If we had been given that, we could have
constructed our own "from the car" analysis, albeit one depending
on the HSCA data.

The more one studied the HSCA analysis of the trajectory, the
more woefully blurred and doubtful its method and conclusions
became. Even the footnotes became interesting in this regard. They
reveal that when Canning gave his testimony in September of 1978 he
believed the inshoot-outshoot path was level through the head. The
trajectory netted Oswald. By March of 1979 he'd been informed that
the outshoot was lower than previously thought. The shot must have
come down at an angle 5 degrees steeper than he had calculated in
1978. His 1979 trajectory still netted Oswald.

In 1964, to accommodate what the Warren Commission believed
about the inshoot-outshoot, the Commission simply decreed a forward head tilt of 59 degrees.

This is not meant to imply that Canning did not say what he
honestly believed. He pointed out to the committee the discomforting
news that the trajectory of the head shot bullet did not fit with the
windshield damage that the committee would maintain was caused
by "the bullet" after it exited from the skull (op. cit. page 200). That
was something Donahue had maintained for years.

It should be noted that Donahue allowed the HSCA confusions to
entrap him into a confusion of his own as he tried to compare his
numeric estimates of head orientations to those of the committee.
Because Donahue had for years been judging the position and attitude
of Kennedy's head relative to the car (and he used more than Z-312;
he used the Altgens and Moorman photos, too), he did not appreciate
that the committee's pronouncement about the head rotation differs
even more than he thought from his own. In effect, the committee's
judgment that Kennedy was rotated 25 degrees away from Zapruder's
line of view meant that he was rotated 27 to 30 degrees away from
the straight-ahead line of the car, depending on how far Zapruder
was from being at a right angle to the car. We left this confusion
uncorrected in the manuscript, which is meant to be a chronicle of
Donahue's thinking on those matters. Donahue has over the years
tested several different degrees of rotation and all of them accommodate a line of fire from the AR-15. We checked his calculations on
these. They do require different outshoots but all are within the exit
portal, and Donahue has always resisted the notion that one *could*
pinpoint a single outshoot.

We are aware that the fact the HSCA report was flawed does not
prove Donahue's thinking is flawless. We are further aware that the
inability to be absolutely sure about numerous measurements and

estimates is a difficulty for Donahue too, but his reconstruction
survives more variations of estimates than the HSCA's does. For
example, by insisting on that farthest forward, farthest down point in
the exit portal as the outshoot, the HSCA is maintaining a thesis that
crumbles with the slightest increase of slope, or change in rotation
either way.

Consider this single vulnerability in the HSCA trajectory analysis:
It depends entirely on the assumption that Zapruder held his camera
perfectly vertical. The HSCA's own much ridiculed "jiggles" analysis (aimed at trying to identify when he jumped because he heard the
shots) cites many times when the camera jittered in his hand. Still
the HSCA used a straight-to-the-earth plumb line attributing a no-tilt
attitude to the camera. A skeptical viewer looking at Z-312 might ask
why, when the limousine is still to Zapruder's left, and it is going
down a 3-degree slope, the front of the car appears to be slightly
higher than the back. Is it possible Zapruder has his camera tilted
slightly to the right?

Up until now, the report of the Hearings of the House Select
Committee has been the most detailed, careful, authoritative study
available of the ballistics issues involved in the assassination of
Kennedy. It was significant to us that Donahue's technical analysis
proved more trustworthy than the HSCA's.

The trajectory analysis is only a small part of the HSCA report but
it aptly serves as one of the benchmarks of cogency against which to
compare Donahue's argument. In our judgment, Donahue more than
survives the test of comparison. We have talked about only the
trajectory analysis here, but his argument from the performance of
the bullet will alone seem to many to be decisively powerful. Every
aspect of his commentary on this seemed to us a telling point against
the belief that the head bullet wound could have been caused by a
cartridge from the Mannlicher-Carcano. Despite the initially startling
thrust of his theory, we did not find the disqualifying leaps of
irrationality that soon burst out of the hull and sink so many vessels
of fantasy about what happened in Dallas. And we could not find in
Donahue a flurry of errors such as those in the HSCA report. Because
his theory of the ballistics facts bore up under inspection better than
the benchmark—and not just in the matter of trajectory—we thought
it deserved to be considered seriously by the vast public whose
instincts still tell them that the true story of Dallas has never come
out.

Donahue's ballistics argument is the strongest yet put forth, and it
accounts for all of the essential data accounted for by the government
theories plus a good deal more. Plus, his reconstruction explains
many details from Dallas that *no* one has otherwise explained. Some
of these are summarized in chapter 17, but others are sprinkled
through the book. They begin before the head shot, with his description of the first shot as a ricochet. Reading that section we can for

the first time explain the presence of metal fragments embedded in the *outside* of Kennedy's skull, John Connally's insistence to this day that the first shot did not hit him even if Kennedy *did* look hit, Roy Kellerman's insistence he heard Kennedy cry "My God, I'm hit!" when a throat shot would seem to make that impossible, Glen Bennett's firm assertion that he saw the second shot, not the first, hit Kennedy in the back, windshield damage too high to be caused by a bullet coming down into the back of the car at 16 degrees, and the presence on the front floor of the car of violently deformed bullet fragments that appeared to have no human blood or tissue on them.

For those who wonder what Lee Harvey Oswald might have had in mind when he declared he was just a "patsy," Donahue's theory allows an answer that does not entail the likes of a New Orleans conspiracy: Oswald, thinking himself to be a lone gunman, nevertheless sees Kennedy killed by a shot he knows he didn't fire. But he is the only one arrested. He does not know how they did it, but he is convinced, wrongly, that somehow he has been used.

Through all this examination of what amounted to the technical factors at Dallas, we knew we had not yet touched on the aspect of Donahue's thesis that would excite the greater skepticism: There were nine other people in that follow-up car (eight, after Hill ran forward to the presidential limousine); why had none of them ever said anything? Did Donahue or Menninger ever ask them?

Yes, they did ask them, or at any rate they tried.

As the potential publishers of Donahue's thesis, we were intensely concerned about this entire area of inquiry—the matters that were not technical but human. Before looking for the answers we had to get our questions straight. The first were: What did the others around Hickey know? Indeed, what did Hickey know?

We read the statements of all of the agents. (They were published in the Warren Commission Report, and are reprinted in Appendix A of this book. The surviving agents were interrogated in 1978 but the HSCA never released any of those papers.) The statements are startling in their variety of ear- and eyewitness accounts. The agents testify to hearing different numbers of shots, from different directions. Dealey Plaza, with its many reflecting facades, was an echo chamber, reflecting cheering crowds, motorcycles, shots, and cries of horror. To this was added the mind-scrambling shock of seeing the President being shot before their eyes. (Glen Bennett, sitting next to Hickey, testified that he actually saw the neck shot hit Kennedy's back.)

The first question was, could the explosive sound of an AR-15 possibly go off within a few feet of these men and they not register it, or, at any rate, believe it came from elsewhere? The strict answer is yes, it is possible. Since starting its investigation, the St. Martin's team has heard numerous accounts of shooting experiences that corroborate that possibility.

More than that, we've heard two first-person accounts from people who *themselves* discharged a rifle and were unaware of it. This implies that the possibility exists that Hickey himself might have, in that most head-jangling moment of his life, fired his gun and never realized it. What the mind registers in a moment of such utter extremity is unpredictable. Suppose Roy Kellerman was right. It would mean that the President of the United States cried, "My God, I'm hit!" and four out of five people in the car with him were unaware of it.

There were eyewitnesses along Elm Street who claimed they heard a gunshot sound that originated right there in the plaza. But others said no, it was from the grassy knoll. There were two shots, three shots, four shots. They all sounded alike. No, one sounded markedly different. They were evenly spaced in time. No, the last two shots were almost simultaneous, ba-bang.

It seems unlikely to most of us that his fellow agents—or some of them—and even Hickey himself would not be aware of the AR-15 going off, but the possibility exists. We are never told if or when or by whom a post event gun examination was carried out.

Inevitably we are pushed to consider the next possibility: that at least some others in the follow-up car were aware that the AR-15 went off. (Where did the ejected AR-15 shell go? It ejects weakly forward, and, Donahue believes, probably fell on the floor of the car.)

If they were aware, where did they think the shot went? In Donahue's reconstruction, Hickey, jumping to his feet on the soft seat cushion of a moving car, tipped backward while clutching the AR-15. The chance of his accidental shot hitting the President probably seemed so remote that they never actually considered it. (Donahue, when asked why he immediately assumed the shot was accidental and not intentional, says that the chances of such a shot being planned and controllably executed are so small that he simply could never take that scenario seriously. Asked if the chances of an accidental shot hitting the President in the head twenty-four feet away did not seem equally small, he says of course they do—until you consider the evidence. First, he points out, he didn't approach his investigation with any idea that it would lead to the AR-15. He considered the data, and the data led him to the follow-up car. You cannot convince any experienced shooter—and certainly not one who as a firearms expert has regularly testified in court about bizarre coincidences that have produced gunshot fatalities—that the apparent unlikelihood of the result of an accidental shot should be enough to persuade him it didn't happen. Any large gathering of shooters telling what they've seen in their day will teem with stories of unlikely but true accidental shots and hits—some hilarious, some tragic.)

If another agent knew the AR-15 went off, and he figured it went skyward, just possibly he would judge it an irrelevant but potential nasty complication to any subsequent investigation, and thus not worth mentioning. We can know none of this—*if* anyone knew, who that anyone might be, what went through his mind.

Donahue and Menninger *tried* to know. The book recounts their efforts to contact the other car occupants, and, repeatedly, George Hickey.

At St. Martin's, before making the final decision to publish, we felt we had to make our own efforts.

On November 1, 1991, we sent the following letter to George Hickey:

Dear Mr. Hickey:

St. Martin's Press is scheduled to publish a book called [*Mortal Error: The Shot That Killed JFK*] by Bonar Menninger. In that book journalist Bonar Menninger presents Howard Donahue's thesis concerning the death of President John F. Kennedy.

As we believe you know: Mr. Donahue's thesis is that the bullet that struck the President in the head was not fired by Lee Harvey Oswald. Rather, Donahue believes, the bullet came from the AR-15 rifle in the Secret Service follow-up car. According to Mr. Donahue, the Secret Service rifle was accidentally fired by you when you picked up the gun in response to Oswald's shots and fell backwards.

Mr. Donahue's thesis is based on a sifting of the available ballistics, medical and other evidence. It is premised among other things on Donahue's contention that the behavior of the bullet in the President's skull was much more consistent with that of a bullet fired from an AR-15 rifle than from a Mannlicher-Carcano rifle such as the one used by Oswald, and on an analysis of the trajectory of the bullet, as well as on a number of other factors.

I want to emphasize that Mr. Donahue is by no means accusing you of any wrongdoing. In Mr. Donahue's view, the shot was a tragic accident. Mr. Donahue also believes that the President would in all likelihood have died anyway as a result of the pre-existing wound caused by one of the shots fired by Oswald even if the bullet in question had not hit the President in the head.

We recognize that in the past you have declined to speak to Mr. Donahue or Mr. Menninger or to respond to press reports on Mr. Donahue's thesis. However, the situation is perhaps now different from what it was when they first contacted you. The difference is that the book—which has been under contract to St. Martin's Press—is now scheduled for national publication early in 1992 barring my receipt of new data invalidating Donahue's thesis.

We would very much urge you to reconsider your decision not to speak on this subject. We would be happy to make reasonable arrangements at our expense for Mr. Menninger to interview you. (If you agree to an interview by Mr. Menninger, he would thereafter provide you with a copy of the transcript of what was said in the interview and a chance to supplement it.) Alternatively, if you prefer, you can respond directly to me.

Any information in any form that you are willing and able to provide that would shed light one way or the other on the validity of Mr. Donahue's thesis would be greatly appreciated. Please be assured that we will carefully consider anything that you have to say.

The assassination of John F. Kennedy has never been a happy subject, but for almost thirty years it has remained an important subject—and a lively one. The liveliness will be increased sharply in 1992 with the Oliver Stone movie on the event. The nation has been wracked, and will be wracked anew, by numerous conspiracy theories. It is my view that if a publisher has in hand a proposed book that may lead at last to the truth of what happened in Dallas, and the extinction of false accusations of intentional murder by people other than Oswald, it is the publisher's duty to make this information available. But, because your actions are an integral part of Donahue's thesis, I would not be comfortable going to press without making this last determined effort to tell you that the book is scheduled and urge you to come forward.

I would appreciate hearing from you at your earliest convenience. You may telephone me collect or write to me at this address.

Sincerely,

Hickey did not respond. Instead, an assistant director of the United States Secret Service called St. Martin's. We conveyed to him that if anyone could produce anything that invalidated Donahue's thesis we wouldn't publish the book. He replied to that by saying Donahue's thesis was impossible because Hickey was in a jump seat facing backward. This, we knew, was not the case, and we said so. (In a later call the assistant director conceded that he had been in error.) We asked if he could put us in touch with others in the follow-up car that day, and he stated that he would ensure that that happened at once. The impression we received was that he would pursue the agents because the new testimony they would supply would be useful in judging Donahue's thesis unworthy of publication.

Subsequently, Dave Powers, not a Secret Service agent but Kennedy's friend who was in the follow-up car, called St. Martin's. The man at the Secret Service had talked to him and asked him to call. Powers denied the AR-15 went off, and he sounded totally sincere when he said it. But his reliability was eroded by other things he said. He declared that Bonar Menninger was a liar; Powers had never talked to him. (Subsequently presented with Menninger's careful records of the call, he conceded he had talked to Menninger.) Powers said he turns down "seven, eight calls a day" on the subject. In any case, he said, Donahue's story was impossible because the bullet would have hit him or Ken O'Donnell sitting next to him. Not if Hickey was standing on the back seat, we said. (In a later talk with Menninger, Powers claimed the bullet would have had to hit him because *he stood up* before the head shot. Menninger demurred, noting that Powers never mentioned that detail in any of his earlier testimony to the government, nor was there any other evidence of his standing.)

For the first time, we began to understand Donahue's reaction over the years as he tried to get a hearing and found himself dismissed on the basis of palpable nonfacts. We have warned Donahue and Menninger that is likely to happen again after the book is published. We tried to convey to the Secret Service assistant director that if, when invited to provide information that would blow Donahue's story out of the water, the best that could be found was a nonexistent back-facing jump seat or Powers' statements, the effect was not to dissuade us from publishing. If anything, what we noted was that Donahue had survived yet another attempt to discredit his argument.

Eventually we did receive a communiqué from another occupant of the Secret Service vehicle, Samuel Kinney, the driver of the follow-up car: "I was driving the car at the time," his letter said, "and I can assure you that there was not a gun fired from the U.S.S.S. follow-up car." After receiving his letter we called Kinney. He explained that he was facing forward through all three shots. His statement that no shot was fired from his car was based, he said, on the conviction that the sound would have told him. He said he was never called before the Warren Commission hearings, and that the FBI had never questioned him. The HSCA did send two men in 1978 to interview him, but he did not know what happened to their report or transcript.

In fact another agent had stated, back in 1963, that no shot was fired from the follow-up car. William McIntyre, who was on the running board next to Hickey, said in his November 29, 1963, statement, "I would estimate that all three shots were fired within five seconds. After the second shot, I looked at the President and witnessed his being struck in the head by the third and last shot. By that time, Mr. Roberts had used the radio in our car to direct the vehicles to a hospital. Most, if not all the agents in the follow-up car had drawn their weapons, and Agent Hickey was handling the AR-15. None of us could determine the origin of the shots, and no shots were fired by any agent."

In an earlier written statement on November 22, McIntyre did not include that detail. Evidently, most of the written statements were prepared for the Chief of the Secret Service, James J. Rowley. Someone seems to have required several to be rewritten, and the Warren Report reprints a kind of patchwork.

Hickey is mentioned several times in these statements, other than by McIntyre.

Rufus Youngblood (who was in a car *behind* the follow-up car): "I heard an explosion and I noticed movements in the Presidential car were very abnormal and, at practically the same time, the movements in the Presidential follow-up car were abnormal. . . . During this time I heard two more explosion noises and observed SA Hickey in the Presidential follow-up car poised on the car with AR-15 rifle looking towards the buildings."

Glen Bennett: ". . . the Motorcade entered an intersection and proceeded down a grade. . . . At this point I heard what sounded like a fire-cracker. I immediately looked from the right/crowd physical area/ and looked towards the President who was seated in the right rear seat of his limousine open convertible. At the moment I looked at the back of the President I heard another fire-cracker noise and saw the shot hit the President about four inches down from the right shoulder. A second shot followed immediately and hit the right rear high [sic] of the President's head. I immediately hollered "he's hit" and reached for the AR-15 located on the floor of the rear seat. Special Agent Hickey had already picked up the AR-15. We peered towards the rear. . . ." (Note in passing that Bennett asserts clearly that the *second* shot hit Kennedy's back.)

Emory Roberts, agent in charge of the follow-up car: "I turned around a couple of times, just after the shooting and saw that some of the Special Agents had their guns drawn, I know I drew mine, and saw SA Hickey in rear seat with the AR-15, and asked him to be careful with it." Elsewhere in his statement Robert has Hickey placed in the right-rear seat, and Bennett in the left.

All these statements were taken in November and sent on by Rowley to the Warren Commission seven months later, in June 1964. One that arrived at the Commission earlier and possibly by another route was that of Agent Winston Lawson, who was in the lead car, the car preceding the President's (Lawson was looking back at the motorcade): "I heard the first loud, sharp report and in more rapid succession two more sounds like gunfire. . . . I noticed Agent Hickey standing up in the follow-up car with the automatic weapon and first thought he had fired at someone."

In late 1991 the assistant director of the Secret Service approached a number of surviving agents—how many, we do not know—with a description of Donahue's picture of what had happened in Dealey Plaza. He evidently urged them to write St. Martin's to deny Donahue's story. The only one we heard from was Samuel Kinney, who was Hickey's roommate in Dallas that day. For whatever reason, the Secret Service assistant director was unable to cause any other agent to come forward and say that Donahue was wrong.

We at St. Martin's do not unanimously feel that Donahue has proved his AR-15 case beyond a shadow of a doubt. His conviction is strong but we cannot say his argument absolutely precludes the possibility that he is wrong. Our own search was begun in an effort to uncover anything that might disqualify that argument. It was in that pursuit that we approached Hickey and talked with the Secret Service. Not only did we find nothing to invalidate Donahue's thesis, but with each passing week our respect grew for him and his ability to cite increasing amounts of evidential support for different aspects of his argument. We now feel that Donahue's command of and reasoning about the hard facts of Dealey Plaza are the strongest that we have seen, and if we cannot attest to certainty it may be because of a natural reluctance to concede that such bad luck, so unlikely and chaotic an accident, can prevail in this world. But to *dis*believe solely because it was a long shot is its own species of irrationality.

At last, what about Hickey?

No matter what crosses the mind as one tries to interpret his muteness in the face of the *Sun* article, Reppert's approaches, the Donahues', Menninger's, and our own, we cannot validly draw conclusions from the fact that he would not respond. He had a right to remain silent. He had no duty to reply to anyone, including us.

But ultimately we were driven to consider Donahue's question: What was he, Donahue, to do? Should Hickey's silence silence him too? He did not think so. He honestly believed he had the solution to the most tangled, festering mystery of our times. His efforts to turn the case file over to an appropriate government forum, the HSCA, were rejected for reasons he thought so groundless as to be irresponsible. Donahue took no delight in what his solution said, but he thought it was the truth, and that it was important.

On the first page of this chapter we said that fairness to Hickey was a necessity as we considered our decision about whether or not to publish. We now feel that every reasonable effort at fairness has been made. If we go forth without absolute agreement with Donahue's conviction that he has found the truth, we do so because we totally agree that what he has uncovered is important.

Very few American Presidents have been killed while in office. And of these, only one—John Kennedy—died under circumstances that were so clouded with doubt. In the years following his death, that doubt has ripened into suspicions, accusations, and a pervasive paranoia. Today, almost three decades after Dallas, the virulent miasma of alleged conspiracy is perhaps stronger than it has ever been. In January of 1992, CBS News conducted a poll revealing that 77 percent of those polled believed that Oswald was not alone in the killing. Seventy-five percent said there was an official cover-up in the case. The notion that the government comprises a share of "rascals" is a Mark Twain level of cynicism that is tolerable. But that the government is a cabal of murderers is a view that, until Kennedy's death, was alien to America, and it can be poisonous to our society.

Was there a miniconspiracy if Hickey's shot did kill the President?

Possibly. But only possibly, and even then conceivably of minimal proportions. If Hickey fired that bullet, there's no telling how few people may have been aware of it, including, we insist, the possibility that Hickey himself did not know. And certainly, if some did know, there's no necessity to believe that *everyone* in the follow-up car knew. In the ultimate clamor of that day, even in the small community of that car it is hard to find more than two or three who seem to have registered the same impressions.

So if there *was* a conspiracy, we do not know who was involved. Do not say it is impossible that such a secret could be held for long by a multiple of people. That prejudice is based solely on the evidence of secrets that have not been kept. If throughout history scores of secrets about major events *have* been kept by a small multitude, how would you know?

The conspiracy paranoia aside, the question of how President Kennedy died has been a legitimate concern and preoccupation for a generation. If it can be answered, the country deserves that answer.

As we considered all these things it became clearer that we were facing not a *decision* to publish but an *obligation* to publish. The dimensions of our tragedy in 1963 were not unique in our nation's history, but its aftermath was—and is. We believe there are people or sealed papers out there whose evidence finally made public will settle Donahue's question one way or another, and that means they may finally settle and put to rest the most damaging misgiving of our age. We believe Donahue's thesis needs to be explored honestly by an unbiased government body. His position is sound enough, his conclusion important enough, to deserve that—and so does the American public. We do not think that will happen if we do not publish this book.

If it takes data heretofore held back to prove Donahue wrong, we will not feel that he or Menninger has done other than what he should in revealing his story. Their work has been honest, careful, and worthy. If new testimony, provoked by this book, proves them right, it will be a justification hard but fully earned by them. And an America till now unmoored by a floodtide of doubt and suspicion will owe Howard Donahue and Bonar Menninger a portion of gratitude.

THOMAS MCCORMACK, Chairman
St. Martin's Press

Appendix A

Testimony and Written Statements by Secret Service Agents Regarding Events of November 22, 1963

Warren Commission, Vol. II, pages 132–144
Warren Commission, Vol. XVII, pages 630–634
Warren Commission, Vol. XVIII, pages 722–784

TESTIMONY OF CLINTON J. HILL, SPECIAL AGENT, SECRET SERVICE

Mr. SPECTER. Mr. Hill, would you state your full name for the record, please?

Mr. HILL. Clinton J. Hill.

Mr. SPECTER. How old are you, sir?

Mr. HILL. Thirty-two.

Mr. SPECTER. What is your educational background?

Mr. HILL. I went to secondary educational high school in Washburn, N. Dak., and then went on to Concordia College, Moorehead, Minn. I was a history and education major, with a minor in physical education.

Mr. SPECTER. What year were you graduated?

Mr. HILL. 1954.

Mr. SPECTER. What have you done since the time of graduation from college, Mr. Hill?

Mr. HILL. I went into the Army in 1954; remained in the Army until 1957. Then I couldn't determine what I wanted to do, whether to go to law school or not, and I took a couple of odd jobs. I worked for a finance company at one time. Then I went to work for the Chicago, Burlington & Quincy Railroad as a special agent in the spring of 1958, and entered the Secret Service in September 1958.

Mr. SPECTER. You have been with the Secret Service since September 1958 to the present time?

Mr. HILL. Yes; I have.

Mr. SPECTER. Will you outline for the Commission your duties with the Secret Service during your tenure there?

Mr. HILL. I entered the Secret Service in Denver, and during that period I did both investigative and protection work. I was assigned to Mrs. Doud, the mother-in-law of President Eisenhower. I attended the Treasury Law Enforcement School during my first year, and was sent to the White House for a 30-day temporary assignment at the White House in June 1959. In November of 1959, November 1, I was transferred to the White House on a permanent basis as a special agent assigned to the White House detail. I have been at the White House since that time.

Mr. SPECTER. Now, were you assigned to duties on the trip of President Kennedy to Texas in November 1963?

Mr. HILL. Yes, sir; I was.

Mr. SPECTER. Did you have any special duty assigned to you at that time?

Mr. HILL. Yes, sir.

Mr. SPECTER. In connection with the trip?

Mr. HILL. I was responsible for the protection of Mrs. Kennedy.

Mr. SPECTER. And, in a general way, what does that sort of an assignment involve?

Mr. HILL. I tried to remain as close to her at all times as possible, and in this particular trip that meant being with the President because all of their doings on this trip were together rather than separate. I would go over her schedule to make sure she knows what she is expected to do; discuss it with her; remain in her general area all the time; protect her from any danger.

Mr. SPECTER. Would you tell us, in a general way, what were the activities of the President and Mrs. Kennedy on the morning of Friday, November 22, before they arrived in Dallas?

Mr. HILL. I went to the fifth floor, I believe it was, where the President and Mrs. Kennedy were staying in the Texas Hotel in Fort Worth at 8:15 in the morning. President Kennedy was to go downstairs and across the street to make a speech to a gathering in a parking lot. I remained on the floor during the period the President was gone.

It was raining outside, I recall. About 9:25 I received word from Special Agent Duncan that the President requested Mrs. Kennedy to come to the mezzanine, where a breakfast was being held in his honor, and where he was about to speak. I went in and advised Mrs. Kennedy of this, and took her down to where the President was speaking; remained with her adjacent to the head table in this particular area during the speech; and accompanied she and the President back up to the, I believe it was, the fifth floor of the hotel, their residential area; remained on that floor until we left, went downstairs, got into the motorcade, and departed the hotel for the airport to leave Fort Worth for Dallas.

We were airborne approximately 11:20, I believe, in Air Force 1. I was in the aft compartment, which is part of the residential compartment, and we arrived in Dallas at 11:40.

Mr. SPECTER. Would you describe, in a general way, what the President and Mrs. Kennedy did upon arrival in Dallas?

Mr. HILL. They debarked the rear ramp of the aircraft first, followed by Governor and Mrs. Connally, various Congressmen and Senators. And Special Agent in Charge Kellerman and myself went down the ramp. There was a small reception committee at the foot of the ramp, and somebody gave Mrs. Kennedy some red roses, I recall. I walked immediately to the followup car and placed my topcoat, which is a raincoat, and small envelope containing some information concerning the Dallas stop in the followup car, returning to where the President and Mrs. Kennedy were at that time greeting a crippled lady in a wheelchair.

Mr. SPECTER. What do you estimate the size of the crowd to have been at Dallas that morning?

Mr. HILL. At the airport?

Mr. SPECTER. Yes, sir.

Mr. HILL. It is rather difficult to say. They were behind a chain-link fence, not on the airport ramp itself, and they were jammed up against the fence holding placards, and many young people in the crowd. I would say there were probably 2,000 people there.

Mr. SPECTER. At approximately what time did the motorcade depart from Love Field to Dallas?

Mr. HILL. Approximately 11:55.

Mr. SPECTER. Do you know approximately how many automobiles there were in the motorcade?

Mr. HILL. No, sir; I do not.

Mr. SPECTER. In which car in the motorcade were you positioned?

Mr. HILL. I was working the followup car, which is the car immediately behind the Presidential car.

Mr. SPECTER. And how many cars are there ahead of the followup car, then, in the entire motorcade?

Mr. HILL. There was a lead car ahead of the President's car, the President's car, then this particular followup car.

Mr. SPECTER. Do you know whether there was any car in advance of the car termed the lead car?

Mr. HILL. There could have been a pilot car, but I am not sure.

Mr. SPECTER. Now, approximately how far in front of the President's car did the lead car stay during the course of the motorcade?

Mr. HILL. I would say a half block, maybe.

Mr. SPECTER. And how far was the President's car in front of the President's followup car during the course of the motorcade?

Mr. HILL. Approximately 5 feet.

Mr. SPECTER. Is there some well-established practice as to the spacing between the President's car and the President's followup car?

Mr. HILL. It would depend upon speed. We attempt to stay as close to the President's car as practical. At high rates of speed it is rather difficult to stay close because of the danger involved. Slow speeds, the followup car stays as close as possible so that the agents on the followup car can get to the Presidential car as quickly as possible.

Mr. SPECTER. What was the first car to the rear of the President's followup car?

Mr. HILL. The Vice-Presidential automobile.

Mr. SPECTER. What car was immediately behind the Vice President's automobile?

Mr. HILL. The Vice-Presidential followup car.

Mr. SPECTER. Do you know what cars in the Dallas motorcade followed the Vice President's followup car?

Mr. HILL. Well, I couldn't say which car any individual rode in after that particular automobile, but I could say they were occupied by members of the staff, both President Kennedy's and Vice President Johnson's; Congressmen and Senators who were on this particular trip; newspaper personnel who were on this trip.

Mr. SPECTER. Would you identify the occupants of the President's followup car and indicate where each was in the automobile.

Mr. HILL. The car itself was driven by Special Agent Sam Kinney, and Assistant to the Special Agent in Charge Emory Roberts was riding in the right front seat. I was assigned to work the left running board of the automobile, the forward portion of that running board. McIntyre was assigned to work the rear portion of the left running board. Special Agent John Ready was assigned the forward portion of the right running board; Special Agent Paul Landis was assigned the rear portion of the right running board. There were two jump seats, and they were occupied by two Presidential aides, Mr. O'Donnell and Mr. Powers. Mr. Powers was sitting on the right-hand side; Mr. O'Donnell on the left. The rear seat was occupied, left rear by Special Agent Hickey, right rear, Special Agent Bennett.

Mr. SPECTER. How were the agents armed at that time?

Mr. HILL. All the agents were armed with their hand weapons.

Mr. SPECTER. And is there any weapon in the automobile in addition to the hand weapons?

Mr. HILL. Yes. There is an AR-15, which is an automatic rifle, and a shotgun.

Mr. SPECTER. And where is the AR-15 kept?

Mr. HILL. Between the two agents in the rear seat.

Mr. SPECTER. How about the shotgun; where is that kept?

Mr. HILL. In a compartment immediately in front of the jump seats.

Mr. SPECTER. Is the President's followup car a specially constructed automobile.

Mr. HILL. Yes, sir; it is.

Mr. SPECTER. And what is the make and model and general description of that vehicle?

Mr. HILL. It is a 1955 Cadillac, nine-passenger touring sedan. It is a convertible type.

Mr. SPECTER. Was that automobile flown in specially from Washington for the occasion?

Mr. HILL. Yes; it was, sir.

Mr. SPECTER. Do you know how that automobile was transported to Dallas, Tex.?

Mr. HILL. Generally, it is flown in a C-130 by the Air Force. I am not sure how on this particular occasion.

Mr. SPECTER. Will you describe, in a general way, the composition of the crowds en route from Love Field down to the center of Dallas, please?

Mr. HILL. Well, when we left Love Field, we went away from the crowd to get to the exit point at Love Field, and there were no crowds at all, and then we, departing Love Field, found the crowds were sporadic. There were people here and there. Some places they had built up and other places they were thinned out. The speed of the motorcade was adjusted accordingly. Whenever there were large groups of people, the motorcade slowed down to give the people an opportunity to view the President. When there were not many people along the side of the street, we speeded up. We didn't really hit the crowds until we hit Main Street.

Mr. SPECTER. What is your best estimate of the maximum speed of the automobile from the time you left Love Field until the time you arrived at downtown Dallas?

Mr. HILL. I would say we never ran any faster than 25 to 30 miles per hour.

Mr. SPECTER. What is your best estimate of the minimum speed during this same interval?

Mr. HILL. Twelve to fifteen miles per hour. We did stop.

Mr. SPECTER. On what occasion did you stop?

Mr. HILL. Between Love Field and Main Street, downtown Dallas, on the right-hand side of the street there were a group of people with a long banner which said, "Please, Mr. President, stop and shake our hands." And the President requested the motorcade to stop, and he beckoned to the people and asked them to come and shake his hand, which they did.

Mr. SPECTER. Did the President disembark from his automobile at that time?

Mr. HILL. No; he remained in his seat.

Mr. SPECTER. At that time what action, if any, did you take?

Mr. HILL. I jumped from the followup car and ran up to the left rear portion of the automobile with my back toward Mrs. Kennedy viewing those persons on the left-hand side of the street.

Mr. SPECTER. What action was taken by any other Secret Service agent which you observed at that time?

Mr. HILL. Special Agent Ready, who was working the forward portion of the right running board, did the same thing, only on the President's side, placed his back toward the car, and viewed the people facing the President. Assistant in Charge Kellerman opened the door of the President's car and stepped out on the street.

Mr. SPECTER. What action was taken by Special Agent McIntyre, if you know?

Mr. HILL. I do not know.

Mr. SPECTER. How about Special Agent Landis?

Mr. HILL. I do not know.

Mr. SPECTER. What is your normal procedure for action in the event the President's car is stopped, as it did in that event?

Mr. HILL. Special Agent McIntyre would normally jump off the car and run to the forward portion of the left-hand side of the car; Special Agent Landis would move to the right-hand forward portion of the automobile.

Mr. SPECTER. Did anything else which was unusual occur en route from Love Field to the downtown area of Dallas?

Mr. HILL. Before we hit Main Street?

Mr. SPECTER. Yes, sir.

Mr. HILL. Not that I recall.

Mr. SPECTER. Did you have any occasion to leave the President's followup car at any time?

Mr. HILL. When we finally did reach Main Street, the crowds had built up to a point where they were surging into the street. We had motorcycles running adjacent to both the Presidential automobile and the followup car, as well as in front of the Presidential automobile, and because of the crowds in the street, the President's driver, Special Agent Greer, was running the car more to the left-hand side of the street more than he was to the right to keep the President as far away from the crowd as possible, and because of this the motorcycles on the left-hand side could not get past the crowd and alongside the car, and they were forced to drop back. I jumped from the followup car, ran up and got on top of the rear portion of the Presidential automobile to be close to Mrs. Kennedy in the event that someone attempted to grab her from the crowds or throw something in the car.

Mr. SPECTER. When you say the rear portion of the automobile, can you, by referring to Commission Exhibit No. 345, heretofore identified as the President's automobile, specify by penciled "X" where you stood?

Mr. HILL. Yes, sir [indicating].

Mr. SPECTER. Will you describe for the record just what area it is back there on which you stood?

Mr. HILL. That is a step built into the rear bumper of the automobile, and on top of the rear trunk there is a handguard which you grab for and hang onto when you are standing up.

Mr. SPECTER. Are identical objects of those descriptions existing on each side of the President's car?

Mr. HILL. Yes, sir; they do.

Mr. SPECTER. Did you have any other occasion en route from Love Field to downtown Dallas to leave the followup car and mount that portion of the President's car?

Mr. HILL. I did the same thing approximately four times.

Mr. SPECTER. What are the standard regulations and practices, if any, governing such an action on your part?

Mr. HILL. It is left to the agent's discretion more or less to move to that particular position when he feels that there is a danger to the President; to place himself as close to the President or the First Lady as my case was, as possible, which I did.

Mr. SPECTER. Are those practices specified in any written documents of the Secret Service?

Mr. HILL. No; they are not.

Mr. SPECTER. Now, had there been any instruction or comment about your performance of that type of a duty with respect to anything that President Kennedy himself had said in the period immediately preceding the trip to Texas?

Mr. HILL. Yes, sir; there was. The preceding Monday, the President was on a trip in Tampa, Fla., and he requested that the agents not ride on either of those two steps.

Mr. SPECTER. And to whom did the President make that request?

Mr. HILL. Assistant Special Agent in Charge Boring.

Mr. SPECTER. Was Assistant Special Agent in Charge Boring the individual in charge of that trip to Florida?

Mr. HILL. He was riding in the Presidential automobile on that trip in Florida, and I presume that he was. I was not along.

Mr. SPECTER. Well, on that occasion would he have been in a postion comparable to that occupied by Special Agent Kellerman on this trip to Texas?

Mr. HILL. Yes, sir; the same position.

Mr. SPECTER. And Special Agent Boring informed you of that instruction by President Kennedy?

Mr. HILL. Yes, sir; he did.

Mr. SPECTER. Did he make it a point to inform other special agents of that same instruction?

Mr. HILL. I believe that he did, sir.

Mr. SPECTER. And, as a result of what President Kennedy said to him, did he instruct you to observe that Presidential admonition?

Mr. HILL. Yes, sir.

Mr. SPECTER. How, if at all, did that instruction of President Kennedy affect your action and—your action in safeguarding him on this trip to Dallas?

Mr. HILL. We did not ride on the rear portions of the automobile. I did on those four occasions because the motorcycles had to drop back and there was no protection on the left-hand side of the car.

Mr. SPECTER. When the President's automobile was proceeding in downtown Dallas, what was the ordinary speed of the automobile, based on your best estimate?

Mr. HILL. We were running approximately 12 to 15 miles per hour, I would say.

Mr. SPECTER. I show you a document which we have marked as Commission Exhibit No. 354, which is an aerial photograph identical with the photograph already marked as Commission Exhibit No. 347.

(The photograph referred to was marked Exhibit No. 354 for identification.)

Mr. SPECTER. I ask you if, referring only to Exhibit 354, you are able to identify what that scene is.

Mr. HILL. Yes, sir; I am.

Mr. SPECTER. Are you able to indicate the route which the President's motorcade followed through that area?

Mr. HILL. Yes, sir; I am.

Mr. SPECTER. And what does that scene depict—what city is it?

Mr. HILL. That is Dallas, Tex. It shows Main Street, Houston Street, and Elm Street.

Mr. SPECTER. Will you write on the picture itself where Main Street is? Would you now write, as best you can, which street is Houston Street?

Mr. HILL. Yes, sir.

Mr. SPECTER. And would you now write which street is Elm?

Mr. HILL. Yes, sir.

(At this point, Representative Ford entered the hearing room.)

Mr. SPECTER. Now, would you indicate, if you know, which is a generally northerly direction on that picture?

Mr. HILL. Yes, sir.

Mr. SPECTER. All right. What was the condition of the crowd as the motorcade made a right-hand turn off of Main Street onto Houston?

Mr. HILL. The crowd was very large on Main Street, and it was thinning down considerably when we reached the end of it, and turned right on Houston Street. Noticeably on my side of the car, which was the left-hand side of the street.

Mr. SPECTER. And what is your best estimate as to the speed of the President's car at the time it made the right-hand turn onto Houston Street?

Mr. HILL. In the curve?

Mr. SPECTER. The speed—in the curve itself; yes.

Mr. HILL. We were running generally 12 to 15 miles per hour. I would say that in the curve we perhaps slowed to maybe 10 miles per hour.

Mr. SPECTER. And how far behind the President's car was the Presidential followup car as the turn was made onto Houston Street?

Mr. HILL. Four to five feet, at the most.

Mr. SPECTER. I show you a photograph of a building which has already been marked as Commission Exhibit No. 348, and ask you if at this time you can identify what that building is.

Mr. HILL. I believe I can, sir; yes.

Mr. SPECTER. And what building is it?

Mr. HILL. It is the Texas School Book Depository.

Mr. SPECTER. Now, does that building appear on the Commission Exhibit No. 354?

Mr. HILL. Yes, sir; it does.

Mr. SPECTER. Did you have any occasion to notice the Texas School Book Depository Building as you proceeded in a generally northerly direction on Houston Street?

Mr. HILL. Yes, sir. It was immediately in front of us and to our left.

Mr. SPECTER. Did you notice anything unusual about it?

Mr. HILL. Nothing more unusual than any other building along the way.

Mr. SPECTER. What is your general practice, if any, in observing such buildings along the route of a Presidential motorcade?

Mr. HILL. We scan the buildings and look specifically for open windows, for people hanging out, and there had been, on almost every building along the way, people hanging out, windows open.

Mr. SPECTER. And did you observe, as you recollect at this moment, any open windows in the Texas School Depository Building?

Mr. HILL. Yes, sir; there were.

Mr. SPECTER. Are you able to recollect specifically which windows were open at this time?

Mr. HILL. No, sir; I cannot.

Mr. SPECTER. What was the condition of the crowd along the streets, if any, along Elm Street, in front of the Texas School Book Depository Building?

Mr. HILL. On the left-hand side of the street, which is the side I was on, the crowd was very thin. And it was a general park area. There were people scattered throughout the entire park.

Mr. SPECTER. Now, what is your best estimate of the speed of the President's automobile as it turned left off of Houston onto Elm Street?

Mr. HILL. We were running still 12 to 15 miles per hour, but in the curve I believe we slowed down maybe to 10, maybe to 9.

Mr. SPECTER. How far back of the President's automobile was the Presidential followup car when the President's followup car had just straightened out on Elm Street?

Mr. HILL. Approximately 5 feet.

Mr. SPECTER. Now, as the motorcade proceeded at that point, tell us what happened.

Mr. HILL. Well, as we came out of the curve, and began to straighten up, I was viewing the area which looked to be a park. There were people scattered throughout the entire park. And I heard a noise from my right rear, which to me seemed to be a firecracker. I immediately looked to my right, and, in so doing, my eyes had to cross the Presidential limousine and I saw President Kennedy grab at himself and lurch forward and to the left.

Mr. SPECTER. Why don't you just proceed, in narrative form, to tell us?

Representative BOGGS. This was the first shot?

Mr. HILL. This is the first sound that I heard; yes, sir. I jumped from the car, realizing that something was wrong, ran to the Presidential limousine. Just about as I reached it, there was another sound, which was different than the first sound. I think I described it in my statement as though someone was shooting a revolver into a hard object—it seemed to have some type of an echo. I put my right foot, I believe it was, on the left rear step of the automobile, and I had a hold of the handgrip with my hand, when the car lurched forward. I lost my footing and I had to run about three or four more steps before I could get back up in the car.

Between the time I originally grabbed the handhold and until I was up on the car, Mrs. Kennedy—the second noise that I heard had removed a portion of the President's head, and he had slumped noticeably to his left. Mrs. Kennedy had jumped up from the seat and was, it appeared to me, reaching for something coming off the right rear bumper of the car, the right rear tail, when she noticed that I was trying to climb on the car. She turned toward me and I grabbed her and put her back in the back seat, crawled up on top of the back seat and lay there.

Mr. SPECTER. Now, referring to Commission Exhibit No. 354, would you mark an "X", as best you can, at the spot where the President's automobile was at the time the first shot occurred?

Mr. HILL. Approximately there.

Mr. SPECTER. And would you mark a "Y" at the approximate position where the President's car was at the second shot you have described? What is your best estimate of the speed of the President's car at the precise time of the first shot, Mr. Hill?

Mr. HILL. We were running between 12 to 15 miles per hour, but no faster than 15 miles per hour.

Mr. SPECTER. How many shots have you described that you heard?

Mr. HILL. Two.

Mr. SPECTER. Did you hear any more than two shots?

Mr. HILL. No, sir.

Mr. SPECTER. And what is your best estimate of the speed of the President's automobile at the time of the second shot?

Mr. HILL. Approximately the same speed as that of the first—although at the time that I jumped on the car, the car had surged forward. The President at that time had been shot in the head.

Mr. SPECTER. When, in relationship to the second shot, did the car accelerate—that is, the President's car?

Mr. HILL. Almost simultaneously.

Mr. SPECTER. You testified just a moment ago that the President grabbed at himself immediately after the first noise which you described as sounding like a firecracker.

Mr. HILL. Yes, sir.

Mr. SPECTER. Would you tell us with more particularity in what way he grabbed at himself?

Mr. HILL. He grabbed in this general area.

Mr. SPECTER. You are indicating that your right hand is coming up to your—to the throat?

Mr. HILL. Yes, sir.

Mr. SPECTER. And the left hand crosses right under the right hand.

Mr. HILL. To the chest area.

Mr. SPECTER. To the chest area. Was there any movement of the President's head or shoulders immediately after the first shot, that you recollect?

Mr. HILL. Yes, sir. Immediately when I saw him, he was like this, and going left and forward.

Mr. SPECTER. Indicating a little fall to the left front.

Mr. HILL. Yes, sir.

Representative BOGGS. This was after a head wound?

Mr. HILL. No, sir.

Representative BOGGS. Before the head wound?

Mr. HILL. Yes, sir; this was the first shot.

Mr. SPECTER. Now, what is your best estimate on the timespan between the first firecracker-type noise you heard and the second shot which you have described?

Mr. HILL. Approximately 5 seconds.

Mr. SPECTER. Now, did the impact on the President's head occur simultaneously, before, or after the second noise which you have described?

Mr. HILL. Almost simultaneously.

Representative FORD. Did you see the President put his hands to his throat and chest while you were still on the followup car, or after you had left it?

Mr. HILL. As I was leaving. And that is one of the reasons I jumped, because I saw him grab himself and pitch forward and to the left. I knew something was wrong.

Representative FORD. It was 5 seconds from the firecracker noise that you think you got to the automobile?

Mr. HILL. Until I reached the handhold, had placed my foot on the left rear step.

Mr. SPECTER. When, in relationship to the second shot, did Mrs. Kennedy move out of the rear seat?

Mr. HILL. Just after it.

Mr. SPECTER. You say that it appeared that she was reaching as if something was coming over to the rear portion of the car, back in the area where you were coming to?

Mr. HILL. Yes, sir.

Mr. SPECTER. Was there anything back there that you observed, that she might have been reaching for?

Mr. HILL. I thought I saw something come off the back, too, but I cannot say that there was. I do know that the next day we found the portion of the President's head.

Mr. SPECTER. Where did you find that portion of the President's head?

Mr. HILL. It was found in the street. It was turned in, I believe, by a medical student or somebody in Dallas.

Mr. SPECTER. Did you have any difficulty maintaining your balance on the back of the car after you had come up on the top of it?

Mr. HILL. Not until we turned off to enter the Parkland Hospital.

Mr. SPECTER. Now, what action did you take specifically with respect to placing Mrs. Kennedy back in the rear seat?

Mr. HILL. I simply just pushed and she moved—somewhat voluntarily—right back into the same seat she was in. The President—when she had attempted to get out onto the trunk of the car, his body apparently did not move too much, because when she got back into the car he was at that time, when I got on top of the car, face up in her lap.

Mr. SPECTER. And that was after she was back in the rear seat?

Mr. HILL. Yes, sir.

Mr. SPECTER. And where were the President's legs at that time?

Mr. HILL. Inside the car.

Mr. SPECTER. Now, what, if anything, did you observe as to the condition of Governor Connally at that time?

Mr. HILL. After going under this underpass, I looked forward to the jump seats, where Mrs. Connally and Governor Connally were sitting. Mrs. Connally had been leaning over her husband. And I had no idea that he had been shot. And when she leaned back at one time, I noticed that his coat was unbuttoned, and that the lower portion of his abdomen was completely covered with blood.

Mr. SPECTER. When was it that you first observed that?

Mr. HILL. Just after going under the underpass.

Mr. SPECTER. Were you able to observe anything which was occurring on the overpass as the President's motorcade moved toward the overpass?

Mr. HILL. From the time I got on the back of the Presidential limousine, I didn't really pay any attention to what was going on outside the automobile.

Mr. SPECTER. Had you noticed the overpass prior to the time you got on the Presidential automobile?

Mr. HILL. Yes; I had scanned it.

Mr. SPECTER. And do you recollect what, if anything, you observed on the overpass at that time?

Mr. HILL. There were some people there, but I also noticed there was a policeman there.

Mr. SPECTER. Approximately how many people would you say were there?

Mr. HILL. Very few, I would say—maybe five, six.

Mr. SPECTER. And how were you able to identify that there was a policeman there?

Mr. HILL. He was wearing the uniform—presumably a policeman.

Mr. SPECTER. What color uniform was it?

Mr. HILL. I think it was blue of some shade.

Mr. SPECTER. Did you identify it at that time as being of the identical color which other Dallas policemen were wearing whom you had observed in the area?

Mr. HILL. That's correct, sir.

Mr. SPECTER. Can you characterize the type of acceleration which the car made after it started to speed forward—that is, the Presidential car.

Mr. HILL. Well, the initial surge was quite violent, because it almost jerked me off the left rear step board. Then after that it was apparently gradual, because I did not notice it any more.

Mr. SPECTER. What is your best estimate of the distance from the time of the shooting to Parkland Hospital?

Mr. HILL. In time or—

Mr. SPECTER. Time and distance.

Mr. HILL. Distance, I have no idea.

Mr. SPECTER. How about time?

Mr. HILL. I would say roughly 4 minutes.

Mr. SPECTER. Did Mrs. Kennedy say anything as you were proceeding from the time of the shooting to Parkland Hospital?

Mr. HILL. At the time of the shooting, when I got into the rear of the car, she said, "My God, they have shot his head off." Between there and the hospital she just said, "Jack, Jack, what have they done to you," and sobbed.

Mr. SPECTER. Was there any conversation by anybody else in the President's automobile from the time of the shooting to the arrival at Parkland Hospital?

Mr. HILL. I heard Special Agent Kellerman say on the radio, "To the nearest hospital, quick."

Mr. SPECTER. Any other comment?

Mr. HILL. He said, "We have been hit."

Mr. SPECTER. Now, was there any other comment you heard Special Agent Kellerman make?

Mr. HILL. Not that I recall.

Mr. SPECTER. Did Special Agent Greer say anything?

Mr. HILL. No, sir.

Mr. SPECTER. Mrs. Connally say anything?

Mr. HILL. No, sir.

Representative BOGGS. Was Governor Connally conscious?

Mr. HILL. Yes, sir; he was.

Mr. SPECTER. Did Governor Connally say anything?

Mr. HILL. No, sir.

Mr. SPECTER. Did President Kennedy say anything?

Mr. HILL. No, sir.

Mr. SPECTER. What is your best estimate on the speed at which the President's car traveled from the point of the shooting to Parkland Hospital?

Mr. HILL. It is a little bit hard for me to judge, since I was lying across the rear portion of the automobile. I had no trouble staying in that particular position—until we approached the hospital, I recall, I believe it was a left-hand turn and I started slipping off to the right-hand portion of the car. So I would say that we went 60, maybe 65 at the most.

Mr. SPECTER. Were you able to secure a handhold or a leghold or any sort of a hold on the automobile as you moved forward?

Mr. HILL. Yes, sir. I had my legs—I had my body above the rear seat, and my legs hooked down into the rear seat, one foot outside the car.

Mr. SPECTER. What is your best estimate of the time of the assassination itself?

Mr. HILL. Approximately 12:30.

Mr. SPECTER. I am not sure whether I asked you about this—about how long did it take you to get from the shooting to the hospital?

Mr. HILL. Approximately 4 minutes.

Mr. SPECTER. What did you observe as to President Kennedy's condition on arrival at the hospital?

Mr. HILL. The right rear portion of his head was missing. It was lying in the rear seat of the car. His brain was exposed. There was blood and bits of brain all over the entire rear portion of the car. Mrs. Kennedy was completely covered with blood. There was so much blood you could not tell if there had been any other wound or not, except for the one large gaping wound in the right rear portion of the head.

Mr. SPECTER. Did you have any opportunity to observe the front part of his body, to see whether there was any tear or rip in the clothing on the front?

Mr. HILL. I saw him lying there in the back of the car, when I was immediately above him. I cannot recall noticing anything that was ripped in the forward portion of his body.

Mr. SPECTER. What action, if any, did you take to shield the President's body?

Mr. HILL. I kept myself above the President and Mrs. Kennedy on the trip to Parkland.

Mr. SPECTER. Did you do anything with your coat upon arrival at Parkland Hospital to shield the President?

Mr. HILL. Yes, sir. I removed it and covered the President's head and upper chest.

Mr. SPECTER. What, if anything, did you observe as to Governor Connally's condition on arrival at Parkland?

Mr. HILL. He was conscious. There was a large amount of blood in the lower abdominal area. He was helped from the automobile to the stretcher, and I do not recall him saying anything, but I know that he was conscious. He was wheeled immediately into, I think, emergency room No. 2.

Mr. SPECTER. And who was removed first from the automobile?

Mr. HILL. Governor Connally.

Mr. SPECTER. How long after the President's car arrived at Parkland Hospital did medical personnel come to the scene to remove the victims?

Mr. HILL. Seconds. They were there when we were there almost—almost simultaneously with the arrival.

Mr. SPECTER. Do you know where President Kennedy was taken in the hospital?

Mr. HILL. Yes, sir. I accompanied he and Mrs. Kennedy to the emergency room.

Mr. SPECTER. Now, tell us what you did at the hospital from the time of arrival on, please.

Mr. HILL. I went into the emergency room with the President, but it was so small, and there were so many people in there that I decided I had better leave and let the doctors take care of the situation. So I walked outside; asked for the nearest telephone; walked to the nearest telephone. About that time Special Agent in Charge Kellerman came outside and said, "Get the White House."

I asked Special Agent Lawson for the local number in Dallas of the White House switchboard, which he gave to me. I called the switchboard in Dallas; asked for the line to be open to Washington, and remain open continuously. And then I asked for Special Agent in Charge Behn's office. Mr. Kellerman came out of the emergency room about that time, took the telephone and called Special Agent in Charge Behn that we had had a double tragedy; that both Governor Connally and President Kennedy had been shot. And that was about as much as he said. I then took the telephone and shortly thereafter Mr. Kellerman came out of the emergency room and said, "Clint, tell Jerry this is unofficial and not for release, but the man is dead." Which I did. During the two calls, I talked to the Attorney General, who attempted to reach me, and told him that his brother had been seriously wounded; that we would keep him advised as to his condition.

Mr. SPECTER. Where was Mrs. Kennedy all this time, if you know?

Mr. HILL. Immediately upon arrival, she went into the emergency room. And a few minutes afterward, she was convinced to wait outside, which she did, remained there the rest of the period of time that we were there.

Mr. SPECTER. And was there any pronouncement that the President had died?

Mr. HILL. Not that I know of. Apparently there was. I was requested by Mr. O'Donnell, one of the Presidential assistants, to obtain a casket, because they wanted to return to Washington immediately. I contacted the administrator of the hospital and asked him to take me where I could telephone the nearest mortuary, which I did, requested that their best available casket be brought to the emergency entrance in my name immediately.

Mr. SPECTER. And what action was taken as a result of that request by you?

Mr. HILL. The casket did arrive from the O'Neal Mortuary, Inc., in their own hearse, which we then wheeled into the emergency room. I left the emergency room and asked that two of our agents, Special Agent Sulliman and Assistant Special Agent in Charge Stout clear all the corridors, and I checked the closest and most immediate route to the ambulance. We took the body from the hospital and departed the Parkland Hospital about 2:04 p.m. The ambulance was driven by Special Agent Berger. Special Agent in Charge Kellerman and Assistant Special Agent in Charge Stout were riding in the front seat; Mrs. Kennedy, Dr. Burkley, the President's body, and myself rode in the rear portion of the ambulance.

Mr. SPECTER. Approximately how long did it take you to reach the airplane at Love Field?

Mr. HILL. We arrived at Love Field at 2:14.

Mr. SPECTER. And were you present during the swearing-in ceremonies of President Johnson?

Mr. HILL. I was aboard the aircraft; yes, sir.

Mr. SPECTER. Did you witness those ceremonies?

Mr. HILL. Well, the Presidential compartment was so small that not all persons on the aircraft could get in. I was in the forward portion of the aircraft, right adjacent to the area that the President was sworn in.

Mr. SPECTER. Do you know the time of the swearing in?

Mr. HILL. 2:38.

Mr. SPECTER. And what time did the Presidential aircraft depart?

Mr. HILL. 2:47.

Mr. SPECTER. Do you know what time it arrived in the Washington area?

Mr. HILL. 5:59, I believe, sir.

Mr. SPECTER. And where did it land?

Mr. HILL. We landed at Andrews Air Force Base.

Mr. SPECTER. And what action, if any, in connection with this matter did you take following landing?

Mr. HILL. I assisted Mrs. Kennedy and the Attorney General, who had joined her at that time, into the ambulance bearing the President's body, and I entered the automobile immediately behind the ambulance with Dr. John Walsh, Mrs. Kennedy's physician, and members of President Kennedy's staff.

Mr. SPECTER. And where did you go then?

Mr. HILL. Immediately to Bethesda Naval Hospital.

Mr. SPECTER. And did you stay with the President's family at that time?

Mr. HILL. When we arrived there, I went to the 17th floor with Mrs. Kennedy, and I remained with Mrs. Kennedy except for one time when I was requested to come to the morgue to view the President's body.

Mr. SPECTER. And did you view the President's body?

Mr. HILL. Yes, sir.

Mr. SPECTER. What action did you take following the time you viewed the President's body in the morgue?

Mr. HILL. After the viewing of the President's body?

Mr. SPECTER. Yes.

Mr. HILL. I returned to the 17th floor and remained with Mrs. Kennedy until we departed the hospital.

Representative BOGGS. May I ask a question? At the hospital in Texas, you had seen—had you seen the whole body, or just the back of the President's head?

Mr. HILL. I had seen the whole body, but he was still cold when I saw him.

Representative BOGGS. At the morgue in Bethesda he was not cold?

Mr. HILL. Yes, sir; the autopsy had been completed, and the Lawler Mortuary Co. was preparing the body for placement in a casket.

Representative BOGGS. At this time did you see the whole body?

Mr. HILL. Yes, sir.

Representative BOGGS. Did you see any other wound other than the head wound?

Mr. HILL. Yes, sir; I saw an opening in the back, about 6 inches below the neckline to the right-hand side of the spinal column.

Representative BOGGS. Was there a frontal neck injury?

Mr. HILL. There was an area here that had been opened but—

Mr. SPECTER. You are indicating—

Mr. HILL. In the neck. It was my understanding at that time that this was done by a tracheotomy.

Mr. SPECTER. What else, if anything, of importance did you do between the time you viewed the body in the morgue until the termination of your duties on that date, Mr. Hill?

Mr. HILL. We handled all communications on the 17th floor, up to the 17th floor, for Mrs. Kennedy, members of her family, Cabinet members who were there at that time, and secured the 17th floor for all personnel. No one was permitted there that we did not know.

Mr. SPECTER. What time did you leave the 17th floor?

Mr. HILL. I believe, sir, it was 3:56, but I am not sure of the exact time.

Mr. SPECTER. Where did you go from there?

Mr. HILL. We went downstairs to the rear of the hospital, where the body was placed in a naval ambulance. I entered an automobile immediately behind the ambulance. Mrs. Kennedy and the Attorney General got into the rear of the ambulance with the body.

Mr. SPECTER. And from there, where did you go?

Mr. HILL. I accompanied them to the White House.

Mr. SPECTER. And did that mark the termination of your duties for that day?

Mr. HILL. No, sir. I remained on duty until approximately 6:30 in the morning; went home, changed clothes, and came back.

Mr. SPECTER. I believe you testified as to the impression you had as to the source of the first shot. To be sure that the record is complete, what was your reaction as to where the first shot came from, Mr. Hill?

Mr. HILL. Right rear.

Mr. SPECTER. And did you have a reaction or impression as to the source of point of origin of the second shot that you described?

Mr. HILL. It was right, but I cannot say for sure that it was rear, because when I mounted the car it was—it had a different sound, first of all, than the first sound that I heard. The second one had almost a double sound—as though you were standing against something metal and firing into it, and you hear both the sound of a gun going off and the sound of the cartridge hitting the metal place, which could have been caused probably by the hard surface of the head. But I am not sure that that is what caused it.

Mr. SPECTER. Are you describing this double sound with respect to what you heard on the occasion of the second shot?

Mr. HILL. The second shot that I heard; yes, sir.

Mr. SPECTER. Now, do you now or have you ever had the impression or reaction that there was a shot which originated from the front of the Presidential car?

Mr. HILL. No.

Mr. SPECTER. That is all I have.

The CHAIRMAN. Congressman Ford, any questions you would like to ask?

Representative FORD. No.

Representative BOGGS. I have no questions, Mr. Chief Justice.

The CHAIRMAN. Mr. Craig.

Mr. CRAIG. No, thank you, Mr. Chief Justice.

The CHAIRMAN. If not, thank you very much. We appreciate your coming.

Mr. HILL. Thank you, Mr. Chief Justice.

(Warren Commission, Vol. II, pages 132–144)

THE ASSASSINATION OF PRESIDENT JOHN F. KENNEDY ON NOVEMBER 22, 1963, AT DALLAS, TEXAS

Statement of Special Agent Winston G. Lawson, United States Secret Service, concerning his activities and official duties on November 22, 1963, and until his arrival in Washington, D.C., on November 23, 1963:

On Friday, November 22, 1963, I handled general advance details, talked over final arrangements with Mr. Jack Puterbaugh; Mr. Art Balas, White House Communications Agency; SAs Hickey and Kinney, and talked to various individuals on the phone before departing the Sheraton-Dallas Hotel. One of those who contacted me by phone was ASAIC Kellerman in Fort Worth concerning car seating and instructions as to whether the bubble top on the President's car was to be used. I also spoke with SAIC Sorrels, Dallas office, on the phone concerning his taking SAs Hickey and Kinney to the airport. I departed the Sheraton-Dallas Hotel with SA David Grant.

At about 8:50 a.m. we arrived at the Dallas Trade Mart. I looked over the security of the parking lot and area where the President was to enter the building. Inside the building I checked on details of the luncheon, answered various questions from interested parties, talked with Agent Steuart already on duty at head table, and left Agent Grant to complete the final preparations and survey for the President's visit and departed for Love Field.

I arrived at Love Field shortly after 9:30 a.m. and checked to see if police security was in effect on a special hole cut in fence for our motorcade's use. I also located the motorcade vehicles and drivers who had been asked to arrive by 9:30 a.m. I checked with Major Nedbal, USAF Advance Officer, on positioning of airplanes and other information. Questions of various press, Host Committee, political committee, communications and press technicians had to be answered. I started forming the motorcade, parking the vehicles and busses in proper positions, instructed drivers, checked and gave instructions to police at press area. I answered the security phone on a number of occasions and talked with Agent Hill in Fort Worth concerning Dallas weather conditions. The weather cleared and the President's car was placed in position for departure from airport without the bubble top covering it. I met some members of Greeting Committee and checked over flowers to be presented to Mrs. Kennedy and other ladies. I checked with Chief Curry as to location of Lead Car and had WHCA portable radio put in and checked. I also checked to see if escort vehicles were in position down the apron from reception area and checked to see if police were posted for crowd control.

About this time the press plane arrived and was met by me. White House Press and Transportation Staff were given instructions. I learned sound equipment, Presidential Seal, flags and a special chair had been sent by them direct to Trade Mart from Fort Worth, and so the police escort and vehicles arranged for these items to be taken to Trade Mart were not needed. Traveling press were requested to go either to their busses or press area.

AF #2 then arrived and I met agents arriving on this plane. Those agents scheduled to be taken by police vehicles to the Trade Mart were shown to these vehicles with instructions to report to Agent Grant at Trade Mart. Agent Bennett was reminded that he would be working Presidential follow-up car on the movement. I then went with those members of AF #2 party who wanted to greet the President's plane and the local Reception Committee to a point near where President's plane would be spotted.

The President's plane, AF #1, was spotted and I positioned myself at bottom of the rear ramp across from Vice President Johnson and others greeting the President. I walked along behind the President as he spoke to this group and continued on to the fence with him. The follow-up car agents and ASAIC Kellerman were with him along the fence and watching the members of the press, so I checked to see if the motorcade was ready to leave when the President was. The motorcade inched forward and many members of it entered their cars. I instructed others to hurry to their vehicles and returned to area where President, Mrs. Kennedy, and others were still proceeding along the fence. The President and Mrs. Kennedy were soon guided towards their car, and after seeing the follow-up car agents were around his car keeping members of press and others out of the way, and doing their other normal functions, I ran to the Lead Car and joined SAIC Sorrels, Chief Curry, and Sheriff Decker.

The motorcade proceeded over the scheduled route from the airport. During the course of the trip I was watching crowd conditions along the route, requesting Chief Curry to give specific instructions to escort vehicles, keeping Lead Car in proper position in front of President's car depending on its speed and crowd conditions, watching for obstructions or other hazards, and in general performing normal duties of advance agent in the Lead Car. Chief Curry was giving instructions at my suggestion to escort vehicles for keeping crowd out of street, blocking traffic in certain areas, requesting pilot vehicle to speed or slow up, and giving orders needed for us to proceed unhampered.

The President's car made one unscheduled stop, apparently at his direction, which was not uncommon. This lasted only a few moments and motorcade proceeded on. On a few occasions I noticed agents leap off the follow-up car to intercept someone or when they thought someone was trying to reach the President's car. They were able to return to positions on the follow-up car.

The motorcade proceeded at about 15–20 miles per hour until the very heavy crowd concentration in the downtown area, when it slowed to approximately 10 miles per hour.

At the corner of Houston and Elm Streets I verified with Chief Curry that we were about five minutes from the Trade Mart and gave this signal over my portable White House Communications radio. We were just approaching a railroad overpass and I checked to see if a police officer was in position there and that no one was directly over our path. I noticed a police officer but also noticed a few persons on the bridge and made motions to have these persons removed from over our path. As the Lead Car was passing under this bridge I heard the first loud, sharp report and in more rapid succession two more sounds like gunfire. I could see persons to the left of the motorcade vehicles running away. I noticed Agent Hickey standing up in the follow-up car with the automatic weapon and first thought he had fired at someone. Both the President's car and our Lead Car rapidly accelerated almost simultaneously. I heard a report over the two-way radio that we should proceed to the nearest hospital. I noticed Agent Hill hanging on to the rear of the President's vehicle. A motorcycle escort officer pulled alongside our Lead Car and said the President had been shot. Chief Curry gave a signal over his radio for police to converge on the area of the incident. I requested Chief Curry to have the hospital contacted that we were on the way. Our Lead Car assisted the motorcycles in escorting the President's vehicle to Parkland Hospital.

Upon our arrival there at approximately 12:34 p.m., I rushed into the emergency entrance, met persons coming with two stretchers and helped rush them outside. Governor Connally was being removed from the car when the stretchers arrived and he was placed on the first one. Mr. Powers, myself and one or two others placed President Kennedy on a stretcher and we ran pushing the stretcher into the emergency area which hospital personnel directed us to. I remained outside the door where the President was being treated and requested a nurse to find someone who would know hospital personnel who should be admitted to the President's room. Other agents, in addition to some members of the White House staff, then stationed themselves at this door. ASAIC Kellerman and myself went to an office in emergency area and used a phone to contact the White House Dallas switchboard, who in turn contacted SAIC Behn, White House Detail in Washington. Mr. Kellerman informed Mr. Behn what had happened and we kept that line open to Mr. Behn's office during our stay at Parkland Hospital. I went outside into a corridor and noticed that agents had established security to the emergency area then proceeded to rear of hospital to make sure police security was keeping general public from the immediate area. Upon returning to the emergency room office, I again assisted in keeping line to Washington open, talked with Mr. Behn in Washington, requested the Dallas White House switchboard to contact Austin, Texas, where the 12 p.m. (midnight) to 8:00 a.m. Secret Service shift was resting and instruct those agents to take first available plane back to Washington, D.C. A few minutes later I learned a special Air Force plane would take them from Bergstrom AFB (Austin, Texas) to Washington, D.C., and requested the Dallas White House switchboard to notify those agents of this change. It was then I learned that Mrs. Kennedy wished to return to Washington, D.C., with the body of President Kennedy immediately, and I returned to rear of hospital to see if enough motorcade vehicles remained for transportation of agents, staff and others needing transportation to the airport.

Vice President Johnson had already been taken to Love Field and was aboard AF #1. The President's car and the Secret Service follow-up car had already been taken to Love Field for loading aboard the special Air Force plane.

I requested the police to be ready to escort us to the airplanes and drivers to have their cars ready. Arrangements had already been made by someone else for a hearse to transport the coffin. Returning inside I learned the Medical Examiner could not release the body and located Sheriff Decker, who had returned to his office, by phone. I believe Dr. Burkley, the President's White House physician, talked with the Sheriff. The President's body was released and the coffin placed in a hearse from the O'Neill Mortuary. At about 2:04 p.m. agents accompanied the President's body and Mrs. Kennedy in the hearse, and other agents rode in a Lincoln automobile behind this hearse. Other staff members rode in other cars. I rode in a police car ahead of the hearse, and motorcycles escorted us to Love Field position of AF #1. We arrived at AF #1 at about 2:15 p.m. I helped remove the coffin from the hearse and place it aboard AF #1.

I remained outside the airplane until it departed for Washington, D.C., after Vice President Johnson was sworn in as President by Federal Judge Sarah Hughes.

Police and agents had removed all general public and press from the immediate area.

While waiting for the departure of AF #1, FBI Agent Vincent Drain, Dallas office, told me SAC Gordon Shanklin, FBI, Dallas, Texas, had some information. I spoke with Mr. Shanklin on the phone and he told me that an individual who had been arrested for the investigation of the killing of a police officer that afternoon had worked at the Texas Book Depository Building. I asked Mr. Shanklin to relay this to an agent on duty in the Dallas Secret Service office and then requested Chief Curry, who was with me, to speak with Mr. Shanklin on the phone.

After the departure of President Johnson and the body of President Kennedy aboard AF #1 at approximately 2:47 p.m., I proceeded to Police Headquarters with Chief Curry and Agent David Grant. En route we learned SAIC Sorrels was at Police Headquarters. Upon our arrival there I reported to SAIC Sorrels and remained at Police Headquarters under his direction.

At approximately 11:00 p.m. Inspector Kelley, Chief's Office, United States Secret Service, arrived and at approximately 1:00 a.m., on November 23, 1963, he requested me to return to Washington, D.C., on a special plane which was returning evidence from the Dallas Police in the killing of Police Officer Tippit and President Kennedy. I went to the FBI Dallas office, met FBI Agent Drain again, and proceeded with him and the packaged evidence to Carswell AFB. I departed Carswell AFB aboard USAF plane #276 at 3:10 a.m., C.S.T., November 23, 1963, and arrived at Andrews AFB at 6:30 a.m., E.S.T.

[signature]
Winston G. Lawson
Special Agent, U. S. Secret Service

December 1, 1963

(Warren Commission, Vol. XVII, pages 630–634)

TREASURY DEPARTMENT
UNITED STATES SECRET SERVICE
WASHINGTON, D.C. 20220

Office of the Chief   JUNE 11, 1964

Mr. J. Lee Rankin
General Counsel
President's Commission on the
   Assassination of President Kennedy
Washington, D.C.

Dear Mr. Rankin:

There are attached statements made by Secret Service personnel, named below, shortly after November 22, 1963, of their recollection of the events surrounding the assassination of President Kennedy.

William R. Greer	Thomas L. Johns
Roy H. Kellerman	Jerry D. Kivett
Samuel A. Kinney	Warren W. Taylor
Emory P. Roberts	Stewart G. Stout, Jr.
Clinton J. Hill	David B. Grant
William T. McIntyre	Samuel E. Sulliman
John D. Ready	Ernest E. Olsson, Jr.
Paul E. Landis, Jr.	John Joe Howlett
Glen A. Bennett	Andrew E. Berger
George W. Hickey, Jr.	Robert A. Steuart
Rufus W. Youngblood	Richard E. Johnsen

There are also attached three statements taken from Joe Henry Rich, Hurchel Jacks, and Milton T. Wright, members of the Texas Highway Patrol, who were assigned as drivers to the motorcade on November 22, 1963, in Dallas.

Statements by Special Agent in Charge Sorrels and Special Agent Winston Lawson have been previously made a part of the Commission's records.

Very truly yours,
[signature]
James J. Rowley

Attachments

WILLIAM R. GREER'S REPORT ON DALLAS, TEXAS

November 22, 1963. 11:35 AM. I arrived at Love Field, Dallas, Texas aboard USAF Plane #26000 from Fort Worth, Texas. My assignment at Dallas was to drive the President's Lincoln Convertible Limousine.

When I got off the plane, I went to where the President's Limousine and the Cadillac Followup Automobile were parked. I had the President's coats and hat and placed them on the front seat.

After the President and Mrs. Kennedy had shook hands with some of the people at the airport the President, Mrs. Kennedy, Governor and Mrs. Connally entered the automobile with the President seated on the right side of the rear seat and Mrs. Kennedy sitting on the left side, Governor Connally sat on the right jump seat in front of the President and Mrs. Connally sat on the left jump seat. ASAIC Kellerman sat on the right front seat and I was driving.

After we left the airport, we drove several miles at speeds ranging from 15 to 30 miles per hour depending on the crowds. When we reached the business section of

Dallas the crowds were very large and the motorcycle Police along side the President's automobile had a hard time keeping the people back.

When we came to a point where the crowd had thinned out, there was a right turn for about half a block and then a left turn. At this point, I would say the President's automobile was traveling about 12 to 15 miles per hour.

A short distance ahead, the street passed under a railroad or expressway. A building stood on the right side of the street, that would have been the last building we would have had to pass before entering the underpass.

The President's automobile was almost past this building and I was looking at the overpass that we were about to pass under in case someone was on top of it, when I heard what I thought was the backfire of a motorcycle behind the President's automobile. After the second shot, I glanced over my right shoulder and saw Governor Connally start to fall, I knew then that something was wrong and I immediately pushed the accelerator to the floor and Mr. Kellerman said, get out of here.

We rushed up to the police escort and I called to the motorcycle police, Hospital. Mr. Kellerman was calling to the lead automobile on the radio to get to the nearest hospital fast. I drove as fast as I could to the hospital and helped to get the President into the emergency room. I guarded the emergency room door until the doctors and nurses had completed their duty. I then drove an official automobile behind the ambulance to Love Airfield, Dallas. I boarded USAF Plane #26000 and returned to Andrews AFB, Wash. D.C. From Andrews AFB, I drove the U.S. Navy ambulance with the President's Body, accompanied by Mrs. Kennedy and the Attorney General to the U.S. Naval Medical Center.

I assisted Mr. Kellerman while the autopsy was being performed and then drove the ambulance with the President's body to the White House.

[signature]
William R. Greer

THE ASSASSINATION OF PRESIDENT JOHN F. KENNEDY ON NOVEMBER 22, 1963, AT DALLAS, TEXAS

The President with Mrs. Kennedy and official party arrived at Love Field, Dallas, Texas, aboard AF #1 (USAF 26000) at 11:40 a.m. (cst). After receiving members of the official reception party, the President and Mrs. Kennedy walked over to a fenced area and shook hands with many of the people who had gathered there to view their arrival. At the conclusion of greeting the gathering, the President, Mrs. Kennedy, Governor and Mrs. Connally entered the presidential limousine (special car: bubble-top, 1961 Lincoln Continental, seven-passenger, four-door convertible sedan). The President sat on the right rear seat with Mrs. Kennedy to the left of him. Governor Connally sat on the right jump seat and Mrs. Connally sat on the left jump seat. I rode in the front (right side) and William Greer drove the vehicle.

In the Secret Service follow-up car, 1956 Cadillac touring sedan (top down), driven by SA Samuel Kinney, ATSAIC Emory Roberts rode in the right front seat, SA John Ready stood on the right front running board, SA Paul Landis on right rear running board, SA Clinton J. Hill on left front running board and William McIntyre on left rear running board. SA Glen Bennett rode in the right rear seat and SA George Hickey on the left rear seat. Mr. Kenneth O'Donnell and Mr. David Powers (White House staff) rode the left and right jump seats respectively.

Behind the follow-up car was the Vice President's car with Vice President and Mrs. Johnson and Senator Yarborough in the rear seat. SA Rufus Youngblood rode in the right front seat and a police officer drove the car. The following vehicles were four cars of congressional members, press cars, VIP bus and then press busses.

We departed Love Field at 11:55 a.m., along the planned motorcade route, enroute to a luncheon at the Trade Mart, given by the Democratic Citizens Council, scheduled for 12:30 p.m. cst. As the motorcade completed the main thoroughfare through Dallas, we made a sharp right turn, for about a ½ block, then a curved left turn into a slight downhill grade, entering an area with little or no spectators. We were still traveling at the normal rate of speed of from 12 to 15 miles per hour when I heard a noise, similar to a firecracker, exploding in the area to the rear of the car, about 12:30 p.m.

Immediately I heard what I firmly believe was the President's voice, "My God, I'm hit!" I turned around to find out what happened when two additional shots rang out, and the President slumped into Mrs. Kennedy's lap and Governor Connally fell into Mrs. Connally's lap. I heard Mrs. Kennedy shout, "What are they doing to you?"

I yelled at William Greer (the driver) to "Step on it, we're hit!" and grabbed the mike from the car radio, called to SA Lawson in the police lead car that we were hit and to get us to a hospital.

With SA Lawson riding in the police car they quickly formed the accompanying escort for the motorcade around our limousines and sped us through the streets to the emergency entrance of Parkland Memorial Hospital. Sometime during the ride to the hospital while looking back into the car I noticed SA Hill hanging on to the back of the car, laying across the trunk. When we got to the hospital I called to the agents to get two stretchers. The special agents of the follow-up car with the police ran into the hospital, obtained two stretchers on wheels. We placed the Governor on the first one at which time I noticed he was conscious and I spoke to him saying, "Governor, everything is going to be all right." His eyes were wide open and he nodded his head in agreement. Just before we removed the President, SA Hill took off his coat, placed it over the President's head and chest and we placed him on the stretcher. Both were taken into separate emergency rooms. The hospital staff appeared quickly and went immediately to work. I accompanied the President to the emergency room. His eyes were closed but I could see no visible damage to his face. The room was crowded with the medical people so I immediately walked out into a doctor's room, asked SA Lawson for the phone number of the White House switchboard in Dallas. SA Hill dialed the number to the White House operator in Washington and I talked with Gerald A. Behn, Special Agent in Charge, White House Detail. I informed him that we had an incident in Dallas, the President and Governor Connally had been shot and both were in emergency rooms at the Parkland Memorial Hospital. This I believe was about 12:38 p.m. cst. This direct telephone line from Dallas to SAIC Behn at Washington was kept open from this time until the plane departed. SAIC Behn was kept informed of all proceedings, plans or desires of both Mrs. Kennedy and President Johnson.

We immediately secured the corridors and the emergency room area, furnished the blood type of the President to the medical staff upon their request. It should be noted that Vice President and Mrs. Johnson were placed in a separate room away from the emergency room. Some time later SA Warren Taylor came to me and said the Vice President wanted to see me. Mr. Johnson asked me the condition of the President and the Governor. I advised him that the Governor was taken up to surgery, that the doctors were still working on the President. He asked me to keep him informed of his condition. SA Kinney entered the emergency room area when I returned there and asked if it would be all right to drive the President's car and the follow-up car back to the airport, load them aboard the plane. I said "Yes" and told him to return the cars to Washington, D.C.

The 4 to 12 shift (ATSAIC Stout, etc.) joined us at the emergency room and the 8 to 4 shift (ATSAIC Roberts, etc.) immediately joined the Vice President and Mrs. Johnson.

Through Dr. Burkley, President's physician, we were advised officially of the death of the President which was registered on the death certificate as 1 p.m. cst. Between 1 p.m., and our departure from the hospital at 2:04 p.m. cst., a casket was obtained and with Mrs. Kennedy, SA Hill and Dr. Burkley riding in the hearse with the casket, SA Berger (Stout and Kellerman in front seat) drove the hearse with police escort to Love Field.

The Vice President and Mrs. Johnson had preceded us with Roberts shift to the airport and when we had arrived, the field had been secured and we rushed to AF 26000. All available special agents carried the casket from the ambulance up the rear steps and placed it in the rear section of the plane. When we boarded the plane, Vice President Johnson and his party were aboard the plane. The services of Federal Judge Sarah T. Hughes was obtained, she was brought into the plane, and Vice President Johnson was administered the oath of office and sworn in as President at 2:38 p.m.

At 2:47 p.m., USAF 26000 was airborne for Washington, D.C., arriving at Andrews Air Force Base at 5:58 p.m., est.

While airborne, arrangements were made for a Naval ambulance from the New Naval Medical Center at Bethesda to be available at the airport. Upon landing we removed the casket, placed it into the ambulance. At the airport, Chief Rowley advised me that two FBI agents, Francis O'Neill, Jr., and James Siebert, had been assigned to this case and to allow them into the morgue at the U.S. Naval Hospital. I told Chief Rowley the cars would arrive at Andrews at about 8 p.m., and suggested he assign field agents to them to completely go over them for any evidence that might be found.

Mrs. Kennedy, Robert Kennedy and General McHugh sat in the rear of the ambulance; SAs Greer, Landis and myself with Dr. Burkley rode in the front to Bethesda, with a police escort. The body was immediately taken to the morgue and the family was assigned rooms in the Towers of the Center. Hill and Landis remained with Mrs. Kennedy in her quarters and William Greer and I remained in the morgue and viewed the autopsy examinations which were performed by Vice Admiral Gallway, Commanding Officer, NNMC, Chief Pathologist Cdr. James Humes, Lt. Col. Pierre A. Finck who is Chief, Military Environmental Pathology Division and Chief of Wound Ballistics, Pathology Branch, and J. Thornton Boswell, Cdr. Medical Corps, USN, together with the Naval Medical Staff. SA O'Leary was also in the morgue briefly. Agents O'Neill and Siebert were present.

During the night Joseph Gawlers Sons, Inc., funeral directors, were notified by Robert Kennedy and Sargent Shriver and a new coffin was obtained. After the completion of the autopsy and before the embalming I summoned SA Hill down to the morgue to view the body and to witness the damage of the gunshot wounds. The embalming was performed after the autopsy by the staff of Joseph Gawlers.

Prior to our departure from the Naval Hospital I received all film, x-rays, that were used during this autopsy, and upon arrival at the White House I turned them over to SAIC Bouck.

We left the hospital at 3:56 a.m. in the Navy ambulance and with police escort motored to the White House. Mrs. Kennedy and Robert Kennedy rode in the hearse, SA Greer drove, Kellerman in the front seat, SAs Hill and Landis with members of the family rode in cars following the ambulance. We arrived at the White House at 4:24 a.m. The body was placed in the East Room.

On Wednesday, November 27, 1963, FBI Agents O'Neill and Siebert were given an oral statement along the lines of this report.

[signature]
Roy H. Kellerman
Assistant Special Agent in Charge
11-29-63

UNITED STATES GOVERNMENT

Memorandum

TO : Chief   DATE: November 30, 1963

FROM : ASAIC Kellerman—1-16

SUBJECT: Security measures taken for the late President Kennedy, and President Johnson, from Parkland Memorial Hospital, Dallas, Texas, to the US Naval Hospital, Bethesda, Maryland and to The White House on November 22 and 23, 1963.

When the late President Kennedy and the official motorcade departed Love Field, Dallas, Texas, on November 22, 1963, SA's Lawton (8-4) and Rybka (Garage) remained at the airport, to effect security at the plane during our absence.

On arrival at the emergency room at the Parkland Memorial Hospital, Dallas, Texas, the agents who worked the Secret Service follow-up car (ATSAIC Roberts shift) were utilized to cover the entrances and corridors leading to the emergency room. Shortly thereafter ATSAIC Stout (4P-12P) and his shift reported to me at the emergency room for instructions.

I then conferred with ASAIC Rufus Youngblood (who was in charge of security for the then Vice President Johnson), and told him to take ATSAIC Roberts and his shift to supplement his agents, and that I would take ATSAIC Stout and his agents with me until we returned to Washington, D.C. This change of shifts was immediately made at the hospital.

Vice President Johnson departed the Parkland Memorial Hospital prior to the departure of the body of President Kennedy, with ATSAIC Roberts shift working the Secret Service follow-up car. On their arrival at Love Field, ATSAIC Roberts and his shift completely secured the area where the President's plane was spotted.

Enroute to Washington, D.C., aboard AF #1 (USAF 26000) another conference was held with ASAIC Youngblood, where he was informed that he would have ATSAIC Stout and his shift with him on their arrival at Andrews AFB, Washington, D.C. I also informed him that I was accompanying the body of the late President Kennedy to the US Naval Hospital, Bethesda, Maryland, and would have with me Special Agents Hill, Landis, Greer and O'Leary.

When we arrived at Andrews AFB, Washington, D.C., the body of the late President Kennedy was placed in a US Navy ambulance, which was driven by SA Greer to the US Naval Hospital, Bethesda, Maryland with SA Landis and Dr. George Burkley and myself in the front seat. Mrs. Kennedy along with Mr. Robert Kennedy and General McHugh rode in the rear of the ambulance. SA's Hill and O'Leary rode in an accompanying vehicle.

At the US Naval Hospital, SA's Hill and Landis remained with Mrs. Kennedy near her quarters, located in the Towers of the Center. SA's Greer and O'Leary and myself accompanied the body to the morgue. SA O'Leary remained in the morgue only briefly.

SA Greer and myself remained with the body in the US Naval Hospital along with Agents Francis O'Neill, Jr., and James Siebert of the Federal Bureau of Investigation, witnessing the autopsy performed by members of the US Navy Medical Corps, and the embalming services done by the staff of Joseph Gawlers, Funeral Directors, Washington, D.C.

At 3:56 a.m., on Saturday, November 23, the body of the late President Kennedy was transported in a US Navy ambulance from the US Naval Hospital, Bethesda, Maryland, to the White House, with SA Greer driving the ambulance and myself riding in the front seat. Mrs. Kennedy and Mr. Robert Kennedy rode in the rear of the ambulance. SA's Hill and Landis rode in accompanying vehicles.

We arrived at the White House at 4:24 a.m., and the body was placed in the East Room.

THE TRIP AND ASSASSINATION OF PRESIDENT KENNEDY IN DALLAS, TEXAS, NOVEMBER 22, 1963

NOVEMBER 21, 1963:

I, Special Agent Kinney and Special Agent Hickey arrived Love Field in Dallas, Texas at 6:05 pm. We were on a Air Force plane C-130, #12373. Capt. Roland H. Thomason AC, USAF. On board this cargo craft was the President's Limousine, 100-X and Secret Service car 679-X. Upon arrival, I was met by SAIC Forrest V. Sorrels, (Dallas Field Office) and Special Agent Winston G. Lawson, (White House Detail), that was doing the Dallas advance of the President's visit. I and SA Hickey proceeded to unload the two cars and were escorted to the garage that was located under the main terminal of the airport. The arrangements were made for over night security of cars and policemen from Dallas force were put on duty thru the night. SAIC Sorrels, SA Lawson, SA Hickey and myself then proceeded to the Sheraton Hotel in downtown Dallas where reservations had been by SA Lawson. After checking in the hotel, we had changed clothes and at approx. 8:30 pm, I met with SA Lawson, SA Hickey, Mr. Jack Puterbugh and Warrant Officer Bales USA WHC. We then proceeded to dinner. On the way to dinner we stopped enroute at the place where President Kennedy was to luncheon on Nov. 22, 1963. We spent approx. 30 min. checking the seating and speaking stands. After securing the Mart, we proceeded to have dinner. After dinner approx. 2 hours, we then returned to the Sheraton Hotel and made our arrangements for the following day, Nov. 22, as to the time and place to meet for transportation to Love Field for the following days activities and turned to our rooms for the night.

NOVEMBER 22, 1963:

SA Hickey and I arose from our beds about 7:00 am. We dressed and packed our bags, then went down to the lobby and checked out of the hotel. We went to the coffee shop for our breakfast. At approx. 8:00 am we went into the lobby to wait transportation to Love Field. At approx. 8:30 am SAIC Sorrels picked SA Hickey and I up in front of the Sheraton hotel and we went to Love Field. We arrived there approx. 9:00 am. SA Sorrels took us directly to the two cars with the understanding that he would be back at 11:00 am to escort the cars to their location for the President's arrival at 11:35 am.

SA Hickey and I proceeded with our duties of getting the two cars ready for the day, which consisted of cleaning, checking oil, water and batteries. Then a security check. We had the tops down on both cars. It had rained all night and was raining when we arrived at the airport. I had on two occasions gone outside to check the weather. The last check at approx. 10:30 am, the sky had cleared and that meant to us that the bubble-top would stay off.

At approx. 11:00 am SA Sorrels came to the garage to escort SA Hickey and me to the location. At this time SA Hickey stayed with the two cars and I was helping SA Lawson and SA Sorrels line up the motorcade, placing the some ten cars that were to be used.

When the President arrived at approx. 11:40 am I took my place behind the driver wheel in the follow-up car 679-X. After a few greetings by the President we proceeded on with the motorcade thru downtown Dallas and on to the Shopping Mart where the President was to have lunch. We had gone about 30 to 40 min. and just made a right turn off Main St. and on block, a left turn onto Elm St. A five min signal had been given to agents waiting at the Mart.

As we completed the left turn and on a short distance, there was a shot. At this time I glanced from the taillights of the President's car, that I use for guaging distances for driving. I saw the President lean toward the left and appeared to have grabbed his chest with his right hand. There was a second of pause and then two more shots were heard. Agent Clinton Hill jumped from the follow-up car and dashed to the aid of the President and First Lady in the President's car. I saw one shot strike the President in the right side of the head. The President then fell to the seat to the left toward Mrs. Kennedy. At this time I stepped on the siren and gas pedal at the same time. Agent Greer driving the President's car did the same. The lead car (ahead of the Pres. car) and motorcycles were told to go to the nearest hospital. The President's car and 679-X then proceeded to the hospital at a high rate of speed, taking approx. 6 min. Upon arrival I jumped from my car and ran to the right rear of the President's car, where I assisted in removing Gov. Connally and the President.

After all had been removed from the President's car I opened the trunk of the car and put on the bubble-top and a canvas cover. This took approx. 20 to 30 min. I asked for a motorcycle to escort the President's car and 679-X back to Love Field. We left promptly not stopping enroute to Love Field. On the way to the airport I called by radio to Maj. Nedbaugh, USAF, to have C-130 crew at the plane with ramp down for loading of the two cars. This was carried and the cars were loaded and the plane secured, awaiting our orders to depart Love Field enroute to Andrews

Air Force Base, Maryland. The plane departed Love Field at 3:35 pm. We arrived AAFB, Md at 8:05 pm. We were met at AAFB by 4 or 5 agents from the Washington, Field Office and some 6 motorcycles. We were then escorted non-stop to the White House garage. After reaching the garage the cars were secured by an all night watch by White House Police and Secret Service agents, pending an investigation.

Statement made Nov. 30, 1963 By:

[signature]
Samuel A. Kinney
Special Agent
White House Detail
U.S. Secret Service
Washington, D.C.

Confidential

I was driving SS 679-X, follow-up. As we turned off Main Street (left) about 4 minutes from our destination of Trade Mart. The first shot was fired as we were going into an underpass. The first shot was fired, I glanced from the taillight of SS-100-X, at the President and it appeared that he had been shot because he slumped to the left. Immediately he sat up again.* At this time the second shot was fired and I observed hair flying from the right side of his head. With this, simultaneously with the President's car, we stepped on the gas. I released the siren at that time. I did hear three shots but do not recall which shots were those that hit the President.

At this time Clint Hill jumped off and ran to the President's car, jumped on the back, and laid out across the trunk in a prone position where he rode the entire trip to the hospital.

Pulling up parallel to the lead car, we were notified we were heading for the hospital, whereupon the motorcycle escort, the lead car, President's car and follow-up proceeded to the hospital at a high rate of speed. We pulled into the emergency entrance of the hospital whereupon Gov. Connally was removed and then the President, and taken inside.

After this, maybe 15 or 20 minutes later, I put the bubble and canvas cover on the car, assisted by SA Hickey. Then under motorcycle escort, both cars proceeded to Love Field, whereupon I notified the crew to get the ramp down and we drove the cars onto the plane and secured them, awaiting departure.

[signature]
Samuel A. Kinney
Special Agent
11-22-63

U.S. TREASURY DEPARTMENT   U. S. Secret Service
Washington, D.C.

TO   : Chief James J. Rowley   November 29, 1963.

FROM   : ATSAIC Emory P. Roberts, The White House Detail.

SUBJECT: Schedule of events prior to and after the assassination of President John F. Kennedy in Dallas, Texas on Friday November 22, 1963.

11:25 a.m.   The President and Mrs. Kennedy with members of the Presidential Party departed Carswell A.F.B., Texas via USAF 26,000 (Jet, also known as AF 1) enroute to Love Field, Dallas, Texas.

The following members of the United States Secret Service were aboard this aircraft. ASAIC Roy T. Kellerman, in charge of White House Detail for the Texas trip, SA Clinton Hill in charge of Mrs. Kennedy's security, SA William Greer, Presidential driver, ATSAIC Emory P. Roberts, in charge of 8 am–4 p.m. shift, with

SA's John Ready, Donald Lawton and William McIntyre. SA John O'Leary was also aboard AF 1. Special Agent Glen Bennett of the 8 a.m.–4 p.m. shift arrived Dallas, Texas aboard USAF 6970.

11:40 a.m.   Presidential Plane arrived Love Field, Dallas, Texas, which was five minutes late according to schedule, as we were due there at 11:35 a.m.

After the usual greeting of approximately 20 people, upon deplaning, the President and Mrs. Kennedy walked to roped off area and shook hands with a number of the assembled persons gathered there, and autographed a few papers and pamphlets. I accompanied the President, as well as other Special Agents while he greeted the people. The President and Mrs. Kennedy returned to their car.

11:55 a.m.   The President (right rear seat), Mrs. Kennedy (left rear seat) Governor John Connally (of Texas) (right jump seat) Mrs. Connally (left jump seat) ASAIC Roy T. Kellerman front seat, with SA William Greer driving, (SS car 100-X—top removed) departed Love Field.

SA Donald Lawton of 8 a.m.–4 p.m. shift remained at Love Field with SA Warner and Rybka to set up security for the President's departure for Bergstrom AFB, Austin, Texas. The Presidential aircraft was due to depart Dallas at 2:35 p.m.

The following persons departed Love Field in Secret Service Follow-up car, 679-X and were located in and on running boards of car as follows:

ATSAIC Emory P. Roberts—front seat—operating radio.
SA Samuel Kinney—driving (did an excellent job)
Mr. Kenneth O'Donnell, Appointment Secretary to the President, left jump seat.
Mr. David Powers, Presidential Aide, right jump seat.
SA Glen Bennett, left rear seat.
SA George Hickey, right rear seat (manning AR-15 (rifle)
SA Clinton Hill, left running board, front.
SA William McIntyre, left running board, behind Hill.
SA John D. Ready, right running board, front.
SA Paul Landis, right running board behind Ready.

Note: On shift report for Nov. 22, 1963, I listed SA Rybka as riding in center of rear seat, which was in error, as he was not in car. As mentioned above, he remained at Love Field.

The Presidential motorcade toured downtown Dallas, through huge crowds, that were sometimes so close, that motorcycles of the Dallas Police Department had to drop back from flanking the Presidential and Secret Service cars, so the two cars could get through. On several occasions the Special Agent working the running boards of the Follow-up car "hit" the ground and ran along side of the President's car; and SA Hill climbed on rear step of the President's car (left rear) where he remained until the crowd thinned and motorcycles had returned to their positions, flanking the rear of the President's car.

The Presidential motorcade was enroute to Trade Mart to attend Luncheon, sponsored by the Dallas Citizens Council, The Dallas Assembly and the Graduate Research Center of the Southwest.

12:29 p.m.   SA Winston Lawson (Advance Agent for Dallas stop) riding in lead car, gave "five minutes away," signal via radio, meaning five minutes away from Trade Mart. I immediately wrote 12:35 p.m. on Itinerary, as the time of arrival at Trade Mart.

12:30 p.m.   First of three shots fired, at which time I saw the President lean toward Mrs. Kennedy. I do not know if it was the next shot or third shot that hit the President in the head, but I saw what appeared to be a small explosion on the right side of the President's head, saw blood, at which time the President fell further to his left. Mrs. Kennedy was leaning toward the President, however, she immediately raised up in the seat and appeared to be getting up on back of same. About this time I saw SA Clinton Hill trying to get on left rear step of the President's car. He got aboard and climbed up over the back of the car and placed himself over the President and Mrs. Kennedy. After SA Hill got on rear step of the President's car, it appeared that SA John Ready was about to follow and go for the right rear step, however, I told him not to jump, as we had picked up speed, and I was afraid he could not make it.

It is estimated that we were traveling approximately 15–20 miles per hour at the time of the shooting and it is believed that the follow-up car was approximately 20–25 feet behind the President's car.

The crowd was very sparse, in fact only a few people were along the motorcade route at the time of the shooting.

Just after the third shot was fired, I picked up the car radio and said "Halfback (code name for SS. Follow-up car) to Lawson, the President has been hit, escort us to the nearest hospital, fast but at a safe speed." I repeated the message, requesting to be cautious, meaning the speed. I had in mind Vice President Johnson's safety, as well as the President's, if he was not already dead.

The Vice President's car was approximately one-half block behind the Secret Service car, at the time of the shooting, and some of us waved for it to close in closer to the Secret Service car. The Vice President's car quickly closed the gap.

When I turned around to wave the Vice President's car to come closer, at same time, trying to determine where shots had come from, I said, pointing to SA McIntyre, "They got him, they got him," continuing I said "You (meaning McIntyre) and Bennett take over Johnson as soon as we stop." (meaning the hospital)

I turned around a couple times, just after the shooting and saw that some of the Special Agents had their guns drawn, I know I drew mine, and saw SA Hickey in rear seat with the AR-15, and asked him to be careful with it.

12:34 p.m.   Presidential motorcade arrived at Parkland Hospital. (I did not look at my watch, however, I overheard someone at the hospital say that it took four minutes to get there.)

Upon arrival at Parkland Hospital, I immediately ran to President Kennedy. Mrs. Kennedy was lying over him. I said to Mrs. Kennedy to let us get the President. She said in effect that she was not going to move. I got one look at the President's head and remarked to ASAIC Kellerman, "You stay with the President, I'm taking some of my men for Johnson." SA's McIntyre and Bennett were already with Vice President Johnson, having joined SAIC Rufus Youngblood and other Special Agents assigned to the Vice President, as the Vice President arrived at the hospital.

The first thing we did, was request a room for the Vice President. After getting the Vice President and Mrs. Johnson in a room, at the hospital, I said in effect to the Vice President, in the presence of Mrs. Johnson, Mr. Cliff Carter, Executive Assistant to the Vice President and SAIC Youngblood, as well as others, that I did not think the President could make it and suggested that we get out of Dallas as soon as possible.

We (SAIC Youngblood and myself) suggested that he (Vice President) think it over, as he would have to be sworn in. I suggested that we leave Dallas via AF 1, and SAIC Youngblood agreed and suggested that we return to the White House.

SAIC Youngblood can give more details, as I left the Vice President from time to time, once to get Mr. Kenneth O'Donnell, as the Vice President did not want to leave Dallas, without permission or suggestion from someone on the President's Staff. I located Mr. O'Donnell in hallway, near room where President Kennedy was.

While trying to locate Mr. O'Donnell for the Vice President, I came across ASAIC Roy Kellerman, who was assisting someone to fill in the President's blood type on a card. I remarked, that it was the same as mine Blood Group O, Rh Positive. Kellerman had card in his hand which he got from his wallet with the President's blood type.

At this time, I explained to Mr. Kellerman that the Vice President would probably leave for Washington very soon aboard AF 1.

I returned with Mr. O'Donnell to the Vice President, and while Mr. O'Donnell and the Vice President were talking, I mentioned to ASAIC Johns to check if the car (President's) was impounded. (I know that the word "evidence" was used.) SAIC Johns left immediately.

Shortly after arrival at the Parkland Hospital, I asked C.W.O. Ira Gearhart, White

House Communication Agency, (Courier for President) to step into room next to Vice President Johnson, and stay with him.

One of the Special Agents assigned to Vice President Johnson called the airport and requested the Presidential plane to stand by to take Vice President Johnson to Washington, D.C.

I contacted the White House Signal Board and advised them to cancel all the other stops that had been planned for the President. I saw SA Richard Johnson (4–12 shift) in hallway and asked him to augment V.P. Detail, which he did.

I had made arrangements with the Dallas Police, in front of the Parkland Hospital to have an unmarked police car for the Vice President and two other cars for other passengers and Secret Service, to take the Vice President and Mrs. Johnson to the airport. SA Lem Johns double checked this.

I left the Vice President a second time upon the request of Mrs. Johnson, as she had stated that she would like to see Mrs. Kennedy. After Inquiry of an agent in hallway, I located Mrs. Kennedy and asked her, if it would be alright if Mrs. Johnson came to see her, to which she replied "yes." I returned to the room where the Vice President were and told Mrs. Johnson.

Mrs. Johnson followed me, with two Special Agents accompanying her.

Mrs. Johnson spent a very short time with Mrs. Kennedy, who was sitting in a chair outside of room where the President was. I returned to room where the Vice President was, with Mrs. Johnson.

I left again, this time upon request of the Vice President to double check with Mr. Kenneth O'Donnell, if it would be O.K. for the Vice President to take AF 1 and return to Washington, D.C. I located Mr. O'Donnell in hallway and he said "yes".

The Vice President was informed that Mr. O'Donnell stated that he could leave. The Vice President said in effect, that he didn't want to leave without the approval of a staff member or the Secret Service.

At 1:15 p.m. (according to my watch) the Vice President, in the presence of Mrs. Johnson, Mr. Cliff Carter, SAIC Youngblood and others, was informed by me, that the President was dead. Vice President Johnson said to Mr. Carter to make a note of it and someone mentioned the time as 1:13 p.m. Mr. Malcolm Kilduff, Assistant Press Secretary to President Kennedy came into the room about that time and it was decided that he would not release the death of the President, until the now President Johnson had left the hospital.

1:35 p.m. The now President Johnson, and I believe Mr. Cliff Carter departed Parkland Hospital in an unmarked police car, accompanied by SAIC Youngblood. As far as I know, SAIC Youngblood never left Vice President's side, from time of shooting to arrival at USAF 1, which was spotted at Love Field, awaiting for Vice President Johnson.

Mrs. Johnson rode in police car, directly behind President Johnson accompanied by Congressman Brooks, and SA's Warren Taylor, Jerry Kivett and Glen Bennett.

Follow-up car was driven by a Dallas Policeman, accompanied by another policeman and SA John Ready in front seat; rear seat ATSAIC Roberts, SA McIntyre and C.W.O. Gearhart, WHCA Courier.

SA Johns followed in another police car.

1:40 p.m. President and Mrs. Johnson arrived at Love Field and immediately boarded AF 1. Special agents were posted strategically in and around the aircraft. SA's Lawton and Rybka joined us upon arrival at airport, in effecting security. All blinds on aircraft were immediately drawn. I do not know who requested that this be done, however, I assisted in closing them.

We learned that Mrs. Kennedy was enroute to AF 1, however, we could not confirm same, then we heard that President Kennedy's body was also being brought to the aircraft. I informed Colonel Swindel (Aircraft Commander) and other members of AF 1, that we would not leave or do anything, until we cleared same with SAIC Youngblood. As we had a few too many people aboard USAF 1, I did ask a couple to get off.

After the arrival of Mrs. Kennedy and President Kennedy's body, I was informed by Col. James Swindel that a Federal Judge Hughes (woman) was enroute to AF 1, to swear in President Johnson. I immediately informed the police present and requested SA Ready to go to gate, to make sure that the Judge got in. When I saw Judge Hughes coming toward the aircraft, I went to meet her and escorted her to the front ramp and cleared her to go aboard, as no one was allowed to go aboard the aircraft, unless they were known personally or cleared by Secret Service. I did not go aboard and waited at bottom on ramp.

Upon arrival of ASAIC Kellerman with Mrs. Kennedy and President Kennedy's body, he advised me that the 4–12 shift (ATSAIC Stout's) would return to Washington, D.C. aboard AF 1. It is to be noted that SA Bennett of my shift (8 am–4 p.m.) also returned to Washington, D.C. via A.F. 1.

2:40 p.m. Approximately, SAIC Gerald A. Behn, in Charge of the White House Detail called Love Field, from Washington, D.C. and requested that I give him the time that A.F. 1 departed for Washington, D.C. I advised Mr. Behn that Judge Hughes was aboard swearing in President Johnson, and advised Mr. Behn when Judge Hughes departed A.F. 1.

2:47 p.m. A.F. 1 departed for Washington, D.C. with President and Mrs. Johnson, Mrs. Kennedy and President Kennedy's body.

I might mention that I assigned the Special Agents to the follow-up car, and each knew his assignment. For instance, SA Hill was assigned to work left rear of President's car (where Mrs. Kennedy was sitting), SA Ready was assigned to work the right rear of the President's car, then SA Landis was to work right front and SA McIntyre was to work the left front. As far as I can remember, SA Hill was the only one that had to jump on rear step of the President's car, while touring downtown Dallas, however, SA Ready would have done the same thing, if motorcycle was not at the President's corner of car.

3:15 p.m. ATSAIC Roberts, SA's Ready, Lawton, and McIntyre departed Love Field, Dallas, Texas via USAF 6970, and arrived Washington, D.C. (Andrews AFB) at 6:35 p.m.

Approved: [signature]
                                                          Emory P. Roberts
Gerald A. Behn   Assistant to the Special Agent in Charge
Special Agent in Charge.

Nov. 22, 1963.

At 11:55 a.m. this date The President, Mrs. Kennedy, Gov. and Mrs. Connally of Texas (Kellerman—Greer) departed Love Field, Dallas Texas in SS 100-X (top removed).

F.U. car—Kinney driving—Roberts front seat, jump seat on left side Ken O'Donnell, jump seat right side, Dave Powers, rear seat left Bennett, center Rybka and right rear—Hickey.

Left running board: Hill on the front, McIntyre behind him.
Right   ″   ″   : Front Ready, behind him Landis.
We had received a 5-minute away signal (radio) from Lawson (in lead car) meaning 5 minutes from Trade Mart—where the President was going.

About 1 minute later at 12:30 p.m. two or three shots were fired, at which time I saw the President lean over on Mrs. Kennedy. I knew he was hit. Just as the first or second shot was fired Hill ran from follow-up car to President's car—jumped aboard and placed himself over Mrs. Kennedy and the President.

Upon seeing the President shot, I radioed Lawson to escort us to the nearest hospital fast but at a safe speed.

During the downtown motorcade the streets were lined with people, however, in the area where the shots rang out, the crowd was very sparse, in fact only a few people.

It is estimated that we were traveling about 20–25 miles an hour at the time of the shooting, and it is believed that the follow-up car was approx. 25 feet behind the President's car.

I could not determine from what direction the shots came, but felt they had come from the right side.

I immediately asked everyone on car to look to see if they could determine where the shots came from,—no one seemed to know.

[signature]
Emory P. Roberts.

THE ASSASSINATION OF PRESIDENT JOHN F. KENNEDY ON NOVEMBER 22, 1963, AT DALLAS, TEXAS

Statement of Special Agent Clinton J. Hill, United States Secret Service, concerning his activities and official duties on November 22, 1963. Statement dated November 30, 1963.

I, Clinton J. Hill, Special Agent, United States Secret Service, arrived at Love Field, Dallas, Texas, at 11:40 a.m. on November 22, 1963, from Fort Worth, Texas, aboard Air Force No. One (USAF #26000) with President and Mrs. John F. Kennedy. President and Mrs. Kennedy debarked the aircraft first from the rear ramp followed by Governor and Mrs. John Connally and by three or four Congressmen and Senators, and then myself and ASAIC Roy H. Kellerman.

Upon alighting, President and Mrs. Kennedy were greeted by a small reception committee and Mrs. Kennedy was presented a bouquet of red roses. I ran over to the Secret Service Follow-up car immediately upon my arrival and placed my topcoat and a small folder containing information on this Dallas stop of the Texas trip on the floor of the car. I then went back to where the President and Mrs. Kennedy were greeting an elderly lady in a wheel chair.

The general public was restricted from the ramp area of Love Field by a permanent chain-link fence. There were a number of photographers and correspondents on the ramp area covering the arrival.

The President noticed the large number of people being restrained by the fence and walked over to the crowd and began shaking hands. He moved from his right to his left down the fence. Mrs. Kennedy accompanied him. I remained very close to Mrs. Kennedy observing the outstretched hands of well-wishers to make sure no weapons were extended toward Mrs. Kennedy and that nothing was handed to her. I accompanied Mrs. Kennedy behind the President along the fence and then to the Presidential automobile which was waiting to take President and Mrs. Kennedy and Governor and Mrs. John Connally to the Trade Mart for a luncheon, after a 45-minute motorcade through downtown Dallas.

President and Mrs. Kennedy entered the automobile with the President getting into the right rear seat and Mrs. Kennedy into the left rear seat. Mrs. Connally got into the left jump seat and Governor Connally into the right jump seat. SA William Greer was driving the automobile with ASAIC Roy H. Kellerman in the right front seat. I went to the left rear side of the Presidential automobile and stood on the airport ramp along side where Mrs. Kennedy was sitting.

As the Presidential automobile began to move forward at 11:55 a.m. I walked along side of the left rear of the automobile for about 150 feet, and since there were no people at all on the airport ramp I went back to the automobile immediately behind the Presidential Automobile and mounted the forward portion of the left running board.

SA Sam Kinney was driving this Secret Service Follow-up car which was a 1955 Cadillac 9-passenger convertible specifically outfitted for use by the Secret Service. ATSAIC Emory Roberts was sitting in the right front seat and operating the two-way radio. SA John Ready was on the forward portion of the right hand running board; SA William McIntyre on the rear portion of the left hand running board; SA Paul E. Landis on the rear portion of the right hand running board; Mr. Kenneth O'Donnell, Presidential Appointment Secretary, was seated on the left side of the second seat; Mr. Dave Powers, Presidential Receptionist, was seated on the right side of the second seat; SA George Hickey was seated on the left side of the third seat; and SA Glen Bennett was seated on the right side of the third seat.

The Presidential Follow-up car was followed by a 1964 Lincoln 4-door convertible occupied by Vice-President and Mrs. Lyndon Johnson, Senator Ralph Yarborough, with ASAIC Rufus Youngblood in the right front seat. This automobile was followed by a Secret Service follow-up car for the Vice President, and then came automobiles occupied by photographers, correspondents, Senators and Congressmen.

Preceding the Presidential automobile was a Dallas Police Department Lead car in which SA Winston Lawson of the Secret Service was riding. Police motorcycles preceded and flanked the motorcade. There were two police motorcycles on the left side of the President's Secret Service follow-up car running abreast of one another between the automobile and the crowd of people.

My instructions for Dallas were to work the left rear of the Presidential automobile and remain in close proximity to Mrs. John F. Kennedy at all times. The agent assigned to work the left rear of the Presidential automobile rides on the forward portion of the left hand running board of the Secret Service follow-up car and only moves forward to walk alongside the Presidential automobile when it slows to such a pace that people can readily approach the auto on foot. If the crowd is very heavy, but the automobile is running at a rather rapid speed, the agent rides on the left rear of the Presidential automobile on a step specifically designed for that purpose.

As the motorcade moved from Love Field through downtown Dallas toward the Trade Mart, there were four (4) occasions before we reached the end of Main Street where I moved from the forward portion of the left running board of the follow-up car to the rear step of the Presidential automobile. I did this because the motorcycles that were along the left hand side of the follow-up car were unable to move up alongside the President's car due to the crowd surging into the street. The motorcycles were forced to drop back and so I jumped from the Follow-up car and mounted the President's car. I remained in this position until the crowd thinned and was away from the President's automobile, allowing the motorcycles to once again move up alongside of the automobile. When we approached the end of Main Street the crowd was noticeably less dense than had been the case prior to that point.

The motorcade made a right hand turn onto Elm Street. I was on the forward portion of the left running board of the follow-up car. The motorcade made a left hand turn from Elm Street toward an underpass. We were traveling about 12 to 15 miles per hour. On the left hand side was a grass area with a few people scattered along it observing the motorcade passing, and I was visually scanning these people when I heard a noise similar to a firecracker. The sound came from my right rear and I immediately moved my head in that direction. In so doing, my eyes had to cross the Presidential automobile and I saw the President hunch forward and then slump to his left. I jumped from the Follow-up car and ran toward the Presidential automobile. I heard a second firecracker type noise but it had a different sound— like the sound of shooting a revolver into something hard. I saw the President slump more toward his left.

I jumped onto the left rear step of the Presidential automobile. Mrs. Kennedy shouted, "They've shot his head off;" then turned and raised out of her seat as if she were reaching to her right rear toward the back of the car for something that had blown out. I forced her back into her seat and placed my body above President and Mrs. Kennedy. SA Greer had, as I jumped onto the Presidential automobile, accelerated the Presidential automobile forward. I heard ASAIC Kellerman call SA Lawson on the two-way radio and say, "To the nearest hospital, quick." I shouted as loud as I could at the Lead car, "To the hospital, to the hospital."

As I lay over the top of the back seat I noticed a portion of the President's head on the right rear side was missing and he was bleeding profusely. Part of his brain was gone. I saw a part of his skull with hair on it lying in the seat. The time of the shooting was approximately 12:30 p.m., Dallas time. I looked forward to the jump seats and noticed Governor Connally's chest was covered with blood and he was slumped to his left and partially covered up by his wife. I had not realized until this point that the Governor had been shot.

When we arrived at Parkland Memorial Hospital, Dallas, I jumped off the Presidential automobile, removed my suit coat and covered the President's head and upper chest with it. I assisted in lifting the President from the rear seat of the automobile onto a wheel type stretcher and accompanied the President and Mrs. Kennedy into the Emergency Room. Governor Connally had been placed in an Emergency Room across the hall.

I exited the Emergency Room almost immediately because of the large number of doctors and nurses in the room, which was quite small. I asked a nurse standing outside of the Emergency Room in which the President was lying to please have everyone except those Medical Staff members necessary leave the emergency ward. She immediately began screening medical staff members.

I asked for the nearest telephone. ASAIC Kellerman exited the Emergency Room and told me to contact the White House in Washington and to keep the line open continually. I asked SA Lawson for the telephone number of the Dallas White House switchboard and he gave it to me. I dialed the Dallas White House operator and told him to connect me with the White House in Washington and to keep this line open continuously. He did so.

ASAIC Kellerman came out of the Emergency Room again and took the telephone and asked for SAIC Gerald A. Behn, Secret Service, The White House, Washington. This was approximately 12:39 p.m. Kellerman told Behn that there had been a double tragedy; that the President and Governor Connally had both been shot and that I would keep him advised. I took over the telephone and told Mr. Behn that the situation was extremely critical. The operator cut into the line and said The Attorney General wanted to talk to me. He asked me what the situation was and I advised him that the President had been injured very seriously and that I would keep him advised as to his condition.

Mr. Kellerman came back out of the Emergency Room and said, "Clint, tell Gerry that this is not for release and not official, but the man is dead." I told that to Mr. Behn and then requested that he immediately contact the Attorney General and other members of the President's family so that he could advise them of the situation rather than having them hear it over some news media.

I then received a request from Mr. O'Donnell to obtain a casket immediately so that we could transport the body back to Washington, D.C., as quickly as possible. I contacted the Hospital Administrator and asked for the name of the nearest mortuary. He said it would be O'Neil, Inc. I telephoned them and identified myself and requested that they bring the best casket immediately available at the mortuary to the Parkland Memorial Hospital Emergency Entrance and deliver it to me. The casket arrived in about twenty minutes at approximately 1:40 p.m. We wheeled it immediately into the Emergency Room where the President's body lay.

I advised the Air Force Aide that we wanted Air Force No. One moved to a different location at Love Field and to have it secured completely away from the view of the General Public. I requested that no press be admitted to the area in which Air Force One was to be placed. I requested SA David Grant to notify the Dallas Police that we did not want to use the same entrance to Love Field that previously had been planned. I then went with the Hospital Administrator and checked the shortest and most direct route from the Emergency Room to the emergency platform where the O'Neil hearse was waiting. I advised ATSAIC Stuart Stout of the route and requested that it be cleared of personnel.

The President's body, accompanied by Mrs. Kennedy, exited the Emergency Room at approximately 1:58 p.m. and proceeded to the emergency entrance platform. The casket was placed in the back of the O'Neil, Inc., hearse and Mrs. Kennedy, Admiral George Burkley (the President's Physician), and I entered the back of the hearse with the casket. SA Andrew Berger drove the hearse; ATSAIC Stuart Stout rode in the center front seat and ASAIC Kellerman rode in the right front seat.

We departed Parkland Memorial Hospital at 2:04 p.m. SA Lawson rode in the Dallas Police Department Lead Car. A Secret Service follow-up car followed immediately behind the hearse. The motorcade arrived at Air Force One, Love Field, at 2:14 p.m.

At 2:18 p.m the casket was placed aboard Air Force One with Mrs. Kennedy accompanying it. The casket was situated in the left rear corner of the aircraft where four seats had been removed. Mrs. Kennedy sat in one of the two seats immediately across the aisle from the casket.

The aircraft could not immediately depart because Vice-President Johnson had to be sworn in as the 36th President of the United States and it was necessary to wait for a Judge to arrive to do this. All personnel on Air Force One including Mrs. Kennedy were requested to witness the swearing in ceremony which took place in the Presidential Compartment of Air Force One at 2:38 p.m. I also attended.

I departed Love Field, Dallas, aboard Air Force One at 2:47 p.m. en route to Andrews Air Force Base, Maryland. I arrived at Andrews Air Force Base at 5:58 p.m. I assisted in moving the casket bearing the President's body from Air Force One to a U.S. Navy ambulance. Mrs. Kennedy got in the back of the ambulance with the casket as did Attorney General Robert Kennedy, who had joined Mrs. Kennedy aboard Air Force One upon arrival at Andrews Air Force Base. General Godfrey McHugh also rode in the back of the ambulance. The ambulance was driven by SA Greer with ASAIC Kellerman, SA Landis, and Admiral Burkley riding in the front seat. I followed in the car immediately behind the ambulance with Dr. John W. Walsh, Dave Powers, Kenneth O'Donnell and Larry O'Brien.

The motorcade departed Andrews Air Force Base for Bethesda Naval Hospital, Bethesda, Maryland, at 6:10 p.m. We were escorted by motorcycle police officers. The motorcade arrived Bethesda Naval Hospital at 6:55 p.m. Mrs. Kennedy, the Attorney General, SA Landis and I went immediately inside and via elevator to the 17th Floor of the hospital, the location of the Presidential Suite. Members of the immediate family and close friends were waiting in the suite.

The President's body was taken to the morgue at the hospital, accompanied by ASAIC Kellerman, SA Greer, and Admiral Burkley, for an autopsy. SA Landis and I secured the 17th Floor of the hospital and remained there with Mrs. Kennedy. We established a communications system with the White House and handled all telephone calls both incoming and outgoing, screening each and every call. Any person attempting to reach the 17th Floor was also screened.

At approximately 2:45 a.m., November 23, I was requested by ASAIC Kellerman to come to the morgue to once again view the body. When I arrived the autopsy had been completed and ASAIC Kellerman, SA Greer, General McHugh and I viewed the wounds. I observed a wound about six inches down from the neckline on the back just to the right of the spinal column. I observed another wound on the right rear portion of the skull. Attendants of the Joseph Gawler Mortuary were at this time preparing the body for placement in the casket. A new casket had been obtained from Gawler Mortuary in which the body was to be placed.

I went back to the 17th Floor of the hospital at approximately 3:10 a.m. The President's body was taken from the U.S. Naval Hospital, Bethesda, Maryland, at 3:56 a.m., accompanied by Mrs. Kennedy and Attorney General Kennedy, in the rear of a U.S. Navy ambulance driven by SA Greer. ASAIC Kellerman rode in the right front seat. I rode in the right front seat of a White House limousine immediately behind the ambulance. The motorcade was accompanied by motorcycle police and arrived at the White House at 4:24 a.m. The casket was taken immediately to the East Room and placed in the center of the room on a catephalt.

[signature]
Clinton J. Hill
Special Agent
U.S. Secret Service

THE WHITE HOUSE DETAIL
November 29, 1963

The following events regarding the assassination of the late President Kennedy, are outlined to the best of my knowledge. No statement is based upon information released by any form of news media.

On Friday, Nov. 22, 1963, I was working on the 8 am to 4 pm shift of the Secret Service White House Detail, and was under the supervision of ATSAIC Emory Roberts. Other agents working that day were Jack Ready, Don Lawton, Glen Bennett, and two agents assigned to Mrs. Kennedy, Clint Hill and Paul Landis.

The Presidential aircraft, AF 1, arrived at Dallas Love Field, Dallas, Texas, at approximately 11:40 am on Nov. 22, 1963. The above-mentioned agents departed the front of the aircraft and assumed protective positions around the President when he departed the rear exit of AF 1. The President walked close to a large crowd and shook hands with the people for approximately 5 or 10 minutes. He then stepped into the Presidential limousine, an open car, and was seated to the right of Mrs. Kennedy, in the rear seat. Governor Connally and his wife were seated in the jump seats of the car, directly in front of the President and Mrs. Kennedy. The Governor was seated to the right of his wife. ASAIC Roy Kellerman was seated in the right front seat of the limousine.

As the motorcade departed Love Field, the President's car was closely followed by the Secret Service follow-up car, which maintained its position throughout the events of the day. Agent Roberts was seated in the front seat of the follow-up car, next to the driver. Kenneth O'Donnell was seated to the left of David Powers, in the jump seats of the car. Agents George Hickey, a driver, and Glen Bennett, were in the rear seat, with Bennett on Hickey's right. Agents Ready and Landis rode the right running board, with Landis behind Ready, and agent Clint Hill and I rode the left running board, Hill being in front of me.

The motorcade was scheduled to last approximately 45 minutes. As we passed through downtown Dallas, crowds were quite heavy, and two motorcycles, on either flank of the Presidential vehicle, were of considerable assistance in keeping the motorcade clear.

As the motorcade cleared the main downtown area, it made a right turn, went approximately one block, and then executed a left turn. After this turn, there was essentially no crowd, and green expanses of lawn stretched to the right and left of the motorcade.

Directly in front of us was an underpass with a green sign with white lettering, stating "Entering Thornton Freeway".

The Presidential vehicle was approximately 200 feet from the underpass when the first shot was fired, followed in quick succession by two more. I would estimate that all three shots were fired within 5 seconds. After the second shot, I looked at the President and witnessed his being struck in the head by the third and last shot. By that time, Mr. Roberts had used the radio in our car to direct the vehicles to a hospital. Most, if not all the agents in the follow-up car had drawn their weapons, and agent Hickey was handling the AR-15. None of us could determine the origin of the shots, and no shots were fired by any agent.

Upon arrival at the hospital, agent Bennett and I escorted then Vice-President Johnson into a vacant treatment room. Agents Youngblood and Kivett stayed with him while agent Taylor and I stood nearby. Agent Bennett established security outside the door to the room.

The shooting occured at approximately 12:25 pm, and we had reached the hospital at approximately 12:30 pm.

Shortly after 1:30 pm, the Vice-President and Mrs. Johnson were taken to Love Field and placed aboard AF 1. Agents Lawton, Ready, and I established security around the aircraft. Within a short time, Mrs. Kennedy, accompanying the body of President Kennedy, arrived at Love Field, and boarded AF 1. AF 1 then departed Dallas, Texas, at what I think was about 2:15 pm.

At 3:15 pm, agents Roberts, Lawton, Ready, and I departed Dallas, Texas via AF 6970, the back-up plane, and arrived at Andrews Air Force Base at 6:30 pm. We all then returned to the White House, and submitted summarized reports of the day's events to Mr. Roberts.

[signature]
William T. McIntyre
Special Agent
U.S. Secret Service

November 22, 1963

On this date, at approximately 12:30 pm, at Dallas, Texas, I was assigned the post of the left rear area on the running board of the Secret Service Follow-up car. At this time, the President and Mrs. Kennedy were riding in the Presidential limousine, about 30 feet in front of my position.

As we approached the underpass leading to the Thornton Freeway, there was little, if any crowd present. I heard three shots fired and observing the President, noticed that he had been struck by at least one bullet, I thought in the head.

I recall a rolling lawn to the right of the area where the President was shot, and seem to also recall an expanse of lawn to the left of the Presidential vehicle.

I attempted to locate the origin of the shots, but was unable to do so. Both the Presidential vehicle and the Secret Service follow-up car immediately sped to the hospital.

[signature]
William T. McIntyre
Special Agent
White House Detail

DALLAS, TEXAS—NOVEMBER 22, 1963—FRIDAY

I, John D. Ready, Special Agent, United States Secret Service, Washington, D.C. arrived at Love Field, Dallas, Texas, at approximately 11:40 a.m., Friday, November 22, 1963 on board the Presidential Aircraft (USAF#1). Upon arrival, I left the aircraft and went to the Press Area (photographers and newsmen) located near the Presidential ramp at the rear of the plane. Here President John F. Kennedy greeted a group of persons and then walked to the fenced off spectator area. I followed the President and Mrs. Kennedy. After 10–15 minutes, the President, Mrs. Kennedy, Governor Connally (State of Texas) and Mrs. Connally entered the Presidential limousine, the motorcade departed Love Field and proceeded on its scheduled route. During this motorcade I held a post on the right frontdoor running-board of the U.S. Secret Service follow-up car.

Several times enroute the President's car stopped and the President shook hands with the crowds. In the downtown, heavily conjested, area of Dallas, a teen-age male came forth from the crowds on my right side. I left the follow-up car, chased the youth several yards before running him into the crowds on the right side. We departed the downtown area and the crowds diminished noticeably.

At about 12:30 p.m. we began the approach to the Thornton Freeway traveling about 20–25 MPH in a slight incline. I was about 25–30 feet from President Kennedy who was located in the right rear seat. I heard what appeared to be fire-crackers going off from my position. I immediately turned to my right rear trying to locate the source but was not able to determine the exact location.

At this time the U.S. Secret Service follow-up car seemed to slow and I heard someone from inside this car say: "he's shot". I left the follow-up car in the direction of the President's car but was re-called by ATSAIC Emory Roberts (Secret Service) as the cars increased their speeds. I got back on the car and seated myself beside Mr. Roberts in the right front seat. The cars proceeded to the hospital several miles distance.

On my arrival at the Parkland Hospital, Dallas, hospital personnel were awaiting the arrival of President Kennedy. After the President was taken to the emergency room, I was posted by ASAIC Kellerman (Secret Service), at the door entrance. I remained on this post until notified by ATSAIC Roberts that we were leaving for Love Field with President Johnson. I departed the hospital in a Dallas Police Cruiser to the rear of President Johnson.

Upon my arrival at Love Field I boarded the Presidential Aircraft (USAF#1), expecting to depart immediately. It was at this time that I was notified that Mrs. Kennedy and the late President were returning to Washington, D.C. on this plane.

ATSAIC Roberts asked me to set-up the airport security which I did. Mrs. Kennedy arrived and we were relieved by the 4–12 shift who then boarded the Presidential aircraft.

At 3:15 p.m. I departed Love Field, Dallas, Texas for Washington, D.C. on the Vice-Presidential aircraft (USAF#2).

[signature]
John D. Ready
Special Agent
White House Detail.

Friday, November 22, 1963
7:25 p.m.

On Friday, November 22, 1963 in Dallas, Texas, I was working the US Secret Service follow-up car about 25–30 feet to the rear of President and Mrs. Kennedy, Gov. and Mrs. Connolly of Texas. At about 12:30 p.m. I heard what sounded like fire crackers going off from my post on the right front running board. The President's car slowed, someone in the follow-up car stated he was shot, and I left to run to the President's car. At that time I was recalled to the follow-up car and took the right front seat aside of ATSAIC Roberts, and proceeded to a hospital several miles distant.

The shooting occurred as we were approaching the Thornton Freeway, traveling about 20–25 miles per hour in a slight incline. There appeared to be no spectators on the right side of the road-way.

After the initial shot I attempted to locate the area from where they had come from but was not able to. It appeared that the shots came from my right-rear side.

[signature]
John D. Ready
Special Agent
1-16

THE ASSASSINATION OF PRESIDENT JOHN F. KENNEDY ON NOVEMBER 22, 1963, AT DALLAS, TEXAS

Statement of Special Agent Paul E. Landis, Jr., United States Secret Service, concerning his activities and official duties on November 22, 1963.

On November 22, 1963, I arrived at Love Field Airport, Dallas, Texas, at 11:35 a.m., having traveled from Ft. Worth, Texas, to Dallas, Texas, on board U.S. Air Force Flight #6970. Upon my arrival I disembarked from the aircraft and immediately walked to where the motorcade vehicles were parked. Special Agent Sam Kinney was the first person that I recognized, and I remember speaking to him and standing by the Follow-up car and jokingly asking him if he could tell me where the Follow-up car was.

After speaking to Sam, I walked over to Special Agent Win Lawson just to double check to see if I was still assigned to working the Follow-up car as had previously been arranged. He was standing by the front right fender of the car in which the President would be riding, and he told me that I was still to ride in the Follow-up car.

Only a very few moments later the President's Aircraft was pulling up to its mooring spot and I moved up to where I would be near the President and First Lady when they disembarked from the aircraft.

There appeared to be a very large crowd at the airport and most of the people were restrained behind a chain-link fence which was about four or five feet high. On the opposite side of the fence from the crowd there was a very narrow sidewalk and curbing which ran along the fence-line.

There were several people on the same side of the fence as the President but most of them were photographers.

As soon as the President and First Lady disembarked from the Aircraft, Mrs. Kennedy was presented a bouquet of roses. The President was also presented what appeared to be two hand-drawn charcoal portraits of himself and Mrs. Kennedy in a black leather and glass folding frame. I believe that this was given to him by a lady wearing a red coat.

Just after the President received the black leather frame I held out my hand and he handed it to me. I had been standing just off to Mrs. Kennedy's left, slightly in front of her. She was on the left side of the President.

At this time the President and First Lady started walking towards the crowd which was restrained behind the fence. On the way, they did stop for a few seconds to talk to an elderly lady in a wheel chair who was on the field area about thirty feet from where the above presentations were made.

They then walked over to the crowd and walked along the fence from their right to their left. At first I was in front of the President, clearing a pathway through the photographers and observing the crowd reaching over the fence; but I noticed that Mrs. Kennedy was moving along slower and becoming separated from the President so I asked another agent, I don't recall who, to move up where I was and I dropped back to assist Special Agent Clinton Hill who was next to Mrs. Kennedy. I continued to keep a pathway clear for Mrs. Kennedy, removing small hand signs that had been dropped in her pathway on the sidewalk and occasionally cautioning to watch out for the curbing. At one point, where the direction of the fence made a right angle turn to the left of the way we were moving, I do remember reaching up and holding a fairly large flag away that someone was waving over the fence. Only a few feet further and the fence and sidewalk made another 90 degree turn in the direction in which we were originally moving.

At this point we stopped momentarily and started in the direction of the cars which were slightly behind us and had been moving along towards us. Mrs. Kennedy asked where the President was and SA Hill noticed him continuing along the fence shaking hands with the crowd; so Mrs. Kennedy returned to the fence and did the same.

Only a short distance later the President and First Lady stopped shaking hands and entered their automobile. I stood by the right rear side until the car started moving and then hopped on the right rear portion of the right running board of the Follow-up car. I was standing with my right leg on the running board and my left leg up over and inside the Follow-up car. I stayed in this position until we were leaving the Airport area and remarked that, "I might as well get all the way in," and I did so. I glanced at my watch but I don't recall the time.

Special Agents Glen Bennett and George Hickey were seated to my left respectively in the rear of the Follow-up car. Mr. David Powers was seated directly in front of me in the center portion of the Follow-up car and Mr. Kenneth O'Donnell was seated on Mr. Power's left. Special Agent Sam Kinney was driving and ATSAIC Roberts was seated in the right front seat. Special Agents John Ready, Clinton Hill, and Tim McIntyre were standing on the right front, left front, and left rear portions of the running board, respectively.

The motorcade had not proceeded far when ATSAIC Roberts asked me to get back on the outside running board, "Just in case," which I immediately did. The crowd was about two deep along each side of the road and I would guess that we were traveling about twenty miles per hour.

As the motorcade proceeded towards the main business section of downtown Dallas I watched the crowd for anyone trying to run towards the President's car or any person who might be holding anything harmful in his hands. I observed the rooftops and windows of the buildings along the route. On the outskirts of town most of the buildings were of a one or two story type structure and very few people were on the rooftops. The crowd was three or more deep along the street as we proceeded towards downtown Dallas with most intersections more heavily crowded. The outskirts seemed to consist mostly of used car lots, junk dealers, auto parts stores, and this typical type of neighborhood. At one intersection there were some Cuban Pickets but I don't recall exactly what their signs said except that they did have "Cuba" on them.

A little further towards town some people had a sign asking the President to please stop and shake hands, which he saw as he passed and stopped. I immediately ran up to his car as it stopped and assumed a position next to him and observed the crowd as it merged on the car, especially watching the hands. Most of the people were children but I do remember one of the adult ladies who was holding the sign, remarking, "It worked, our sign worked!"

At various places along the route I remember Mr. Dave Powers standing up and taking movies of the President's car and the crowd.

The closer we came to downtown Dallas the larger the crowds became. At several places they were forcing their way into the street and there was just barely enough room for the cars to get through. There were two motorcycle escorts on each side of the President's and the Follow-up car and in several instances the crowd was so close that the motorcycles could not get through and had to drop completely behind the Follow-up car. During these instances SA Clint Hill would run up and jump on the left rear bumper of the President's car and he would ride there until the crowd was further back away from the President's car.

Just before we reached the heart of downtown Dallas, I remember noticing some new looking, very high, multi-storied skyscrapers and I remarked to Jack Ready that there were even people way up on the roof of one. I think the motorcade made a right turn onto Main Street, as that is the only street sign I saw and remembered. I remember thinking to myself that about every town I know of has a Main Street.

I'm not sure how far we traveled on Main Street, but I do know that this is where the crowd seemed heaviest. The buildings were tall on both sides of the street but I didn't notice many people in the windows. I continued to scan the crowds on the street and the buildings along the route. I glanced at the President's car somewhere along Main Street and saw Clint Hill again standing on the left rear bumper behind Mrs. Kennedy who was seated to the President's left. Governor Connally was seated in front of the President and Mrs. Connally was in front of Mrs. Kennedy.

The crowd lined both sides of the street and in several places was right out into the street leaving barely enough room to get through.

Not long after we turned onto Main Street there was one boy who, I would say, was in his early teens who ran out from the crowd after the President's and Follow-up cars had passed and tried to overtake the President's car. I saw him coming and tapped SA Ready on the shoulder and pointed towards him. He was carrying a camera. SA Ready jumped off the running board, overtook the boy and pushed him back into the crowd.

When we reached the end of Main Street we turned right and approached a gradual left turn. As we approached the intersection and while we were turning left, the crowd seemed to thin and almost disappear around the turn. I then made a quick surveillance of a building which was to be on the President's right once the left turn was completed. It appeared to be the last one in sight. It was a modernistic type building, approximately eight stories high, and it had large glass windows. I also seem to recollect orange paneling or siding. None of the windows were open, and I did not see anyone standing by them. I surmised that the building was closed or that all its employees were out on the street corner.

As the President's car continued around the corner, I continued to survey the crowd along the righthand side of the road and noticed that it was fairly scattered, with hardly enough people to form a single line. I continued to look ahead to an overpass over the route we were traveling. At approximately this point, I would say, the President's car and the Follow-up car had just completed their turns and both were straightening out.

At this moment I heard what sounded like the report of a high-powered rifle from behind me, over my right shoulder. When I heard the sound there was no question in my mind what it was. My first glance was at the President, as I was practically looking in his direction anyway. I saw him moving in a manner which I thought was to look in the direction of the sound. I did not realize that President Kennedy had been shot at this point.

I immediately returned my gaze, over my right shoulder, toward the modernistic building I had observed before. With a quick glance I saw nothing and immediately started scanning the crowd at the intersection from my right to my left. I observed nothing unusual and began to think that the sound had been that of a fire cracker but I hadn't seen any smoke. In fact, I recall Special Agent Jack Ready saying, "What was it? A Fire Cracker?" I remarked, "I don't know; I don't see any smoke." So far the lapsed period of time could not have been over two or three seconds.

All during this time I continued to scan the crowd, returning my gaze towards the President's car. It must have been another second or two before the next shot was fired because, as I recall having seen nothing out of the ordinary, I then thought that maybe one of the cars in the motorcade had had a blowout that had echoed off the buildings. I looked at the right front tire of the President's car and saw it was all right. I then glanced to see the right rear tire, but could not because the Follow-up car was too close.

I also thought of trying to run and jump on the President's car but did not think I could make it because of the speed at which we were traveling. I decided I had better stay where I was so that I would at least be near the First Lady, to whom I am assigned. I think that it was at this point that I thought, "Faster, Faster, Faster," thinking that we could not get out of the area soon enough. However, I don't have any idea as to how fast we were then moving.

I had drawn my gun, but I am not sure exactly when I did this. I did leave my suit coat unbuttoned all during the motorcade movement, thinking at the time that I could get to my gun faster this way, if I had to.

I glanced towards the President and he still appeared to be fairly upright in his seat, leaning slightly toward Mrs. Kennedy with his head tilted slightly back. I think Mrs. Kennedy had her right arm around the President's shoulders at this time. I also remember Special Agent Clinton Hill attempting to climb onto the back of the President's car.

It was at this moment that I heard a second report and it appeared that the President's head split open with a muffled exploding sound. I can best describe the sound as I heard it, as the sound you would get by shooting a high powered bullet into a five gallon can of water or shooting into a melon. I saw pieces of flesh and blood flying through the air and the President slumped out of sight towards Mrs. Kennedy.

The time lapse between the first and second report must have been about four or five seconds.

My immediate thought was that the President could not possibly be alive after being hit like he was. I still was not certain from which direction the second shot came, but my reaction at this time was that the shot came from somewhere towards the front, right-hand side of the road.

I did not notice anyone on the overpass, and I scanned the area to the right of and below the overpass where the terrain sloped towards the road on which we were traveling. The only person I recall seeing clearly was a Negro male in light green slacks and a beige colored shirt running from my left to right, up the slope, across a grassy section, along a sidewalk, towards some steps and what appeared to be a low stone wall. He was bent over while running and I started to point towards him, but I didn't notice anything in his hands and by this time we were going under the overpass at a very high rate of speed. I was looking back and saw a motorcycle policeman stopping along the curb approximately adjacent to where I saw the Negro running.

After we rode under the overpass I again looked at the President's car and saw Special Agent Clint Hill lying across the trunk. He was looking back towards the Follow-up car shaking his head back and forth and gave a thumbs-down sign with his hand.

ATSAIC Roberts asked if anyone got the exact time of the shooting and someone said "about 12:30 p.m.;" then someone told me to get inside the car and pulled me by the arm. My sun glasses fell off and Special Agent Bennett handed them to me. By now we were on an Expressway and a few people were standing in spots along the way waving as we went by.

ATSAIC Roberts was telling the other agents in the Follow-up car to cover Vice-President Johnson as soon as we stopped.

Sometime around 12:37 p.m. we arrived at Parkland Memorial Hospital. I immediately ran to the left rear side of the President's car, reached over and tried to help Mrs. Kennedy up by taking hold of her shoulders. She did not want to let go of President Kennedy whose head she held in her lap and she was bending over him. She said something like, "No, I want to stay with him!"

Agent Hill had in the meantime opened the left rear door of the Presidential Convertible, stepped inside and took Mrs. Kennedy by the arm. She released the President and someone said, "Cover up his head." Agent Hill took off his suit coat and covered up the President's head. I also remember Mr. Powers leaning in the car and saying, "Oh, No!, Mr. President! Mr. President!"

By this time someone was lifting the President's body out of the right side of the car. Agent Hill helped Mrs. Kennedy out of the car, and I followed. Mrs. Kennedy's purse and hat and a cigarette lighter were on the back seat. I picked these three items up as I walked through the car and followed Mrs. Kennedy into the hospital.

The President's body was taken directly to an Emergency Room, and I think I remember Mrs. Kennedy following the people in but coming out almost immediately. The door to the Emergency Room was closed and I stayed by Mrs. Kennedy's side. Someone, in the meantime, had brought a chair for Mrs. Kennedy to sit in and she sat just outside of the Emergency Room. There were several people milling around and with the help of a nurse we cleared all unauthorized personnel out of the immediate area.

Someone came out of the Room that the President was in and asked if anyone knew his Blood Type. ASAIC Kellerman and SA Hill immediately reached for their wallets. ASAIC Kellerman gave the man the information first.

At one point someone else came out of the President's Room again and said he was still breathing. Mrs. Kennedy stood up and said, "Do you mean he may live?" No one answered.

Most of the time while in the hospital I stayed right next to Mrs. Kennedy. Twice,

I believe, she went into the Room where the President was; however, I remained outside by the door. A short time later I still remember several people standing around, and I asked a doctor for help in clearing the area.

At approximately 2:00 p.m. the President's body was wheeled from the hospital in a coffin into an ambulance. Special Agent Andrew Berger drove the ambulance; ASAIC Kellerman and ATSAIC Stout were in the front seat. Mrs. Kennedy, Admiral Burkley, and Agent Hill rode in the rear of the ambulance with the President's body.

I rode in the Follow-up car behind the ambulance which departed the hospital at 2:04 p.m.

At 2:14 p.m., the President's body arrived at Love Field Airport and several Secret Service agents immediately carried it on board U.S. Air Force No. One via the rear door. I followed on board behind Mrs. Kennedy and then moved to the forward section of the plane. I witnessed the swearing in of President Johnson at 2:39 p.m. in the center compartment on board Air Force #1, and at 2:47 p.m. departed Love Field Airport, Dallas, Texas, via Air Force No. One, with Mrs. Kennedy and the body of the late President Kennedy.

Upon our arrival at Andrews Air Force Base, Md., at 5:58 p.m. I helped carry the late President Kennedy's coffin from Air Force #1. The body was placed in an ambulance which departed Andrews Air Force Base at approximately 6:10 p.m., driven by Special Agent William Greer. ASAIC Kellerman, Admiral Burkley, and I rode in the front seat of the ambulance. Mrs. Kennedy and Attorney General Robert Kennedy rode in the rear of the ambulance with President Kennedy's body.

The above party arrived at Bethesda Naval Hospital, Bethesda, Md., at approximately 6:55 p.m. Special Agent Hill and I escorted Mrs. Kennedy to the 17th Floor where we immediately secured the area. Only hospital personnel assigned to the area, Kennedy family members and friends, and authorized personnel were allowed in the area.

I only left the 17th Floor twice while Mrs. Kennedy was there. Once, to find ASAIC Kellerman in the hospital morgue and give him a telephone message from Chief Rowley. The other time was to find a White House driver.

At 3:56 a.m., on November 23, 1963, Mrs. Kennedy and Attorney General Robert Kennedy departed Bethesda Naval Hospital via ambulance, accompanying the late President John F. Kennedy's body to the White House. Special Agent William Greer was driving and ASAIC Kellerman accompanied. Special Agent Clinton Hill rode in the first limousine behind the ambulance and I rode in the second limousine.

The above Party arrived at the White House at 4:24 a.m.

[signature]
Paul E. Landis, Jr.
Special Agent
U.S. Secret Service

TREASURY DEPARTMENT
UNITED STATES SECRET SERVICE

The Assassination of President John F. Kennedy as it appeared to Paul E. Landis, Jr., Special Agent, U. S. Secret Service.

I was assigned to work the follow-up car from Love Field Airport, Dallas, Texas. My position was on the right rear portion of the running board. Special Agent John Ready was on the running board ahead of me. SAs Hill and McIntyre were on the left-hand running board. SAs Bennett and Hickey were in the rear seat. Mr. Kenneth O'Donnell and Dave Powers were in the middle seats, and ATSAIC Roberts was in the front seat, and Sam Kinney was driving.

I remember the motorcade reaching the end of Main Street, in downtown Dallas, Texas, turning right and approaching a gradual left turn. As the President's car approached the intersection to make the left turn, the crowd appeared to thin down and almost end. As we reached the intersection I made a quick surveillance of a building on the right side of the route, which appeared to be the last one that the President would pass. It was a modernistic building, about eight stories high with large glass windows. None of the windows were open, and I did not notice anyone standing by the windows. My first thought was that the building was either closed or that all of its employees were on the street corner.

As the President's car continued around the corner, I returned my gaze to the crowd along the right-hand side of the route and noticed that it was fairly scattered. I continued to look ahead to what appeared to be an overpass over the route we were traveling. At this point the President's car and follow-up car had just completed its turn and both were straightening out.

At this moment I heard what sounded like the report of a high-powered rifle from behind me. My first glance was at the President, as my eyes were almost straight ahead at that time. I did not realize that the President had been shot at this point. I saw him moving and thought he was turning in the direction of the sound. I immediately returned my gaze to the building which I had observed before, at a quick glance saw nothing and dropped my eyes to the crowd at the intersection, scanning it quickly from right to left. I saw nothing out of the ordinary and thought that the sound might have been a fire cracker, but I couldn't see any smoke. In fact, I think I recall Special Agent Jack Ready saying, "What was it? A fire cracker?" I remarked "I don't know, I don't see any smoke." All during this time I was scanning the crowd and returning my gaze to the President's car. By then I think I had my gun out, but I do not recall exactly when it was drawn. I then thought that maybe one of the cars in the motorcade had had a blowout that had echoed off the buildings. I looked at the front right tire of the President's car and saw it was alright and glanced to see the right rear tire but could not as the follow-up car was too close. In fact, from my position on the running board of the follow-up car I could not see the rear bumper of the President's car. I glanced back towards the President, he still appeared upright in his seat, leaning slightly towards Mrs. Kennedy. It was at this moment that I heard a second report and saw the President's head split open and pieces of flesh and blood flying through the air. I also remember Special Agent Clinton Hill attempting to climb onto the back of the car at the time the second shot was fired. I would guess that the time between the first and second shot was approximately four or five seconds.

My reaction at this time was that the shot came from somewhere towards the front, but I did not see anyone on the overpass, and looked along the right-hand side of the road. By this time we were almost at the overpass, and the only person I recall seeing was a negro male in light green slacks and a beige colored shirt running across a grassy section towards some concrete steps and what appeared to be a low stone wall. He was in a bent over position, and I did not notice anything in his hands.

By now both the President's car and the follow-up car were traveling at a high rate of speed. As we passed under the overpass, I was looking back and saw a motorcycle policeman stopping approximately where I saw the negro running. I do not recall hearing a third shot.

[signature]
Paul E. Landis, Jr.
Special Agent
November 27, 1963

TREASURY DEPARTMENT
UNITED STATES SECRET SERVICE
FIELD FORCE

Protective Assignment of S/A Bennett on 11/22/63
at Dallas, Texas

Air Force Two landed at Love Field, Dallas, Texas at 11:35 A.M. Upon deplaning, I covered the fence and press areas. The President's plane arrived at

approximately 11:38 A.M. I stayed with the President and First Lady during the
time they greeted the crowd on the apron and along the fence. The greeting lasted
for about 10 minutes and the President/First Lady entered their car and the
motorcade planned to depart. I asked while moving towards the follow-up car what
position I should take; Mr. Roberts informed me that I should take the right rear
seat of the follow-up. I took this position and held it during the entire motorcade. I
left this rear seat position at one point in the trip to assist in getting well-wishers
away from the President's auto. About thirty minutes after leaving Love Field,
about 12:25 P.M., the Motorcade entered an intersection and then proceeded down
a grade. At this point the well-wishers numbered but a few; the motorcade
continued down this grade enroute to the Trade Mart. At this point I heard what
sounded like a fire-cracker. I immediately looked from the right/crowd/physical
area/and looked towards the President who was seated in the right rear seat of his
limousine open convertible. At the moment I looked at the back of the President I
heard another fire-cracker noise and saw the shot hit the President about four
inches down from the right shoulder. A second shot followed immediately and hit
the right rear high of the President's head. I immediately hollered "he's hit" and
reached for the AR-15 located on the floor of the rear seat. Special Agent Hickey
had already picked-up the AR-15. We peered towards the rear and particularly the
right side of the area. I had drawn my revolver when I saw S/A Hickey had the AR-
15. I was unable to see anything or one that could have fired the shots. The
President's car immediately kicked into high gear and the follow-up car followed.
The President's auto and the follow-up proceeded to the Parkland Hospital. Upon
arriving at the hospital's parking lot, I was instructed by ASAIC Roberts to stay
with the Vice-President who had followed us into the parking lot. I immediately
went to the Vice-President's auto and accompanied him to a room on the ground
floor of the hospital. I then continued with the Vice-President back to Washington,
D.C. where I was relieved.

> [signature]
> Glen A. Bennett
> Special Agent
> 11-23-63

> Saturday
> November 30, 1963

TO   : Gerald A. Behn, Special Agent in Charge, White House Detail, United
States Secret Service

FROM : George W. Hickey, Jr., Special Agent, White House Detail, White House
garage, United States Secret Service

SUBJECT: Activities of S.A. George W. Hickey, Jr. from the time he arrived at Love
Airfield, Dallas, Texas, Thursday, November 21, 1963, to the time he
departed from the above Love Airfield, Friday, November 22, 1963

REPORT : *Thursday, November 21, 1963*
I arrived at Love Airfield, Dallas, Texas at 6:05 p.m. via U.S.A.F. C 130
plane #12373. U.S.A.F. flight order number 597, dated November 15,
1963 giving the names and rank of the crew of the above plane is attached
to this report and initialed by me this date. S.A. Samuel Kinney was the
senior agent aboard this plane which was being used in Presidential
support to transport Secret Service Cars 100X and 679X. We were met at
the airport by S.A.I.C. Forest V. Sorrels of the Dallas Field Office and
S.A. Winston G. Lawson, the advance agent for the White House Secret
Service Detail. S.A. Kinney unloaded 679X and I unloaded 100X from
the plane. The drivers of the above cars accompanied by agents Sorrels
and Lawson then drove to the garage beneath the airport's main terminal
building where security was placed on the cars by the Dallas Police
Department as arranged by S.A.I.C. Sorrels.
Agents Kinney, Hickey, Lawson and Sorrels then drove in a Dallas

field office car to the Sheraton Hotel in Dallas where reservations had
been made for us. Agent Kinney and I then went to our room to wash and
change clothes before dinner.

We met with Agent Lawson, Warrant Officer Arthur Bales of the White
House Signal Agency and Jack Puterbaugh, a Democratic National
Committee man for that area at about 8:30 p.m. at the hotel, and drove to
the Dallas Trade Mart where the President was to speak the next day. The
premises were checked by Agent Lawson for final security details. At
about 9:15 p.m. we departed and went to dinner. Finished about 11:00
p.m. and proceeded back to the Sheraton Hotel where we parted
company and went to our respective rooms.

Friday, November 22, 1963
Awoke about 7:00 a.m., washed, packed suitcase, checked out of hotel
and had breakfast. About 8:30 a.m. Agent Sorrels met Agent Kinney and
me outside the hotel and drove to the airport arriving about 9:00 a.m. We
went directly to the garage and relieved the police of the security of the
cars. Washed and cleaned both cars and checked outside, inside and
underneath for security violations—none found. We drove the cars to the
area where the President was to be met about 11:00 a.m. Cars were kept
under close observation until the arrival of the President, when Agent
William Greer of the White House Detail took over control of 100X and
Agent Kinney 679X.

The President and his party then proceeded up to the fence holding the
crowd back and greeted and shook hands with them. I assisted Agents on
the detail to make a path for them and helped Agent Greer keep the cars
abreast of the President as he moved along the length of the fence.

After the President and his party entered and were seated in 100X I
entered 679X as I had been instructed to do by Agent Lawson. I was
seated in the rear left side seat. The shift leader, Emory Roberts, had
instructed me to take control of the AR15 rifle whenever I was riding in
679X as an extra man. I did this and had the ammunition clip inserted in
the rifle and placed the rifle within easy reach of me.

The motorcade then left the airport and proceeded along the parade
route. Just prior to the shooting the Presidential car turned left at the
intersection and started down an incline toward an underpass followed by
679X. After a very short distance I heard a loud report which sounded
like a firecracker. It appeared to come from the right and rear and seemed
to me to be at ground level. I stood up and looked to my right and rear in
an attempt to identify it. Nothing caught my attention except people
shouting and cheering. A disturbance in 679X caused me to look forward
toward the President's car. Perhaps 2 or 3 seconds elapsed from the time I
looked to the rear and then looked at the President. He was slumped
forward and to his left, and was straightening up to an almost erect sitting
position as I turned and looked. At the moment he was almost sitting
erect I heard two reports which I thought were shots and that appeared to
me completely different in sound than the first report and were in such
rapid succession that there seemed to be practically no time element
between them. It looked to me as if the President was struck in the right
upper rear of his head. The first shot of the second two seemed as if it
missed because the hair on the right side of his head flew forward and
there didn't seem to be any impact against his head. The last shot seemed
to hit his head and cause a noise at the point of impact which made him
fall forward and to his left again.

Possibly four or five seconds elapsed from the time of the first report
and the last.

At the end of the last report I reached to the bottom of the car and
picked up the AR 15 rifle, cocked and loaded it, and turned to the rear. At
this point the cars were passing under the over-pass and as a result we

had left the scene of the shooting. I kept the AR 15 rifle ready as we proceeded at a high rate of speed to the hospital.

Agent Clint Hill was riding across the rear and the top of 100X in a horizontal position. He looked into the rear of 100X and turned toward 679X and shook his head several times. I received the impression that the President at the least was very seriously injured. A few moments later shift leader Emory Roberts turned to the rest of us in the car and said words to the effect that when we arrive at the hospital some of us would have to give additional protection to the Vice President and take him to a place of safety. He assigned two of the agents in the car to this duty. I was told to have the AR 15 ready for use if needed.

When we arrived at the hospital the President and Governor Connally were taken inside and about the same time the Vice President had arrived. I requested him to come into the hospital to a place of safety and he was surrounded by his detail and the other assigned agents, and myself and led into the hospital. When he entered I returned the gun to 679X as ordered by Agent Roberts.

By this time a great number of police had arrived with newsmen and others in the motorcade, and Agent Kinney and I stood by the cars. Agent Kinney requested that I go and see if I could find out what was to be done with the cars. As I was on my way into the hospital to do this, Mr. Kenneth O'Donnell asked me to take him to where the President was as he could not get by the police. I did this and he joined Mrs. Kennedy and Mr. Dave Powers outside the President's operating room.

Agent John D. Ready was stationed outside this room and he requested that I take his place for a few moments and to allow no unauthorized persons to enter or linger outside the door and to care for Mrs. Kennedy if necessary. I did this until Agent Ready returned and relieved me.

As I was leaving to go back to the area where Agent Roberts was, Mr. Dave Powers asked me to get a priest which I did. Agent Roberts informed me to wait until later when a decision might be made about the cars. Upon returning to the vehicles, I assisted Agent Kinney to put the tops on the cars.

A short time later Agent Roy Kellerman told Agent Kinney and me to take the cars to the plane and stand by for orders. Agent Kinney drove 679X and I 100X to the plane and loaded them and secured the plane, allowing no one to enter except the regular crew.

After Airforce #1 left, we received orders to depart for Washington, D.C. and return the cars to the garage and preserve any evidence that might be in them. Departed Love Airfield, Dallas, Texas via U.S.A.F. plane #12373 at 3:35 p.m.

The above report has been initialed by the below signed on each of its four pages, including the attached flight sheet.

[signature]
George W. Hickey, Jr.
Special Agent, U.S.S.S.

Just prior to the shooting I was seated in the rear of SS-679-X on the left side. As 100-X made the turn and proceeded a short distance I heard what seemed to me that a firecracker exploded to the right and rear. I stood partially up and turned to the rear to see if I could observe anything. Nothing was observed and I turned around and looked at the President's car. The President was slumped to the left in the car and I observed him come up. I heard what appeared to be two shots and it seemed as if the right side of his head was hit and his hair flew forward. I then reached down, picked up the AR 15, cocked and loaded it and stood part way up in the car and looked about. By this time, 100-X and 679-X had passed under the overpass and was proceeding at a high rate of speed towards the hospital.

Clint Hill who was lying on the trunk of the President's car looked into the car and then looked back at us and shook his head. Emory Roberts then turned around and said to words of this effect that we had to take care of the Vice President. He assigned two agents to go to him the minute we arrived at the hospital. He told me to stand by with the AR 15 in case there was any danger to the Vice President when we arrived at the hospital.

I did this, and after the Vice President was escorted into the hospital, I returned the gun to the car. Kenneth O'Donnell asked me to take him into the hospital. He couldn't get by the local police. I took him into the area where the President was and assisted the agent outside the door to keep the people away who didn't belong there. I was then relieved and went back to the cars where I assisted Agent Kinney to put the plastic top on 100-X. We were then told by Roy Kellerman to take the cars to the plane and stand by. I drove 100-X to the plane, loaded it in company with Agent Kinney. We stood by until the plane took off.

> [signature]
> George W. Hickey
> Special Agent
> 11-22-63

UNITED STATES GOVERNMENT   1-22-614.0
Memorandum

                                                            U.S. Secret Service

TO   : Chief   DATE: November 29, 1963

FROM   : SAIC Youngblood—Vice Presidential Detail

SUBJECT: Statement of SAIC Rufus W. Youngblood, Vice Presidential Detail (office 1-22), concerning details of events occurring in Dallas, Texas, on November 22, 1963.

At 11:35 a.m., AF-2 plane arrived at Love Field airport, Dallas, Texas. The Vice President, Mrs. Johnson, and others were aboard this plane including ATSAIC Thomas L. Johns, SA Warren W. Taylor, and myself of the Vice Presidential Detail (office 1-22). SA Jerry D. Kivett of the Vice Presidential Detail was on the ground in Dallas ahead of us.

We arrived before the Presidential aircraft, and the Vice President and Mrs. Johnson were met by numerous dignitaries when they disembarked from the plane. ATSAIC Johns, SA Taylor and myself were staying in the immediate vicinity of Vice President and Mrs. Johnson. SA Kivett was working intermittently with us and also keeping up with location of cars, the other airplane, etc.

Prior to the arrival of the Presidential aircraft, I led the Vice President and Mrs. Johnson to the reception line, and when AF-1 was in position and the ramp was in place, led them to the foot of the ramp. They greeted the President and the First Lady upon their arrival. We later followed the Presidential couple and when the Presidential couple went along the fence to greet the public, we did likewise but in a separate group. During this time, I was always in close proximity to the Vice President; Warren Taylor was in close proximity to Mrs. Johnson; and we were both being assisted by Johns and Kivett. When the President took his position in the Presidential vehicle, we did likewise in the Vice Presidential vehicle. The following persons were in the Vice Presidential vehicle when the motorcade departed from the airport at approximately 11:50 a.m., CST.

In the front seat: The driver, Herschel Jacks, Texas Highway Patrol
Other side front seat: ASAIC Youngblood
Rear seat, behind driver: Senator Ralph W. Yarborough
Rear seat, middle: Mrs. Johnson
Rear seat, behind ASAIC Youngblood: The Vice President

The above vehicle was a 4-door Lincoln convertible with the top down. I had a shoulder strap (DCN) portable 2-way radio with me on "Baker" frequency.

The following persons loaded into the Vice Presidential follow-up car:

The driver
ATSAIC Johns
SA Warren W. Taylor
SA Kivett
Mr. Cliff Carter, member of the Vice President's staff

ATSAIC Johns had a portable radio which was the companion of the one I had—also on "Baker" frequency. This Vice Presidential follow-up car also had a portable, 2-way radio set on "Charlie" frequency.

When we departed from the airport, the motorcade order was:

Lead car
Presidential car
Presidential follow-up car
Vice Presidential car
Vice Presidential follow-up car
Other cars—press, dignitaries, busses, etc.

During the motorcade, the order listed above was not changed and remained so until we arrived at the hospital.

Upon leaving the airport, we were proceeding to the Trade Mart and were due to arrive there at 12:30 p.m. We were proceeding at a slow pace to this destination, which was entirely normal due to the large crowds of people along both sides of the motorcade route. During our motorcade, the Presidential vehicle made some stops to greet well-wishers. Our speed and the stops were naturally controlled by the Presidential car. I was working both in and out of the Vice Presidential car on these stops. To my recollection, the Vice President did not leave the vehicle during the motorcade. Several times during the motorcade, I was in radio contact with the Vice Presidential follow-up car concerning times, distances, etc.

During the motorcade, I instructed our driver to keep some distance (about two or three car lengths) behind the Presidential follow-up car while we were going at slow speeds.

The motorcade had just cleared the congested downtown area and made a right turn. I recall observing an illuminated clock sign on a building—the time was 12:30 p.m., which was the time we were due to be at the Trade Mart. The motorcade then made a left turn, and the sidewalk crowds were beginning to diminish in size. I observed a grassy plot to my right in back of the small crowd of bystanders on the sidewalk; some tall buildings; a downhill grade ahead where the street went under what appeared to be a railroad overpass. We were about two car lengths behind the Presidential follow-up car at this time.

I heard an explosion—I was not sure whether it was a firecracker, bomb, bullet, or other explosion. I looked at whatever I could quickly survey, and could not see anything which would indicate the origin of this noise. I noticed that the movements in the Presidential car were very abnormal and, at practically the same time, the movements in the Presidential follow-up car were abnormal. I turned in my seat and with my left arm grasped and shoved the Vice President, at his right shoulder, down and toward Mrs. Johnson and Senator Yarborough. At the same time, I shouted "get down!" I believe I said this more than once and directed it to the Vice President and the other occupants of the rear seat. They all responded very rapidly. I quickly looked all around again and could see nothing to shoot at, so I stepped over into the back seat and sat on top of the Vice President. I sat in a crouched position and issued orders to the driver. During this time, I heard two more explosion noises and observed SA Hickey in the Presidential follow-up car poised on the car with the AR-15 rifle looking toward the buildings. The second and third explosions made the same type of sound that the first one did as far as I could tell, but by this time I was of the belief that they definitely were shots—not bombs or firecrackers. I am not sure that I was on top of the Vice President before the second shot—he says I was. All of the above related events, from the beginning at the sound of the first shot to the sound of the third shot, happened within a few seconds.

In my crouched position, I observed the people on the streets to scatter; heard some shouts; saw the motorcade increase speed, and I knew we were making a rapid evacuation. I shouted to the driver to stick with them and stay close. We then began moving very fast. I then called on my portable radio, which I had with me, to the Vice Presidential follow-up car and ordered them to switch to "Charlie" frequency. As I switched to "Charlie," I heard some transmission from the Presidential follow-up car. From fragments of what I heard and what I saw, I knew that the President had suffered injury. I could see an agent (who had previously run from the Presidential follow-up car, although I did not observe this when it happened) lying across the trunk turtle of the Presidential car above the President and Mrs. Kennedy. I heard enough radio transmission to know we were headed for a hospital. I could also see the agents in the Presidential follow-up car waving our car to come up close, and I told our driver to stay as close and go as fast as he could without having a wreck.

This driver wasn't talkative and he wasn't excitable. He responded to everything I said. He did an excellent job.

During this ride to the hospital, I had some brief conversations with the Vice President and Senator Yarborough in response to their questions. I told the Vice President that the President must have been shot or wounded, but I did not know his condition. I told the Vice President and Mrs. Johnson to follow me and the agents as closely and quickly as possible when we got to our destination. They agreed to do this.

When we got to the hospital, my agents (SA's Kivett and W. Taylor) from the Vice Presidential follow-up car were on the ground by the time we stopped. Also, some agents from the Presidential follow-up car were coming back to assist us. We left the car immediately (Vice President and Mrs. Johnson and myself) and, surrounded by agents, went into the hospital and quickly into a corner of a large room with partitions. We did not stop to look at or for the Presidential car occupants. Senator Yarborough did not go with us. I told one agent (Glen Bennett, Protective Research Section) to stop any traffic into the room unless he knew the person to be a member of our party. Vice President and Mrs. Johnson and myself were in the corner of the room while SA's Kivett and W. Taylor were securing the room by evacuating a couple of occupants and closing blinds, shades, etc. They remained in our immediate proximity. We were shortly joined by ATSAIC Johns, Congressman Thornberry, Congressman Brooks, and Cliff Carter. ATSAIC Roberts, White House Detail, came in and told us that the President was badly wounded and probably would not live. I advised the Vice President that we should evacuate the hospital and go to the airplane and return to Washington, D.C., and the White House.

At this time I had no knowledge of whether the actions that caused the President to be shot were the work of one man, a small group, or what. I felt that the safest place for him, and in the best interests of all concerned, was in the White House. Others who were present also concurred. We were later joined by ASAIC Kellerman who reported the President's condition was very critical. Ken O'Donnell came to the room and told us the same thing, and said we should return to Washington.

During all of this time, many things occurred and I don't recall now the exact order. I talked to Mrs. Johnson and obtained information about Lynda and Lucy, and told SA Kivett to make the necessary calls to have them placed under Secret Service protection. Mrs. Johnson left the room briefly on two occasions, accompanied by SA's Kivett and W. Taylor. I had several conversations with the Vice President about moving the airplane, and at one time he considered moving it to Carswell Air Force Base and driving this distance. We also considered just moving it to another location at Love Field, and this is what I told SA Kivett to have them do, and to have enough fuel for cross-country flight. I told the Vice President that we would drive to the airport with he and Mrs. Johnson in separate cars; that I wanted him to stay down below window level; and that Mrs. Johnson would be accompanied by agents.

I had previously told ATSAIC Johns in the presence of the Vice President that he should go out of the hospital and get two cars on a stand-by, preferably unmarked police cars with police drivers who were familiar with Love Field, etc. I told him we would not return to the motorcade cars. I also told him that we would take an unknown route, and to make sure the drivers were thoroughly familiar with the area. ATSAIC Johns reported back that he had this set up.

The Vice President and I were both questioning the feasibility of leaving the hospital by the same way in which we had entered it. I told ATSAIC Johns to check on the various exits from which we might enter the cars and make a hasty evacuation, and to get cars at other exits if this could be worked out. While he was gone, ASAIC Kellerman and Mr. Ken O'Donnell came into the room. We learned that the President had died.

The Vice President was concerned about wanting to leave quickly as he had been advised to do, and which he now felt that he should, but he was also very much concerned about leaving without Mrs. Kennedy. It was finally agreed, at the advice of Mr. O'Donnell and others of us, that we would leave the hospital and go to AF-1 (President Kennedy's former airplane), with Mr. O'Donnell and others bringing Mrs. Kennedy as soon as they could remove the body. We were told that Mrs. Kennedy would not leave without President Kennedy's body.

While we were in this room, we were visited by Malcolm Kilduff of the White House Press Secretary's office. I also recall other White House staff people coming in, among whom I think were Mr. Larry O'Brien and, I believe, Mr. Dave Powers. I remained in the room with the Vice President at all times. Mrs. Johnson made some notes regarding the situation.

We started to leave the room and to evacuate the hospital, and since ATSAIC Johns had not returned, I grabbed one of the agents and told him to run ahead and get the cars ready, and we started out.

As soon as we got outside, we loaded into an unmarked police car—the driver of which was Jesse Curry, Chief of Police, Dallas. The Vice President and I got into the back seat. He got in first and slumped below window-level, and I got in after him. Congressman Homer Thornberry got in the front seat. I was seated behind Congressman Thornberry.

Mrs. Johnson was in the company of SA's Kivett and W. Taylor, and also Congressman Brooks. SA Glen Bennett had also been working very closely with our group since our arrival at the hospital, and he got in the car with Mrs. Johnson.

I ordered the driver (Chief Curry) to drive out and head for Love Field. Congressman Albert Thomas was walking, and seeing Congressman Thornberry, he called out for us to stop and pick him up. I don't believe he saw the Vice President. I told the driver to continue but by this time Congressman Thomas was by the side of the car. The Vice President ordered the driver to stop, whereupon we immediately took the Congressman aboard and proceeded again. Congressman Thomas got in the front seat with Congressman Thornberry being moved over closer to the driver. The Vice President then requested that Congressman Thornberry climb over into the back seat, which he did. Congressman Thornberry took a position on the window side behind the driver. We then had the Vice President in the middle of the back seat.

We were momentarily blocked by traffic which was coming onto the hospital access road—a delivery truck, I believe. Rapid police assistance got us through this obstacle, and we continued to the airport. We had motorcycle escort which began using sirens. We asked Chief Curry to stop them from using sirens, which he did by use of his radio.

When we approached the apron at Love Field, I called on my portable radio that we would board AF-1 rapidly and to be ready to receive us aboard. They replied that the plane was ready.

The Vice President and I practically ran up the ramp, followed by the others. I gave several orders to agents and Air Force crewmen about checkpoints at front and rear of plane, and pulling down all shades.

The Vice President went to the stateroom area, and Mrs. Johnson joined us there. Congressmen Thornberry, Brooks, and Thomas were also there. The Vice President told me to observe all of the events that I could, and to tell my agents to make notes, and also to tell any of his staff to do likewise. I passed these instructions on to my agents. I went everywhere the Vice President did, and was present when he called Attorney General Kennedy. He asked the Attorney General about the legal aspects of taking the oath of the President, such as when, where, and who should administer it. The Vice President placed calls to the office of Federal Judge Hughes, and he received a call from the Justice Department. He instructed Marie Fehmer to take down the wording of the oath. The Vice President had another phone conversation with the Attorney General. The Vice President advised me and others that Judge Sara Hughes would be coming to the plane, and I advised other agents and had them pass the word to local security officials. He also asked me to check on the status and location of Mrs. Kennedy and the President's body, and inform him of their estimated time of arrival.

Mrs. Kennedy and the President's body arrived at the plane ahead of Judge Hughes. The Vice President and Mrs. Johnson went to Mrs. Kennedy's bedroom to comfort her.

When Judge Hughes arrived, the oath was administered, and Cecil Stoughton, White House photographer, took photos of this event. His photos show most of those who witnessed this event within the stateroom and thru the passageway door leading to the front of the plane. There were some other witnesses who were not in the pictures since we were on the side of the stateroom where the photographer was. These persons included myself, an Air Force steward, and an agent who was stationed at the rear of the plane with the President's body.

The oath of office was administered at approximately 2:40 p.m., CST. Judge Hughes and Chief Curry disembarked from the plane, and the plane was airborne from Love Field, Dallas, at 2:47 p.m., CST, enroute to Andrews Air Force Base.

The foregoing account of events is true and accurate to the best of my recollections.

[signature]
Rufus W. Youngblood
Special Agent in Charge, 1-22

UNITED STATES GOVERNMENT   1-22-614.0
Memorandum

U.S. Secret Service
TO   : Chief   DATE: November 29, 1963
FROM   : ASAIC Thomas L. Johns—Vice Presidential Detail
SUBJECT: Statement regarding events in Dallas, Texas, on Friday, November 22, 1963.

This personal statement is being submitted at the direction of SAIC Rufus W. Youngblood, Vice Presidential Detail, office 1-22.

On Friday, November 22, 1963, I was assigned to the Vice Presidential Detail, office 1-22, and was working the movements of Vice President Johnson during his travels on this date with ASAIC Youngblood. ASAIC Youngblood was riding the Vice President's car on all movements and I worked the Vice Presidential follow-up car. Special Agent Warren W. Taylor was also working all Vice Presidential movements on this date, and was assigned to Mrs. Johnson. SA Taylor rode the Vice Presidential follow-up car when Mrs. Johnson rode in the car with the Vice President.

On this same date, the Vice President and party arrived Love Field, Dallas, Texas, at 11:35 a.m., CST. President Kennedy and party arrived Love Field at 11:38 a.m., CST, and at 11:50 a.m., CST, the Presidential and Vice Presidential motorcades departed Love Field en route to the Trade Mart where the President was to speak.

The motorcade and security personnel were as follows:

President's car
Secret Service follow-up car
Vice President's car: ASAIC Youngblood
Vice Presidential security car: ATSAIC Johns, and SA's Taylor and Kivett

The Vice Presidential security car was a 1963 or 1964 Mercury 4-door sedan driven by a man whom I believe to be an employee of the Texas Department of Public Safety. Mr. Cliff Carter, Aide to Vice President Johnson, was seated in the middle front seat; SA Kivett, who was the Vice Presidential Detail's advance man for Fort Worth–Dallas, was seated in the right front seat; SA Taylor was seated in the left rear seat; and I was seated in the right rear seat of this car.

The motorcade had passed through the downtown section of Dallas, and at approximately 12:35 p.m., CST, I heard two "shots," not knowing whether they were firecrackers, backfire, or gun shots. These two shots were approximately two or three seconds apart, and at this time we were on a slight downhill curve to the right. On the right-hand side of the motorcade from the street, a grassy area sloped upward to a small 2 or 3-foot concrete wall with sidewalk area. When the shots sounded, I was looking to the right and saw a man standing and then being thrown or hit to the ground, and this together with the shots made the situation appear dangerous to me. I estimate that the motorcade was going approximately 12 to 14 miles per hour at this time, and I jumped from the security car and started running for the Vice President's car. I felt that if there was danger due to the slow speed of the motorcade, I would be of more assistance and in a more proper location with the Vice President's car. Before I reached the Vice President's car, a third shot had sounded and the entire motorcade then picked up speed and I was left on the street at this point. I obtained a ride with White House movie men and joined the Vice President and ASAIC Youngblood at the Parkland Hospital.

I did not have any trouble keeping my balance when getting out of the security car, and it is on this that I base the estimated speed of the motorcade. Also, as the door of the security car opened to the rear, I lost some time in getting out and starting to run for the Vice President's car.

At no time did I see any details concerning persons in President Kennedy's car, as his security car was a large one with agents standing on the running boards and this obscured my view of the President's car.

I arrived at Parkland Hospital at approximately 12:45–12:50 p.m. and immediately joined ASAIC Youngblood with Vice President Johnson. In a few minutes I was directed by ASAIC Youngblood (at the request of Vice President Johnson) to go to ASAIC Kellerman and ask him to give a report on the condition of President Kennedy to Vice President Johnson. I found ASAIC Kellerman and conveyed this message to him, and then I returned to close proximity of Vice President Johnson. Mr. Ken O'Donnell came to the Vice President and advised that President Kennedy was in a "bad way" and advised Vice President Johnson to return to Washington, D.C. Those present with Vice President Johnson were Mrs. Johnson, Congressman Homer Thornberry, ASAIC Youngblood and, most of the time, Congressman Jack Brooks and Special Agents Jerry Kivett and Warren Taylor.

ASAIC Youngblood then requested that I obtain transportation (cars) for the Vice President, and to have drivers who were thoroughly familiar with any and all routes from the hospital to Love Field, and to have added police protection placed at Love Field. I went outside the hospital and spoke to an inspector—highest ranking police officer. We discussed cars for use of the Vice President, and possibly other members of his party, and he offered the use of several unmarked police cars. Chief Curry, Dallas Police, then joined us, and in further discussion they stated that they would send a large police detail to Love Field and "completely secure it." The Police Inspector himself then stated that he would drive Vice President Johnson to the airport.

I returned to the Vice President and ASAIC Youngblood and heard Ken O'Donnell inform Vice President Johnson that President Kennedy had died. To the best of my knowledge I believe that the Vice President learned from Mr. O'Donnell that Mrs. Kennedy was getting a casket, and would proceed as soon as she could to AF-1 for return to Washington, D.C., with President Johnson on the same plane.

At the request of ASAIC Youngblood, I then went and got the hospital building superintendent, and with him started looking and checking out another exit to use from the hospital. I was gone about ten minutes, and when I returned to last location in the hospital of the Vice President and ASAIC Youngblood, I learned that they had just departed the hospital en route to AF-1.

I went outside the hospital, and with Mr. Cliff Carter and Mr. Jack Valenti, staff member and friend of Vice President Johnson, respectively, and Captain Cecil Stoughton, I obtained a police car and driver, and all of us drove to Love Field, and I went aboard AF-1 and rejoined the Vice President and ASAIC Youngblood.

I then conferred with Col. James Swindal, pilot of AF-1, and a decision was made to remove seats from small rear compartment of AF-1 for use of Mrs. Kennedy and the casket containing President Kennedy's body. Also, passengers on board were identified and a manifest started at front entrance to AF-1, the rear entrance being reserved for Mrs. Kennedy.

Via radio-telephone, I then talked with SAIC Behn, White House Detail, Washington, D.C., and informed him that Mrs. Kennedy and the body of President Kennedy would accompany the Vice President back to Washington, D.C.

At approximately 2:30 p.m., Federal Judge Sarah Hughes came aboard AF-1, and gave the Presidential Oath of Office to Vice President Johnson, witnessed by all at the request of the Vice President.

AF-1 then departed Love Field, Dallas, Texas, immediately following the above, at 2:50 p.m., CST, en route for Andrews Air Force Base, Maryland, and I was aboard the plane.

[signature]
Thomas L. Johns
ASAIC, 1-22

UNITED STATES GOVERNMENT   1-22-614.0
Memorandum

U.S. Secret Service

TO   : Chief   DATE: Nov. 29, 1963

FROM   : SA Jerry D. Kivett—Vice Presidential Detail

SUBJECT: Statement regarding events in Dallas, Texas, on Friday, November, 1963.

I arrived Love Field, Dallas, Texas, at approximately 10:30 a.m., CST, from Fort Worth, Texas. I was driven from Fort Worth by SA Warner, Dallas Field Office, and SA Shannon was also in the car. SA Shannon had worked the previous midnight at Fort Worth and was catching a commercial flight from Dallas to Austin in order to work the following midnight at the LBJ Ranch.

Upon arrival at Love Field, I immediately contacted SA Lawson, and assisted him in advance arrangements prior to the arrival of the President and the Vice President. I assisted him in arranging motorcade cars and various other duties as he directed. I contacted the local representative of Continental Airlines and obtained four pillows to be used in case the President and his party wanted to sit on the back of the convertible. I was in constant contact with Art Bales as to the exact location and time of arrival of the Vice President and Presidential aircraft. I also conferred with Mr. Jack Peuterball (phonetic), political advance officer, on who was going to greet the Vice President when he arrived.

AF-2, with the Vice President and party aboard, arrived at 11:35 a.m., CST. I was at the foot of the ramp when Vice President and Mrs. Johnson and party disembarked. Vice Presidential Detail agents accompanying the Vice President were ASAIC Youngblood, ATSAIC Johns, and SA Taylor. Other White House Detail agents were also on board. The Vice President was greeted by the local committee consisting of 15 persons. ASAIC Youngblood and ATSAIC Johns remained in close proximity to the Vice President; SA Taylor remained in close proximity to Mrs. Johnson; and I was making sure that the Vice President and others moved to the proper area to greet the President, and also was keeping an eye on the Presidential plane so as to advise ASAIC Youngblood of its location.

AF-1, with the President and party aboard, arrived at 11:40 a.m., CST. The Vice President was at the foot of the ramp to greet President and Mrs. Kennedy when they descended the steps of the plane. After the President was greeted by the reception committee (same committee that greeted the Vice President), he walked past his automobile and up to the crowd which was behind a waist-high cyclone fence. He and Mrs. Kennedy began to shake hands with those assembled there. The Vice President and Mrs. Johnson also went past their cars to the fence and also started shaking hands. ASAIC Youngblood and ATSAIC Johns remained in close proximity to the Vice President, with SA Taylor in close proximity to Mrs. Johnson. I was alternating between remaining in close proximity to the Vice President and seeing that the Vice President's car and follow-up car were staying right behind the Presidential car and follow-up car as President and Mrs. Kennedy and Vice President and Mrs. Johnson moved down the fence to their left shaking hands.

When President and Mrs. Kennedy took their positions in their car, I assisted ASAIC Youngblood and ATSAIC Johns in getting Vice President and Mrs. Johnson in their car. The Vice Presidential car was a 1964 Lincoln convertible with the top down. The driver was Herschel Jacks, Department of Public Safety, and ASAIC Youngblood rode in the right front seat. In the back seat were Senator Yarborough, Mrs. Johnson, and the Vice President—left to right. As the motorcade started moving out, I ran alongside the Vice President's car for approximately 15 to 25 yards and then jumped into the Vice Presidential follow-up car, a 1963 Mercury 4-door sedan. This vehicle was driven by Joe Rich, Department of Public Safety, with Cliff Carter, Executive Assistant to the Vice President, in the middle front seat, and I was in the right front seat. SA Taylor and ATSAIC Johns were in the back seat, left and right sides respectively. The motorcade proceeded out of the airport and along the motorcade route.

The entire route was well lined with people, and on several occasions when the crowds were large, I opened the door of the vehicle to be prepared to get out if necessary.

During the entire parade route, I could not see the Presidential car well, but I could see the Presidential follow-up car and observed the agents standing on the running board.

On one occasion (exact location unknown), the Presidential car stopped and a few well-wishers went over to the car to shake his hand. The stop was very brief and none of the crowd made an attempt to shake the Vice President's hand. During this time I had the door open and was standing halfway out of the car, prepared to go up to the Vice President's car if necessary. During the motorcade, as we moved further downtown, the crowd became increasingly heavy and I noticed numerous persons watching the motorcade from windows of the various buildings we passed. All agents in the Vice Presidential follow-up car were closely observing the crowd both along the streets and watching from the windows.

Approximately three minutes before the assassination, in the very downtown part of Dallas, I observed a young white male approximately 21 years old, running toward the Presidential car. As he got alongside the Presidential follow-up car, SA Ready, who was working the right front running board, jumped down from the follow-up car and forcibly shoved this individual back into the crowd. We continued along the motorcade route and turned off Main Street. At this point, SA Lawson in the lead car gave a "5-minutes to Trade Mark signal"—moments later the first shot was heard.

See additional statement for actions during and after assassination.

[signature]
SA Jerry D. Kivett

STATEMENT BY JERRY D. KIVETT CONCERNING THE EVENTS OF NOVEMBER 22, 1963

November 29, 1963

I was riding in the Vice Presidential follow-up car immediately behind the Vice President's car and the third car behind the President's car. The Vice President's car was a 1964 steel gray Lincoln convertible, borrowed from Ford Motor Company, Dallas, Texas and was driven by Herschel D. Jacks, Texas Department, Public Safety. ASAIC Youngblood was riding in the right front seat of this vehicle. In the back seat were Senator Yarborough, Mrs. Johnson, and the Vice President, left to right. The Vice Presidential follow-up car was a 1963 yellow 4-door Mercury Sedan, also borrowed from Ford Motor Company, driven by Joe H. Rich, Texas Department, Public Safety. Cliff Carter, Executive Assistant to the Vice President, was seated in the middle of the front seat and I was seated in the right front seat. In the rear seat was SA Taylor and ATSAIC Johns, left to right respectively. The motorcade had just made a right turn from Main Street and then made an immediate left turn on to Elm Street. The motorcade was heading slightly downhill toward an underpass. As the motorcade was approximately 1/3 of the way to the underpass, traveling between 10 and 15 miles per hour, I heard a loud noise—someone hollered "What was that?" It sounded more like an extremely large firecracker, in that it did not seem to have the sharp report of a rifle. As I was looking in the direction of the noise, which was to my right rear, I heard another report—then there was no doubt in my mind what was happening—I looked toward the Vice Presidential car, and as I did so, I could see the spectators, approximately 25–50, scattering—some were falling to the ground, some were running up a small hill, and some were just standing there stunned—here I heard the third shot. I could see the President's car, and observed Mrs. Kennedy, who seemed to be standing up in the car and trying to get out. I was getting out of the car to get to the Vice President's car and assist Youngblood; I had reached for my gun but did not draw it for I could not tell where the shots were coming from; when I saw the Presidential car speed down the street, since I could not get to the Vice Presidential car, I fell back into the follow-up car and hollered to the driver to go-go, and the car lurched forward behind the Vice President's car. During this time, I don't know exactly what happened, but it seems that the Vice Presidential follow-up car was moving quite slow. ATSAIC Johns was out of the car (I have no knowledge of what actions he took), and as we moved out, ATSAIC Johns was left. SA Taylor was seated to my left rear, and since all the actions took place on my right, I do not know what action he took. Cliff Carter, to the best of my knowledge remained still in the middle front seat.

Once we left the area, I could see all three cars—the President's car (I could not see any principal party and could only see Clint Hill on the back of the car)—The follow-up car, with some agent holding the AR-15 pointed in the air—The Vice President's car (I could not see the Vice President, but could see ASAIC Youngblood lying over the area where he had been sitting—I don't recall seeing Mrs. Johnson or Senator Yarborough). We were traveling at a high rate of speed. ATSAIC Roberts said over the radio, and this is not a direct quote but to the best of my recollection—To the hospital—to the hospital, as fast as possible—Lawson, are we going to the hospital?—Hurry, he's hit—Then Roberts called to Youngblood, I answered since Youngblood was using Baker frequency with our follow-up car; however, I had a Charlie set in the follow-up car also. Roberts said to cover our man good, I replied that Youngblood had him covered—at this point Youngblood, who had switched his radio to Charlie, answered and stated that he had him covered and to take off, we were right behind them. It took approximately 4 minutes from the time the first shot was fired until we reached the hospital. As soon as we reached the hospital, ASAIC Youngblood and myself ran the Vice President into the Hospital and continued running with him until we reached an isolated room. SA Taylor immediately followed with Mrs. Johnson. As we were taking the Vice President into the hospital, Roberts informed him that the President had been shot and was critically injured and probably would die. Once inside the hospital, we had the Vice President and Mrs. Johnson in an isolated room. We pulled all window shades so as no one would know our exact location. At first it was the Vice President, Mrs. Johnson, Youngblood and myself. Moments later, Emory Roberts came in and said the President would not make it. A discussion followed as to what action would be taken and all agents were in agreement that we should leave the hospital as soon as possible, fly to Washington and go to the White House, which was the safest location for the Vice President to go. The Vice President asked for Congressman Homer Thornberry and Congressman Jack Brooks to join him in the isolated room, he also asked that someone go to get coffee for he and Mrs. Johnson. Cliff Carter who also had come into the room went to get the coffee. Roy Kellerman came into the room and discussed the President's condition with the Vice President. The Vice President did not want to leave the hospital immediately and fly to the White House because he said it would appear presumptuous on his part. ASAIC Youngblood told me to get in touch with Austin, Texas and Washington, D.C. and have agents assigned to the Vice President's daughters immediately. I located a phone which was being manned by a member of a telephone company, who had accompanied the Presidential party and who had an open line to the Signal Board in Washington. I asked first for Chief Rowley, then Chief Paterni and ended up talking to Chief Wildy. I told him to call Austin and have an agent assigned immediately to Lynda Bird Johnson and as she could probably be located at Kinsolving Dormitory, University of Texas. That an agent should also be assigned immediately to Lucy Baines Johnson, who could best be located at National Cathedral for Girls, Washington, D.C. Since I was talking to the Signal Board I asked for Austin, Texas. I talked to SA Paine, advised him to get an agent with Lynda as soon as possible. He put SA Lockwood on the phone and I told him to find Lynda and stay with her until he heard further word and that she was probably at Kinsolving Dormitory, University of Texas. Upon completing these calls, I went back to the room where the Vice President was.

Mrs. Johnson stated that she would like to visit Mrs. Kennedy and Mrs. Connally. Someone, I don't remember who, I think it was a member of the hospital staff, showed Mrs. Johnson to Mrs. Kennedy's location and to Mrs. Connally's location where she visited briefly with each. She was accompanied at all times by SA Taylor and myself. Upon returning to the isolated room where the Vice President was located, I overheard Ken O'Donald tell the Vice President that the President was dead. It was then decided to leave the hospital immediately. ASAIC Youngblood told me to get in touch with Air Force One to advise them to fuel for a cross country flight and to move to another part of the airport. I located a phone which was opened to the Dallas Signal Board and contacted Air Force One, cannot recall who I talked to. I advised them to refuel the plane for a cross country flight, and to move it to another location. I was advised that the plane was refueled and ready to go and that they were in the process of trying to locate another location. I told him to call me back as soon as they moved to a new location. I returned to the room where the Vice President was and Youngblood told me we are leaving right now. We exited from the hospital by the same room we had entered. SA Taylor and myself accompanied Mrs. Johnson, placed her in an unmarked police Sedan and drove immediately behind the car carrying the Vice President to the airport. A car of Secret Service agents followed directly behind us. This vehicle (the one Mrs. Johnson was in) was driven by an uniform police officer, name unknown, with SA

Taylor, SA Bennett, in the front seat; in the rear seat were Congressman Brooks, Mrs. Johnson, and myself, left to right. I requested Mrs. Johnson to crouch down in the seat so that she could not be seen from the outside, she did so immediately. Upon arrival to the airport (Love Field) SA Taylor and myself ran Mrs. Johnson up the ramp into the airplane. Upon instructions from ASAIC Youngblood, all window shades in the airplane were pulled down and check points were established at both doors leading to the Vice President's area of the airplane, (Air Force One). At first the Vice President was put in the State Room, i.e. where the beds were; however he said this was in bad taste and he moved up to the sitting room, i.e. where the table and television set are located. At first inside this area were the Vice President, Mrs. Johnson, Cliff Carter, Marie Fehmer, Jack Valenti, members of the Vice President's staff, Paul Glynn, Vice President's Air Force Valet, ASAIC Youngblood and myself. SA Taylor manned the check point at the front door leading to the State Room and SA Bennett manned the check point at the rear door leading to the State Room. There followed a series of conferences between the Vice President, Congressman Homer Thornberry, Congressman Jack Brooks, and Albert Thomas. The Vice President and the others in the State Room where also watching television accounts of the President's Assassination. I do not recall what necessarily was discussed and at one time or another various members of the White House staff came back to the State Room to talk to the Vice President. It was decided that the plane would remain and wait for Mrs. Kennedy and the President's body. Malcolm Kilduff asked me to inquire of the Vice President if he wanted any press to go back on the plane with him. I inquired of the Vice President wishes in this matter and he said yes, let me talk to Kilduff. I then asked Kilduff to come in and talk to the Vice President. About this time we received word that Mrs. Kennedy and the President's body were on the way. During the discussions that took place in the State Room, the Vice President stated that he had talked with the Attorney General and they agreed that the Vice President should take the oath of office of President of the United States as soon as possible. The Vice President added that he had been able to contact Judge Sarah T. Hughes and she would be at the plane in 10 minutes to administer the oath of office. About this time Mrs. Kennedy and the President's body arrived at the airplane. The Vice President and Mrs. Johnson attempted to console Mrs. Kennedy in the State Room where she was. It cleared of all personnel exception of Vice President, Mrs. Johnson, Mrs. Kennedy, ASAIC Youngblood, and a member or two of the White House staff, exactly who I cannot recall. Judge Hughes soon arrived and prepared to administer the oath of office. The Vice President invited all who wished to observe the proceedings into the State Room. I do not know exactly who was there, but to the best of my knowledge the following persons were there: Vice President, Mrs. Johnson, Mrs. Kennedy, Ken O'Donald, Dave Powers, Congressmen Brooks, Thomas, and Thornberry, Marie Fehmer, Elizabeth Carpenter, Cliff Carter, Jack Valenti, Paul Glynn, ASAIC Youngblood, ATSAIC Johns, myself, Mariam Smith of the United Press International and Captain Stoughton, White House photographer. The Vice President took the oath of office at approximately 2:40 PM in the airplane and it was airborne enroute to Washington, D.C., at 2:47 PM.

The foregoing account of events is to the best of my knowledge.

[signature]
Jerry D. Kivett
Special Agent

UNITED STATES GOVERNMENT   1-22-614.0
Memorandum

U.S. Secret Service
TO   : Chief   DATE: November 29, 1963
FROM   : SA Warren W. Taylor—Vice Presidential Detail
SUBJECT: Statement regarding events in Dallas, Texas, on Friday, November 22, 1963.

On Friday, November 22, 1963, I was working as a Special Agent with the Vice Presidential Detail, U.S. Secret Service, on a special assignment with Mrs. Johnson in Dallas, Texas, for the President's visit there.

At 11:35 a.m., CST, I arrived at Love Field, Dallas, Texas, aboard AF-2 with Vice President and Mrs. Johnson. Vice President and Mrs. Johnson disembarked from the plane and I remained in close proximity to Mrs. Johnson while she and the Vice President went over to a crowd awaiting the President's arrival behind a fence surrounding the field. Vice President and Mrs. Johnson were at the foot of the ramp upon which the President and Mrs. Kennedy disembarked from AF-1 at 11:38 a.m., CST. Again, I was in close proximity to Mrs. Johnson. President and Mrs. Kennedy and Vice President and Mrs. Johnson all went back to the area of the general public and again shook hands for a short period of time. At 11:50 a.m., CST, the Presidential and Vice Presidential motorcades departed Love Field, and at that time I was working the Vice Presidential follow-up car.

The automobile in which I was riding was a late model Ford 4-door sedan driven by an unknown man whom I was later told is an officer with the Texas Department of Public Safety. Special Agent Kivett was riding in the front right seat, and ATSAIC Johns was in the right rear seat. Mr. Cliff Carter, a member of the Vice President's staff, was riding in the middle front seat, and I was in the rear left seat.

On the way to the Trade Mart where the President was to speak, large crowds of people were along the side of the road, and as we entered the downtown area, I observed extremely large crowds along the streets and in all of the windows of large buildings on the route.

Our automobile had just turned a corner (the names of the streets are unknown to me) when I heard a bang which sounded to me like a possible firecracker—the sound coming from my right rear. Out of the corner of my eye and off slightly to the right rear of our car, I noticed what now seems to me might have been a short piece of streamer flying in the air close to the ground, but due to the confusion of the moment, I thought that it was a firecracker going off.

As a matter of course, I opened the door and prepared to get out of the car. In the instant that my left foot touched the ground, I heard two more bangs and realized that they must be gun shots. Also at that instant, the car paused slightly and I heard something over the radio to the effect that something or someone had been shot. At that moment, the car picked up speed and I pulled myself back into the car. During the aforementioned I also noticed that ATSAIC Johns had completely jumped out of our car, and as we sped away, I believe he was knocked to the ground and left in the street. I recall hearing SA Kivett telling the driver to "go, go, stay right behind the car." During all of the aforementioned, I could see ASAIC Youngblood, in the Vice President's car immediately in front of us, jump to the back seat and cover the Vice President.

I was not looking at the President's car at the time and did not notice his car until we were well on our way to Parkland Hospital. When I did point my attention to the President's car, I could only notice SA Hill, White House Detail, lying across the trunk lid of the President's car. At no time subsequent to the first shot did I ever see the President or what had happened to him.

In approximately three minutes from the time of the last shot, we arrived at Parkland Hospital, Dallas. When we arrived at the hospital, I jumped out of the follow-up car, grabbed Mrs. Johnson from her car, and took her as quickly as possible into the hospital, following the Vice President. We went immediately to what I believe was a room in the emergency section of the hospital—a large room divided into sections by curtains hanging from the ceiling to the floor.

Vice President and Mrs. Johnson, accompanied by ASAIC Youngblood and SA Kivett, went immediately to one corner of the room, and I proceeded to move a secretary and an unknown negro male, whom I believe was a patient, out into the hall. I drew all the blinds and checked the entrances to the room. Finding SA Glen Bennett, Protective Research Section, who was temporarily assigned to the White House Detail, stationed at the doors to the above-mentioned room, I stood by inside the room awaiting instructions. During our short stay in the hospital, SA Kivett and myself accompanied Mrs. Johnson to and from a third floor room where she spoke briefly to Mrs. John Connally, wife of the Governor of Texas. Also during our brief stay at the hospital, I was told by ATSAIC Roberts, White House Detail, to call the Dallas White House switchboard and have them notify AF-1 to prepare for an immediate takeoff. I complied with his order and approximately one-half hour later the Vice President and Mrs. Johnson departed the hospital.

SA Kivett and myself stayed with Mrs. Johnson as we left the hospital and we jumped into an unmarked police car which happened to be standing by. The Vice President, accompanied by ASAIC Youngblood, jumped into another car, and we proceeded to the Dallas airport and AF-1. Also riding in the car with Mrs. Johnson, SA Kivett and myself were SA Glen Bennett and Congressman Jack Brooks. An unknown police officer was driving our car.

An escort of two motorcycles accompanied the above two vehicles to Love Field without incident. When we arrived at Love Field, we immediately boarded AF-1 and I maintained a checkpoint in the forward compartment of the aircraft until the aircraft was airborne at approximately 2:50 p.m., CST. Between the time we boarded AF-1 and the time of takeoff, the Vice President was sworn in as President in his cabin. There were no unusual incidents during that period of time.

[signature]
Warren W. Taylor
Special Agent, 1-22

(Warren Commission, Vol. XVIII, pages 722–784)

Appendix B

1968 Panel Review of Photographs, X-Ray Films, Documents and Other Evidence Pertaining to the Fatal Wounding of President John F. Kennedy on November 22, 1963, in Dallas, Texas

At the request of The Honorable Ramsay Clark, Attorney General of the United States, four physicians (hereafter sometimes referred to as The Panel) met in Washington, DC on February 26 and 27 to examine various photographs, X-ray films, documents and other evidence pertaining to the death of President Kennedy, and to evaluate their significance in relation to the medical conclusions recorded in the Autopsy Report on the body of President Kennedy signed by Commander J. J. Humes, Medical Corps, US Navy; Commander J. Thornton Boswell, Medical Corps, US Navy and Lt. Col. Pierre A. Finck, Medical Corps, US Army and in the Supplemental Report signed by Commander Humes.

These appear in the Warren Commission Report at pages 538 to 545.

The four physicians constituting The Panel were:

1) Carnes, William H., MD, Professor of Pathology, University of Utah, Salt Lake City, UT, Member of Medical Examiner's Commission, State of Utah, nominated by Dr. J. E. Wallace Sterling, President of Stanford University.

2) Fisher, Russell S., MD, Professor of Forensic Pathology, University of Maryland and Chief Medical Examiner of the State of Maryland, Baltimore, MD, nominated by Dr. Oscar B. Hunter, Jr., President of the College of American Pathologists.

3) Morgan, Russell H., MD, Professor of Radiology, School of Medicine and Professor of Radiological Science, School of Hygiene and Public Health, The Johns Hopkins University, Baltimore, MD, nominated by Dr. Lincoln Gordon, President of The Johns Hopkins University.

4) Mortiz, Alan R., MD, Professor of Pathology, Case Western Reserve University, Cleveland, OH and former Professor of Forensic Medicine, Harvard University, nominated by Dr. John A. Hannah, President of Michigan State University.

Bruce Bromley, a member of the New York Bar who had been nominated by the President of the American Bar Association and thereafter requested by the Attorney General to act as legal counsel to The Panel, was present throughout The Panel's examination of the exhibits and collaborated with The Panel in the preparation of this report.

No one of the undersigned has had any previous connection with prior investigations of, or reports on this matter, and each has acted with complete and unbiased independence, free of preconceived views as to the correctness of the medical conclusions reached in the 1963 Autopsy Report and Supplementary Report.

PREVIOUS REPORTS

The Autopsy Report stated that X-rays had been made of the entire body of the deceased. The Panel's inventory disclosed X-ray films of the entire body except for the lower arms, wrists and hands and the lower legs, ankles and feet.

The Autopsy Report also described the decedent's wounds as follows:

"The fatal missile entered the skull above and to the right of the external occipital protuberance. A portion of the projectile traversed the cranial cavity in a posterior-anterior direction (see lateral skull roentgenograms) depositing minute particles along its path. A portion of the projectile made its exit through the parietal bone on the right carrying with it portions of cerebrum, skull and scalp. The two wounds of the skull combined with the force of the missile produced extensive fragmentation of the skull, laceration of the superior sagittal sinus and of the right cerebral hemisphere.

The other missile entered the right superior posterior thorax above the scapula and traversed the soft tissues of the suprascapular and the supraclavicular portions of the base of the right side of the neck. This missile produced contusions of the right apical parietal pleura and of the apical portion of the right upper lobe of the lung. The missile contused the strap muscles of the right side of the neck, damaged the trachea and made its exit through the anterior surface of the neck. As far as can be ascertained, this missile struck no bony structures in its path through the body.

In addition, it is our opinion that the wound of the skull produced such extensive damage to the brain as to preclude the possibility of the deceased surviving this injury."

The medical conclusions of the Warren Commission Report (p. 19) concerning President Kennedy's wounds are as follows:

"The nature of the bullet wounds suffered by President Kennedy and the location of the car at the time of the shots establish that the bullets were fired from above and behind the Presidential limousine, striking the President as follows:

President Kennedy was first struck by a bullet which entered at the back of his neck and exited through the lower front portion of his neck, causing a wound which would not necessarily have been lethal. The President was struck a second time by a bullet which entered the right rear portion of his head, causing a massive and fatal wound."

INVENTORY OF MATERIAL EXAMINED

Black and White and Colored Prints and Transparencies

Head viewed from above
#5(9JB), 8(7JB), 13(6JB), 16(10JB), 32, 33, 34, 35, 36, 37

Head viewed from right and above to include part of face, neck, shoulder and upper chest
#3(14JB), 4(13JB), 11(6JB), 12(5JB), 26, 27, 28, 40, 41

Head and neck viewed from left side
#6(3JB), 15(4JB), 17(2JB), 18(1JB), 29, 30, 31

Head viewed from behind
#7(16JB), 14(15JB), 42, 43

Cranial cavity with brain removed viewed from above and in front
#1(18JB), 2(17JB), 44, 45

Back of body including neck
#9(11JB), 10(12JB), 38, 39

Brain viewed from above
#50, 51, 52

Brain viewed from below
#46, 47, 48, 49

The black and white and color negatives corresponding to the above were present and there were also seven black and white negatives of the brain without corresponding prints. These were numbered 19 through 25(JTB) and appeared to represent the same views as #46 through 52. All of the above were listed in a memorandum of transfer, located in the National Archives, and dated Apr. 26, 1965.

X-ray Films

(The films bore the number 21296 and an inscription indicating that they have been made at the US Naval Hospital, Bethesda, MD on 11/22/63.)

Skull, A-P view
#1

Skull, left lateral
#2, 3

Skull, fragments of
#4, 5, 6

Thoracolumbar region, A-P view
#7, 11

Chest, A-P view
#9

Right hemithorax, shoulder and upper arm, A-P view
#8

Left hemithorax, shoulder and upper arm, A-P view
#10

Pelvis, A-P view
#13

Lower femurs and knees, A-P view
#12

Upper legs, A-P view
#14

Bullets

CES 399—A whole bullet

CE 567—Portion of nose of a bullet

CE 569—Portion of base segment of a bullet

CE 840—3 fragments of lead

Motion Picture Films

CE 904—Zapruder film

CE 905—Nix film

CE 906—Muchmore film

Series of single frames (215 through 334) from Zapruder film

Clothing

CE 393—Suit coat

CE 394—Shirt

CE 395—Neck tie

Documents

The Warren Commission's Report and the accompanying volumes of Exhibits and Hearings. (Study of these Documents was limited to those portions deemed pertinent by The Panel.)

EXAMINATION OF PHOTOGRAPHS OF HEAD

Photographs 7, 14, 42, and 43 show the back of the head, the contours of which have been grossly distorted by extensive fragmentation of the underlying calvarium. There is an elliptical penetrating wound of the scalp situated near the midline and high above the hairline. The position of this wound corresponds to the hole in the skull seen in the lateral X-ray film #2.(See description of X-ray films.) The long axis of this wound corresponds to the long axis of the skull. The wound was judged to be approximately six millimeters wide and 15 millimeters long. The margin of this wound shows an ill-defined zone of abrasion.

Photographs 5, 8, 13, 16, 32, 33, 34, 35, 36 and 37 show the top of the head with multiple gaping irregularly stellate lacerations of the scalp over the right parietal, temporal and frontal regions.

Photographs 1, 2, 44 and 45 show the frontal region of the skull and a portion of the internal aspect of the back of the skull. Due to lack of contrast of structures portrayed and lack of clarity of detail in these photographs, the only conclusion reached by The Panel from study of this series was that there was no existing bullet defect in the supraorbital region of the skull.

Photographs 46, 47, 48 and 49 are of the inferior aspect of the brain and show extensive deformation with laceration and fragmentation of the right cerebral hemisphere. Irregularly shaped areas of contusion with minor loss of cortex are seen on the inferior surface of the first left temporal convolution. The orbital gyri on the left show contusion with some underlying loss of cortex. The sylvian fissure on the right side has been opened, revealing a rolled-up mass of arachnoid and blood clot which is dark brown to black in color. The mid-temporal region is depressed and its surface lacerated. The peduncles have been lacerated, probably incident to the removal of the contents from the cranium.

Photographs 50, 51 and 52 show the superior aspect of the brain. The left cerebral hemisphere is covered by a generally-intact arachnoid with evidence of subarachnoid hemorrhage especially over the parietal and frontal gyri and in the sulci. The right cerebral hemisphere is extensively lacerated. It is transected by a broad canal running generally in a posteroanterior direction and to the right of the midline. Much of the roof of this canal is missing, as are most of the overlying frontal and parietal gyri. In the central portion of its base, there can be seen a gray-brown, rectangular structure measuring approximately 13 × 20 mm. Its identity cannot be established by The Panel. In addition to the superficial and deep cortical destruction, it can be seen that the corpus callosum is widely torn in the midline.

These findings indicate that the back of the head was struck by a single bullet travelling at high velocity, the major portion of which passed forward through the right cerebral hemisphere, and which produced an explosive type of fragmentation of the skull and laceration of the scalp. The appearance of the entrance wound in the scalp is consistent with its having been produced by a bullet similar to that of exhibit CE 399. The photographs do not disclose where this bullet emerged from the head, although those showing the interior of the cranium with the brain removed indicate that it did not emerge from the supraorbital region. Additional information regarding the course of the bullet is presented in the discussion of the X-ray films.

Examination of photographs of anterior and posterior views of thorax, and anterior, posterior and lateral views of neck (Photographs 3, 4, 6, 9, 10, 11, 12, 15, 17, 18, 26, 27, 28, 29, 30, 31, 38, 39, 40, 41).

There is an elliptical penetrating wound of the skin of the back located approximately 15 cm. medial to the right acromial process, 5 cm. lateral to the mid-dorsal line and 14 cm. below the right mastoid process. This wound lies approximately 5.5

cm. below a transverse fold in the skin of the neck. This fold can also be seen in a lateral view of the neck which shows an anterior tracheotomy wound. This view makes it possible to compare the levels of these two wounds in relation to that of the horizontal plane of the body.

A well-defined zone of discoloration of the edge of the back wound, most pronounced on its upper and outer margins, identifies it as having the characteristics of the entrance wound of a bullet. The wound with its marginal abrasion measures approximately 7 mm. in width by 10 mm. in length. The dimensions of this cutaneous wound are consistent with those of a wound produced by a bullet similar to that which constitutes exhibit CE 399.

At the site of and above the tracheotomy incision in the front of the neck, there can be identified the upper half of the circumference of a circular cutaneous wound the appearance of which is characteristic of that of the exit wound of a bullet. The lower half of this circular wound is obscured by the surgically produced tracheotomy incision which transects it. The center of the circular wound is situated approximately 9 cm. below the transverse fold in the skin of the neck described in a preceding paragraph. This indicates that the bullet which produced the two wounds followed a course downward and to the left in its passage through the body.

EXAMINATION OF X-RAY FILMS

The films submitted included: an anteroposterior film of the skull (#1), two left lateral views of the skull taken in slightly different projections (#2 and 3), three views of a group of three separate bony fragments from the skull (#4, 5 and 6), two anteroposterior views of the thoracolumbar region of the trunk (#7 and 11), one anteroposterior view of the right hemithorax, shoulder and upper arm (#8), one anteroposterior view of the chest (#9), one anteroposterior view of the left hemithorax, shoulder and upper arm (#10), one anteroposterior view of the lower femurs and knees (#12), one anteroposterior view of the pelvis (#13) and one anteroposterior view of the upper legs (#14).

Skull

There are multiple fractures of the bones of the calvarium bilaterally. These fractures extend into the base of the skull and involve the floor of the anterior fossa on the right side as well as the middle fossa in the midline. With respect to the right frontoparietal region of the skull, the traumatic damage is particularly severe with extensive fragmentation of the bony structures from the midline of the frontal bone anteriorly to the vicinity of the posterior margin of the parietal bone behind. Above, the fragmentation extends approximately 25 mm. across the midline to involve adjacent portions of the left parietal bone; below, the changes extend into the right temporal bone. Throughout this region, many of the bony pieces have been displaced outward; several pieces are missing.

Distributed through the right cerebral hemisphere are numerous small, irregular metallic fragments, most of which are less than 1 mm. in maximum dimension. The majority of these fragments lie anteriorly and superiorly. None can be visualized on the left side of the brain and none below a horizontal plane through the floor of the anterior fossa of the skull.

On one of the lateral films of the skull (#2), a hole measuring approximately 8 mm. in diameter on the outer surface of the skull and as much as 20 mm. on the internal surface can be seen in profile approximately 100 mm. above the external occipital protuberance. The bone of the lower edge of the hole is depressed. Also there is, embedded in the outer table of the skull close to the lower edge of the hole, a large metallic fragment which on the anteroposterior film (#1) lies 25 mm. to the right of the midline. This fragment as seen in the latter film is round and measures 6.5 mm. in diameter. Immediately adjacent to the hole on the internal surface of the skull, there is localized elevation of the soft tissues. Small fragments of bone lie within portions of these tissues and within the hole itself. These changes are consistent with an entrance wound of the skull produced by a bullet similar to that of exhibit CE 399.

The metallic fragments visualized within the right cerebral hemisphere fall into two groups. One group consists of relatively large fragments, more or less randomly distributed. The second group consists of finely divided fragments, distributed in a posteroanterior direction in a region 45 mm. long and 8 mm. wide. As seen on lateral film #2, this formation overlies the position of the coronal suture; its long axis, if extended posteriorly, passes through the above-mentioned hole. It appears to end anteriorly immediately below the badly fragmented frontal and parietal bones just anterior to the region of the coronal suture.

The foregoing observations indicate that the decedent's head was struck from behind a single projectile. It entered the occipital region 25 mm. to the right of the midline and 100 mm. above the external occipital protuberance. The projectile fragmented on entering the skull, one major section leaving a trail of fine metallic debris as it passed forward and laterally to explosively fracture the right frontal and parietal bones as it emerged from the head.

In addition to the foregoing, it is noteworthy that there is no evidence of projectile fragments in the left cerebral tissues or in the right cerebral hemisphere below a horizontal plane passing through the floor of the anterior fossa of the skull. Also, although the fractures of the calvarium extend to the left of the midline and into the anterior and middle fossae of the skull, no bony defect, such as one created by a projectile either entering or leaving the head, is seen in the calvarium to the left of the midline or in the base of the skull. Hence, it is not reasonable to postulate that a projectile passed through the head in a direction other than that described above.

Of further note, when the X-ray films of the skull were presented to The Panel, film #1 had been damaged in two small regions by what appears to be the heat from a spotlight. Also, on film #2, a pair of converging pencil lines had been drawn on the film. Neither of these artifacts interfered with the interpretation of the films.

Neck Region

Films #8, 9 and 10 allowed visualization of the lower neck. Subcutaneous emphysema is present just to the right of the cervical spine immediately above the apex of the right lung. Also, several small metallic fragments are present in this region. There is no evidence of fracture of either scapula or of the calvicles, or of the ribs or of any of the cervical and thoracic vertebrae.

The foregoing observations indicate that the pathway of the projectile involving the neck was confined to a region to the right of the spine and superior to a plane passing through the upper margin of the right scapula, the apex of the right lung and the right clavicle. Any other pathway would have almost certainly fractured one or more bones of the right shoulder girdle and thorax.

Other Regions Studied

No bullets or fragments of bullets are demonstrated in X-rayed portions of the body other than those described above. On film #13, a small round opaque structure, a little more than 1 mm. in diameter, is visible just to the right of the midline at the level of the sacral segment of the spine. Its smooth characteristics are not similar to those of the projectile fragments seen in the X-rays of the skull and neck.

EXAMINATION OF THE CLOTHING

Suit Coat (CE 393)

A ragged oval hole about 15 mm. long (vertically) is located 5 cm. to the right of the midline in the back of the coat at a point about 12 cm. below the upper edge of the coat collar. A smaller ragged hole, which is located near the midline and about 4 cm. below the upper edge of the collar, does not overlie any corresponding damage to the shirt or skin and appears to be unrelated to the wounds or their causation.

Shirt (CE 394)

A ragged hole about 10 mm. long vertically and corresponding to the first one described in the coat, is located 2.5 cm. to the right of the midline in the back of the shirt at a point 14 cm. below the upper edge of the collar. Two linear holes 15 mm. long are found in the overlapping hems of the front of the shirt in a position corresponding to the place where the knot of the necktie would normally be.

Tie (CE 395)

In the front component of the knot of the tie in the outer layer of fabric, a ragged tear about 5 mm. in maximum diameter is located 2.5 cm. below the upper edge of the knot and to the left of the midline.

DISCUSSION

The information disclosed by the joint examination of the foregoing exhibits by the members of The Panel supports the following conclusions:

The decedent was wounded by two bullets, both of which entered his body from behind.

One bullet struck the back of the decedent's head well above the external occipital protuberance. Based upon the observation that he was leaning forward with his head turned obliquely to the left when this bullet struck, the photographs and X-rays indicate that it came from a site above and slightly to his right. This bullet fragmented after entering the cranium, one major piece of it passing forward and laterally to produce an explosive fracture of the right side of the skull as it emerged from the head.

The absence of metallic fragments in the left cerebral hemisphere or below the level of the frontal fossa on the right side together with the absence of any holes in the skull to the left of the midline or in its base and the absence of any penetrating injury of the left hemisphere, eliminate with reasonable certainty the possibility of a projectile having passed through the head in any direction other than from back to front as described in preceding sections of this report.

The other bullet struck the decedent's back at the right side of the base of the neck between the shoulder and spine and emerged from the front of his neck near the midline. The possibility that this bullet might have followed a pathway other than one passing through the site of the tracheotomy wound was considered. No evidence for this was found. There is a track between the two cutaneous wounds as indicated by subcutaneous emphysema and small metallic fragments on the X-rays and the contusion of the apex of the right lung and laceration of the trachea described in the Autopsy Report. In addition, any path other than one between the two cutaneous wounds would almost surely have been intercepted by bone and the X-ray films show no bony damage in the thorax or neck.

The possibility that the path of the bullet through the neck might have been more satisfactorily explored by the insertion of a finger or probe was considered. Obviously, the cutaneous wound in the back was too small to permit the insertion of a finger. The insertion of a metal probe would have carried the risk of creating a false passage in part, because of the changed relationship of muscles at the time of autopsy and in part because of the existence of postmortem rigidity. Although the precise path of the bullet could undoubtedly have been demonstrated by complete dissection of the soft tissue between the two cutaneous wounds, there is no reason to believe that the information disclosed thereby would alter significantly the conclusions expressed in this report.

SUMMARY

Examination of the clothing and of the photographs and X-rays taken at autopsy reveal that President Kennedy was struck by two bullets fired from above and behind him, one of which traversed the base of the neck on the right side without striking bone and the other of which entered the skull from behind and exploded its right side.

The photographs and X-rays discussed herein support the above-quoted portions of the original Autopsy Report and the above-quoted medical conclusions of the Warren Commission Report.

WILLIAM H. CARNES, MD
RUSSELL S. FISHER, MD
RUSSELL H. MORGAN, MD
ALAN R. MORITZ, MD

Appendix C

Excerpts from Interviews Conducted by the House Select Committee on Assassinations with Drs. Humes, Petty, Angel, Baden, Boswell, and Loquvam

From the Appendix to the Hearings before the Select Committee on Assassinations of the U.S. House of Representatives, Ninety-fifth Congress, Second Session, March 1979, Volume VII, pages 243–255, U.S. Government Printing Office, 1979.

Dr. HUMES. There was what we interpreted to be an exit wound, in the location to which I point. The bone that would correspond and complete that circle or ellipse, that might have been made by that exit wound, was missing at the time we began the examination. Later on that evening, several hours into the evening, we were presented with another fragment of bone, not the one that you are examining now, and that fragment had a corresponding semicircular defect which almost completed this, what we interpreted to be an exit wound, but not quite. And we never had the privilege of examining the fragments or photographs of this fragment that you now examined until this afternoon, and I was unaware of its existence until about 3 weeks ago. . . .

Dr. PETTY. Dr. Angel, let me show you also this X-ray film of the three fragments that were separate and detached from the body which had been X-rayed here. One of these three fragments—the larger of the three—is the one that apparently helped complete a portion of an outshoot wound, is that correct, Dr. Humes? . . .

Dr. ANGEL. I would have guessed that it might be. Again, I don't see any meningeal vessel markings, but if this exit wound is here and the coronal suture is going up like that, that's conceivable. . . .

Dr. ANGEL. Right. Well, this then could be frontal perfectly well. It doesn't show the meningeal markings, and that's what made me unhappy about it being, well— photo makes more sense—in that case the exit wound must be not very far above the right or near the right pterion, I would think. . . .

Dr. ANGEL. Well, this must be well forward then on the frontal bone, I was interpreting it as being—this itself as being near the pterion.

Dr. BADEN. Yet here is the gap.

Dr. HUMES. That is not frontal bone where that semicircle is—it's either temporal or parietal bone, Dr. Angel.

Dr. ANGEL. I don't see how it can be. That's what it looks like to me.

Dr. HUMES. That's exactly what it is.

Dr. ANGEL. In that case, I'm puzzled by the missing bone here and the angles. Is this to be placed more like this? Now this piece could fit on here and the parietal piece could fit behind that, this piece could. . . .

Dr. ANGEL. I think so, yes. I thought perhaps this was a little more tilted.
Dr. PETTY. Well, perhaps like that.
Dr. HUMES. Negative, I don't think that's true.
Dr. ANGEL. What's bothering me is what part of the flesh is that?
Dr. PETTY. That's the cheek, the right cheek.
Dr. ANGEL. If that's the right cheek then it can't be—has to be more or less.
Dr. PETTY. Yeah.
Dr. ANGEL. It's really hard to be sure, square this with the X-ray which shows so much bone lost in this right frontal area. . . .

Dr. ANGEL. It's not too—that would be just about at the hairline or just above it—and then in front of the temporal line, which I couldn't see, that was what was bothering me. And I couldn't see any temporal line here, and if the temporal is—if this is really the forehead, this scalp directed down as it ordinarily would be, then that makes sense.
Dr. PETTY. I believe it is the forehead, and the scalp is reflected down.
Dr. ANGEL. Yeah. I think that makes sense.
Dr. PETTY. Dr. Humes, would you buy that here is the scalp of photograph No. 44 and reflected down over the face? Right here?
Dr. HUMES. Yes.
Dr. PETTY. And that this then really could very well be the frontal portion?
Dr. HUMES. Right. Now I'm much happier. I will buy that completely. That's where that was.
Dr. PETTY. OK, well—this makes more sense to me.
Dr. HUMES. We reflected the scalp here. This is the exit wound where I thought it was. This is the back of his head here. This is the back of his shoulder.
Dr. PETTY. These two are lined up just about right now. See, this notch is pointing in the same direction here, and this would be in the frontal area and anterior to the coronal suture in all probability. . . .

Dr. PETTY. So that placing the outshoot wound in the right frontal bone toward the coronal suture is probably about where it was.
Dr. HUMES. Uh-huh. . . .

Dr. BADEN. Could I interrupt 1 second? Dr. Angel has to go at this point, but in summary, you are pointing to the skull. The X-rays and the photographs and the X-ray of fragments of bone that was taken by Dr. Humes during the autopsy would indicate that the exit perforation is where?
Dr. ANGEL. Along in here I think, above the temporal line, and that triangular fragment I think would fit from—just short of the fragment down to the edge of the exit perforation and then across this way, fitting in as sort of a triangle in the upper part of the frontal—so I think that's the best fit that I could estimate from seeing the X-rays.
Dr. BADEN. And this would place the exit gunshot wound just anterior and almost incorporated into the lateral aspect of the coronal suture line.
Dr. ANGEL. A little in front of it, yes.
Dr. BADEN. Then it's slightly in front of and just superior to the temporal bone.
Dr. ANGEL. Apparently above the hairline. His hairline was fairly low; he wasn't getting bald like me. So, I think an exit wound about there would fit, then, the fragment that you have.
Dr. BADEN. Just anterior to the coronal suture line?
Dr. ANGEL. Just anterior to the coronal suture line, yes. Well above pterion, far above pterion near the point where the temporal line crosses the coronal suture.
Dr. BADEN. Do you have a name for it?
Dr. ANGEL. Stephanion. . . .

Dr. BOSWELL. Well, this was an attempt to illustrate the magnitude of the wound again. And as you can see it's 10 centimeters from right to left, 17 centimeters from posterior to anterior. This was a piece of 10 centimeter bone that was fractured off of the skull and was attached to the under surface of the skull. There were fragments attached to the skull or to the scalp and all the three major flaps. I guess the—I'm not sure in retrospect what I meant by that. . . .

Dr. DAVIS . . . Now, there is radiopaque material, some of which appears to be even exterior, at least in this view, with continuation of radiopaque fragments in the vertex part of the interior of the head, and also continues straight ahead, and I think there's some more down here in the mid-posterior area. So I think all of us who have done a fair number of investigations like this are well aware that a bullet can split into fragments and one fragment can be deflected outward, another fragment can be deflected inward and slightly upward, and even a third fragment can go straight. There's all sorts of things can happen with bullets when they strike in this manner. I think I can see radiopaque trails going up which could reconcile the testimony. . . .

Dr. DAVIS. What I'm saying—what I'm inferring: in the absence of photographs and specific measurements, we could only conjecture as to how long the tunneling is, but I would envision this as a tunneling first and then entry into the skull.

Dr. LOQUVAM. Gentlemen, may I say something?

Dr. DAVIS. Yes.

Dr. LOQUVAM. I don't think this discussion belongs in this record.

Dr. PETTY. All right.

Dr. HUMES. I agree.

Dr. LOQUVAM. We have no business recording this. This is for us to decide between ourselves; I don't think this belongs on this record.

Dr. PETTY. Well, we have to say something about our feeling as to why we're so interested in that one particular area.

Dr. HUMES. Could I make a comment that I think would be helpful to you, and you can throw out anything I say or whatever? But I feel obligated to make a certain interjection at this point, having heard this theory which I hadn't heard from the committee because I didn't pay that much attention quite frankly. Our attention was obviously directed to what we understood and thought to be clearly a wound of entrance. If such a fragment were to have detached itself from the main mass of the missile, it would have to be a relatively small fragment because the size of the defect in the skull which approximated this point was almost identical with the size of the defect in the skin. Do you follow that line of reasoning?

Dr. PETTY. Yes, that makes sense. I mean, I've seen the same thing.

Dr. DAVIS. I've seen the same thing—bothers me a bit—part of that casing comes off.

Dr. COE. The reason we are so interested in this, Dr. Humes, is because other pathologists have interpreted the——

Dr. LOQUVAM. I don't think this belongs in the damn record.

Dr. HUMES. Well, it probably doesn't.

Dr. LOQUVAM. You guys are nuts. You guys are nuts writing this stuff. It doesn't belong in that damn record.

Dr. BADEN. I think the only purpose of its being in the record is to explain to Dr. Humes what——

Dr. LOQUVAM. Why not turn off the record and explain to him and then go back and talk again.

Dr. BADEN. Well, our problem is not to get our opinions, but to get his opinions.

Dr. LOQUVAM. All right then, keep our opinions off. Here's Charles and Joe talking like mad in the damn record, and it doesn't belong in it. Sorry.

Dr. BADEN. Dr. Humes, realizing our concerns, if there is anything that you or Dr. Boswell can say that can help clarify any further the entrance wound and tract of the bullet in the head, we would be most appreciative.

Dr. HUMES. I think we're at a distinct disadvantage because, as I said, when we cataloged the photographs and numbered them, and spent half a day or day to do it, I'll confess to possibly even overlooking the area to which you gentlemen, and apparently someone else, has directed attention. I would not attempt to make an interpretation of what it represents because I can't at this point. . . .

Dr. BADEN. But in essence you said, as you indicated before, your main goal at the time you did the autopsy was to determine what happened to the President, and the bottom line for you then, as it is now, having reviewed everything and discussed everything, essentially two gunshot wounds from behind struck the President.

Dr. HUMES. Correct.

Dr. BADEN. Now, there may be, as we're going over the photographs and X-rays and all, some room for discussion about precise points, but you feel the essential findings are two gunshot wounds from behind and from above, I take it, or just from behind?

Dr. HUMES. I think behind is probably the most one can say from the anatomic findings.

Appendix D

Trajectory Analysis from the House Select Committee on Assassinations Hearings

(d) Conclusions[3]

(123) *Kennedy's head wounds.*—The bullet that caused Kennedy's head wounds at Zapruder frame 312 came from a point 29° to the right of true north from the President. The bullet was descending at an angle of 16° below horizontal as it approached him. This trajectory intercepted the plane of the Texas School Book Depository approximately 11 feet west of the southeast corner of the building at a point 15 feet above the sixth floor windowsills.

(124) *Kennedy's back and neck wounds.*—The bullet that caused President Kennedy's back and neck wounds came from a point 26° to the right of true north from the President. It was descending at an angle of 21° below horizontal as it approached him. Extending this trajectory from the position President Kennedy occupied at the time of Zapruder frame 190, the trajectory intercepted the plane of the Texas School Book Depository approximately 11 feet west of the southeast corner and 2 feet lower than the sixth floor windowsill.

(125) *Kennedy neck and Connally back wounds.*—The bullet which caused President Kennedy's neck wound and Governor Connally's back wound came from a point of 27° to the right of true north from the President and was descending at an angle of 25° below horizontal.

(126) Given the position of the two men at the time of Zapruder frame 190, the trajectory intercepted the plane of the Texas School Book Depository 2 feet west of the southeast corner and 9 feet above the sixth floor windowsill. Because this trajectory falls within the trajectory range established when President Kennedy's back-neck wounds are used as the reference points for the trajectory line, the Panel concludes that the relative alinement of President Kennedy and Governor Connally within the limousine is consistent with the single bullet theory. Further, since each of these trajectories intersects the plane of the Texas School Book Depository in the vicinity of the southeast corner of the sixth and seventh floors, it is highly probable that the bullets were fired from a location within this section of the building.*

(e) Analysis

(1) The head wound case**

(127) To determine this trajectory, the Panel first had to locate the entrance and exit head wounds as precisely as possible. Figures II-6 and II-7 [see drawing 7] show

---

[3]Explanatory diagrams supporting these conclusions are set forth in the analysis section of this report.

*The above conclusions differ to some extent from the testimony given by Thomas N. Canning before the House Select Committee on Assassinations on Sept. 12, 1978; in each case, the differences reflect new information or analysis resulting from work concluded subsequent to the presentation of preliminary findings at the hearing.

**The interpretation of the head wounds used in defining trajectory reported in testimony on Sept. 12, 1978 differs from this report because the final illustration from the Forensic Pathology Panel showed the exit wound to be 1 centimeter lower than the entrance, rather than level with it as had been concluded earlier. Thus, the resulting trajectory is somewhat steeper.

where the fatal bullet entered the back of President Kennedy's head at a point 9.0 centimeters above the external occipital protuberance. (45) This distance was measured on postmortem X-rays from point to point. The entry point is 1.8 centimeters to the right of the midplane of his skull. The bullet passed forward through his head and exited at the right coronal suture at a point 11 centimeters forward of the entry wound and 5.5 centimeters to the right of the midplane. This exit point was 1 centimeter lower than the entrance wound, using as the exterior vertical reference a line drawn through the President's brow and upper lip. Thus the bullet was traveling 18.6° to the right relative to his midplane and 5.0° downward relative to his facial axis.

(128)   Once these wound locations were established, derivation of the bullet's trajectory still required knowledge of the orientation of Kennedy's head relative to Dealey Plaza. Establishing this relationship from the photographs was most easily accomplished in two steps: (1) finding the position of Kennedy's head relative to the line of sight to Zapruder's camera, and (2) accounting for the orientation of that line relative to the entire Dealey Plaza area.

(129)   The Zapruder and Nix films showed the position both of Kennedy's head and of suitable reference structures in the field of view such as walls, street lights, and curbs. Since Kennedy's head is seen exploding in frame 313 of the Zapruder film, frame 312, which was exposed 0.055 seconds earlier, was considered to be the most important photograph available for this aspect of the trajectory analysis. (See JFK exhibit F-254.) [See illustration 19.]

(130)   The key features to be analyzed in frame 312 with respect to determining the orientation of Kennedy's head, were the lateral and vertical position of his right ear relative to the outline of the head and the overall relationship between his ear, nose and eyebrow. Rather than basing the analysis on a purely subjective interpretation, orientation was determined by comparing these features, as they appeared in an enhanced print of Zapruder frame 312 (see fig. II-8, JFK exhibit F-134), with a series of calibration photographs of a replica of Kennedy's head prepared by the Civil Aeromedical Institute of the FAA's Aeronautical Center.* These calibration photographs were taken from many carefully measured aspects (lines of sight), including several which closely approximated the relative location of Zapruder's camera at frame 312. (See fig. II-9, JFK exhibit F-141.)

(131)   After studying those photographs most closely approximating the correct aspect, it was possible to determine, by comparing the positions of such features as Kennedy's ear relative to other parts of his head, the aspect from which Zapruder's camera viewed Kennedy. On this basis, it was determined that Kennedy was turned partially away from Zapruder—approximately 25° past the 90°, or profile, direction. His head was tilted away from Zapruder by about 15°, and he appeared to be nodding forward by about 11° (clockwise, as viewed by Zapruder).

(132)   In order to obtain a similar set of relationships relative to landmarks in Dealey Plaza, it was necessary to establish the orientation and position of this line of sight. Its direction and the point where it intercepts Kennedy's head were determined by drawing a line on a scaled map of Dealey Plaza between Zapruder, whose position had been derived from other photographs and testimony, and Kennedy at the geographic position on the street corresponding to the limousine's location at the time that Zapruder frame 312 was exposed. The latter was determined by relying on the photogrammetric analysis of the USGS. (46)** (See fig. II-10, JFB exhibit F-133.) The slope of this line was calculated by considering the relative heights of both the pedestal on which Zapruder was standing and of the street at the point where the limousine was located at frame 312, and then measuring the distance between Zapruder and Kennedy.

(133)   The pedestal on which Zapruder stood was 12 feet above the point on Elm

*The construction of the replica and the taking of the calibration photographs are described in addendum A, at pars. 169–176 infra.

**Because Zapruder frame 313 provided better reference points, the USGS used that frame to determine the location of the limousine. Based on the limousine's estimated average speed, an adjustment of 1 foot was made to locate the vehicle at frame 312.

Street occupied by Kennedy at the time of Zapruder frame 312. When both the height at which the camera was held and the height of Kennedy's head above the street were considered (about 5 feet and 4 feet, respectively), the camera was determined to have been about 13 feet higher than Kennedy. The distance between Kennedy and Zapruder was about 70 feet at the time of the fatal shot. (See fig. II-10, JFK exhibit F-133.) Given this height difference and the distance between the two men a line of sight downward from Zapruder to Kennedy was computed to be at an angle of 10°.

(134) Once these factors had been established, the geometric relationship between the line of sight from Zapruder's camera and the trajectory line defined by the inshot and outshoot wounds in Kennedy's head was determined.

(135) A physical reconstruction, consisting of a wooden mockup based on the photographic analysis of Zapruder frame 312, was used. In the mockup, the camera line of sight was represented by a straight dowel. The midplane of Kennedy's head was represented by a flat piece of wood to which the line-of-sight dowel was affixed in a manner reflecting its relative slope and direction. A second straight dowel was installed vertically at the front of the midplane to represent the external facial axis defined by the forehead and upper lip. Finally, to simulate the location of the entry and exit wounds, two short posts were fastened to the midplane 11 centimeters apart and extending 1.8 and 5.5 centimeters outward on the same side as the line-of-sight rod. These posts were fitted with circular tips—one open and the other solid—to serve as sighting points. The positions of the posts relative to the facial axis and line-of-sight rods duplicated the positions of the wounds as located by the Forensic Pathology Panel.

(136) This assembly was then supported on a photographer's tripod in a laboratory so as to duplicate the slope of the line of sight of Zapruder's camera and the inclination of the facial axis simultaneously. The direction of the line of sight in the laboratory was registered by mounting two plumb bobs on the line-of-sight rod and marking their positions on the level floor. The direction of the bullet trajectory in the laboratory was similarly registered by mounting two plumb bobs on separate, movable supports that were positioned to correspond with the circular posts representing the wounds. The resulting angle between these two lines established the angle between the direction of the camera's line of sight and the direction of the bullet's trajectory.

(137) The slope of the bullet's trajectory was deduced by placing markers on the two plumb bobs alined with the two posts (wounds). The difference in height of these two markers above the laboratory floor and the distance between the two plumb bobs were used to calculate the slope of the trajectory.

(138) The direction and slope determined in the laboratory were then related to the real case by incorporating the same data on scale drawings developed from a topographic map of Dealey Plaza. First, the limousine and Kennedy's head were positioned in the drawing. Then the line of sight was drawn between Zapruder and Kennedy's head. Next, the direction angle derived from the laboratory replication was duplicated in order to arrive at the trajectory direction line on the Dealey Plaza map. This line was then extended rearward until it intercepted the face of the first building it encountered—a point approximately 11 feet west of the southeast corner of the Texas School Book Depository. (See fig. II-11.) [See drawing 12.]

(139) In order to show the slope of the trajectory without distortion, it was necessary to develop an oblique elevation view shown in fig. II-12. [See drawing 15.] This view is an orthogonal projection onto a vertical plane parallel to the bullet's trajectory. In this view, the resulting trajectory slope of 16° is shown to intersect the Texas School Book Depository at a point approximately 11 feet west of the southwest corner of the building and 15 feet above the sixth floor windowsills.*

---

*The revision in relative heights of the inshoot and outshoot wounds in Kennedy's head resulted in most of the difference in this trajectory from that presented in testimony before the House Select Committee on Assassinations on September 12, 1978. The remaining revisions resulted from the availability of a superior enhanced reproduction of Zapruder frame 312 for comparison with the calibration photographs.

(140)   A circle with a radius of 23 feet has been drawn around the intersect point in figure II-12 representing the estimated minimum reasonable margin of error for this trajectory analysis.* To derive this estimate of the margin of error, each step in the anlaysis was checked for possible errors. Factors such as the position of Zapruder and Kennedy and the height of the pedestal on which Zapruder stood were not considered significant sources of error. The major uncertainties related to the wound positions and the orientation of Kennedy's head relative to Zapruder.

(141)   For example, of critical importance in comparing calibration photographs with Zapruder frame 312 was the apparent position of Kennedy's right ear in relation to his nose, brow and back of head. An error of 1.0° (equal to about 0.16 centimeter), in positioning the ear on the replica of the head would yield approximatly 1.0° error in the deduced trajectory** if not offset by other factors in interpreting the photographs or elsewhere. Similarly, establishing the relationship of those elements critical in determining the degree to which Kennedy's head was nodding forward (for example, the line from his brow to his upper lip relative to the slope of the street) also required careful and repetitious measurements to minimize errors. All measurements were made repeatedly, using as many independent image cues as could be found. The redundancy of the cues selected and the repetition of the studies, coupled with the probable random direction of any errors introduced, allows the Panel to conclude that a liberal estimate for the margin of error is about 5° (that is, a 23-foot radius about the intersect point at the Texas School Book Depository).

(2)   The back-neck case
(142)   According to the autopsy photographs, the first bullet to strike Kennedy entered his back slightly about his shoulder blade and slightly to the right of his backbone. (See fig. II-13). This bullet passed through soft tissue hitting no bone, and exited at the front of his neck. (47) Independent determinations by the Photographic Evidence Panel showed the entrance wound to be from 4 to 5 centimeters from Kennedy's center plane and the exit wound to be on the center plane or as much as 0.5 centimeters to its left. When seen in the autopsy position, the outshoot wound was described as being at about the same height (or slightly higher) relative to the inshoot wound. The distance between the wounds was determined to be 14 centimeters.

(143)   Based on the acoustics results (48), the camera blur study (49) and the visual observations made by the Photographic Evidence Panel, (50) it was determined that Kennedy was struck by this bullet at a time corresponding approximately to Zapruder frame 190. Accordingly, to determine Kennedy's orientation at that point, frame 190 and adjoining frames were closely scrutinized. (51) (See JFK exhibits JFK F-225-227.)

(144)   The best record of Kennedy's posture, torso inclination, and shoulder "hunching" is a photograph taken by Robert Croft at about the time of Zapruder frame 161. (52) (See fig. II-14, JFK exhibit F-135). This correlation was established by the Photographic Evidence Panel by examining features in the Croft photograph and studying Croft's movements as recorded in the Zapruder film.

(145)   In Croft's picture, Kennedy and other persons in the limousine are seen from a perspective that permits a reasonable determination of their posture and orientation. Kennedy's upper torso/neck region was inferred from this photograph to have been inclined forward at an approximate angle of 11° to 18° relative to a line drawn upward from and perpendicular to the road surface. The range of this angle is well within a much larger range derived from studies of many other photographs taken during the motorcade. Although the Croft photograph corresponds to Zapruder frame 161, there is no indication in the Zapruder movie that Kennedy changed his inclination substantially before he was hit in the back. (53) (See JKF exhibits F-226-242.)

(146)   The Croft photograph also shows Kennedy's torso facing nearly straight forward. At Zapruder frame 190, however, he is seen to turn his head about 60° to

---

*That is to say that the margin of error could be greater.

**A 1-degree error results in a movement of about 4 feet at a range of 250 feet.

his right (see JFK exhibit F-226), and it is reasonable to expect that he also would have rotated his shoulders a small amount in the same direction. Most probably, this rotation was only 5° or less, as judged by the absence of obvious large shifts in body position in the Zapruder movie. Thus, it was assumed that, except for turning his head by about 60° and his torso perhaps by 5°, Kennedy made no major changes in posture after frame 161. This assumption is supported by a photograph taken by Phillip Willis at about the time of Zapruder frame 202.* (See fig. II-15, JFK exhibit F-155.) [See illustration 13.]

(147)   The Panel then had to adjust slightly the wound locations that had been provided based on the autopsy photographs and X-rays because of their difference in body position from that at the time of the shooting. During the autopsy, Kennedy was in an anatomical position with his face tilted as if looking upward about 35°, a posture and conformation significantly different from those at the time of the assassination.

(148)   Appropriate adjustments were made under the direction of Dr. Clyde Snow, a forensic anthropologist at the Civil Aeromedical Institute of the FAA's Aeronautical Center. It was determined that returning Kennedy's head to a normal position relative to his body would, according to laboratory tests on men of similar build, adjust his neck wound down about 1.0 centimeter toward his breastbone. Returning Kennedy's head to the position it was in at the time he was first wounded—about 60° to the right of straight ahead of his torso—caused only a slight change in the position (approximately 0.1 centimeter to the right of its observed position in the autopsy photographs). (54)

(149)   Because the Zapruder film showed that Kennedy had raised his right shoulder slightly so as to place his elbow on the side of the limousine, the resulting movement of skin at the inshoot location was also assessed. It was found that the wound was approximately 0.1 centimeter higher and 0.2 centimeter closer to his midplane than the post mortem photographic observations by themselves indicated. (55) While only the vertical position of the neck wound was substantially altered by these changes in conformation, all the adjustments were included in the analysis of trajectory.

(150)   Using the average locations and adjustments, the back wound was located at a point 4.4 centimeters to the right of and 1.1 centimeters above Kennedy's neck wound at the time of the shot. The bullet was moving from right to left by 18° and downward by 4.0° relative to Kennedy if he were sitting erect (not inclined forward or aft). Since Kennedy was believed to have been turned about 5° to his right relative to the fore-and-aft line of the limousine, it is concluded that the bullet was moving from right to left by 13° relative to the midline of the limousine. By a similar analysis, since Kennedy was inclined slightly forward by approximately 11° to 18° (from true vertical), the downward slope of the trajectory, taking into account the 3° slope of the street, was established at between 18° and 25° (4° plus 11° to 18°, plus 3°). The Panel decided to use an angle of 21° for its analysis.

(151)   The analysis by the USGS of the limousine's motion through Dealey Plaza provided both the location and angular orientation of the limousine at a time corresponding to Zapruder frame 193; (56) adjustments were then made with reference to Zapruder frame 190. (See fig. II-10, JFK exhibit F-133.)

(152)   The direction of the trajectory was then determined by drawing a line on a scaled diagram of Dealey Plaza at a 13° (that is, 18° minus 5°) angle relative to the car and extending it to the rear until it intercepted the first building that it encountered. Assuming frame 190 as the moment of impact, the trajectory line intercepts the Texas School Book Depository approximately 14 feet west of its southeast

---

*Establishing when the Willis photograph was exposed in reference to the Zapruder film was done by the Photographic Evidence Panel by studying the Zapruder film and determining when Willis could actually be seen snapping his picture. In the study of the back/neck wounds trajectory, calibration photographs of the anthropometric dummy were taken but not used (that is, for measurement analysis) because, unlike the head, the torso is quite mobile, and consequently there is no stable relationship between the various body parts. It was decided that to rely on the calibration-photograph technique in this instance would have given a false sense of accuracy to the analysis.

corner. (See fig. II-16). Using an angle of 21°, the slope of the trajectory was then drawn onto a similarly scaled diagram and found to intersect the Texas School Book Depository at a point almost level with the sixth floor windowsill. (See fig. II-17.)

(153)   A circle with a radius of 13 feet has been drawn about the intercept point of the trajectory in figure II-16, reflecting the margin of error. It represents the estimated minimum reasonable margin of error that can be ascribed to this analysis.

(154)   The same kinds of considerations as were discussed for the head wounds case were applicable in assessing the accuracy of the trajectory based on the President's torso wounds. Here the most critical issue was Kennedy's upper torso attitude rather than the orientation of his head. Consequently, different types of problems were encountered.

(155)   The Croft photograph, while quite illustrative of Kennedy's posture, lacked two features noted in Zapruder frame 312. Since the torso is flexible, no clear stable relationship could be established between the photographed exterior and the unseen interior. Further, this picture was taken at least 1.5 seconds before Kennedy was wounded. During this interval, he had turned his head about 60° to his right and may have shifted his torso slightly. Thus, errors of 5° may easily be present in this interpretation. Finally, an accurate determination of his back and neck wound locations was impeded both by the extremely inapprorpiate lighting and composition of the autopsy photographs and by the distortions resulting from the tracheostomy performed at Parkland Memorial Hospital. These latter problems probably contributed little to the uncertainty in trajectory location as compared with the more serious difficulties arising from the poor photographic definition of his posture and position.*

(3)   The single-bullet theory trajectory

(156)   In order to examine the hypothesis that the bullet responsible for Kennedy's back and neck wounds was also responsible for Connally's wounds, a trajectory was constructed based on Kennedy's exit neck wound and the entrance wound in Connally's back. The hypothesis was to be evaluated by determining whether this trajectory lay close enough to the back-neck trajectory to make it reasonable to conclude that both are consistent with the trajectory of one bullet. Necessarily, the margin of error radius for the Kennedy-Connally trajectory would have to intersect the depository at a point within the 13-foot-radius circle of probable accuracy for the back-neck wound trajectory established earlier. Ideally, of course, the two trajectories would line up precisely, but this standard was considered unrealistically high, because, as with Kennedy, Connally's position at the time of this shot could not be precisely established; moreover, each trajectory was subject to its own sources of error.

(157)   In addition to the information that already had been analyzed concerning Kennedy's neck wound, derivation of this trajectory required placement of the location of Connally's entry wound to the back. At the committee's request, Connally agreed to have the position of his back wound redetermined by the Forensic Pathology Panel. His inshot wound was described as being immediately above his right armpit. This description is essentially consistent with figure II-18. (JFK exhibit F-399.) (57)

(158)   In contrast to the analyses involving Kennedy's wound pairs, the two-man wound combination required focusing on the positions of the two men relative to each other and to their surroundings in Dealey Plaza, rather than just on individual details of posture and orientation. This analysis was accomplished by reviewing Zapruder frames 180–207, the Croft photograph, and photographs taken by Hugh Betzner and Phillip Willis, two witnesses who were both standing behind and to the left of the Presidential limousine.

(159)   Two independent determinations of the lateral relationship between the two men were made. The first consisted of a photogrammetric analysis of several pairs of pictures taken from the Zapruder movie between frames 182 and 200. These pairs

---

*The 5° margin of error resulted in a smaller margin-of-error radius than in the head wound trejectory because in this case the limousine was substantially closer to the Texas School Book Depository. (See fig. II-10, JFK exhibit F-133.)

were viewed together in a stereoscopic viewer so that together the pairs would project a single, three-dimensional image that could be evaluated for the relative depths of the objects that they portrayed.* The stereo pairs clearly showed that Kennedy was seated close to the right-hand, inside surface of the car, with his arm resting atop the side of the car and his elbow extending, at times, beyond the body of the car. Connally, on the other hand, was seated well within the car on the jump seat ahead of Kennedy; a gap of slightly less than 15 centimeters separated this seat from the car door. (See fig. II-19.) (*58*)

(160)   The second photographic analysis, which was based primarily on the Betzner and Croft photographs, confirmed these observations. The Betzner photograph (see fig. II-20) [see illustration 14] was determined by the panel to have been taken at the time Zapruder frame 186 was exposed.** Scrutiny of enlarged portions of the area surrounding Kennedy showed the direction in which an extension of the line of sight would travel from Betzner's lens. It goes by the upper right corner of the Secret Service handhold on the left side of the limousine trunk lid, then passes by the extreme tip of Kennedy's left shoulder, and then by the edge of the limousine's rollbar center post (to which the wind-wing window is attached) just ahead to the right rear door at Connally's right.*** This line establishes a boundary to the left of which no part of Kennedy can be seen. Nor are there visible signs of Connally's right shoulder or arm slightly to the left of this boundary (the line of sight is limited by the spectator's arm in the foreground). Therefore, Connally must be seated to the left of this line of sight.

(161)   With these two observations and some supportive evidence drawn from the remaining pictorial evidence, it was possible to outline Kennedy as he would have been seen from directly above. The key additional features used were his posture and inclination, which were derived from the Croft picture (see fig. II-14), and the slight indication of torso rotation to his right, derived from the Zapruder film. Next, a similar outline was drawn for Connally, with his shoulders against the backrest of the jump seat as far to the right as can be justified in view of the Betzner photograph, and turned to his right.

(162)   The direction in which Connally's torso was facing has been determined on the basis of viewing the Zapruder movie and by careful study of a particularly clear stereo pair taken from the movie. The estimates of the angle of his twist vary from 30° to slightly over 45°. The two outlines show the positions of the men relative to one another. (See fig. II-23.) Connally cannot have been sitting very far to the left of this position in view of his location in Zapruder frame 190. (See JFK exhibit F-226.)

(163)   The point-to-point distance between Kennedy's neck and the part of Connally's back that was wounded was determined photogrammetrically in the Croft photograph to be approximately 60 centimeters. The height differential between the two was determined in a similar manner to be 8 centimeters.****

---

*A similar stereophotogrammetric analysis, performed by the Itek Corp. and verified by the photographic evidence panel, indicated that in several stereo pairs Connally was sitting 10.2 to 20.3 centimeters to the left of a line extending straight forward from Kennedy. (see *John Kennedy Assassination Film Analysis*, Itek Corp. (1976), pp. 43–48).

**A first generation print of a photograph taken by Hugh Betzner, very close in time and from a similar vantage point as the Willis No. 5 photograph, was examined by the panel; no enhancement processing was performed as the original negative was never located. The Betzner photograph was correlated to the corresponding Zapruder frame by establishing when a Secret Service agent riding in the car behind Kennedy could be seen in both Zapruder's and Betzner's immediate line of sight.

***Fig. II-21 (JFK exhibit F-136) demonstrates the Betzner photograph line-of-sight analysis. The rollbar center post has a diagonal appearance in the Betzner photograph because it is inclined inward from the side of the car toward the rollbar. See fig. II-22 for a clearer view of the rollbar post, as seen from a similar angle in a photograph taken by James Altgens on Houston St. less than a minute earlier.

****The appearance of an even greater height difference between the two men, as depicted in the Croft photograph, resulted from the more inward position of Connally in the car and the slightly downward line of sight from Croft's camera.

(164)   Using the lateral and longitudinal relationships, given the limousine as the frame of reference (see fig. II-23), the direction in which the bullet was found to have been moving from the rear was 12.7° from right to left relative to the midplane of the car. The direction of the trajectory was thereby determined by drawing a line at a 12.7° angle relative to the car and extending it to the rear until it intersected the first building that it encountered—the Book Depository, at a point approximately 2 feet to the west of the southeast corner of the building, using Zapruder frame 190 for the moment of impact. (See fig. II-24.)

(165)   In deriving the slope of the trajectory, the difference in height between the two wounds, the 60-centimeter distance between them, and the inclination of Elm Street, were taken into account. Kennedy's neck wound was 1.1 centimeters below his first thoracic vertebra; his forward inclination lowered the wound an additional 2.4 centimeters. Connally's inshoot wound was 18 centimeters below his first thoracic vertebra. Thus, if the men had been sitting so that the tops of their heads were at equal heights, Kennedy's wound would have been 14.5 centimeters higher than Connally's.* Then, taking into account that Kennedy was seated approximately 8 centimeters higher than Connally (as observed in the Croft photograph), Kennedy's wound is found to have been 22.5 centimeters higher (14.5 plus 8 centimeters) than Connally's relative to the car. This height difference over a distance of 60 centimeters (point-to-point distance between the wounds) yields a downward slope of about 22° from Kennedy's wound to Connally's. Finally, accounting for the 3° slope of the street, the slope of the trajectory is found to be 25°.

(166)   This means that the bullet was traveling at an angle of 25° below true horizontal as it passed forward from Kennedy's neck to Connally's back.** Using the position of the men at the time of Zapruder 190, if this line is extended toward the rear, it intercepts the depository building about 9 feet above the sixth floor windowsill.*** (See fig. II-25.)

(167)   In figure II-25, a circle of 7 feet radius, representing the estimated minimum reasonable margin of error, has been drawn around the intercept point. It is smaller than those of the other two trajectories simply because the distance between the two wounds (60 centimeters) is more than four times as great as that for the back/neck case (14 centimeters) and five times that for the fatal bullet (11 centimeters). This longer baseline distance admits greater error in wound location and body position, while yielding superior accuracy. The eastern border of the error circle is somewhat better fixed than the western because the right-most position of Connally was better defined than the left-most.

(168)   The consistency of the single-bullet theory trajectory with the back/neck shot trajectory described earlier is illustrated by their similar direction and slope. Note that the intercept point of the single-bullet theory trajectory at the Texas School Book Depository lies very close to the margin of error circle established for the back-neck case. Indeed, the two error circles overlap substantially. (See figs. II-17 and II-25.) Clearly, this analysis supports the single-bullet theory. The reliability of this trajectory in indicating the position of the gunman would be less if it could be shown that the bullet had been deflected as it passed through Kennedy's tissue. Nevertheless, the evidence indicates that the bullet passed near, but did not strike, the right lateral processes of the seventh cervical and first thoracic vertebrae (nor any other bony matter). (59) Consequently, the deflection, if any, was probably negligible.

---

*This analysis makes the assumption that the distance in each man from the top of his head to his first thoracic vetebra is approximately the same.

**This slope is 2° steeper than described in testimony before the committee on September 12, 1978, because the former was based on a 6-centimeter height difference instead of 8 centimeters, as presently interpreted.

***This result differs somewhat from the testimony given before the committee on September 12, 1978, because the adjustment in the height differential between the two men affected the ultimate determination of trajectory slope.

APPENDIX D 333

ADDENDUM A

CALIBRATION PHOTOGRAPHS OF THE REPLICA OF PRESIDENT KENNEDY'S HEAD

(169)   Photographs of Kennedy taken immediately before each shot provide invaluable, albeit imperfect, records of his position and orientation at the time of the assassination. The quantitative interpretation of these photographs was facilitated through detailed comparisons with calibration photographs taken of a full-scale replica of Kennedy's head, upper torso, and arms.

(170)   Calibration photographs may be defined as photographs of a replica that is geometrically and texturally representative of a subject; they are taken under controlled conditions and are used to facilitate quantitative interpretation of photographs of the real subject that were taken under uncontrolled circumstances. Requirements for a good calibration photograph include: accuracy of the replica, photographic distortion similar to that in the real-life photograph under study; comparable positions for the camera and replica; and comparable lighting distribution. The calibration pictures should have somewhat superior photographic qualities in terms of spatial resolution and contrast so that error will not be introduced into the interpretation.

Head replica

(171)   To maximize the accuracy of the replica, the Aeromedical Research Institute of the FAA's Aeronautical Center worked with a group of high-quality photographs from the National Archives. Using dimensions obtained from well characterized X-rays of Kennedy's head taken shortly before the assassination, the size and proportions of his skull and the thickness of overlying tissue (front and rear) were established. Modeling clay was applied to a standard plaster skull until the form of his head was duplicated in many aspects. To achieve improved photographic realism, artificial eyes and a wig were added. The head was then mounted on the neck of a standard FAA anthropometric dummy.

Simulation of lighting and environment

(172)   A single studio light was used to simulate the Sun, with two small studio floodlamps to augment the illumination by the studio skylight of the figure and the neutral background. At the time of the first shot, Kennedy had been facing west. The spotlight was accordingly positioned to the model's left. It was placed about 36° above horizontal from the head, a position comparable to that of the midday November Sun. Similar lighting was arranged for the head-wound shot. In this case the elevation of the spotlight (Sun) was about 56°, compensating for the erect placement of the head on the dummy, and it was placed nearly straight in front because Kennedy had been facing south.

(173)   Camera stations—the various points from which the dummy would be photographed—were marked out on the studio floor in an arc 25 feet from the bridge of the model's nose. Two plumb bobs were suspended beside the figure to provide a precise vertical and angular reference respectively. Beads were installed on each plumbline at a point level with the bridge of the dummy's nose. The elevation of the camera was varied to achieve the desired angles of elevation relative to the dummy. (This caused the actual distance between the camera and the dummy to change slightly.)

(174)   Once the camera stations were established, a series of photographs was taken at varying elevations from each station, with the location of each photograph recorded. The pictures were then compared with an enhanced photograph of Zapruder 312. (See fig. II-8.) The goal was to determine the angular orientation of Kennedy's head relative to his surroundings in Dealey Plaza. Since the positions of the Zapruder and Nix cameras, with which the best pictures had been taken, were known, only the position angles relative to each camera's line of sight and to vertical references visible in the respective pictures had to be found.

(175)   The relative positions of the features of Kennedy's head varied with the viewing aspect. In Zapruder frame 312, part of Kennedy's nose was obscured by his

right cheek because his head was turned slightly away from the camera. His right ear appears slightly forward of where it would have been had he not been facing slightly away. His cheekbone and ear appear slightly elevated in Zapruder frame 312 as the camera was, in effect, viewing the President from slightly "below" because of the inclination of his head to the left.

(176)   All these relationships among features were accounted for simultaneously during comparison with the calibration photographs. Serious impediments to accurate interpretation of the photograph were occasioned by the extremely complicated background to the President's face resulting from Mrs. Kennedy's pink suit and dark blue blouse and by the interior surface of the left side of the limousine. These problems were overcome in part by the use of a computer-enhanced version of Zapruder frame 312. (See fig. II-8.)

(Appendix to the Hearings Before the Select Committee on Assassinations of the U.S. House of Representatives, Ninety-fifth Congress, Second Session, March 1979, Vol. VI, pages 34–58.)

NOTES

1. A CHANCE TELEPHONE CALL

1. Mark Lane, *Rush to Judgment* (New York: Holt, Rinehart & Winston, 1966; Fawcett World Library, 1967), 105–107.

2. Josiah Thompson, *Six Seconds in Dallas* (New York: Bernard Geis Associates, 1967), 294.

3. Ibid., 292.

2. THE WARREN REPORT

1. Harrison Salisbury, "An Introduction to the Warren Commission Report," *Report of the Warren Commission on the Assassination of President Kennedy* (New York: Bantam Books, 1964), xxiii–xxv.

2. Jim Marrs, *Crossfire: The Plot That Killed Kennedy* (New York: Carroll & Graf Publishers, 1989), 464.

3. "Chief of Inquiry—Earl Warren," *The New York Times*, 28 September 1964, p. 14.

4. Marrs, *Crossfire*, 464.

5. Ibid., 468.

6. *Warren Report*, 6.

7. Ibid., 7.

8. Ibid., 8.

9. Ibid., 6–8.

10. Ibid., 8.

11. Marrs, *Crossfire*, 488.

12. *Warren Report*, 123.

13. Ibid., 125.

14. Ibid., 113–114, 126.

15. Ibid., 19–20, 47.

16. Jim Bishop, *The Day Kennedy Was Shot* (New York: Funk & Wagnalls, 1968), 150.

17. *Warren Report*, 61.

18. Ibid., 107–108.

19. Ibid., 107–112.

20. Ibid., 113.

21. Ibid., 87–88.

22. Ibid., 117–118.

23. Ibid., 380.

24. Ibid., 133–134.

25. Ibid., 145–146.

26. Ibid., 155–160.

27. Ibid., 160.

28. Ibid., 156, 158.

29. Ibid., 160–162.

30. Ibid., 165.

31. Ibid., 163.

32. Ibid., 39, 171–172.

33. Ibid., 85–88.

34. Ibid., 351.

35. Ibid., 353.

36. Ibid., 355–356.

37. Ibid., 357.

38. Ibid., 359.

39. Ibid., 359.

40. Ibid., 357, 359–360.

41. Ibid., 361.

42. Ibid., 362–363.

43. Ibid., 364.

44. Ibid., 240.

45. Ibid., 367.

46. Ibid., 368.

47. Ibid., 369.

48. Ibid., 244–247.

49. Ibid., 370.

50. Ibid., 255–256.

51. Ibid., 378–379, 269.

52. Ibid., 388.

53. Ibid., 311.

54. Ibid., 341.

55. Ibid., 311.

56. Ibid., 313.

57. Ibid., 325–326.

58. Ibid., 321.

59. Ibid., 331.

60. Ibid., 335.

3. THE CRITICS

1. Harold Weisberg, *Whitewash II—The FBI–Secret Service Cover-Up* (New York: Dell Publishing Co., 1966), 168.

2. Josiah Thompson, *Six Seconds in Dallas* (New York: Bernard Geis Associates, 1967), vii.

3. Ibid., 66–68.

4. Mark Lane, *Rush to Judgment* (New York: Fawcett World Library, 1966), 63–66.

5. *Warren Commission, Vol. VI*, (Washington, D.C.: U.S. Government Printing Office, 1964), 133–134.

6. Thompson, *Six Seconds in Dallas*, 25.

7. *Warren Commission, Vol. VI*, 243–244.

8. Lane, *Rush to Judgment*, 23–24.

9. Ibid., 24.

10. *Warren Commission, Vol. VI*, 284–289.

11. *Warren Commission, Vol. XXIV*, 522.

12. Jim Marrs, *Crossfire: The Plot That Killed Kennedy* (New York: Carroll & Graf Publishers, 1989), 479.

13. Ibid., 478.

14. *Report of the Warren Commission on the Assassination of President Kennedy* (New York: Bantam Books, 1964), 133–134.

15. Thompson, *Six Seconds in Dallas*, 135.

16. *Warren Commission, Vol. XXIV*, 229.

17. *Warren Commission, Vol. III*, 179.

18. *Warren Commission, Vol. XI*, 226–227.

19. *Warren Report*, 114.

20. Ibid., 295–297.

21. *Warren Commission, Vol. X*, 352–356.

22. *Warren Report*, 577, 593–594.

23. Lane, *Rush to Judgment*, 37.

24. *Warren Report*, 91–92.

25. Marrs, *Crossfire*, 368.

26. Sylvan Fox, *The Unanswered Questions About President Kennedy's Assassination* (New York: Award Books, 1965), 85.

27. Ibid., 47.

28. Ibid., 53.

29. Ibid., 111.

30. Thomas Buchanan, *Who Killed Kennedy?* (New York: MacFadden Books, 1964), 110.

31. Fox, *Unanswered Questions*, 156–157.

32. Harold Weisberg, *Whitewash I—The Report on the Warren Report* (New York: Dell Publishing Co., 1966), 40.

33. Thompson, *Six Seconds in Dallas*, 69–78.

34. Ibid., 86–111.

35. Ibid., 10.

36. Ibid., 137.

37. Richard Warren Lewis and Lawrence Schiller, *The Scavengers and Critics of the Warren Report* (New York: Dell Publishing Co., 1967), 24.

38. Ibid., 145–146.

39. Fox, *Unanswered Questions,* front cover.

40. Thompson, *Six Seconds in Dallas,* xv.

41. Fox, *Unanswered Questions,* 64.

42. Weisberg, *Whitewash,* 287.

43. Buchanan, *Who Killed Kennedy?,* 80.

44. F. Peter Model and Robert J. Groden, *JFK: The Case for Conspiracy* (New York: Manor Books, 1977), 27, 80.

45. John K. Lattimer, *Kennedy and Lincoln—Medical & Ballistic Comparisons of their Assassinations* (New York: Harcourt Brace Jovanovich, 1980), 272.

4. THE SINGLE BULLET THEORY

1. *Report of the Warren Commission on the Assassination of President Kennedy* (New York: Bantam Books, 1964), 21.

2. Ibid., 344.7 (photo section).

3. *Warren Report,* 66.

4. Ibid., 67.

5. Ibid., 66.

6. *Warren Commission, Vol. III,* (Washington, D.C.: U.S. Government Printing Office, 1964), 369–370.

7. *Warren Report,* 68–69.

8. Mark Lane, *Rush to Judgment* (New York: Holt, Rinehart & Winston, 1966; Fawcett World Library, 1967), 37.

9. Jim Marrs, *Crossfire: The Plot That Killed Kennedy* (New York: Carroll & Graf, 1989), 368.

10. F. Peter Model and Robert J. Groden, *JFK: The Case for Conspiracy* (New York: Manor Books, 1977), 57.

11. Marrs, *Crossfire,* 371.

12. Harold Weisberg, *Whitewash I—The Report on the Warren Report* (New York: Dell Publishing Co., 1965), 319.

13. Josiah Thompson, *Six Seconds in Dallas* (New York: Bernard Geis Associates, 1967), 44.

14. *Warren Report,* 91.

15. Marrs, *Crossfire,* 369.

16. Thompson, *Six Seconds in Dallas,* 41.

17. Ibid., 41–42.

18. Ibid., 42.

19. Weisberg, *Whitewash,* 325.

20. David Lifton, *Best Evidence—Disguise and Deception in the Assassination of President Kennedy* (New York: Macmillan Publishing Co., 1980), 534–535.

21. *Warren Report,* 91.

22. Ibid., 501.

23. Thompson, *Six Seconds in Dallas,* 48.

24. Ibid.

25. *Warren Report*, 94–95.

26. Thompson, *Six Seconds in Dallas*, 49.

27. David Lifton, *Best Evidence*, 77.

28. John K. Lattimer, *Kennedy and Lincoln—Medical and Ballistic Comparisons of Their Assassinations* (New York: Harcourt Brace Jovanovich, 1980), 193.

29. *Select Committee on Assassinations, Appendix Vol. VII* (Washington, D.C.: U.S. Government Printing Office, 1979), 34–36, photo section (376.6).

30. Lattimer, *Kennedy and Lincoln*, 204–205.

31. *Warren Commission, Vol. VI*, 3.

32. Weisberg, *Whitewash*, 320–321.

33. Sylvan Fox, *The Unanswered Questions About President Kennedy's Assassination* (New York: Award Books, 1965), 91–92.

34. Thompson, *Six Seconds in Dallas*, 52.

35. Ibid.

36. Lattimer, *Kennedy and Lincoln*, 230–239.

37. *Warren Report*, 95.

38. Ibid.

39. Ibid., 69.

40. Lane, *Rush to Judgment*, 61.

41. *Warren Report*, 104.

42. Lane, *Rush to Judgment*, 61–62.

43. *Warren Report*, 105–106.

44. Lane, *Rush to Judgment*, 64–65.

45. *Warren Report*, 105.

46. Lane, *Rush to Judgment*, 65.

47. *Warren Report*, 98.

48. Thompson, *Six Seconds in Dallas*, 148–149.

49. Ibid., 150.

50. Richard Warren Lewis and Lawrence Schiller, *The Scavengers and Critics of the Warren Report* (New York: Dell Publishing Co., 1967), 176.

51. Thompson, *Six Seconds in Dallas*, 168–169.

52. *Warren Report*, 87.

53. Ibid., 100–102.

54. Ibid., 109.

55. Thompson, *Six Seconds in Dallas*, 71.

56. Ibid.

57. Ibid., 66.

58. Ibid., 67–68.

59. Ibid., 39.

60. Ibid., 39, 40.

5. THE HEAD SHOT

1. *The Report of the Warren Commission on the Assassination of President Kennedy* (New York: Bantam Books, 1964), 106.

2. Ibid., 107.

3. Ibid.

4. Josiah Thompson, *Six Seconds in Dallas* (New York: Bernard Geis Associates, 1967), 136.

5. *Warren Report,* 501–502.

6. Ibid., 83–84.

7. Ibid., 502.

8. Ibid.

9. Ibid., 514–515.

10. Thompson, *Six Seconds in Dallas,* 25.

11. *Warren Commission, Vol. VI,* (Washington, D.C.: U.S. Government Printing Office, 1964), 210–211.

12. Ibid., 211.

13. *The Final Assassinations Report* (New York: Bantam Books, 1979), 228–230.

14. Ibid., 229.

15. Richard Warren Lewis and Lawrence Schiller, *The Scavengers and Critics of the Warren Report* (New York: Dell Publishing Co., 1967), 29–31.

16. *Warren Commission, Vol. VI,* 33.

17. Thompson, *Six Seconds,* 107.

18. *Warren Commission, Vol. VI,* 65.

6. A FORTUITOUS ENCOUNTER

1. Associated Press, "New Oswald Clue Reportedly Found," *The New York Times,* 19 February 1967, p. 43.

2. Gene Roberts, "Figure in Oswald Inquiry is Dead in New Orleans," *The New York Times,* 23 February 1967, p. 22.

3. Ibid.

4. Ibid.

5. Gene Roberts, "Arrests in Kennedy Case Delayed for Months, New Orleans Prosecutor Says," *The New York Times,* 21 February 1967, p. 20.

6. Ibid.

7. Ibid.

8. Gene Roberts, "Figure in Oswald Inquiry Is Dead in New Orleans," *The New York Times,* 23 February 1967, p. 22.

9. Ibid.

10. Gene Roberts, "Businessmen Aid Inquiry on Plot," *The New York Times,* 25 February 1967, p. 56.

11. Associated Press, "Garrison Arrests an Ex-Major in Conspiracy to Kill Kennedy," *The New York Times,* 2 March 1967, p. 24.

12. Gene Roberts, "Suspect in 'Plot' Linked to Oswald," *The New York Times,* 3 March 1967, p. 22.

13. Gene Roberts, "Louisiana A.C.L.U. Scores Garrison," *The New York Times,* 7 March 1967, p. 21.

14. Herblock in *The Washington Post, The New York Times,* 5 March 1967, Sec. IV, p. 9.

15. Robert E. Dallos, "New Witness Alleges That He Was Offered Money to Aid Garrison in Investigation of Assassination," *The New York Times,* 19 June 1967, p. 27.

16. Gene Roberts, "Investigator Quits Garrison's Staff and Assails Inquiry into Plot," *The New York Times,* 27 June 1967, p. 25.

17. Martin Waldron, "Garrison Charges C.I.A. and F.B.I. Conceal Evidence on Oswald," *The New York Times,* 10 May 1967, p. 27.

18. Associated Press, "Garrison Says Kennedy Was Killed in Crossfire," *The New York Times,* 24 May 1967, p. 50.

19. "Garrison Says Some Policemen in Dallas Aided Kennedy Plot," *The New York Times,* 22 September 1967, p. 28.

20. Associated Press, "Garrison Says Assassin Killed Kennedy from Sewer Manhole," *The New York Times,* 11 December 1967, p. 28.

21. Boswell-Clark letter obtained from the Department of Justice under the Freedom of Information Act, 30 January 1990.

22. Robert B. Semple Jr., "Clark Discounts Shaw Conspiracy," *The New York Times,* 3 March 1967, p. 22.

23. Richard Irwin, "Russell Fisher, Pathologist for State, Dies," *Baltimore News-American,* 27 February 1986, page unknown.

24. "Dr. R.H. Morgan, X-Ray Specialist, Dies," *Baltimore News-American,* 27 February 1986, page unknown.

25. Russell Fisher, et al., *1968 Panel Review of Photographs, X-Ray Films, Documents and Other Evidence Pertaining to the Fatal Wounding of President John F. Kennedy on November 22, 1963 in Dallas, Texas,* obtained from the Department of Justice under the Freedom of Information Act on Jan. 31, 1990, pp. 1–2.

7. KENNEDY'S UNKNOWN WOUND

1. John K. Lattimer, *Kennedy and Lincoln—Medical and Ballistic Comparisons of Their Assassinations* (New York: Harcourt Brace Jovanovich, 1980), 214.

2. *The Report of the Warren Commission on the Assassination of President Kennedy* (New York: Bantam Books, 1964), 102.

3. Ibid., 100.

4. Ibid., 108.

5. Ibid.

6. Ibid.

7. Ibid.

8. *Warren Commission, Vol. VII* (Washington, D.C.: U.S. Government Printing Office, 1964), 507–515.

9. *Warren Commission, Vol. VI*, 238.

10. *Warren Commission, Vol. VII*, 291.

11. Jim Marrs, *Crossfire: The Plot That Killed Kennedy* (New York: Carroll & Graf, 1989), 14.

12. Ibid.

13. *Warren Report*, 83.

14. Ibid.

15. Ibid.

16. Ibid.

17. Ibid., 90.

18. Ibid., 111.

19. *Warren Report*, 111.

20. *Warren Commission, Vol. VII*, 486–487.

21. *Warren Commission, Vol. VI*, 165.

22. *Warren Commission, Vol. VII*, 512.

23. *Warren Commission, Vol. VI*, 233.

24. William Manchester, *The Death of a President* (New York: Harper & Row, 1967), 156.

8. MURPHY'S LAW

1. *Warren Commission, Vol. XVIII* (Washington, D.C.: U.S. Government Printing Office, 1964), 758–759.

2. *Warren Commission, Vol. VII*, 517.

3. *The Report of the Warren Commission on the Assassination of President Kennedy* (New York: Bantam Books, 1964), 533.

4. Fred Graham, "Mystery Cloaks Fate of Brain of Kennedy," *The New York Times*, 27 August 1972, p. 1.

5. Thomas W. Lippman, "Court Denies JFK Photos to Garrison," *Washington Post*, 18 January 1969, p. 1.

6. Jim Marrs, *Crossfire: The Plot That Killed Kennedy* (New York: Carroll & Graf, 1989), 514.

7. Associated Press, "Garrison Record Shows Disability" and (no byline) "Aide Responds to Article," *The New York Times*, 30 December 1967, p. 28.

8. Ibid.

9. "District Attorneys Pay for Dinner; Garrison Cancels It," *The New York Times*, 17 March 1968, p. 78.

10. United Press International, "Judge Restrains Shaw Prosecutor," *The New York Times*, 29 May 1968, p. 28.

11. "Louisiana Trial of Shaw Assured," *The New York Times*, 10 December 1968, p. 42.

12. Marrs, *Crossfire*, 507.

13. Ibid., 510.

14. Ibid., 494–497.

15. Ibid., 497–498.

16. Ibid., 502.

17. Ibid., 503.

9. THE DISCOVERY

1. Lawrence M. Blume, Jr., "Spencer—Terror of Civil War!" *Gun Week*, 4 February 1977, p. 1.

2. *Historical Times Illustrated Encyclopedia of the Civil War*, ed. Patricia L. Faust (New York: Harper & Row, 1986), 708.

3. Lawrence M. Blume, Jr., "Spencer—Terror of Civil War!" p. 1.

4. Ibid.

5. Ibid.

6. Bell I. Wiley, *The Common Soldier of the Civil War* (New York: Charles Scribner's Sons, 1975), 35.

7. "Firing Civil War Spencers," *Gun Week*, 4 February 1977, p. 1.

8. William Manchester, *The Death of a President* (New York: Harper & Row, 1967), 159.

9. Ibid., 134.

10. *Warren Commission, Vol. VII* (Washington, D.C.: U.S. Government Printing Office, 1964), 479.

11. Ibid., 439–440.

12. Richard Warren Lewis and Lawrence Schiller, *The Scavengers and Critics of the Warren Report* (New York: Dell Publishing Co., 1967), 32–33.

13. *Warren Commission, Vol. XVIII*, 768.

14. *Warren Commission, Vol. XVII*, 632.

15. *Warren Commission, Vol. XVIII*, 760.

16. *Warren Commission, Vol. XVIII*, 735.

17. *Warren Commission, Vol. XVIII*, 747.

18. *Warren Commission, Vol. II*, 69.

19. *Warren Commission, Vol. VII*, 473.

20. Lewis and Schiller, *The Scavengers and Critics*, 31.

21. *Warren Report*, 111.

22. *Warren Commission, Vol. VI*, 225.

23. Ibid., 237.

24. Mark Lane, *Rush to Judgment* (New York: Holt, Rinehart & Winston, 1966; Fawcett World Library, 1967), 32.

10. BREAKING NEWS

1. Harold Weisberg, *Whitewash I—The Report on the Warren Report* (New York: Dell Publishing Co., 1965), 19.

2. Jim Bishop, *The Day Kennedy Was Shot* (New York: Funk & Wagnalls, 1968), 225.

3. William Manchester, *The Death of a President* (New York: Harper & Row, 1967), 298.

4. Ibid., 300.

5. Ibid., 299.

6. Ibid., 302.

7. Blaine Taylor, "The Case of the Outspoken Medical Examiner," *Maryland State Medical Journal*, March 1977, p. 26.

8. Manchester, *Death of a President*, 304.

9. Ibid., 312–316.

10. Ibid., 319.

11. Ibid.

12. Ibid., 318–319.

13. Frank Cormier, *LBJ—The Way He Was* (Garden City, N.Y.: Doubleday & Co., 1977), 19–20.

14. Ibid., 21.

15. Josiah Thompson, *Six Seconds in Dallas* (New York: Bernard Geis Associates, 1967), 143.

16. *The Report of the Warren Commission on the Assassination of President Kennedy* (New York: Bantam Books, 1964), 170–172.

17. Ibid., 173.

18. Ibid., 172–173.

19. Ibid., 173.

20. Thompson, *Six Seconds in Dallas*, 135.

21. *Warren Commission, Vol. XXIV,* 229.

22. Reprinted by permission of the *Baltimore Sun*. Copyright 1977. All rights reserved.

23. George Lardner, Jr., "National Security Agency: Turning On and Tuning In," *The Washington Post,* 18 March 1990, p. 1.

11. THE HOUSE SELECT COMMITTEE

1. Harold Weisberg, *Whitewash I—The Report on the Warren Report* (New York: Dell Publishing Co., 1965), 286.

2. David Lifton, *Best Evidence—Disguise and Deception in the Assassination of John F. Kennedy* (New York: Macmillan Publishing Co., 1980), 556.

3. Harold Weisberg, *Post Mortem—JFK Assassination Cover-Up Smashed!* (Frederick, Md.: Harold Weisberg, 1975), 16–17.

4. Ibid., 313.

5. Jim Marrs, *Crossfire: The Plot That Killed Kennedy* (New York: Carroll & Graf, 1989), 446.

6. Weisberg, *Post Mortem,* 419–422.

7. Marrs, *Crossfire,* 446.

8. Weisberg, *Post Mortem,* 607.

9. Seymour M. Hersh, "Helms Was Vague in 1973 on Spy Bid," *The New York Times,* 27 December 1974, p. 1.

10. Clifton Daniel, "C.I.A.'s Covert Role: Ford's Defense Runs Against Current Trend," *The New York Times,* 18 September 1974, p. 4.

11. Seymour M. Hersh, "Huge C.I.A. Operation Reported in U.S. Against Antiwar Forces, Other Dissidents in Nixon Years," *The New York Times,* 22 December 1975, p. 1.

12. Clifton Daniel, "C.I.A.'s Covert Role: Ford's Defense Runs Against Current Trend," *The New York Times,* 18 September 1974, p. 4.

13. Walter Rugaber, "Ford Sets Up Commission on C.I.A.'s Domestic Role; A Justice Dept. Inquiry On," *The New York Times,* 5 January 1975, p. 1.

14. John M. Crewdson, "Rockefeller Unit Said to Check Report of C.I.A. Link to Kennedy Assassination," *The New York Times,* 8 March 1975, p. 11.

15. Ibid.

16. "C.I.A. Involvement Is Alleged in Plots to Kill 3 Dictators," *The New York Times,* 10 March 1975, p. 49.

17. Murray Illson, "Johnson in '69 Suspected Foreign Ties With Oswald," *The New York Times,* 26 April 1975, p. 12.

18. "Autopsy Studied Again," *The New York Times,* 26 April 1975, p. 12.

19. Ibid.

20. Cyril H. Wecht, press release of June 12, 1975, reprinted in *The Assassinations: Dallas and Beyond—A Guide to Cover-Ups and Investigations,*" edited by Peter Dale Scott, Paul L. Hoch and Russell Stetler (New York: Random House, 1976), 519–520.

21. Ibid.

22. Marrs, *Crossfire,* 518.

23. F. Peter Model and Robert J. Groden, *JFK: The Case for Conspiracy* (New York: Manor Books, 1976), 1.

24. Edward Cowan, "New Study Urged in Kennedy Death," *The New York Times*, 21 July 1975, p. 27.

25. United Press International, "Dallas Ex–Police Chief Alleges an F.B.I. Cover-Up on Oswald," *The New York Times*, 2 September 1975, p. 12.

26. Ibid.

27. Ibid.

28. Ibid.

29. Martin Waldron, "F.B.I. Chiefs Linked to Oswald File Loss," *The New York Times*, 14 September 1975, p. 1.

30. Nicholas M. Horrock, "Panel Studies F.B.I. Links to Oswald and Ruby in '63," *The New York Times*, 14 October 1975, p. 1.

31. Ibid.

32. Ibid.

33. Associated Press, "Schweiker Predicts Collapse of Warren Report on Kennedy," *The New York Times*, 16 October 1975, p. 28.

34. James R. Phelan, "The Assassination That Will Not Die," *The New York Times Sunday Magazine*, 23 November 1975, p. 110.

35. Martin Waldron, "Schweiker Joins Attack on Warren Report as Clamor for New Inquiry Rises," *The New York Times*, 20 October 1975, p. 16.

36. Ibid.

37. Nicholas M. Horrock, "Warren Panel Aide Calls for 2nd Inquiry into Kennedy Killing," *The New York Times*, 23 November 1975, p. 1.

38. Ibid.

39. James M. Naughton, "Ford Vows Curb on Social Outlays," *The New York Times*, 14 September 1975, p. 1.

40. Nicholas M. Horrock, "Ford Would Sift New Data in Kennedy, King Slayings," *The New York Times*, 27 November 1975, p. 1.

41. Associated Press, "Slain Kennedys Called 'Most Dangerous Men,' " *The New York Times*, 29 January 1976, p. 28.

42. United Press International, "Remarks on Kennedys Explained by Kunstler," *The New York Times*, 24 February 1976, p. 28.

43. William E. Farrell, "A Catholic School Ponders Kennedy and Morality," *The New York Times*, 21 January 1976, p. 39.

44. David Binder, "F.B.I.-C.I.A. Laxity on Kennedy Found," *The New York Times*, 24 June 1976, p. 1.

45. Ibid.

46. Ibid.

47. Associated Press, "House Inquiry into Killing of Kennedys and King Due," *The New York Times*, 15 September 1976, p. 24.

48. "F.B.I. Tried to Kill Rev. King's Reputation," *The New York Times*, 23 November 1975, Sec. 4, p. 1.

49. Ben A. Franklin, "Assassination Panel Names Top Counsel," *The New York Times*, 5 October 1976, p. 17.

50. Ibid.

51. Marrs, *Crossfire*, 520.

52. Ben A. Franklin, "Assassination Panel Names Top Counsel," *The New York Times*, 5 October 1976, p. 17.

53. Marrs, *Crossfire*, 520.

54. David Burnham, "Assassination Study Requests $13 Million," *The New York Times*, 10 December 1976, p. 19.

55. Gaeton Fonzi, "The Last Investigation," *The Third Decade—A Journal of Research on the John F. Kennedy Assassination*, Vol. 1, #1, November 1984, p. 2.

56. Ibid.

57. David Burnham, "Assassination Panel Is Warned on Its Techniques," *The New York Times*, 6 January 1977, p. 15.

58. David Burnham, "New Assassination Panel Is Blocked," *The New York Times*, 12 January 1977, p. B6.

59. Ibid.

60. David Burnham, "Assassination Panel Facing Budget Trim," *The New York Times*, 25 January 1977, p. 17.

61. David Burnham, "House Gives Assassination Panel Authority to Continue Temporarily," *The New York Times*, 3 February 1977, p. 21.

62. David Burnham, "Sprague Ouster Is Upset by Panel on Assassination," *The New York Times*, 10 February 1977, p. 1.

63. Ibid.

64. David Burnham, "Assassination Panel's Fate in Doubt as Sprague Faces New Allegations," *The New York Times*, 12 February 1977, p. 11.

65. Ibid.

66. David Burnham, "Gonzalez, Assailing His Committee, Quits as Assassination Inquiry Head," *The New York Times*, 3 March 1977, p. 1.

67. Richard L. Madden, "House Votes to Keep Assassination Panel After Sprague Quits," *The New York Times*, 31 March 1977, p. 1.

68. Ben A. Franklin, "Sprague Urges Carter to Set Up Inquiry into Murders of Kennedy and Dr. King," *The New York Times*, 12 April 1977, p. 18.

69. Ibid.

70. Wendell Rawls, Jr., "Cornell Professor Is Named as Assassinations Panel Counsel," *The New York Times*, 21 June 1977, p. 21.

71. Wendall Rawls, Jr., "House Inquiry Reported Fruitless on Kennedy-King Assassinations," *The New York Times*, 6 June 1977, p. 1.

72. Ibid., p. 1.

73. Ibid.

12. KATIE DONAHUE FORCES THE ISSUE

1. "Towson Gunsmith Tells Panel JFK Was Killed Accidentally by Secret Service agent," *Baltimore Sun*, 13 July 1977, p. A5.

2. Jim Marrs, *Crossfire: The Plot That Killed Kennedy* (New York: Carroll & Graf, 1989), 524.

3. Ibid., 528.

4. Ibid., 524.

5. Ibid.

6. Ibid., 525.

7. Wendell Rawls, Jr., "Assassination Panel Is Given Right to Bypass House," *The New York Times*, 17 October 1977, p. 15.

8. Ibid.

9. Ibid.

10. G. Robert Blakey and Richard N. Billings, *The Plot to Kill the President* (New York: Times Books, 1981), xiii.

13. BLAKEY'S $5 MILLION FOLLY

1. George Lardner, Jr., " 'Umbrella Man' Was Heckler," *The Washington Post*, 26 September 1978, p. A2.

2. Ibid.

3. Associated Press, "Hill Unit to Open Hearings on JFK," *The Washington Post*, 6 September 1978, A6.

4. George Lardner, Jr., "Connallys Tell of 'Terrible Ride,' *The Washington Post*, 7 September 1978, p. A1.

5. Ibid.

6. *Appendix to Hearings Before the Select Committee on Assassinations, Vol. VII* (Washington, D.C.: U.S. Government Printing Office, 1979), 131.

7. Ibid., 224.

8. Ibid., 132.

9. Ibid.

10. Ibid., 254.

11. George Lardner, Jr., " Warren Commission Findings Backed," *The Washington Post*, 8 September 1978, p. A1.

12. *The Final Assassinations Report* (New York: Bantam Books, 1979), 33.

13. *Appendix to Hearings Before the Select Committee on Assassinations, Vol. VII*, 23.

14. Ibid.

15. Ibid., 23–33.

16. George Lardner, Jr., "New Tests Said to Match Fragments in Kennedy, Connally," *The Washington Post*, 9 September 1978, p. A3.

17. Ibid.

18. Ibid.

19. *Appendix to Hearings Before the Select Committee on Assassinations, Vol. VI*, 32–62.

20. Ibid., 38.

21. *Appendix to Hearings before the Select Committee on Assassinations, Vol. VII*, 176.

22. Ibid., 169.

23. *Committee Appendix, Vol. VII*, 128.

24. Ibid., 169.

25. *Committee Appendix, Vol. VI*, 35–36.

26. George Lardner, Jr., "JFK Panel Gets Evidence of Conspiracy," *The Washington Post*, 21 December 1978, p. A1.

27. G. Robert Blakey, Richard N. Billings, *The Plot to Kill the President: Organized Crime Assassinated J.F.K.—The Definitive Story* (New York: Times Books, 1981), 91–92.

28. George Lardner, Jr., "50-50 Chance of a 4th Shot in Dallas, JFK Panel Is Told," *The Washington Post*, 12 September 1978, p. A2.

29. Ibid.

30. Nancy Smith, "Acoustics Experts Reenact '63 Kennedy Assassination in Dallas," *The Washington Post*, 21 August 1978, p. A3.

31. George Lardner, Jr., "50-50 Chance of a 4th Shot In Dallas, JFK Panel Is Told," *The Washington Post,* 12 September 1978, p. A2.

32. Blakey and Billings, *Plot to Kill the President,* 100.

33. George Lardner, Jr., "Experts Track Mystery JFK Bullet," *The Washington Post,* 22 December 1978, p. A1.

34. Ibid.

35. Ibid.

36. George Lardner, Jr., "Second JFK Gunman, Experts Say," *The Washington Post,* 31 December 1978, p. A1.

37. Michael Baden, *Unnatural Death—Confessions of a Medical Examiner* (New York: Random House, 1989), 21–22.

38. George Lardner, Jr., "Second JFK Gunman, Experts Say," *The Washington Post,* 31 December 1978, p. A1.

39. *Final Assassinations Report,* unnumbered; final two pages of introduction.

40. Ibid., 107.

47. Ibid.

42. David W. Belin, "The Case Against Conspiracy," *The New York Times Magazine,* 15 July 1979, p. 40.

43. *Final Assassinations Report,* 650.

44. Ibid., 651.

45. Ibid., 668–669.

46. Ibid., 669.

47. "Who Shot President Kennedy?" First broadcast Nov. 15, 1988. Produced by Robert Richter for *NOVA*/WGBH.

48. Ibid.

49. Jim Marrs, *Crossfire: The Plot That Killed Kennedy* (New York: Carroll & Graf, 1989), 533.

50. Ibid.

51. *NOVA* broadcast, first aired on P.B.S. November 15, 1988. Produced by WGBH in Boston.

52. Robert Sherrill, "The Body Snatchers," *The Washington Post Book World,* 8 March 1981, p. 5.

53. *Choice,* ed. Jay Martin (Middletown, Conn.: Association of College & Research Libraries, July-August 1981), Vol. 18, Nos. 11/12, 1600.

14. THE AR-15

1. James Fallows, "M-16: A Bureaucratic Horror Story," *Atlantic Monthly,* June 1981, p. 56–65.

2. Ibid.

3. Ibid.

4. Ibid.

5. no byline, "Senate Unit Assails the Army's Policy on Rifle Purchases," *The New York Times,* 5 June 1967, p. 1.

6. Fallows, *Atlantic Monthly,* June 1981.

7. Ibid.

8. Ibid.

9. Ibid.

10. Ibid.

11. Ibid.

12. William Beecher, "Marines' Chief Defends the M-16 Rifle," *The New York Times*, 27 May 1967, p. 3.

13. Fallows, *Atlantic Monthly*, June 1981.

14. William Beecher, "Marines' Chief Defends the M-16 Rifle," *The New York Times*, 27 May 1967, p. 3.

15. Harold Gal, "House Panel Scores Army Procurement in Inquiry on M-16," *The New York Times*, 19 October 1967, p. 1.

15. THE FINAL BREAKTHROUGH

1. Vincent J. M. Di Maio, *Gunshot Wounds—Practical Aspects of Firearms, Ballistics, and Forensic Techniques* (New York: Elsevier Science Publishing Co. Inc., 1985), 145–146.

2. Ibid., 155.

3. John K. Lattimer, *Kennedy and Lincoln—Medical and Ballistic Comparisons of Their Assassinations* (New York: Harcourt Brace Jovanovich, 1980), xvii.

4. Ibid., xix.

5. Ibid., 240.

6. Ibid., 240–245.

7. Ibid., 240–246.

8. Ibid.

9. Ibid., 245.

10. Ibid.

11. Jane E. Brody, "Doctor Analyzes Kennedy Ailment," *The New York Times*, 11 July 1967, p. 39.

12. Ibid.

13. Lattimer, *Kennedy and Lincoln*, 249.

14. Ibid.

15. Ibid., 255.

16. Jim Bishop, *The Day Kennedy Was Shot* (New York: Funk & Wagnalls, 1968), 636–639.

17. *The Report of the Warren Commission on the Assassination of President Kennedy* (New York: Bantam Books, 1964), 88.

18. Bishop, *The Day Kennedy Was Shot*, 499.

16. HOPE DIES HARD

1. John H. Davis, *Mafia Kingfish—Carlos Marcello and the Assassination of John F. Kennedy* (New York: Signet, 1989), 643.

2. *The Final Assassinations Report* (New York: Bantam Books, 1979), 289.

3. *The New Columbia Encyclopedia*, ed. by William H. Harris and Judith S. Levey (New York: Columbia University Press, 1975), 2466.

4. Edmund W. Starling as told to Thomas Sugrue, *Starling of the White House* (New York: Simon and Schuster Inc., 1946), 53–54.

5. George Rush, *Confessions of an Ex-Secret Service Agent—The Marty Venker Story* (New York: Donald I. Fine Inc., 1988), 44.

6. Ibid., 46.

7. Ibid., 155.

8. *Final Assassinations Report*, 22.

9. William Manchester, *The Death of a President* (New York: Harper & Row, 1967), 65.

10. Ibid., 35.

11. Ibid.

12. Martin Arnold, "Visit to New York Disturbed Police," *The New York Times*, 23 November 1963, p. 10.

13. Ibid.

14. Ibid.

15. Manchester, *Death of a President*, 37.

16. "Excerpts from Rowley Testimony," *The New York Times*, 24 November 1964, p. 31.

17. *The Report of the Warren Commission on the Assassination of President Kennedy* (New York: Bantam Books, 1964), 426.

18. "Excerpts from Rowley Testimony, *The New York Times*, 24 November 1964, p. 30.

19. Ibid.

20. Ibid.

21. *Warren Report*, 64.

22. Ibid.

23. *Warren Commission, Vol. II*, 69.

24. Ibid., 427–428.

25. *Final Assassinations Report*, 299.

26. Ibid., 301.

17. TODAY

1. Vincent P. Guinn and John Nichols, "Neutron Activation Analysis of Bullet-Lead Specimens: The President Kennedy Assassination," Submitted for presentation at The American Nuclear Society Annual Meeting, San Diego, CA., 18–23 June, 1978.

INDEX